5th Workshop on Natural Language Processing and Computational Social Sciences (NLPCSS 2022)

Abu Dhabi, United Arab Emirates
7 November 2022

ISBN: 978-1-7138-9145-1

Printed from e-media with permission by:

Curran Associates, Inc.
57 Morehouse Lane
Red Hook, NY 12571

CURRAN ASSOCIATES INC. proceedings.com

Some format issues inherent in the e-media version may also appear in this print version.

Association for Computational Linguistics
209 N. Eighth Street
Stroudsburg, Pennsylvania 18360

Phone: 1-570-476-8006
Fax: 1-570-476-0860

acl@aclweb.org

Additional copies of this publication are available from:

Curran Associates, Inc.
57 Morehouse Lane
Red Hook, NY 12571 USA
Phone: 845-758-0400
Fax: 845-758-2633
Email: curran@proceedings.com
Web: www.proceedings.com

NLPCSS 2022

The Fifth Workshop on Natural Language Processing and Computational Social Science (NLP+CSS)

Held at the 2022 Conference on Empirical Methods in Natural Language Processing

November 7, 2022

The NLPCSS organizers gratefully acknowledge the support from the following sponsors.

Gold

Google

Introduction

Welcome to the Fifth Workshop on Natural Language Processing (NLP) and Computational Social Science (CSS)! This workshop series builds on a successful string of iterations, with many interdisciplinary contributions to make NLP techniques and insights standard practice in CSS research—as well as improve NLP through insights from the social sciences.

We received a record 63 submissions and after a rigorous review process by our committee, we accepted 23 archival entries and 2 non-archival papers. We are also pleased to include 8 Findings of EMNLP papers for presentation at the workshop. This year we have organized a hybrid event with both virtual and in-person components with an evening soirée in Gather Town to allow mingling between folks in different time zones. We continue to be excited to see so many submissions from outside of NLP, and hope to continue the tradition to foster a dialogue between researchers in NLP and these other fields.

We would like to thank the Program Committee members who reviewed the papers this year. They did a heroic job proving some top-notch reviews in a time when reviewing requests are abundant. We would also like to thank the workshop participants both in-person and virtual for the opportunities to connect (or reconnect) and learn from each other. Last, a word of thanks also goes to our sponsor Google, who enabled us to support valuable participation and activities.

David Bamman, Dirk Hovy, Katherine Keith, David Jurgens, Brendan O'Connor, and Svitlana Volkova (Co-Organizers)

Organizing Committee

Organizers

David Bamman, University of California, Berkeley
Dirk Hovy, Bocconi University
David Jurgens, University of Michigan
Katherine Keith, Williams College
Brendan O'Connor, University of Massachusetts Amherst
Svitlana Volkova, Pacific Northwest National Laboratory

Program Committee

Chairs

David Bamman, University of California, Berkeley
Dirk Hovy, Bocconi University
David Jurgens, University of Michigan
Katherine Keith, University of Massachusetts, Amherst
Brendan O'connor, University of Massachusetts Amherst
Svitlana Volkova, Pacific Northwest National Laboratory

Program Committee

Natalie Ahn, UC Berkeley
Kenan Alkiek, University of Michigan
Kristen M. Altenburger, Facebook
Timothy Baldwin, The University of Melbourne
Alon Bartal, Ben-Gurion University
Eric Bell, Self
Chris Biemann, Universität Hamburg
Laura Biester, University of Michigan
Michael Bloodgood, The College of New Jersey
Amanda Buddemeyer, University of Pittsburgh, School of Computing and Information
Aoife Cahill, Dataminr
Marine Carpuat, University of Maryland
Samuel Carton, University of Chicago
Sky Ch-wang, Columbia University
Mohit Chandra, Georgia Institute of Technology
Kaiping Chen, University of Wisconsin-Madison
Zhiyu Chen, Meta
Minje Choi, University of Michigan
Aron Culotta, Tulane University
Walter Daelemans, University of Antwerp, CLiPS
Debarati Das, University of Minnesota Twin Cities
Leon Derczynski, IT University of Copenhagen
Jonathan Dunn, University of Canterbury
Valery Dzutsati, University of Kansas
Micha Elsner, The Ohio State University
Samuel Fraiberger, World Bank
Kathleen C. Fraser, National Research Council Canada
Dan Garrette, Google Research
Nabeel Gillani, MIT
Ann-sophie Gnehm, University of Zurich
Xiaobo Guo, Dartmouth College
Shirley Anugrah Hayati, University of Minnesota
Marti A. Hearst, UC Berkeley
Joseph Hoover, University of Southern California
Tiancheng Hu, ETH Zurich
Rebecca Hwa, University of Pittsburgh
Loring Ingraham, George Washington University

Mali Jin, University of Sheffield
Kristen Johnson, Michigan State University
Kenneth Joseph, University at Buffalo
Shima Khanehzar, University of Melbourne
Sopan Khosla, Amazon Web Services, Amazon Inc
Roman Klinger, University of Stuttgart
Ekaterina Kochmar, University of Bath
Jiazhao Li, University of Michigan
Jinfen Li, Syracuse University
Mingyang Li, University of Pennsylvania
Ruibo Liu, Dartmouth College
Nikola Ljubešić, Jožef Stefan Institute
Julia Mendelsohn, University of Michigan
Rada Mihalcea, University of Michigan
David Mimno, Cornell University
Shubhanshu Mishra, Twitter Inc.
Kunihiro Miyazaki, The University of Tokyo
Jason Naradowsky, University of Tokyo
John Nay, Stanford University - Center for Legal Informatics
Dong Nguyen, Utrecht University
Pierre Nugues, Lund University
Alice Oh, KAIST
Silviu Oprea, University of Edinburgh
Sebastian Padó, Stuttgart University
Shriphani Palakodety, Onai
Elizabeth Palmieri, University of Virginia
Jiaxin Pei, University of Michigan
Massimo Poesio, Queen Mary University of London
Thierry Poibeau, LATTICE (CNRS & ENS/PSL)
Afshin Rahimi, The University of Queensland
Ange Richard, Laboratoire PACTE, Laboratoire Informatique de Grenoble (LIG)
Matīss Rikters, National Institute of Advanced Industrial Science and Technology
Ellen Riloff, University of Utah
Anthony Rios, University of Texas at San Antonio
Molly Roberts, University of California, San Diego
Frank Rudzicz, St Michael's Hospital; University of Toronto, Department of Computer Science
Asad Sayeed, University of Gothenburg
David Schlangen, University of Potsdam
Hope Schroeder, MIT
Djamé Seddah, Inria
Felix Soldner, GESIS - Leibniz Institute for the Social Science
Nikita Soni, Stony Brook University
Mark Steedman, University of Edinburgh
Sara Tonelli, FBK
Oren Tsur, Ben Gurion University
Zijian Wang, AWS AI Labs
Maximilian Weber, Goethe University
Charles Welch, University of Marburg
Swede White, Louisiana State University Dept. of Sociology
Gregor Wiedemann, Leibniz Institute for Media Research | Hans-Bredow-Institute
Steven Wilson, Oakland University

Winston Wu, University of Michigan
Wei Xu, Georgia Institute of Technology
Xiao Xu, NIDI-KNAW / University of Groningen
Ivan Yamshchikov, Max Planck Institute for Mathematics in the Sciences; ISEG & CEMAPRE, University of Lisbon
Michael Yeomans, Imperial College London
Sourabh Zanwar, RWTH Aachen University
Shuang (sophie) Zhai, University of Oklahoma
Yongjun Zhang, Stony Brook University
Tongtong Zhang, Stanford University
Xixuan Zhang, Freie Universität Berlin
Mian Zhong, ETH Zürich
Naitian Zhou, University of Michigan

Keynote Talk: Tackling social challenges with data science and AI

Jisun An
Singapore Management University

Abstract: Artificial Intelligence (AI) and technology have become increasingly embedded in our daily lives. Billions of people interact with AI systems on various online platforms every day. Those tremendous interactions enable us to understand individual or collective human behavior: what people think, what people care about, how people feel, where people go, what people buy, what people do, and with whom people associate. Tools that can extract hidden patterns and insights from large-scale data allow researchers to understand complex social phenomena better. Also, the recent advancement of AI has empowered researchers and practitioners to investigate such massive data in an innovative way. My main research theme is developing AI-based methods and tools to 1) understand, predict, and nudge online human behavior and 2) tackle a wide range of social problems. In this talk, I will introduce two of my work on developing natural language processing methods and models to tackle social challenges.
First, I will introduce our novel technique, 'SemAxis,' to measure semantic changes in words across communities. Using transfer learning of word embeddings, SemAxis offers a framework to examine and interpret words on diverse semantic axes (732 systematically created semantic axes that capture common antonyms, such as safe vs. dangerous). Second, I will present my recent work on tackling anti-Asian hate during COVID-19. We used natural language processing techniques to characterize social media users who began to post anti-Asian hate messages during COVID-19 and build a prediction model to investigate the predictors of those users.

Bio: Jisun An is an Assistant Professor at the School of Computing and Information Systems, Singapore Management University (SMU-SCIS). She is a member of SODA (Social Data and AI) Lab (`https://soda-labo.github.io`), where she develops AI and NLP methods to understand, predict, and nudge online human behavior and to tackle various social problems, from media bias and framing, polarization, online hate, to healthy lifestyle and urban changes. Before joining SMU-SCIS, she was a scientist at Qatar Computing Research Institute, HBKU, and she received her Ph.D. in Computer Science from the University of Cambridge, UK.

Keynote Talk:

Elliot Ash
ETH Zurich

Abstract:

Bio: Elliott Ash is Assistant Professor of Law, Economics, and Data Science at ETH Zurich's Center for Law & Economics, Switzerland. Elliott's research and teaching focus on empirical analysis of the law and legal system using techniques from applied micro-econometrics, natural language processing, and machine learning. Prior to joining ETH, Elliott was Assistant Professor of Economics at University of Warwick, and before that a Postdoctoral Research Associate at Princeton University's Center for the study of Democratic Politics. He received a Ph.D. in economics and J.D. from Columbia University, a B.A. in economics, government, and philosophy from University of Texas at Austin, and an LL.M. in international criminal law from University of Amsterdam.

Keynote Talk: Challenges in NLP for Analyzing Social Media during Emerging Events

Anjalie Field
Stanford University

Abstract: Abstract: Social media has become a driving force in both online and offline events. Given huge volumes of organizations and people who generate text in short time periods, NLP should be a valuable tool in analyzing new data. However, developing NLP approaches that are robust to emerging domains and useable for research questions of interest remains difficult.
In this talk I will review some challenges we have encountered in using NLP to analyze social media during unfolding conflicts and social movements. First, I will present an analysis of emotions in tweets about the Black Lives Matter movement and our findings on how emotion data can shed interesting light on on-the-ground activism. Second, I will present an analysis of Twitter and VK posts in the ongoing Ukraine-Russia war in an attempt to identify propaganda strategies employed by state media. In both parts, I will highlight what worked and what didn't in using state-of-the-art NLP approaches and will suggest some directions for future research.

Bio: Anjalie Field is currently a postdoctoral researcher in the Stanford NLP Group and Stanford Data Science Institute working with Dan Jurafsky and Jennifer Eberhardt and an incoming Assistant Professor in Computer Science at Johns Hopkins University in the Fall of 2023. She completed her PhD at the Language Technologies Institute at Carnegie Mellon University, where she was advised by Yulia Tsvetkov and a member of TsvetShop. She was also a visiting student at the University of Washington in 2021-2022. Her primary interests involve using Natural Language Processing (NLP) to model social science concepts. Her current work is focused on identifying social biases in various domains, including Wikipedia, social media, and social workers' notes.

Table of Contents

Program

Wednesday, December 7, 2022

09:00 - 09:10 *Opening Remarks*

09:10 - 10:00 *Invited Speaker: Anjalie Field*

10:00 - 10:30 *Synchronous Talk Session 1: Influence due to Linguistic Variation*

Professional Presentation and Projected Power: A Case Study of Implicit Gender Information in English CVs
Jinrui Yang, Sheilla Njoto, Marc Cheong, Leah Ruppanner and Lea Frermann

Conditional Language Models for Community-Level Linguistic Variation
Bill Noble and Jean-philippe Bernardy

Predicting Long-Term Citations from Short-Term Linguistic Influence
Jacob Eisenstein, David Bamman and Sandeep Soni

10:30 - 11:00 *Coffee Break*

11:00 - 11:30 *Synchronous Talk Session 2: Political Frames and Stances*

Quotatives Indicate Decline in Objectivity in U.S. Political News
Tiancheng Hu, Manoel Horta Ribeiro, Robert West and Andreas Spitz

Capturing Topic Framing via Masked Language Modeling
Soroush Vosoughi, Weicheng Ma and Xiaobo Guo

Examining Political Rhetoric with Epistemic Stance Detection
Ankita Gupta, Su Lin Blodgett, Justin Gross and Brendan O'connor

11:30 - 12:30 *In-person Poster Session*

Improving the Generalizability of Text-Based Emotion Detection by Leveraging Transformers with Psycholinguistic Features
Sourabh Zanwar, Daniel Wiechmann, Yu Qiao and Elma Kerz

Wednesday, December 7, 2022 (continued)

12:30 - 14:00 *Lunch Break*

14:00 - 15:00 *Invited Speaker: Jisun An*

15:00 - 15:30 *Synchronous Talk Session 2: Heterogenous Real-World Social Data*

Fine-Grained Extraction and Classification of Skill Requirements in German-Speaking Job Ads
Ann-sophie Gnehm, Eva Bühlmann, Helen Buchs and Simon Clematide

Analyzing Norm Violations in Real-Time Live-Streaming Chat
Jihyung Moon, Dong-ho Lee, Hyundong Cho, Woojeong Jin, Chan Young Park, Minwoo Kim, Jay Pujara and Sungjoon Park

Status Biases in Deliberation Online: Evidence from a Randomized Experiment on ChangeMyView
Alan Montgomery, Yohan Jo and Emaad Manzoor

15:30 - 16:00 *Coffee Break*

16:00 - 17:00 *Invited Speaker: Elliot Ash*

17:00 - 20:00 *Break*

20:00 - 21:00 *Virtual Poster Session*

Fine-Grained Extraction and Classification of Skill Requirements in German-Speaking Job Ads
Ann-sophie Gnehm, Eva Bühlmann, Helen Buchs and Simon Clematide

Experiencer-Specific Emotion and Appraisal Prediction
Maximilian Wegge, Enrica Troiano, Laura Ana Maria Oberlaender and Roman Klinger

Understanding Narratives from Demographic Survey Data: a Comparative Study with Multiple Neural Topic Models
Xiao Xu, Gert Stulp, Antal Van Den Bosch and Anne Gauthier

Wednesday, December 7, 2022 (continued)

Human Counts Extraction from Text
Mian Zhong, Shehzaad Dhuliawala and Niklas Stoehr

To Prefer or to Choose? Generating Agency and Power Counterfactuals Jointly for Gender Bias Mitigation
Maja Stahl, Maximilian Spliethöver and Henning Wachsmuth

Conspiracy Narratives in the Protest Movement Against COVID-19 Restrictions in Germany. A Long-term Content Analysis of Telegram Chat Groups.
Manuel Weigand, Maximilian Weber and Johannes Gruber

Conditional Language Models for Community-Level Linguistic Variation
Bill Noble and Jean-philippe Bernardy

Understanding Interpersonal Conflict Types and their Impact on Perception Classification
Charles Welch, Joan Plepi, Béla Neuendorf and Lucie Flek

Examining Political Rhetoric with Epistemic Stance Detection
Ankita Gupta, Su Lin Blodgett, Justin Gross and Brendan O'connor

Linguistic Elements of Engaging Customer Service Discourse on Social Media
Sonam Singh and Anthony Rios

Measuring Harmful Representations in Scandinavian Language Models
Samia Touileb and Debora Nozza

Can Contextualizing User Embeddings Improve Sarcasm and Hate Speech Detection?
Kim Breitwieser

Professional Presentation and Projected Power: A Case Study of Implicit Gender Information in English CVs
Jinrui Yang, Sheilla Njoto, Marc Cheong, Leah Ruppanner and Lea Frermann

Detecting Dissonant Stance in Social Media: The Role of Topic Exposure
Vasudha Varadarajan, Nikita Soni, Weixi Wang, Christian Luhmann, H. Andrew Schwartz and Naoya Inoue

Wednesday, December 7, 2022 (continued)

Improving the Generalizability of Text-Based Emotion Detection by Leveraging Transformers with Psycholinguistic Features

Sourabh Zanwar
RWTH Aachen University
sourabh.zanwar@rwth-aachen.de

Daniel Wiechmann
University of Amsterdam
d.wiechmann@uva.nl

Yu Qiao
RWTH Aachen University
yu.qiao@rwth-aachen.de

Elma Kerz
RWTH Aachen University
elma.kerz@ifaar.rwth-aachen.de

Abstract

In recent years, there has been increased interest in building predictive models that harness natural language processing and machine learning techniques to detect emotions from various text sources, including social media posts, micro-blogs or news articles. Yet, deployment of such models in real-world sentiment and emotion applications faces challenges, in particular poor out-of-domain generalizability. This is likely due to domain-specific differences (e.g., topics, communicative goals, and annotation schemes) that make transfer between different models of emotion recognition difficult. In this work we propose approaches for text-based emotion detection that leverage transformer models (BERT and RoBERTa) in combination with Bidirectional Long Short-Term Memory (BiLSTM) networks trained on a comprehensive set of psycholinguistic features. First, we evaluate the performance of our models within-domain on two benchmark datasets: GoEmotion (Demszky et al., 2020) and ISEAR (Scherer and Wallbott, 1994). Second, we conduct transfer learning experiments on six datasets from the Unified Emotion Dataset (Bostan and Klinger, 2018) to evaluate their out-of-domain robustness. We find that the proposed hybrid models improve the ability to generalize to out-of-distribution data compared to a standard transformer-based approach. Moreover, we observe that these models perform competitively on in-domain data.

1 Introduction

Emotions are a key factor affecting all human behavior, which includes rational tasks such as reasoning, decision making, and social interaction (Parrott, 2001; Loewenstein and Lerner, 2003; Lerner et al., 2015; Bericat, 2016). Although emotions seem to be subjective by nature, they appear in objectively derivable ways in texts. Text-based emotion detection (henceforth TBED) is a branch of sentiment analysis that aims to extract textual features to identify associations with various emotions such as anger, fear, joy, sadness, surprise, etc. TBED is a rapidly developing interdisciplinary field that brings together insights from cognitive psychology, social sciences, computational linguistics, natural language processing (NLP) and machine learning (Canales and Martínez-Barco, 2014; Acheampong et al., 2020a; Alswaidan and Menai, 2020; Deng and Ren, 2021). TBED has a wide range of real-world applications, from healthcare (Cambria et al., 2010a), recommendation systems (Majumder et al., 2019), empathic chatbot development (Casas et al., 2021), offensive language detection (Plaza-del Arco et al., 2021), social data analysis for business intelligence (Cambria et al., 2013; Soussan and Trovati, 2020), and stock market prediction (Xing et al., 2018).

The differentiation of emotions and their classification into specific groups and categories is a subfield of affective research and has yielded several theories and models (Borod et al., 2000; Scherer et al., 2000; Cambria et al., 2012; Sander and Nummenmaa, 2021; Susanto et al., 2020). The grouping of models for the classification of emotions generally differs according to whether emotions are conceived as discrete/categorical or as dimensional. Categorical models of emotions, like Ekman's six basic emotions (anger, disgust, fear, joy, sadness, and surprise) (Ekman, 1992, 1999), assume physiologically distinct basic human emotions. Plutchik's Wheel of Emotion (Plutchik, 1984) is another categorical model that assumes a set of eight discrete emotions expressed in four opposing pairs (joy–sadness, anger–fear, trust–disgust, and anticipation–surprise). Dimensional emotion models, like the Circumplex Model of Russell (1980), groups affective states into a vector space of valence (corresponding to senti-

Proceedings of the Fifth Workshop on Natural Language Processing and Computational Social Science (NLP+CSS), pages 1 - 13
November 7, 2022 ©2022 Association for Computational Linguistics

ment/polarity), arousal (corresponding to a degree of calmness or excitement), and dominance (perceived degree of control over a given situation).

Current approaches to TBED take the advantage of recent advances in NLP and machine learning, with deep learning techniques achieving state-of-the-art performance on benchmark emotion datasets (see Acheampong et al. 2020a for recent reviews). However there still remains the issue of out-of-domain generalizability of the existing emotion detection models. The way emotions are conveyed in texts may differ from domain to domain, reflecting differences in topics, communicative goals, target audience, etc. This makes the deployment of such models in real-world sentiment and emotion applications difficult. The importance of this issue has been increasingly recognized in the TBED literature. For example, Bostan and Klinger (2018) emphasize that "[j]ournalists ideally tend to be objective when writing articles, authors of microblog posts need to focus on brevity", and that "emotion expressions in tales are more subtle and implicit than, for instance, in blogs". To support future transfer learning and domain adaptation work for TBED, the authors constructed a unified, aggregated emotion detection dataset that encompasses different domains and annotation schemes.

In this work, we contribute to the improvement of the generalizability of emotion detection models as follows: We build hybrid models that combine pre-trained transformer language models with Bidirectional Long Short-Term Memory (BiLSTM) networks trained, to our knowledge, on the most comprehensive set of psycholinguistic features. We evaluate the performance of the proposed models in two ways: First, we conduct within-corpus emotion classification experiments (training on one corpus and testing on the same) on two emotion benchmark datasets, GoEmotion (Demszky et al., 2020) and ISEAR (Scherer and Wallbott, 1994), to show that such hybrid models outperform pre-trained transformer models. Second, we conduct transfer learning experiments on six popular emotion classification datasets of the Unified Emotion Dataset (Bostan and Klinger, 2018) to show that our approach improves the generalizability of emotion classification across domains and emotion taxonomies. The remainder of the paper is organized as follows: In Section 2, we briefly review recent related work on TBED. Then, in Section 3, we present popular benchmark datasets for emotion detection. Section 4 details the extraction of psycholinguistic features using automated text analysis based on a sliding window approach. In Section 5, we describe our emotion detection models, and in Section 6, we present our experiments and discuss the results. Finally, we conclude with possible directions for future work in Section 7.

2 Related Work

In this section, we focus on previous TBED research conducted on two popular benchmark datasets (GoEmotions, ISEAR) to compare the performance of our models with state-of-the-art emotion recognition models, as well as previous attempts to improve generalizability using transfer learning techniques.

Current work on TBED typically utilizes a variety of linguistic features, such as word or character n-grams, affect lexicons, and word embeddings in combination with a supervised classification model (for recent overviews see, Sailunaz et al., 2018; Acheampong et al., 2020b; Alswaidan and Menai, 2020). While earlier approaches relied on shallow classifiers, such as a naive Bayes, SVM or MaxEnt classifier, later approaches increasingly relied on deep learning models in combination with different word embedding methods. For example, Polignano et al. (2019) proposed an emotion detection model based on the use of long short-term memory (LSTM) and convolutional neural network (CNN) mediated through the use of a level of attention in combination with different word embeddings (GloVe, Pennington et al. 2014, and Fast-Text, Bojanowski et al. 2017).

In experiments performed on the ISEAR dataset, Dong and Zeng (2022) proposed a text emotion distribution learning model based on a lexicon-enhanced multi-task convolutional neural network (LMT-CNN) to jointly solve the tasks of text emotion distribution prediction and emotion label classification. The LMT-CNN model is an end-to-end multi-module deep neural network that utilizes semantic information and linguistic knowledge to predict emotion distributions and labels. Based on comparative experiments on nine commonly used emotion datasets, Dong and Zeng (2022) showed that the LMT-CNN model can outperform two previously introduced deep-neural-network-based models: TextCNN, a convolutional neural network for text emotion classification (Kim, 2014) and MT-CNN (Zhang et al., 2018), a multi-task convolutional neural network model that simultaneously predicts the distribution of text emotion and the dominant emotion of the text (see Table 1 for numerical details on the performance of these models on the datasets used in the present work). In recent years, TBED research has increasingly relied on transformer-based pre-trained language models (Acheampong et al., 2020a; Demszky et al., 2020; **?**): For example, Acheampong et al. (2020a) perform comparative analyses of BERT (Devlin et al., 2019), RoBERTA (Liu et al., 2019), DistilBERT (Sanh et al., 2019), and XLNet (Yang et al., 2019) for text-based emotion recognition on the ISEAR dataset. While all models were found to be efficient in detecting emotions from text, RoBERTa achieved the highest performance with a detection accuracy of 74.31%. The currently best-performing model on the ISEAR dataset, reaching a micro-average F1 score of 75.2%, is Park et al. (2021). In this work a RoBERTa-Large model was finetuned to learn conditional VAD distributions – obtained from the NRC-VAD lexicon (Mohammad, 2018) – through supervision of categorical labels. The learned VAD distributions were then used to predict the emotion labels for a given sentence.

For the recently introduced GoEmotions dataset, Demszky et al. (2020) already provided a strong baseline for modeling emotion classification by fine-tuning a BERT-base model. Their model achieved an average F1-score of 64% over an Ekman-style grouping into six coarse categories. **?** conducted comparative experiments with additional transformer-based models – BERT, DistilBERT, RoBERTa, XLNet, and ELECTRA (Clark et al., 2020) – on the GoEmotions dataset. As in the case of ISEAR, the best performance was achieved by RoBERTa, with an F1-score of 49% on the full GoEmotions taxonomy (28 emotion categories).

Previous TBED work has also proposed combinations of different approaches. For example, Seol et al. (2008) proposed a hybrid model that combines emotion keywords in a sentence using an emotional keyword dictionary with a knowledge-based artificial neural network that uses domain knowledge. To our knowledge, however, almost no TBED research has investigated hybrid models that combine transformer-based models with (psycho)linguistic features (see, however, De Bruyne et al. 2021, for an exception in Dutch). This is surprising, as such an approach has been successfully applied in related areas, for example personality prediction (Mehta et al., 2020; Kerz et al., 2022).

The available research aimed at improving the generalizability of transformer-based models using transfer learning techniques has so far focused on demonstrating that training on a large dataset of one domain, say Reddit comments, can contribute to increasing model accuracy for different target domains, such as tweets and personal narratives. Specifically, using three different finetuning setups – (1) finetuning BERT only on the target dataset, (2) first finetuning BERT on GoEmotions, then perform transfer learning by replacing the final dense layer, and (3) freezing all layers besides the last layer and finetuning on the target dataset –, Demszky et al. (2020) showed that the GoEmotions dataset generalizes well to other domains and different emotion taxonomies in nine datasets from the Unified Emotion Dataset (Bostan and Klinger, 2018).

3 Datasets

We conduct experiments on a total of eight datasets. The within-domain experiments are performed on two benchmark corpora: The GoEmotions dataset (Demszky et al., 2020) and the International Survey on Emotion Antecedents and Reactions (ISEAR) dataset (Scherer and Wallbott, 1994). GoEmotions is the largest available manually annotated dataset for emotion prediction. It consists of 58 thousand Reddit comments, labeled by 80 human raters for 27 emotion categories plus a neutral category. While 83% of the items of the dataset have received a single label, GoEmotions is strictly speaking a multilabel dataset, as raters were free to select multiple emotions. The dataset has been manually reviewed to remove profanity and offensive language towards a particular ethnicity, gender, sexual orientation, or disability. The ISEAR dataset is a widely used benchmark dataset consisting of personal reports on emotional events written by 3000 people from different cultural backgrounds. It was constructed by collecting questionnaires answered by people that reported on their own emotional events. It contains a total of 7,665 sentences labeled with one of seven emotions: joy, fear, anger, sadness, shame, guilt and disgust. The transfer-learning experiments are conducted on six benchmark datasets from Unified Emotion Dataset (Bostan and Klinger, 2018) that were chosen based on their diversity in size and domain: (1) The **AffectiveText** dataset (Strapparava and Mihalcea, 2007) consists of 1,250 news headlines. The annotation schema follows Ekman's basic emotions, complemented by valence. It is multi-label annotated via expert annotation and emotion categories are assigned a score from 0 to 100. (2) The **CrowdFlower** dataset consists of 39,740 tweets annotated via crowdsourcing with one label per tweet. The dataset was previously found to be noisy in comparison with other emotion datasets (Bostan and Klinger, 2018). (3) The dataset **Electoral-Tweets** (Mohammad et al., 2015) targets the domain of elections. It consists of over 100,000 responses to two detailed online questionnaires (the questions targeted emotions, purpose, and style in electoral tweets). The tweets are annotated via crowdsourcing. (4) The Stance Sentiment Emotion Corpus **SSEC** (Schuff et al., 2017) is an annotation of 4,868 tweets from the SemEval 2016 Twitter stance and sentiment dataset. It is annotated via expert annotation with multiple emotion labels per tweet following Plutchik's fundamental emotions. (5) The Twitter Emotion Corpus **TEC** (Mohammad, 2012) consists of 21,011 tweets. The annotation schema corresponds to Ekman's model of basic emotions. They collected tweets with hashtags corresponding to the six Ekman emotions: #anger, #disgust, #fear, #happy, #sadness, and #surprise, therefore it is distantly single-label annotated. (6) The Emotion-Stimulus dataset (Ghazi et al., 2015) has 1,549 sentences with their emotion analysed. The set of annotation labels comprises of Ekman's basic emotions with the addition of shame. (7) The $\text{ISEAR}_{\text{UED}}$ dataset that is part of the Unified Emotion Dataset has 5,477 sentences with single emotion annotations. This dataset is a filtered version of the original ISEAR dataset described above. Bostan and Klinger (2018) filter and keep the texts with the labels anger, disgust, joy, sadness and fear for the Unified Emotion Dataset.

4 Sentence-level measurement of psycholinguistic features

The datasets were automatically analyzed using an automated text analysis (ATA) system that employs a sliding window technique to compute sentence-level measurements (for recent applications of this tool across various domains, see Qiao et al. (2020) for fake news detection, Kerz et al. (2021) for predicting human affective ratings) and Wiechmann et al. (2022) for predicting eye-moving patterns during reading). We extracted a set of 435 psycholinguistic features that can be binned into four groups: (1) features of morpho-syntactic complexity (N=19), (2) features of lexical richness, diversity and sophistication (N=77), (3) readability features (N=14), and (4) lexicon features designed to detect sentiment, emotion and/or affect (N=325). Tokenization, sentence splitting, part-of-speech tagging, lemmatization and syntactic PCFG parsing were performed using Stanford CoreNLP (Manning et al., 2014).

The group of **morpho-syntactic complexity features** includes (i) surface features related to the length of production units, such as the average length of clauses and sentences, (ii) features of the type and frequency of embeddings, such as number of dependent clauses per T-Unit or verb phrases per sentence and (iii) the frequency of particular structure types, such as the number of complex nominals per clause. This group also includes (iv) information-theoretic features of morphological and syntactic complexity based on the Deflate algorithm (Deutsch, 1996). The group of **lexical richness, diversity and sophistication features** includes six different subtypes: (i) lexical density features, such as the ratio of the number of lexical (as opposed to grammatical) words to the total number of words in a text, (ii) lexical variation, i.e. the range of vocabulary as manifested in language use, captured by text-size corrected type-token ratio, (iii) lexical sophistication, i.e. the proportion of relatively unusual or advanced words in a text, such as the number of words from the New General Service List (Browne et al., 2013), (iv) psycholinguistic norms of words, such as the average age of acquisition of the word (Kuperman et al., 2012) and two recently introduced types of features: (v) word prevalence features that capture the number of people who know the word (Brysbaert et al., 2019; Johns et al., 2020) and (vi) register-based n-gram frequency features that take into account both frequency rank and the number of word n-grams ($n \in [1, 5]$). The latter were derived from the five register subcomponents of the Contemporary Corpus of American English (COCA, 560 million words, Davies, 2008): spoken, magazine, fiction, news and academic language (see Kerz et al., 2020, for details see e.g.). The group of **readability features** combines a word familiarity variable defined by a prespecified vocabulary resource to estimate semantic difficulty along with a syntactic variable, such as average sentence length. Examples of these measures include the Fry index (Fry, 1968) or the

SMOG (McLaughlin, 1969). The group of **lexicon-based sentiment/emotion/affect features** was derived from a total of ten lexicons that have been successfully used in personality detection, emotion recognition and sentiment analysis research: (1) The Affective Norms for English Words (ANEW) (Bradley and Lang, 1999), (2) the ANEW-Emo lexicons (Stevenson et al., 2007), (3) DepecheMood++ (Araque et al., 2019), (4) the Geneva Affect Label Coder (GALC) (Scherer, 2005), (5) General Inquirer (Stone et al., 1966), (6) the LIWC dictionary (Pennebaker et al., 2001), (7) the NRC Word-Emotion Association Lexicon (Mohammad and Turney, 2013), (8) the NRC Valence, Arousal, and Dominance lexicon (Mohammad, 2018), (9) SenticNet (Cambria et al., 2010b), and (10) the Sentiment140 lexicon (Mohammad et al., 2013).

5 Modeling Approach

We construct a total of five models: (1) a fine-tuned Bidirectional Encoder Representations from Transformers (BERT) model, (2) a fine-tuned RoBERTA model (Robustly Optimized BERT pre-training Approach), (3) a bidirectional neural network classifiers trained on sentence-level measurements of psycholinguistic features described in Section 3.1, and (4) and (5) two hybrid models integrating BERT and RoBERTa predictions with the psycholinguistic features. We train all models in a multi-label classification setup. For the within-domain evaluation of the models on the GoEmotions dataset, we follow the procedure specified in Demszky et al. (2020): That is, we filtered out emotion labels selected by only a single annotator. The 93% of the original were randomly split into train (80%), dev (10%) and test (10%) sets. These splits are identical to those used by Demszky et al.. In the transfer learning setting geared to show that our modeling approach improves generalization across domains and taxonomies, we perform experiments on each of the six emotion benchmark datasets presented in section 3 using four approaches: with/without finetuning on target dataset and with/without the inclusion of the label 'neutral'. The performance of these models is evaluated using 5 times repeated 5-fold crossvalidation using a 80/20 split to counter variability due to weight initialization. We report performance metrics averaged over all runs. All models are implemented using PyTorch (Paszke et al., 2019). Unless specifically stated otherwise, we use 'BCELoss' as our

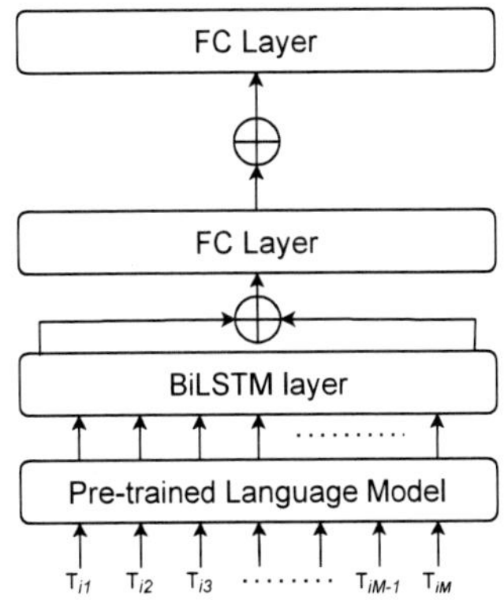

Figure 1: Structure diagram of transformer-based emotion detection models

loss function, 'AdamW' as optimizer, with learning rate 2×10^{-5} and weight decay of 1×10^{-5}

5.1 Transformer-based models (BERT, RoBERTa)

We used the pretrained 'bert-base-uncased' and 'roberta-base' models from the Huggingface Transformers library (Wolf et al., 2020). The models consist of 12 Transformer layers with hidden size 768 and 12 attention heads. We run experiments with (1) a linear fully-connected layer for classification as well as with (2) an intermediate bidirectional LSTM layer with 256 hidden units (Al-Omari et al., 2020) (BERT-BiLSTM). The following hyperparameters are used for fine-tuning: a fixed learning rate of 2×10^{-5} is applied and $L2$ regularization of 1×10^{-6}. All models were trained for 8 epochs, with batch size of 4 and maximum sequence length of 512 and dropout of 0.2. We report the results from the best performing models, i.e. RoBERTa-BiLSTM and BERT-BiLSTM.

5.2 Bidirectional LSTM trained on psycholinguistic features (PsyLing)

As a model based solely on psycholinguistic features, we constructed a 2-layer bidirectional long short-term model (BiLSTM) with a hidden state dimension of 32, which is depicted in Figure 2. The input to the model is a sequence $CM_1^N = (CM_1, CM_2 \ldots, CM_N)$, where CM_i, the output of the ATA-system, for the ith sentence of a document, is a 435 dimensional vector and N is the sequence length. To predict the labels of a sequence, we concatenate the last hidden states of the last layer in forward ($\overrightarrow{h_n}$) and backward directions ($\overleftarrow{h_n}$). The resulting vector $h_n = [\overrightarrow{h_n}|\overleftarrow{h_n}]$ is

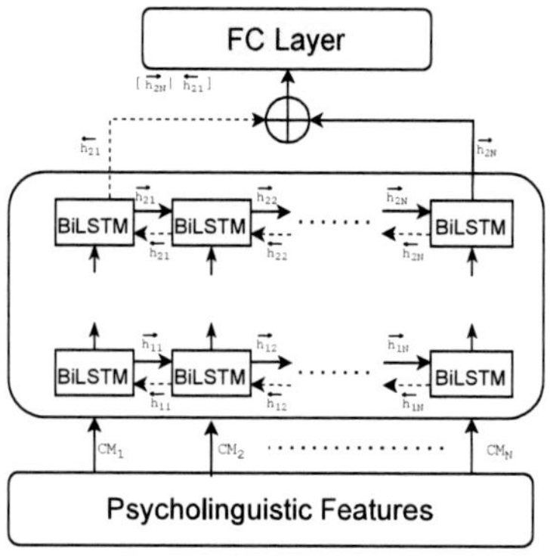

Figure 2: Structure diagram of BiLSTM emotion detection model trained on psycholinguistic features

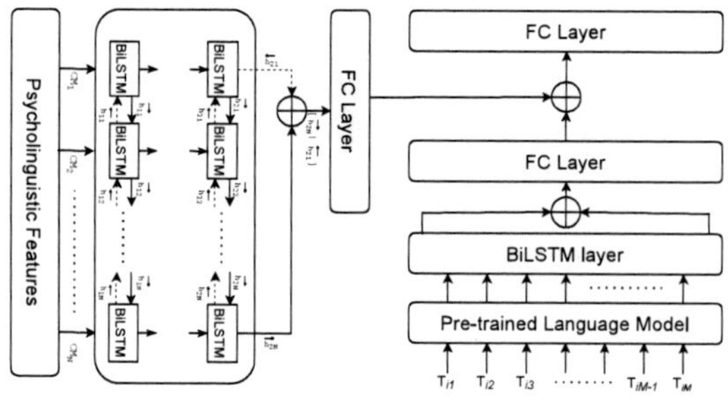

Figure 3: Structure diagram of hybrid emotion detection models

then transformed through a 2-layer feedforward neural network, whose activation function is Rectifier Linear Unit (ReLU). The output of this is then passed to a Dense Fully Connected Layer with a dropout of 0.2, and finally fed to a final fully connected layer. The output of this is a K dimensional vector, where K is the number of emotion labels.

5.3 Hybrid models (BERT+PsyLing, RoBERTa+PsyLing)

We assemble the hybrid models by (1) obtaining a set of 256 dimensional vector from the PsyLing model and then (2) concatenating these features along with the output from the pre-trained transformer-based model part. To obtain the output of the pre-trained transformer-based model, the given text is fed to a pre-trained language model, its outputs are passed through a 2-layer BiLSTM with hidden size of 512. This is further passed through a fully connected layer to obtain a 256 dimensional vector. This concatenated vector is then fed into a 2-layer feedforward classifier. To obtain the soft labels (probabilities that a text belongs to the corresponding emotion label), sigmoid was applied to each dimension of the output vector.

6 Results

The models were evaluated using accuracy, precision, recall and F1 scores as the performance metrics. The results of the within-domain classification experiments on the GoEmotion and ISEAR datasets are shown in Table 1 (detailed results on all metrics are provided in see Table 4 in the appendix). We focus here on the discussion of F1 scores. For both datasets and for both transformer-based models, we find that the proposed hybrid models outperform the standard transformer-based baseline models: Specifically, in the case of the GoEmotions dataset, the hybrid models (BERT+PsyLing, RoBERTa+PsyLing) exhibit an increase in F1 score of +2% relative to their respective baseline models. In the case of the ISEAR dataset, the RoBERTa+PsyLing model show an increase in F1 score of +2% relative to RoBERTa, while the BERT+PsyLing model show an increase in F1 score of +1% relative to BERT. Our hybrid models show improvements in all emotion categories, except for anger, where they are on par with their respective baseline models. These results indicate that integrating transformer-based models with BiLSTM trained on psycholinguistic features can improve emotion classification within two distinct domains: an online domain (Reddit) as well as the domain of reports of personal events. On the GoEmotion dataset, our best-performing hybrid model, RoBERTa+PsyLing, outperforms the previous SOTA model Roberta-EMD (Park et al., 2021) by +9.9% macro-F1. On the ISEAR dataset, both hybrid models outperform two of the three CNNs presented in Dong and Zeng (2022), TextCNN and MT-CNN, and are competitive with the lexicon-enhanced multi-task CNN (LMT-CNN). In fact, both hybrid models outperform the LMT-CNN on two of the five emotion categories, with an increase on the joy category of +10.31% F1 (LMT-CNN vs. BERT-PsyLing) and an increase on the fear category of +4.05% F1 (LMT-CNN vs. BERT-PsyLing). The results of the comparisons with previous deep-learning TBED models on the two benchmark datasets thus indicate that the proposed approach constitutes a valuable framework for future TBED efforts.

An overview of the results of the out-of-domain experiments is presented in Table 2. Table 3 shows

	GoEmotion Dataset						
Model	Anger	Disgust	Sadness	Surprise	Fear	Joy	Average
RoBERTa-EMD (Park et al., 2021)	–	–	–	–	–	–	61.1
BERT	70	48	64	72	72	90	68
RoBERTa	70	49	63	69	71	90	69
PsyLing	50	24	40	40	34	80	45
BERT+PsyLing (ours)	**71**	49	**65**	72	72	91	70
RoBERTa+PsyLing (ours)	70	**50**	**65**	**74**	**73**	**92**	**71**
	ISEAR Dataset						
TextCNN (Dong and Zeng, 2022)	62.14	65.22	76.39	–	72.09	73.97	69.96
MT-CNN (Dong and Zeng, 2022)	65.68	67.63	77	–	74.25	72.09	71.33
LMT-CNN (Dong and Zeng, 2022)	**66.54**	**70.64**	**80.68**	–	74.95	74.69	73.5
RoBERTa-EMD (Park et al., 2021)	**–**	**–**	**–**	**–**	**–**	**–**	**75.2**
BERT	56	65	71	-	77	84	71
RoBERTa	60	69	71	-	72	84	71
PsyLing	38	36	48	-	48	57	45
BERT+PsyLing (ours)	58	**70**	70	-	78	**85**	72
RoBERTa+PsyLing (ours)	**64**	69	**73**	-	**79**	79	73

Table 1: Results on the two benchmark datasets (GoEmotion (top), ISEAR (bottom)). All scores represent macro-averages of F1 scores(in %).

	Model	TEC	Crowdfl.	$\text{ISEAR}_{\text{UED}}$	elect-tweet	affect-text	SSEC	emo-stimulus
Train GoEmo	BERT	29	**23**	44	26	36	19	53
w/o finetuning	RoBERTa	**31**	**23**	44	**29**	39	21	56
w/o neutral	PsyLing	22	18	25	16	23	11	38
	BERT+PsyLing	**31**	**23**	44	27	36	21	56
	RoBERTa+PsyLing	29	**23**	**47**	27	**40**	**22**	**61**
w/o finetuning	BERT	20	26	35	23	13	16	41
with neutral	RoBERTa	22	27	34	**25**	14	**18**	47
	PsyLing	16	20	17	13	10	08	23
	BERT+PsyLing	21	27	35	24	15	17	45
	RoBERTa+PsyLing	**23**	**28**	**36**	**25**	**16**	17	**49**
with finetuning	BERT	55	31	63	36	54	**32**	92
w/o neutral	RoBERTa	**56**	30	**65**	34	53	**32**	**94**
	PsyLing	34	23	41	32	36	24	46
	BERT+PsyLing	55	32	**65**	39	**57**	**32**	**94**
	RoBERTa+PsyLing	**56**	**31**	**65**	**41**	**57**	**32**	**94**
with finetuning	BERT	46	33	55	33	44	29	96
with neutral	RoBERTa	44	**34**	**56**	30	46	30	95
	PsyLing	24	24	35	28	29	30	53
	BERT+PsyLing	**47**	34	55	34	**48**	31	**97**
	RoBERTa+PsyLing	46	**34**	**56**	**34**	47	**33**	96

Table 2: Results on transfer learning experiments. Values are macro-averaged F1 scores (in %).

Dataset	BERT	RoBERTa	PsyLing	BERT + PsyLing	RoBERTa + PsyLing	Bostan and Klinger, 2018
TEC	63	64	45	**67**	64	48
CrowdFlower	46	**47**	41	**47**	**47**	24
$\text{ISEAR}_{\text{UED}}$	76	**78**	49	**78**	**78**	52
elect-tweet	**62**	**62**	58	**62**	**62**	31
affect-text	63	63	48	**67**	**67**	64
SSEC	58	60	45	58	60	**67**
emo-stimulus	94	96	55	**97**	**97**	**97**

Table 3: Comparison of performance with Bostan and Klinger (2018). Values are micro-averaged F1 scores (in %).

comparisons of the results of our best performing model, RoBERTa+PsyLing, in the finetuning setting without the neutral label with the results of maximum entropy classifiers trained on with bag-of-words (BOW) features from Bostan and Klinger (2018). The results in Table 2 reveal that the RoBERTa+PsyLing hybrid model was the best performing model across all four experimental settings. Performance was generally observed to be highest in the finetuning setting without the neutral label. Importantly, the results in Table 2 reveal that the integration of psycholinguistic features matched or improved the performance of the models across all settings, with increases in F1 scores of up to 7% relative to a standard transformer-based approach. The results in Table 3 indicate that our hybrid models pretrained on GoEmotions outperform the results of the baseline models provided by Bostan and Klinger (2018) on five of the seven emotion datasets (TEC, CrowdFLower, $\text{ISEAR}_{\text{UED}}$, elect-tweet, and affect text), with increases in performance of up to 31%. The hybrid models tied the near-perfect performance of the baseline model on the emo-stimulus dataset and fell short only on the SSEC dataset. A possible reason for the relatively low performance of our models on the latter may be due to the fact that the SSEC was rated based on Plutchik's fundamental emotions.

7 Conclusion

This paper proposed approaches for text-based emotion detection that leverage transformer models in combination with Bidirectional Long Short-Term Memory networks trained on a comprehensive set of psycholinguistic features. The results of transfer learning experiments performed on six out-of-domain emotion datasets demonstrated that the proposed hybrid models can substantially improve model generalizability to out-of-distribution data compared to a standard transformer-based model. Moreover, we found that these models perform competitively on in-domain data. In future work, we intend to extend this line of work to dimensional emotion models as well as to models that jointly solve the tasks of emotion label classification and text emotion distribution prediction.

Ethical Considerations

The datasets used in this study may contain biases, are not representative of global diversity and may contain potentially problematic content. Potential biases in the data include: Inherent biases in user base biases, the offensive/vulgar word lists used for data filtering, inherent or unconscious bias in assessment of offensive identity labels. All these likely affect labeling, precision, and recall for a trained model.

References

Francisca Adoma Acheampong, Nunoo-Mensah Henry, and Wenyu Chen. 2020a. Comparative analyses of bert, roberta, distilbert, and xlnet for text-based emotion recognition. In *2020 17th International Computer Conference on Wavelet Active Media Technology and Information Processing (ICCWAMTIP)*, pages 117–121. IEEE.

Francisca Adoma Acheampong, Chen Wenyu, and Henry Nunoo-Mensah. 2020b. Text-based emotion detection: Advances, challenges, and opportunities. *Engineering Reports*, 2(7):e12189.

Hani Al-Omari, Malak A. Abdullah, and Samira Shaikh. 2020. Emodet2: Emotion detection in english textual dialogue using bert and bilstm models. In *2020 11th International Conference on Information and Communication Systems (ICICS)*, pages 226–232.

Nourah Alswaidan and Mohamed El Bachir Menai. 2020. A survey of state-of-the-art approaches for emotion recognition in text. *Knowledge and Information Systems*, 62(8):2937–2987.

Oscar Araque, Lorenzo Gatti, Jacopo Staiano, and Marco Guerini. 2019. Depechemood++: a bilingual emotion lexicon built through simple yet powerful techniques. *IEEE transactions on affective computing*.

Eduardo Bericat. 2016. The sociology of emotions: Four decades of progress. *Current Sociology*, 64(3):491–513.

Piotr Bojanowski, Edouard Grave, Armand Joulin, and Tomas Mikolov. 2017. Enriching word vectors with subword information. *Transactions of the association for computational linguistics*, 5:135–146.

Joan C Borod et al. 2000. *The neuropsychology of emotion*. Oxford University Press.

Laura-Ana-Maria Bostan and Roman Klinger. 2018. An analysis of annotated corpora for emotion classification in text. In *Proceedings of the 27th International Conference on Computational Linguistics*, pages 2104–2119.

Margaret M Bradley and Peter J Lang. 1999. Affective norms for english words (ANEW): Instruction manual and affective ratings. Technical report, Technical report C-1, the center for research in psychophysiology ....

Charles Browne et al. 2013. The new general service list: Celebrating 60 years of vocabulary learning. *The Language Teacher*, 37(4):13–16.

Marc Brysbaert, Paweł Mandera, Samantha F McCormick, and Emmanuel Keuleers. 2019. Word prevalence norms for 62,000 english lemmas. *Behavior research methods*, 51(2):467–479.

Erik Cambria, Amir Hussain, Catherine Havasi, and Chris Eckl. 2010a. Sentic computing: Exploitation of common sense for the development of emotion-sensitive systems. In *Development of multimodal interfaces: active listening and synchrony*, pages 148–156. Springer.

Erik Cambria, Andrew Livingstone, and Amir Hussain. 2012. The hourglass of emotions. In *Cognitive behavioural systems*, pages 144–157. Springer.

Erik Cambria, Dheeraj Rajagopal, Daniel Olsher, and Dipankar Das. 2013. Big social data analysis. *Big data computing*, 13:401–414.

Erik Cambria, Robyn Speer, Catherine Havasi, and Amir Hussain. 2010b. Senticnet: A publicly available semantic resource for opinion mining. In *2010 AAAI fall symposium series*.

Lea Canales and Patricio Martínez-Barco. 2014. Emotion detection from text: A survey. In *Proceedings of the workshop on natural language processing in the 5th information systems research working days (JISIC)*, pages 37–43.

Jacky Casas, Timo Spring, Karl Daher, Elena Mugellini, Omar Abou Khaled, and Philippe Cudré-Mauroux. 2021. Enhancing conversational agents with empathic abilities. In *Proceedings of the 21st ACM International Conference on Intelligent Virtual Agents*, pages 41–47.

Kevin Clark, Minh-Thang Luong, Quoc V. Le, and Christopher D. Manning. 2020. ELECTRA: Pre-training text encoders as discriminators rather than generators. In *8th International Conference on Learning Representations, ICLR 2020, Addis Ababa, Ethiopia, April 26-30, 2020*. OpenReview.net.

Mark Davies. 2008. The Corpus of Contemporary American English (COCA): 560 million words, 1990-present.

Luna De Bruyne, Orphée De Clercq, and Véronique Hoste. 2021. Emotional robbert and insensitive bertje: Combining transformers and affect lexica for dutch emotion detection. In *Workshop on Computational Approaches to Subjectivity, Sentiment and Social Media Analysis*, pages 257–263.

Dorottya Demszky, Dana Movshovitz-Attias, Jeongwoo Ko, Alan Cowen, Gaurav Nemade, and Sujith Ravi. 2020. GoEmotions: A dataset of fine-grained emotions. In *Proceedings of the 58th Annual Meeting of the Association for Computational Linguistics*, pages 4040–4054, Online. Association for Computational Linguistics.

Jiawen Deng and Fuji Ren. 2021. A survey of textual emotion recognition and its challenges. *IEEE Transactions on Affective Computing*.

Peter Deutsch. 1996. Rfc1951: Deflate compressed data format specification version 1.3.

Jacob Devlin, Ming-Wei Chang, Kenton Lee, and Kristina Toutanova. 2019. BERT: Pre-training of deep bidirectional transformers for language understanding. In *Proceedings of the 2019 Conference of the North American Chapter of the Association for Computational Linguistics: Human Language Technologies, Volume 1 (Long and Short Papers)*, pages 4171–4186, Minneapolis, Minnesota. Association for Computational Linguistics.

Yuchang Dong and Xueqiang Zeng. 2022. Lexicon-enhanced multi-task convolutional neural network for emotion distribution learning. *Axioms*, 11(4):181.

Paul Ekman. 1992. Are there basic emotions? *Psychological review*, 99 3:550–3.

Paul Ekman. 1999. Basic emotions. *Handbook of cognition and emotion*, 98(45-60):16.

Edward Fry. 1968. A readability formula that saves time. *Journal of reading*, 11(7):513–578.

Diman Ghazi, Diana Inkpen, and Stan Szpakowicz. 2015. Detecting emotion stimuli in emotion-bearing sentences. In *International Conference on Intelligent Text Processing and Computational Linguistics*, pages 152–165. Springer.

Brendan T Johns, Melody Dye, and Michael N Jones. 2020. Estimating the prevalence and diversity of words in written language. *Quarterly Journal of Experimental Psychology*, 73(6):841–855.

Elma Kerz, Yu Qiao, and Daniel Wiechmann. 2021. Language that captivates the audience: predicting affective ratings of ted talks in a multi-label classification task. In *Proceedings of the Eleventh Workshop on Computational Approaches to Subjectivity, Sentiment and Social Media Analysis*, pages 13–24.

Elma Kerz, Yu Qiao, Daniel Wiechmann, and Marcus Ströbel. 2020. Becoming linguistically mature: Modeling english and german children's writing development across school grades. In *Proceedings of the Fifteenth Workshop on Innovative Use of NLP for Building Educational Applications*, pages 65–74.

Elma Kerz, Yu Qiao, Sourabh Zanwar, and Daniel Wiechmann. 2022. Pushing on personality detection from verbal behavior: A transformer meets text contours of psycholinguistic features. In *Proceedings of the 12th Workshop on Computational Approaches to Subjectivity, Sentiment & Social Media Analysis*, pages 182–194, Dublin, Ireland. Association for Computational Linguistics.

Yoon Kim. 2014. Convolutional neural networks for sentence classification. In *Proceedings of the 2014 Conference on Empirical Methods in Natural Language Processing (EMNLP)*, pages 1746–1751, Doha, Qatar. Association for Computational Linguistics.

Victor Kuperman, Hans Stadthagen-Gonzalez, and Marc Brysbaert. 2012. Age-of-acquisition ratings for 30,000 English words. *Behavior research methods*, 44(4):978–990.

Jennifer S Lerner, Ye Li, Piercarlo Valdesolo, and Karim S Kassam. 2015. Emotion and decision making. *Annual review of psychology*, 66:799–823.

Yinhan Liu, Myle Ott, Naman Goyal, Jingfei Du, Mandar Joshi, Danqi Chen, Omer Levy, Mike Lewis, Luke Zettlemoyer, and Veselin Stoyanov. 2019. Roberta: A robustly optimized bert pretraining approach. *arXiv preprint arXiv:1907.11692*.

G. Loewenstein and J.S. Lerner. 2003. *The role of affect in decision making*, pages 619–642. Oxford University Press, Oxford.

Navonil Majumder, Soujanya Poria, Devamanyu Hazarika, Rada Mihalcea, Alexander Gelbukh, and Erik Cambria. 2019. Dialoguernn: An attentive rnn for emotion detection in conversations. In *Proceedings of the AAAI Conference on Artificial Intelligence*, volume 33, pages 6818–6825.

Christopher Manning, Mihai Surdeanu, John Bauer, Jenny Finkel, Steven Bethard, and David McClosky. 2014. The stanford corenlp natural language processing toolkit. In *Proceedings of 52nd annual meeting of the association for computational linguistics: system demonstrations*, pages 55–60.

G Harry McLaughlin. 1969. Clearing the smog. *Journal of Reading*.

Yash Mehta, Samin Fatehi, Amirmohammad Kazameini, Clemens Stachl, Erik Cambria, and Sauleh Eetemadi. 2020. Bottom-up and top-down: Predicting personality with psycholinguistic and language model features. In *2020 IEEE International Conference on Data Mining (ICDM)*, pages 1184–1189. IEEE.

Saif Mohammad. 2012. # emotional tweets. In * *SEM 2012: The First Joint Conference on Lexical and Computational Semantics–Volume 1: Proceedings of the main conference and the shared task, and Volume 2: Proceedings of the Sixth International Workshop on Semantic Evaluation (SemEval 2012)*, pages 246–255.

Saif Mohammad. 2018. Obtaining reliable human ratings of valence, arousal, and dominance for 20,000 english words. In *Proceedings of the 56th Annual Meeting of the Association for Computational Linguistics (Volume 1: Long Papers)*, pages 174–184.

Saif Mohammad, Svetlana Kiritchenko, and Xiaodan Zhu. 2013. Nrc-canada: Building the state-of-the-art in sentiment analysis of tweets. In *Proceedings of the seventh international workshop on Semantic Evaluation Exercises (SemEval-2013)*, Atlanta, Georgia, USA.

Saif M Mohammad and Peter D Turney. 2013. Crowdsourcing a word–emotion association lexicon. *Computational intelligence*, 29(3):436–465.

Saif M Mohammad, Xiaodan Zhu, Svetlana Kiritchenko, and Joel Martin. 2015. Sentiment, emotion, purpose, and style in electoral tweets. *Information Processing & Management*, 51(4):480–499.

Sungjoon Park, Jiseon Kim, Seonghyeon Ye, Jaeyeol Jeon, Hee Young Park, and Alice Oh. 2021. Dimensional emotion detection from categorical emotion. In *Proceedings of the 2021 Conference on Empirical Methods in Natural Language Processing*, pages 4367–4380.

W Gerrod Parrott. 2001. *Emotions in social psychology: Essential readings*. Psychology Press.

Adam Paszke, Sam Gross, Francisco Massa, Adam Lerer, James Bradbury, Gregory Chanan, Trevor Killeen, Zeming Lin, Natalia Gimelshein, Luca Antiga, Alban Desmaison, Andreas Kopf, Edward Yang, Zachary DeVito, Martin Raison, Alykhan Tejani, Sasank Chilamkurthy, Benoit Steiner, Lu Fang, Junjie Bai, and Soumith Chintala. 2019. Pytorch: An imperative style, high-performance deep learning library. In H. Wallach, H. Larochelle, A. Beygelzimer, F. d'Alché-Buc, E. Fox, and R. Garnett, editors, *Advances in Neural Information Processing Systems 32*, pages 8024–8035. Curran Associates, Inc.

James W Pennebaker, Martha E Francis, and Roger J Booth. 2001. Linguistic inquiry and word count: Liwc 2001. *Mahway: Lawrence Erlbaum Associates*, 71(2001):2001.

Jeffrey Pennington, Richard Socher, and Christopher D Manning. 2014. Glove: Global vectors for word representation. In *Proceedings of the 2014 conference on empirical methods in natural language processing (EMNLP)*, pages 1532–1543.

Flor Miriam Plaza-del Arco, Sercan Halat, Sebastian Padó, and Roman Klinger. 2021. Multi-task learning with sentiment, emotion, and target detection to recognize hate speech and offensive language. *arXiv preprint arXiv:2109.10255*.

Robert Plutchik. 1984. Emotions: A general psychoevolutionary theory. *Approaches to emotion*, 1984(197-219):2–4.

Marco Polignano, Pierpaolo Basile, Marco de Gemmis, and Giovanni Semeraro. 2019. A comparison of word-embeddings in emotion detection from text using bilstm, cnn and self-attention. In *Adjunct Publication of the 27th Conference on User Modeling, Adaptation and Personalization*, pages 63–68.

Yu Qiao, Daniel Wiechmann, and Elma Kerz. 2020. A language-based approach to fake news detection through interpretable features and brnn. In *Proceedings of the 3rd international workshop on rumours and deception in social media (RDSM)*, pages 14–31.

James A Russell. 1980. A circumplex model of affect. *Journal of personality and social psychology*, 39(6):1161.

Kashfia Sailunaz, Manmeet Dhaliwal, Jon Rokne, and Reda Alhajj. 2018. Emotion detection from text and speech: a survey. *Social Network Analysis and Mining*, 8(1):1–26.

David Sander and Lauri Nummenmaa. 2021. Reward and emotion: an affective neuroscience approach. *Current Opinion in Behavioral Sciences*, 39:161–167.

Victor Sanh, Lysandre Debut, Julien Chaumond, and Thomas Wolf. 2019. Distilbert, a distilled version of bert: smaller, faster, cheaper and lighter. *arXiv preprint arXiv:1910.01108*.

Klaus R Scherer. 2005. What are emotions? and how can they be measured? *Social science information*, 44(4):695–729.

Klaus R Scherer and Harald G Wallbott. 1994. Evidence for universality and cultural variation of differential emotion response patterning. *Journal of personality and social psychology*, 66(2):310.

Klaus R Scherer et al. 2000. Psychological models of emotion. *The neuropsychology of emotion*, 137(3):137–162.

Hendrik Schuff, Jeremy Barnes, Julian Mohme, Sebastian Padó, and Roman Klinger. 2017. Annotation, modelling and analysis of fine-grained emotions on a stance and sentiment detection corpus. In *Proceedings of the 8th Workshop on Computational Approaches to Subjectivity, Sentiment and Social Media Analysis*, pages 13–23.

Yong-Soo Seol, Dong-Joo Kim, and Han-Woo Kim. 2008. Emotion recognition from text using knowledge-based ann. In *ITC-CSCC: International Technical Conference on Circuits Systems, Computers and Communications*, pages 1569–1572.

Tariq Soussan and Marcello Trovati. 2020. Improved sentiment urgency emotion detection for business intelligence. In *International Conference on Intelligent Networking and Collaborative Systems*, pages 312–318. Springer.

Ryan A Stevenson, Joseph A Mikels, and Thomas W James. 2007. Characterization of the affective norms for english words by discrete emotional categories. *Behavior research methods*, 39(4):1020–1024.

Philip J Stone, Dexter C Dunphy, and Marshall S Smith. 1966. The general inquirer: A computer approach to content analysis.

Carlo Strapparava and Rada Mihalcea. 2007. Semeval-2007 task 14: Affective text. In *Proceedings of the Fourth International Workshop on Semantic Evaluations (SemEval-2007)*, pages 70–74.

Yosephine Susanto, Andrew G Livingstone, Bee Chin Ng, and Erik Cambria. 2020. The hourglass model revisited. *IEEE Intelligent Systems*, 35(5):96–102.

Daniel Wiechmann, Yu Qiao, Elma Kerz, and Justus Mattern. 2022. Measuring the impact of (psycho-)linguistic and readability features and their spill over effects on the prediction of eye movement patterns. In *Proceedings of the 60th Annual Meeting of the Association for Computational Linguistics (Volume 1: Long Papers)*, pages 5276–5290, Dublin, Ireland. Association for Computational Linguistics.

Thomas Wolf, Julien Chaumond, Lysandre Debut, Victor Sanh, Clement Delangue, Anthony Moi, Pierric Cistac, Morgan Funtowicz, Joe Davison, Sam Shleifer, et al. 2020. Transformers: State-of-the-art natural language processing. In *Proceedings of the 2020 Conference on Empirical Methods in Natural Language Processing: System Demonstrations*, pages 38–45.

Frank Z Xing, Erik Cambria, and Roy E Welsch. 2018. Natural language based financial forecasting: a survey. *Artificial Intelligence Review*, 50(1):49–73.

Zhilin Yang, Zihang Dai, Yiming Yang, Jaime Carbonell, Russ R Salakhutdinov, and Quoc V Le. 2019. Xlnet: Generalized autoregressive pretraining for language understanding. *Advances in neural information processing systems*, 32.

Yuxiang Zhang, Jiamei Fu, Dongyu She, Ying Zhang, Senzhang Wang, and Jufeng Yang. 2018. Text emotion distribution learning via multi-task convolutional neural network. In *IJCAI*, pages 4595–4601.

A Appendix

Table 4: Detailed Results on the two benchmark datasets (GoEmotion (top), ISEAR (bottom))

		GoEmotion Dataset						
Model	Metric	Anger	Disgust	Sadness	Surprise	Fear	Joy	Average
RoBERTa-EMD (Park et al 2021)	F1	–	–	–	–	–	–	61.1
	Pre	69	38	53	68	68	88	64
BERT	Rec	71	65	80	77	76	91	77
	F1	70	48	64	72	72	90	68
	Pre	70	62	79	78	71	88	75
RoBERTa	Rec	71	41	53	62	70	93	65
	F1	70	49	63	69	71	90	69
	Pre	48	28	47	43	42	80	48
PsyLing	Rec	53	22	34	38	29	80	43
	F1	50	24	40	40	34	80	45
	Pre	69	65	68	73	81	90	74
BERT+PsyLing (ours)	Rec	71	40	63	69	56	90	65
	F1	**71**	49	**65**	72	72	91	70
	Pre	69	65	68	73	81	90	74
RoBERTa+PsyLing (ours)	Rec	71	40	63	69	56	90	65
	F1	70	**50**	**65**	**74**	**73**	**92**	**71**
		ISEAR Dataset						
	Pre	61.36	63.5	76.64	–	70.67	79.3	70.29
TextCNN (Dong & Zeng 2022)	Rec	70.84	64.24	74.21	–	71.66	64.59	69.11
	F1	62.14	65.22	76.39	–	72.09	73.97	69.96
	Pre	61.31	64.68	80.27	–	72.16	81.13	71.91
MT-CNN (Dong & Zeng 2022)	Rec	71.62	64.46	77.37	–	73.66	69.36	71.29
	F1	65.68	67.63	77	–	74.25	72.09	71.33
	Pre	62.28	66	82.07	–	72.5	82.15	73
LMT-CNN (Dong & Zeng 2022)	Rec	72.38	65.1	79.34	–	74.4	71.64	72.57
	F1	**66.54**	**70.64**	**80.68**	–	74.95	74.69	73.5
RoBERTa-EMD (Park et al 2021)	F1	**–**	**–**	**–**	**–**	**–**	**–**	**75.2**
	Pre	51	74	74	-	83	84	73
BERT	Rec	63	60	69	-	74	86	70
	F1	56	65	71	-	77	84	71
	Pre	58	68	77	-	93	86	77
RoBERTa	Rec	61	66	64	-	62	77	66
	F1	60	69	71	-	72	84	71
	Pre	26	35	37	-	46	62	41
PsyLing	Rec	62	34	63	-	48	53	41
	F1	38	36	48	-	48	57	45
	Pre	55	73	72	-	80	84	73
BERT+PsyLing (ours)	Rec	62	68	68	-	77	86	72
	F1	58	**70**	70	-	78	**85**	72
	Pre	66	72	79	-	80	80	75
RoBERTa+PsyLing (ours)	Rec	66	66	68	-	77	77	71
	F1	**64**	69	**73**	-	**79**	79	73

Fine-Grained Extraction and Classification of Skill Requirements in German-Speaking Job Ads

Ann-Sophie Gnehm and **Eva Bühlmann** and **Helen Buchs** and **Simon Clematide**
Department of Sociology and Department of Computational Linguistics
University of Zurich
{gnehm,buehlmann,buchs}@soziologie.uzh.ch, simon.clematide@cl.uzh.ch

Abstract

Monitoring the development of labor market skill requirements is an information need that is more and more approached by applying text mining methods to job advertisement data. We present an approach for fine-grained extraction and classification of skill requirements from German-speaking job advertisements. We adapt pre-trained transformer-based language models to the domain and task of computing meaningful representations of sentences or spans. By using context from job advertisements and the large ESCO domain ontology we improve our similarity-based unsupervised multi-label classification results. Our best model achieves a mean average precision of 0.969 on the skill class level.

1 Introduction

How skill demand evolves over time in the labor market has always been a main research question in social sciences. Research has however been hampered by the following limitations: Skills were mostly measured on the supply side (what workers bring, not what employers ask for) and only on an aggregated level (by occupations) and/or cross-sectional (one data point in time). Furthermore, most data focused on a selection of skills, since defining and measuring skills is difficult (Biagi and Sebastian, 2020). Job advertisement data can help to overcome such shortcomings by providing time-series measurements on the job level, including all labor market skill requirements (Buchmann et al., 2022a). Not surprisingly, social science has thus lately shown great interest in applying text mining methods to job advertisements (job ads in the following).

Our main goals are to, first, extract spans of text in Swiss German-speaking job ads that specify workers' skill requirements: Specifically, educational requirements, work experiences or skills, and language competences. Second, we classify the extracted spans onto the large, fine-grained *European Skills, Competences, Qualifications and Occupations Ontology* (ESCO).[1] Third, we show the value of the data-driven extraction results in evaluations and initial social science analyses.

Our general idea is to use, in an unsupervised approach, the semantic similarity between ontological concepts and text spans in job ads for fine-grained classification of job ad skills to the ESCO skill ontology. We rely on state-of-the-art pre-trained transformer-based language models (foundational models) and experiment with adaptations to the job ad domain and to the task of computing the semantic similarity on sentence or span level. Additionally, we assess different methods to exploit the textual content and terminological richness of the ESCO ontology for fine-tuning the foundational language models. And, we show how providing additional textual context from the job ads and/or the ontology improves the similarity scores between skill requirement spans in job ads and their corresponding concepts from the ontology.

Our contributions include a definition of skill requirement mention types and annotation guidelines for fine-grained extraction, and an exploration of NLP methods for improving semantic similarity measures for matching job ad text snippets with ESCO terminology. We contribute further sentence-level language representation models that are adapted to the job ad domain and skill-related expressions, and we incorporate terminological variability from a large ontology into the model.

Section 2 discusses related work. Section 3 describes our data. Our approaches, experiments, and results for extracting skills are explained in Section 4, and for classification in Section 5. Section 6 shows initial sociological analyses on the extracted data. Section 7 summarizes our main findings and directions for future work.

[1] See https://esco.ec.europa.eu/en/about-esco/what-esco, (European Commission. Directorate General for Employment, Social Affairs and Inclusion., 2017)

Proceedings of the Fifth Workshop on Natural Language Processing and Computational Social Science (NLP+CSS), pages 14 - 24
November 7, 2022

2 Related Work

2.1 Skill Extraction from Job Ads

For the US and UK job market, recent studies investigate changing skill requirements in jobs ads (Deming and Kahn, 2018; Hershbein and Kahn, 2018; Azar et al., 2018), with newer research pointing out the importance of new skills entering jobs and altering required skill combinations within professions (Acemoglu et al., 2022; Atalay et al., 2020). However, these approaches use mostly proprietary data, where extraction is not fully documented. Recently, Zhang et al. (2022b) worked on fine-grained skill classification using their English and Danish *Kompetencer* dataset. They use the ESCO API to retrieve 100 candidates per manually annotated skill span and select the best candidate for their silver standard annotation by minimal Levenshtein distance. Fine-tuning a multilingual BERT-style model on their small in-domain and in-language training material resulted in big improvements compared to their few-shot setup.

2.2 NLP Methods for Improving Semantic Similarity Measures

Continued in-domain pre-training: Masked language modeling (MLM) on domain or task-specific data is often and successfully applied for adapting general-domain language models to specific domains or even tasks (see Gururangan et al. (2020) for an overview, or Gnehm et al. (2022) and Zhang et al. (2022a) for applications on job ads.)

Sentence-level fine-tuning: Reimers and Gurevych (2019) were the first to adapt pre-trained transformer-based language models with supervised training on natural language inference (NLI) and semantic textual similarity (STS) datasets. Resulting Sentence-BERT (SBERT) models can be used to efficiently compare semantic similarities on the sentence level. Many subsequent approaches leverage more self-supervised training to lower data requirements, often by using unlabeled data and by synthetically creating pairs of similar sentences from a single source sentence (Giorgi et al., 2021; Gao et al., 2021; Wang et al., 2021). Differences between the approaches in architectures and training objectives are discussed in Section 5.2.

3 Experimental Data

3.1 Job Ad Data

We use the Swiss Job Market Monitor (SJMM) dataset consisting of representative yearly samples of print and online job ads from Switzerland from 1950 up to now.[2] Being representative and longitudinal, the data is ideal for research on the evolution of skill requirements. In our experiments, we focus on German-speaking job ads from 1990-2021 (n=53k).

3.2 Ontological and Terminological Data

ESCO: We use the German data of the multilingual ESCO ontology (v1.1.0), comprising 14.5k skill concepts. Each concept is represented by a **preferred term** (e.g., *use spreadsheets software*), often complemented by **alternative terms** (synonyms as *use spreadsheets programs*) or **hidden terms** (outdated terms or specific products, *Microsoft Office Excel*).

In total, the 14.5k ESCO concepts are expressed by 20k terms, and include **knowledge** (e.g., *pharmacotherapy*), **skills** in a narrower sense (an ability as *apply change management*), **language skills** (*understand spoken French*), and **transversal skills**, also referred to as core or soft skills (*negotiate compromises*). These four fields are hierarchically structured into 638 classes (max. depth of 3 with 475 classes on the lowest level). The concepts are internally ordered by broader/narrower relationships and are linked to these classes directly or via broader concepts. ESCO is multi-hierarchical and a concept may have several broader concepts (e.g., *aviation meteorology* belongs to the broader concepts *meteorology* and *transport services*). Overall, 29.3% of concepts (30.5% of terms) fall into more than one class.

Swiss databases:[3] We dispose of Swiss terminology on professions and qualifications that has been linked to ESCO **knowledge** classes (e.g., the term *architect* belongs to the ESCO class *architecture and town planning*). This adds 39k terms (20.5k concepts) to 102 knowledge classes and should help identify Swiss educational requirements. Here the class ambiguity is much lower, only 0.1% of concepts (0.4% of terms) belong to more than one class.

Custom terminology additions: We add a handful of terms to cover a few Swiss-specific high-

[2] See https://www.swissubase.ch (Buchmann et al., 2022b)

[3] Swiss Federal Statistical Office, data available on request

You have successfully completed your studies in computer science[EDU] or an equivalent IT education[EDU].

We expect from you:

- Experience in software development[EXP]
- Good knowledge of an object-oriented programming language like C# or Java[EXP]
- German as native language[LNG], good knowledge of English[LNG]

Figure 1: Example extraction of EDU, EXP, LNG spans (examples translated from German to English)

	Precision	Recall	F-score
EXP	0.856	0.831	0.843
EDU	0.861	0.859	0.861
LNG	0.885	0.914	0.899

Table 1: Skill extraction results per skill span type on final test set (n=200 ads)

frequency abbreviations, which are not represented as such in the ontology, e.g., 'KV' for 'kaufmännische/r Angestellte/r' (*commercial clerk*).

4 Skill Extraction

4.1 Coarse Skill Span Extraction

We first trained a model to extract text spans from the ads that contain skill requirements. Three span types were defined for this coarser task: **education** (EDU), **experiences** (EXP), and **language skills** (LNG). EDU spans include requirements for both formal and informal education and further training. EXP spans contain all required experiences and knowledge, which are not specified in terms of specific education. LNG spans describe requirements for the language skills of the applicants. Figure 1 shows an annotated example.

We annotated 2,000 ads iteratively with the annotation tool *prodigy*[4]. To start, a domain expert annotated a sample of around 100 ads to refine the annotation guidelines and train an initial model. Then, we built the rest of the training data in 7 iterations, where the same annotator corrected each time roughly 250 ads pre-annotated by the model. We retrained the model after every iteration using 80% of available data as training, 10% as development, and 10% as test set.

EDU

You have successfully completed[QUALIFIER] your studies[CONTAINER] in computer science[SKILL] or an equivalent[QUALIFIER] IT-education[SkillContainer].

EXP

Experience[CONTAINER] in software development[SKILL]

Good[QUALIFIER] knowledge[CONTAINER] of an object-oriented programming language[SKILL] like C#[SKILL] or Java[SKILL]

Figure 2: Examples for fine-grained extraction of QUALIFIER, CONTAINER, and SKILL areas in EDU and EXP spans (examples translated from German to English)

	Precision	Recall	F-score
EXP			
QUALIFIER	0.953	0.968	0.960
SKILL	0.910	0.915	0.913
CONTAINER	0.940	0.973	0.956
EDU			
QUALIFIER	0.947	0.989	0.968
SKILL	0.940	0.951	0.945
CONTAINER	0.922	0.936	0.929
SkillContainer	0.874	0.908	0.891

Table 2: Fine-grained skill area extraction results on final test set (n=200 ads)

We treated the extraction and classification of skill spans as a named-entity-recognition-like problem and trained a transition-based NER model (Lample et al., 2016) using *spaCy*[5]. We used *jobBERT-de*[6], a German transformer model adapted to the domain of job ads (Gnehm et al., 2022), to compute contextualized input representations for the downstream NER component.

4.2 Fine-Grained Skill Area Extraction

Within the extracted EDU and EXP spans, different content aspects are present, as shown in Figure 1 and 2. In addition to information about the specific **skill area**, they also specify the **qualitative level** of a skill, or mention also generic **skill re-**

[4]https://prodi.gy

[5]https://spacy.io. We used the default settings of the components *spacy-transformers.TransformerModel.v1* and *spacy.TransitionBasedParser.v2*

[6]https://huggingface.co/agne/jobBERT-de

quirement containers. To better capture the core content of the skills, a more fine-grained skill area extraction model has been trained for both the EXP and the EDU spans. The training data was created the same way as for coarse-grained extraction (see Section 4.1). Formally, these models split the spans into different areas: QUALIFIER, SKILL, CONTAINER, and SkillContainer. The last category was introduced only in the EDU domain to capture compounds that contain both skill area and container information. In German, such compounds occur frequently, e.g., 'Handelsdiplom' (*commercial diploma*), 'Bürolehre' (*office apprenticeship*). Figure 2 shows how the EDU and EXP spans from Figure 1 are refined accordingly.

4.3 Results

Table 1 shows the results for the skill span extraction on the final test set (n=200 ads). For LNG, it performs best with an F-score of 0.899, while EXP performs least well with 0.843. This reflects the higher complexity of the EXP span task. Table 2 reports the performance of the fine-grained skill area extraction. In general, all categories perform very well, with F-scores above 0.9. Only the SkillContainer category scores slightly worse with 0.891.

5 Fine-Grained Unsupervised Multi-Label Classification of Skill Requirements

5.1 Task Definition

In order to map a skill mention of a job ad to one or more fitting ESCO concepts, we perform a semantic similarity lookup, comparable to an information retrieval setting, where, for a given query (job ad skill), we search for the most relevant items (ontology skill concepts). The problem can thus be understood as an unsupervised, fine-grained multi-label classification task.

Contextualizing job ad terms: As introduced in Section 4, we use skill areas for our query. However, isolated skill areas without surrounding job ad text can be too generic or ambiguous, potentially leading to unsuitable matches. To mitigate this issue, we contextualize each skill area with available surrounding skill areas of the same span.[7] After embedding these contextualized text spans with an SBERT model, we calculate a vector representation for each skill area by averaging the vector representation of each token. Contextualization helps us find more exact skill concepts, e.g., if we query *project management*, we receive *project management* as top suggestion, but if we query *project management* with its context *IPMA, PMI, HERMES*, we find the more specific concept *IT project management methods*. It helps further dealing with incomplete skill areas, as they occur for instance in elliptic enumerations: Querying *Motor vehicle* in its context *Motor vehicle, liability, property insurance* returns *insurance types* as top suggestion.[8]

Contextualizing ontology terms: In the lookup, we use all available ontology terms (see Section 3.2). As preprocessing, we remove information on educational levels in the Swiss data, such that – as for the job ads – only a skill area remains (e.g. *florist (Federal Professional Certificate)* is transformed to *florist)*. Ontology terms can also be ambiguous by themselves, and many belong to more than one skill class (see Section 3.2). Therefore, we contextualize ontology terms too, and use the hierarchical ontology structure by inserting its class label for each term as context. For embedding with SBERT models, we represent these term and class combinations in the form '<term> (<class label>)'.[9] For each term, a vector representation is calculated in the same way as described above for the job ad terms. To give an example, with contextualized ontology terms, querying the job ad skill *SAP developer ABAP*, we find that *SAP ABAP* in the class *Software and applications development* is more similar than *SAP ABAP* in the class *Using digital tools for collaboration and productivity*.

5.2 Semantic Skill Representation Approaches

The quality of the results of the vector similarity search depends crucially on a suitable vector space representation of the skill descriptions from the job ads and from the ontology. Therefore, we experiment with several state-of-the-art approaches for improving the vector similarity of general BERT language representation models by applying continued pretraining and fine-tuning techniques.

MLM on job ad texts: Masked language mod-

[7]In total, we have 131k areas from 78k EXP spans, and 81k areas from 74k EDU spans available. The 39k LNG spans were not further split up.

[8]ESCO queried with the model sts-gbert.

[9]After initial experiments, 173 knowledge class labels were replaced by custom labels using a language less formulaic and more common for job ads, e.g., *services in the field of transportation* was replaced by *transportation services*.

eling (Devlin et al., 2019) on in-domain texts has been successfully used for adaptation of general-domain BERT models to special domain language use (Gururangan et al., 2020). We assess the benefit of continued in-domain language model pretraining by comparing *GBERT-base*[10], a small version of the German state-of-the-art model (Chan et al., 2020), with a version of the same model that is adapted to the domain of German-speaking job ads, and was trained on a job ad dataset including the data used here, *jobGBERT*[11] (Gnehm et al., 2022).

TSDAE on skill spans: In the transformer-based sequential denoising auto-encoder (TSDAE) approach (Wang et al., 2021), meaningful sentence embeddings are learned by denoising corrupted input. An encoder produces a fixed-size vector representation for an input sentence with deleted words, from which a decoder learns to reconstruct the uncorrupted sentence. By giving the decoder only the fixed-size sentence representation and no word embeddings as input, a bottleneck is introduced that forces the encoder to provide a good semantic sentence representation. We use TSDAE to learn embeddings for our domain-specific skill terminology. As training data, we use all skill spans from our job ad data (216k), and skill terms and descriptions (split into sentences) from our ontology data (107k). Since our spans are shorter than the sentences used in the original approach (2.2 vs. 10.6 tokens on average), we experimented with smaller deletion rates and found a rate of 0.4 best performing. All other parameters are set as in Wang et al. (2021).

STS on general-domain data: Reimers and Gurevych (2019) use Siamese BERT Networks for training sentence embeddings on sentence pairs which are labeled with a cosine similarity score indicating their semantic similarity. Sentence vector representations are calculated by mean pooling over token embeddings. Then, by computing the similarity of the two sentence vectors and by comparing it against the gold similarity score, better semantic sentence representations are learned. No such labeled data is available for our domain, but we assess the benefits of fine-tuning our sentence embeddings on general-domain data for German by using the translated *STSBenchmark* dataset (May, 2021) (5k sentence pairs). We train with hyperparameters set as in Reimers and Gurevych (2019).

[10]https://huggingface.co/deepset/gbert-base

[11]https://huggingface.co/agne/jobGBERT

EXP skill: ***attracting new customers**, acquisition*		
skill concept suggestions	A	B
recruitment methods (marketing and advertisement)	0.5	0.5
customer insight (marketing and advertisement)	0.5	0
find new clients (entrepreneurial skills)	1	1
recruitment and hiring (personnel recruitment)	0	0
EDU skill: ***bio lab technician***		
skill concept suggestions	A	B
biologist (biology)	0.5	0.5
biology technician (biology)	1	0.5
biology lab technician (chemical technology)	1	1
biology teaching assistant (specialist subject teachers)	0	0
LNG skill: ***English** (very good in spoken and written)*		
skill concept suggestions	A	B
teach English as a foreign language (teaching)	0	0
understand written English (languages)	1	1
English speaking skills (languages)	1	1
English teacher (specialist subject teachers)	0	0

Table 3: Evaluation examples of skill concept suggestions (class labels in brackets) for an EDU, an EXP, and an LNG job ad skill (in bold italics, context in italics) by two annotators A and B (examples translated from German to English).

MNR on ontology data: Sentence embeddings are learned by training Siamese networks with multiple negative ranking (MNR) loss (Henderson et al., 2017). This is a supervised approach, but training data requirements are low since only pairs of similar sentences are needed. Dissimilar sentence pairs are created by using other examples from the same batch of training sentences. The relative distances between sentence pairs are then learned using a ranking loss function. We leverage our ontology data by creating positive text pairs in which we combine alternative or hidden terms, as well as the phrases describing them, each with their preferred label. In this way, we seek to incorporate knowledge of terminological variations within the ontology into sentence embeddings. We expect this approach to be the most beneficial since it is using data specific to our domain and task in a supervised fashion.

5.3 Experiments and Evaluation

Evaluation data: To be able to evaluate models on our fine-grained unsupervised multi-label classification task, we created a small amount of gold standard data. We selected a random sample of 25 job ad skill terms and in addition compiled a challenge sample of 15 terms covering some difficult cases (e.g., formulations that are specific to Switzerland). For these 40 terms, we did a contextualized ontology lookup as described in Section 5.1 using all our different SBERT models (see below), and evaluated the ten first suggestions of all models.

Annotators assigned scores of 0 for inadequate, 0.5 for acceptable, and 1 for highly appropriate suggestions. We evaluated the suggestions on the class level and for the random sample also on the concept level. Table 3 shows examples for evaluation on concept level. A total of 494 class suggestions were rated by 3 annotators each and 685 concept suggestions were rated by 2 annotators each. For the random sample, Krippendorff's alpha on the class level is 0.83, on concept level 0.814, and for the challenge set on class level 0.73. This indicates good agreement for the random and satisfactory agreement for the challenge sample (Krippendorff, 2004).

Experiments: We evaluate combinations of the presented SBERT training approaches with some restrictions: MLM on domain data only makes sense as the first step, since it affects the foundational model on the token level. STS after TSDAE is more effective than vice versa, according to Wang et al. (2021), and domain-oriented (MNR) is applied after general-domain (STS) fine-tuning.[12] This leads to a total of 14 tested model configurations: Starting from a general (gbert) or domain-adapted (jobgbert) LM, we optionally train with TSDAE (model name prefix: tsdae-), followed by optional STS (prefix: sts-), followed by optional MNR (prefix: mnr-). A model with only STS training on a general-domain LM (sts-gbert in the following) corresponds to a vanilla or baseline SBERT model. For selected models, we further perform an ablation study to estimate the effects of contextualizing job ad skills and/or ontology skills for similarity queries.

We use the created gold standard data to evaluate fine-grained unsupervised skill classification with mean average precision over the first ten concept or class suggestions (mAP@10), see Equation 1, where Q are the queries, (25 in our case for the random sample), m is the number of accepted suggestions, and k is the cutoff rank (10 in our case).[13] Mean average precision considers the ranking capabilities of models (are more appropriate suggestions presented first?) and does not unfairly penalize models when too few suitable items are available (less than ten items for mAP@10) (Manning et al., 2008).

$$MAP(Q) = \frac{1}{|Q|}\sum_{j=1}^{|Q|}\frac{1}{m_{\mathrm{j}}}\sum_{k=1}^{m_{\mathrm{j}}} Precision(R_{\mathrm{jk}}) \tag{1}$$

A conventional recall evaluation (are all relevant ontology concepts among the suggestions?) is not applicable in this scenario with 638 classes and 35k concepts. However, we examine mentions with very low similarities to ontology concepts.

5.4 Results and Discussion

Fine-grained skill classification performance: In classification from job ads to ESCO, the best model on class level is mnr-sts-jobgbert with 0.969 mAP@10, on concept level mnr-sts-tsdae-jobgbert with 0.908 mAP@10 (see Table 4). As expected, evaluation scores are lower on concept than on class level, since it is much harder to find an appropriate concept out of 35k possibilities than an appropriate class out of 638. Performance differences between models are often small, but it is noticeable that the best models at both levels include MNR as pre-training. MNR seems thus to have a strong positive impact on performance, while the effect of other pre-training steps is less obvious, and including additional pre-training does not ensure higher performance compared to vanilla sts-gbert.

On the challenge test set (not shown in Table 4), all models experience a performance drop compared to the random sample, but to varying degrees. For instance, the sts-gbert model with general-domain pre-training only achieves mAP@10 of 0.763. Compared to the random sample this is a loss of 15.1 percentage points (pp in the following). Our best models mnr-sts-tsdae-jobgbert and mnr-sts-jobgbert reach both mAP@10 of 0.9, which means a smaller performance drop of 6.2 and 6.9pp respectively. Hence, extensive SBERT fine-tuning also pays off for classifying more difficult cases.

The mapping of EDU and LNG terms is, in general, easier than the mapping of EXP terms, with models reaching on average mAP@10 of 0.952 and 0.938 versus 0.878 (on class-level, see Table 4). Interestingly, model performance can vary considerably across different skill types, suggesting that fine-tuning approaches may have type-specific effects (see discussion below).

Impact of different SBERT fine-tuning steps: To assess different sentence embedding fine-tuning steps, we estimate their effects on mean average

[12] In MNR we used batch-size of 32 after pre-tests with batch sizes 16, 32, 64. If not specified differently in Section 5.2, all other parameters are set as in the original approaches.

[13] We considered a suggestion as true positive if at least one annotator gave a score of 1, or at least two annotators a score of 0.5.

Class Level								
Model	**ALL**	**R**	**EDU**	**R**	**EXP**	**R**	**LNG**	**R**
mnr-sts-jobgbert	**0.969**	**1**	0.977	5	**0.945**	**1**	**1.000**	**1**
mnr-sts-tsdae-jobgbert	0.961	2	0.977	5	0.944	2	0.963	9
mnr-gbert	0.958	3	0.987	2	0.929	3	0.957	10
mnr-tsdae-jobgbert	0.957	4	0.983	3	0.924	4	0.968	8
mnr-sts-tsdae-gbert	0.954	5	0.983	3	0.902	6	0.998	2
mnr-jobgbert	0.941	6	0.940	11	0.923	5	0.976	6
mnr-tsdae-gbert	0.940	7	0.967	8	0.890	9	0.988	5
sts-tsdae-gbert	0.935	8	**0.996**	**1**	0.856	10	0.970	7
sts-jobgbert	0.914	9	0.926	12	0.899	7	0.919	11
mnr-sts-gbert	0.903	10	0.865	14	0.893	8	0.998	2
tsdae-gbert	0.879	11	0.968	7	0.786	14	0.887	13
sts-gbert (baseline)	0.876	12	0.870	13	0.826	11	0.990	4
sts-tsdae-jobgbert	0.872	13	0.947	10	0.787	13	0.890	12
tsdae-jobgbert	0.821	14	0.948	9	0.790	12	0.631	14
mean	0.920		0.952		0.878		0.938	
stdev	0.044		0.041		0.059		0.096	
Concept Level								
Model	**ALL**	**R**	**EDU**	**R**	**EXP**	**R**	**LNG**	**R**
mnr-sts-tsdae-jobgbert	**0.908**	**1**	0.923	5	**0.865**	**1**	0.963	8
mnr-gbert	0.897	2	**0.950**	**1**	0.825	3	0.934	10
mnr-tsdae-jobgbert	0.889	3	0.947	2	0.791	6	0.968	7
mnr-sts-jobgbert	0.886	4	0.874	10	0.842	2	**1.000**	**1**
sts-tsdae-gbert	0.868	5	0.928	4	0.758	8	0.970	6
sts-gbert (baseline)	0.867	6	0.878	8	0.795	5	0.990	4
mnr-sts-gbert	0.866	7	0.864	13	0.803	4	0.998	2
mnr-sts-tsdae-gbert	0.866	7	0.929	3	0.737	9	0.998	2
mnr-jobgbert	0.854	9	0.872	12	0.790	7	0.943	9
mnr-tsdae-gbert	0.838	10	0.904	7	0.698	11	0.987	5
sts-jobgbert	0.819	11	0.877	9	0.710	10	0.919	11
tsdae-gbert	0.777	12	0.916	6	0.570	12	0.912	12
sts-tsdae-jobgbert	0.716	13	0.857	14	0.543	13	0.780	13
tsdae-jobgbert	0.676	14	0.874	10	0.516	14	0.600	14
mean	0.838		0.900		0.732		0.926	
stdev	0.069		0.032		0.113		0.110	

Table 4: Mean Average Precision (mAP@10) of the models on the random sample, evaluated on class (upper part) and concept level (lower part). Model names end with general (gbert) or domain-specific (jobgbert) LM used as starting point, each subsequent training step is prepended on the left (last step leftmost). The columns labeled 'R(ank)' denote the systems' ranking. The systems are ordered by the overall (ALL) classification performance.

	ALL	EDU	EXP	LNG
constant	0.856	0.904	0.801	0.869
MLM	-0.004	0.008	0.011	-0.058
TSDAE	-0.002	0.040	-0.030	-0.033
STS	0.024	-0.013	0.030	0.085
MNR	0.079	0.032	0.108	0.115
R2	0.616	0.348	0.733	0.643

Table 5: Linear model B-coefficients of SBERT fine-tuning steps on mAP@10 scores (class level)

Model	Context	ALL	EDU	EXP	LNG
mnr-sts-tsdae-jobgbert	all	0.908	0.923	0.865	0.963
	job ad	0.903	0.920	0.850	0.976
	ontology	0.890	0.937	0.805	0.963
	none	0.872	0.944	0.747	0.976
sts-gbert	all	0.867	0.878	0.795	0.990
	job ad	0.730	0.730	0.712	0.763
	ontology	0.852	0.901	0.735	0.990
	none	0.759	0.815	0.700	0.763

Table 6: mAP@10 for 2 selected models with different query contextualization (evaluated at concept level)

precision in a linear model (see Table 5). Over all terms, MNR raises the mAP@10 score by 7.9pp, and STS by 2.4pp, while the effects of MLM and TSDAE are small and negative.

Examining different skill types, we see that MNR is especially helpful for EXP (10.8pp) and LNG (11.5pp), much less for EDU (3.2pp). For EDU terms, the terminology is comprehensive thanks to Swiss data on educational terms, and these terms also have little class ambiguity (see Section 3.2). Thus, the smaller effect of MNR in classifying EDU terms can be explained by the fact that less needs to be learned about the ontology or the term variations. STS's strong effect on LNG (8.5pp) may reflect that this task is closer to general knowledge (e.g., *mother tongue* is similar to language proficiency), whereas EDU and EXP mapping requires domain knowledge, and barely profits from general-domain training material. TSDAE is only effective for EDU classification. Educational degrees represented in the ontology are often mentioned verbatim in job ads. We assume it is the small gap between ontology and job ad language which makes this simple fine-tuning so helpful. MLM effects are minor, but EXP classification, the most difficult task, benefits (1.1pp) from pre-training on job ad texts. In sum, MNR is the most beneficial method, but for certain term types, performance gains are observed with all approaches.

Effect of contextualization: We assess the benefits of query contextualization in ablation experiments where we omit the job ad skill span context, the ontology context, or both.[14] We compare our best model on concept level, mnr-sts-tsdae-jobgbert with sts-gbert, which has only undergone general-domain fine-tuning. Table 6 shows performance drops for both, but sts-gbert is much more affected than mnr-sts-tsdae-jobgbert (-10.8 vs -3.6pp when omitting all context). The example in Table 7 shows how mnr-sts-tsdae-jobgbert suggests appropriate skill concepts independent of contextualization, whereas sts-gbert fails without context. Examination of different term types shows that mnr-sts-tsdae-jobgbert benefits from query contextualization only for EXP mapping – the most diffi-

[14]For this ablation experiment, additional 89 skill concept suggestions were evaluated by one annotator.

Model	Context	Skill Concept	Similarity
mnr-sts-tsdae-jobgbert	all	Banking and Finance	0.722
	none	Bankier (*banker*)	0.732
sts-gbert	all	Banking Consultant	0.809
	none	Bankknecht (*butcher's assistant*)	0.782

Table 7: Most similar skill concept suggestion for the job ad expression *Bank* with and without its context *Financial Consulting, Management*

cult task –, whereas for LNG and EDU, the model seems to have incorporated enough domain knowledge during fine-tuning. As for which context is more helpful, omitting ontology context is much more detrimental to sts-gbert (-13.7pp) than omitting job ad context (-1.5pp), whereas for mnr-sts-tsdae-jobgbert, dropping job ad context is worse (-1.8 vs -0.5pp). Again, this indicates that suitable fine-tuning can effectively incorporate ontology knowledge into the model.

Low-similarity cases: We examine the 5% of EDU and EXP skills that each have the lowest similarities to ESCO concepts using mnr-sts-tsdae-jobgbert.[15] For EDU, these cases consist mainly of terms that are not skill areas at all, but containers e.g., 'Diplomabschluss' (*diploma*), rare abbreviations (*CFA (Chartered Financial Analyst)*), and generic terms like 'technisch' (*technical*).[16] For EXP, we also find mainly generic terms (*implementation*) as well as skills not covered by the ontology (e.g., *knowing a place* or *working abroad*). In a random sample of 20 low-similarity cases each for EDU and EXP, we find that for both types, 4 out of 20 skill span extractions were flawed. In the remaining cases, the precision of the first suggestion at the class level is very low, 0.594 for EDU and 0.313 for EXP. Finally, inspecting the 20 cases with the lowest similarities, none of the EDU terms and only 7 out of 20 EXP terms qualify as proper skill areas. It is in favor of our model that we find low similarities between ESCO concepts and flawed extractions or job ad skills not represented in the ontology. For practical application, the results suggest applying a minimum similarity threshold, and we use 0.5 as the default threshold.

Term selection: mAP@10 as a measure considers that the ontology may not comprise 10 acceptable suggestions for every skill area. However, for the application, a suitable cut-off value must be found for each case, since the number of acceptable ontology terms indeed varies greatly.[17] In a gradient-based approach, we aim to select term suggestions until a drop in similarities is observed, i.e., we cut off where the gradient of the probability distribution is minimal. This way, we consider on average three ontology terms for each skill term. In comparison to considering only the most similar term, we lose on average 3.6pp of the evaluation score on the concept level, which we regard as a reasonable trade-off for application.

6 Downstream Sociological Analysis

Labor market changes: It is commonly believed that digital technologies have changed the demand for skills to perform tasks in the labor market in the past decades. Recent literature points to the importance of new skills entering jobs and altering the required skill combinations (Acemoglu et al., 2022). It also emphasizes that most of the changes in skill demand take place within and not across occupations (Bisello et al., 2019; Freeman et al., 2020). According analyses require time series data on skill demand at the job level that includes valid measures of all skills required in the labor market. Such data has been, however, extremely scarce.

Illustrative analyses: To illustrate the usefulness of our job ads data for social sciences, we present some selected analyses. First, we calculate correlations between occupation-skill matrices that ESCO provides and those resulting from the SJMM data. At the 1-digit level of the international standard classification of occupations (ISCO-08)[18], for example, the correlation is as high as 0.87, underscoring the validity of our skill extractions. Second, we illustrate within-occupation change in skill demand with an example: the evolution of skill requirements in the occupational field of technicians and engineers. To aggregate fine-grained, multi-hierarchical ESCO skill classes, we used a clustering approach.[19] The resulting 48 clusters are then applied to the SJMM job level data, generating for each job ad indicators of how strongly the text represents each skill cluster. To keep the picture detailed as well as simple, only three interesting clusters for this occupation are shown in Figure 3.

Figure 3 confirms – for our example – that

[15]Mean similarity of the first suggestion is 0.446 for EXP and 0.473 for EDU.

[16]The German word 'technisch' (*technical*) appears in 377 ontology terms or descriptions, from 183 different classes.

[17]For instance, five concepts were accepted for *acquiring new customers*, but only one for *fire department*.

[18]https://isco-ilo.netlify.app/en/isco-08/

[19]We applied HDBSCAN (Campello et al., 2013) (min. size=3, epsilon=0.0 and alpha=1.0) over skill class vectors (averaged skill term vectors per class).

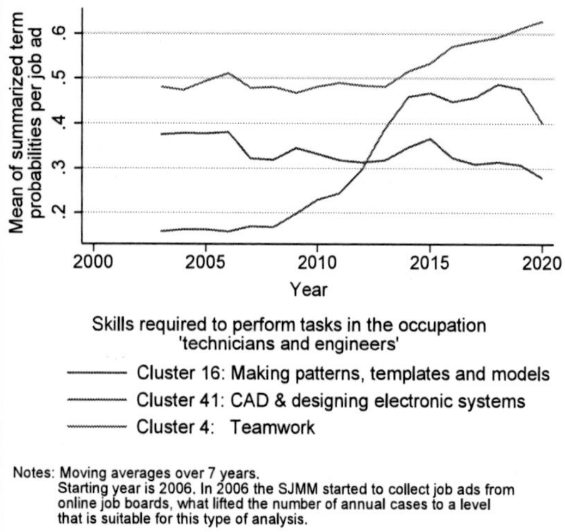

Figure 3: Illustration of within-occupation evolution of skill requirements

the type of required skills changed within occupations over time. Skills for *making patterns, templates and models* were highly required shortly after the turn of the century. Across the following 15 years, the demand for these mainly manual and non-digital skills declined. In contrast, the demand for *CAD and designing electronic systems* was nearly nonexistent and then increased sharply. These skills are related to digital technologies and newly entered the occupation. After their entry, also other elements of the required skill combination seem to change, e.g., demand for *teamwork skills* is increasing (see Figure 3). This is in line with the literature, which suggests that digital technologies lead to more flexible, team-based settings (Autor et al., 2002).

7 Conclusion

Our two-step approach of first extracting text spans expressing language skills, experience, and educational requirements, followed by further subdividing these into skill areas, containers, and qualifiers, allowed us to achieve broad coverage of fine-grained competency classifications. By grouping skill areas from the same span for transformer-based vector representation, we provide relevant context that helps find appropriate ESCO ontology concepts for each job ad skill area.

For fine-grained classification, our domain and task-specific SBERT learning steps boost performance – best models reaching mAP@10 of 0.969 on class and 0.908 on concept level – and also help deal with more difficult cases encountered in the challenge sample. While infusing terminological variation from the ontology into the model with MNR is by far the most effective, all different pre-training and fine-tuning steps are beneficial to some extent.

Analyses on low-similarity cases and our gradient-based selection approach showed that similarity values of our best models can be used to select the most relevant ontology concepts and avoid mismatches.

In future work, models could be further fine-tuned with curated task-specific training material (similar to our evaluation data) to improve classification for the most difficult task, experience classification (EXP). The next steps in social science analyses could be to assess how required skill combinations evolve within occupations, which occupations shift towards more specialized or diversified requirements, or to which extent the skill requirements of some occupations become more alike.

Limitations

Job ad texts are influenced by conventions, social norms, and the effects of their publication media. This potentially affects the performance of our approach in different social settings, e.g., for German-language job ads from other countries.

Furthermore, the average number of skill requirements per ad grows over time. The extent to which this is due to changes in labor market structure, social norms, recruiting practices, or publication media remains to be investigated.

Our SBERT fine-tuning aimed at enabling valid skill classification for job ads from the last three decades. Therefore, the application to future job ads might require periodic updates of models with newer data. And, while our experiments on the classification task show expected and explainable results, analyses could still benefit from a larger test set.

Acknowledgements

We would like to thank the anonymous reviewers for their helpful comments and suggestions. This work is supported by the Swiss National Science Foundation (grant number 407740 187333).

References

Daron Acemoglu, David Autor, Jonathon Hazell, and Pascual Restrepo. 2022. Artificial intelligence and jobs: evidence from online vacancies. *Journal of Labor Economics*, 40(S1):S293–S340.

Enghin Atalay, Phai Phongthiengtham, Sebastian Sotelo, and Daniel Tannenbaum. 2020. The Evolution of Work in the United States. *American Economic Journal: Applied Economics*, 12(2):1–34.

David H. Autor, Frank Levy, and Richard J. Murnane. 2002. Upstairs, downstairs: Computers and skills on two floors of a large bank. *ILR Review*, 55(3):432–447.

José A. Azar, Ioana Marinescu, Marshall I. Steinbaum, and Bledi Taska. 2018. Concentration in US Labor Markets: Evidence From Online Vacancy Data.

Federico Biagi and Raquel Sebastian. 2020. Technologies and "routinization". *Handbook of Labor, Human Resources and Population Economics*, pages 1–17.

Martina Bisello, Eleonora Peruffo, Enrique Fernández-Macías, and Riccardo Rinaldi. 2019. How computerisation is transforming jobs: Evidence from the eurofound's european working conditions survey. Technical report, JRC working papers series on Labour, Education and Technology.

Marlis Buchmann, Helen Buchs, Felix Busch, Simon Clematide, Ann-Sophie Gnehm, and Jan Müller. 2022a. Swiss Job Market Monitor: A Rich Source of Demand-Side Micro Data of the Labour Market. *European Sociological Review*.

Marlis Buchmann, Helen Buchs, Eva Bühlmann, Felix Busch, Ann-Sophie Gnehm, Yanik Kipfer, Urs Klarer, Jan Müller, Marianne Müller, Stefan Sacchi, Alexander Salvisbert, and Anna von Ow. 2022b. *Stellenmarkt-Monitor Schweiz 1950 – 2021*. Soziologisches Institut der Universität Zürich.

Ricardo JGB Campello, Davoud Moulavi, and Jörg Sander. 2013. Density-based clustering based on hierarchical density estimates. In *Pacific-Asia conference on knowledge discovery and data mining*, pages 160–172. Springer.

Branden Chan, Stefan Schweter, and Timo Möller. 2020. German's next language model. In *Proceedings of the 28th International Conference on Computational Linguistics*, pages 6788–6796, Barcelona, Spain (Online). International Committee on Computational Linguistics.

David Deming and Lisa B Kahn. 2018. Skill requirements across firms and labor markets: Evidence from job postings for professionals. *Journal of Labor Economics*, 36(S1):S337–S369.

Jacob Devlin, Ming-Wei Chang, Kenton Lee, and Kristina Toutanova. 2019. BERT: Pre-training of Deep Bidirectional Transformers for Language Understanding. In *Proceedings of the 2019 Conference of the North American Chapter of the Association for Computational Linguistics: Human Language Technologies, Volume 1 (Long and Short Papers)*, pages 4171–4186, Minneapolis, Minnesota. Association for Computational Linguistics.

European Commission. Directorate General for Employment, Social Affairs and Inclusion. 2017. *ESCO handbook: European skills, competences, qualifications and occupations*. Publications Office, LU.

Richard B. Freeman, Ina Ganguli, and Michael J. Handel. 2020. Within-occupation changes dominate changes in what workers do: A shift-share decomposition, 2005–2015. *AEA Papers and Proceedings*, 110:394–99.

Tianyu Gao, Xingcheng Yao, and Danqi Chen. 2021. SimCSE: Simple Contrastive Learning of Sentence Embeddings. In *Proceedings of the 2021 Conference on Empirical Methods in Natural Language Processing*, pages 6894–6910, Online and Punta Cana, Dominican Republic. Association for Computational Linguistics.

John Giorgi, Osvald Nitski, Bo Wang, and Gary Bader. 2021. DeCLUTR: Deep Contrastive Learning for Unsupervised Textual Representations. In *Proceedings of the 59th Annual Meeting of the Association for Computational Linguistics and the 11th International Joint Conference on Natural Language Processing (Volume 1: Long Papers)*, pages 879–895, Online. Association for Computational Linguistics.

Ann-Sophie Gnehm, Eva Bühlmann, and Simon Clematide. 2022. Evaluation of transfer learning and domain adaptation for analyzing german-speaking job advertisements. In *Proceedings of the Language Resources and Evaluation Conference*, pages 3892–3901, Marseille, France. European Language Resources Association.

Suchin Gururangan, Ana Marasović, Swabha Swayamdipta, Kyle Lo, Iz Beltagy, Doug Downey, and Noah A. Smith. 2020. Don't Stop Pretraining: Adapt Language Models to Domains and Tasks. In *Proceedings of the 58th Annual Meeting of the Association for Computational Linguistics*, pages 8342–8360, Online. Association for Computational Linguistics.

Matthew Henderson, Rami Al-Rfou, Brian Strope, Yunhsuan Sung, Laszlo Lukacs, Ruiqi Guo, Sanjiv Kumar, Balint Miklos, and Ray Kurzweil. 2017. Efficient Natural Language Response Suggestion for Smart Reply. ArXiv:1705.00652 [cs].

Brad Hershbein and Lisa B Kahn. 2018. Do recessions accelerate routine-biased technological change? evidence from vacancy postings. *American Economic Review*, 108(7):1737–72.

Klaus Krippendorff. 2004. Reliability in Content Analysis.: Some Common Misconceptions and Recommendations. *Human Communication Research*, 30(3):411–433.

Guillaume Lample, Miguel Ballesteros, Sandeep Subramanian, Kazuya Kawakami, and Chris Dyer. 2016. Neural architectures for named entity recognition. In *Proceedings of the 2016 Conference of the North American Chapter of the Association for Computational Linguistics: Human Language Technologies*, pages 260–270, San Diego, California. Association for Computational Linguistics.

Christopher D. Manning, Prabhakar Raghavan, and Hinrich Schütze. 2008. *Introduction to information retrieval.* Cambridge University Press, New York. OCLC: ocn190786122.

Philip May. 2021. Machine translated multilingual sts benchmark dataset.

Nils Reimers and Iryna Gurevych. 2019. Sentence-BERT: Sentence Embeddings using Siamese BERT-Networks. In *Proceedings of the 2019 Conference on Empirical Methods in Natural Language Processing and the 9th International Joint Conference on Natural Language Processing (EMNLP-IJCNLP)*, pages 3980–3990, Hong Kong, China. Association for Computational Linguistics.

Kexin Wang, Nils Reimers, and Iryna Gurevych. 2021. TSDAE: Using Transformer-based Sequential Denoising Auto-Encoder for Unsupervised Sentence Embedding Learning. In *Findings of the Association for Computational Linguistics: EMNLP 2021*, pages 671–688, Punta Cana, Dominican Republic. Association for Computational Linguistics.

Mike Zhang, Kristian Jensen, Sif Sonniks, and Barbara Plank. 2022a. SkillSpan: Hard and Soft Skill Extraction from English Job Postings. In *Proceedings of the 2022 Conference of the North American Chapter of the Association for Computational Linguistics: Human Language Technologies*, pages 4962–4984, Seattle, United States. Association for Computational Linguistics.

Mike Zhang, Kristian Nørgaard Jensen, and Barbara Plank. 2022b. Kompetencer: Fine-grained skill classification in danish job postings via distant supervision and transfer learning. In *Proceedings of the Language Resources and Evaluation Conference*, pages 436–447, Marseille, France. European Language Resources Association.

Experiencer-Specific Emotion and Appraisal Prediction

Maximilian Wegge, Enrica Troiano, Laura Oberländer and **Roman Klinger**
Institut für Maschinelle Sprachverarbeitung, University of Stuttgart
{firstname.lastname}@ims.uni-stuttgart.de

Abstract

Emotion classification in NLP assigns emotions to texts, such as sentences or paragraphs. With texts like "I felt guilty when he cried", focusing on the sentence level disregards the standpoint of each participant in the situation: the writer ("I") and the other entity ("he") could in fact have different affective states. The emotions of different entities have been considered only partially in emotion semantic role labeling, a task that relates semantic roles to emotion cue words. Proposing a related task, we narrow the focus on the experiencers of events, and assign an emotion (if any holds) to each of them. To this end, we represent each emotion both categorically and with appraisal variables, as a psychological access to explaining why a person develops a particular emotion. On an event description corpus, our experiencer-aware models of emotions and appraisals outperform the experiencer-agnostic baselines, showing that disregarding event participants is an oversimplification for the emotion detection task.

1 Introduction

Computational emotion analysis from text includes various subtasks, with the most prominent one being emotion classification or regression. Its goal is to assign an emotion representation to textual units, and the way this is done typically depends on the domain of the data, the practical application of the task, and the psychological theories of reference: emotions can be modelled as discrete labels, in line with theories of basic emotions (Ekman, 1992; Plutchik, 2001), as valence–arousal value pairs that define an affect vector space where to situate emotion concepts (illustrated, e.g., by Posner et al., 2005), or as appraisal spaces that correspond to the cognitive evaluative dimensions underlying emotions[1] (Scherer, 2005; Smith and Ellsworth, 1985). Irrespective of the adopted representations, most work in the field detects emotions from a single perspective – either to recover the emotion that the writer of a text likely expressed (e.g., with respect to emotion categories and intensities (Mohammad et al., 2018), and cognitive categories (Hofmann et al., 2020)), or to predict the emotion that the text elicits in the readers (e.g., using news articles, Strapparava and Mihalcea, 2007; Bostan et al., 2020). Only a few approaches combine or compare the reader's with the writer's perspective (Buechel and Hahn, 2017, i.a.). However, none of them looks at the perspectives of the *participants* in events (both mentioned or implicit) as described by a text.

Focusing on such perspectives separately is essential to develop an all-round account of the affective implications that events have. It would emphasize how the facts depicted in text are amenable to different "emotion narratives", by pushing one or the other perspective in the foreground. For instance, a possible interpretation for the sentence "As the waiter yelled at her, the expression on my mother's face made all the staff look repulsed", could be: "my mother"→sadness, "the waiter"→anger, and "the staff"→disgust. There, one entity is responsible for an event (screaming), one is influenced by it, and the third is affected by the emotion emerging in the other (the facial expression, which can be seen as an event in itself).

Our goal is close to emotion role labeling, a special case of semantic role labeling (SRL) (Mohammad et al., 2018; Kim and Klinger, 2018). SRL addresses the question "Who did What to Whom, Where, When, and How?" (Gildea and Jurafsky, 2000), emotion SRL asks "Who feels what, why, and towards whom?" (Kim and Klinger, 2018), mainly to detect causes of emotion-eliciting events (Ghazi et al., 2015) for certain entities. Here, we tackle a variation of this question, namely, "Who feels what and under which circumstances?". The circumstances refer to the explanation pro-

[1] They are similar to a valence–arousal space, but the dimensions correspond to evaluations of events (i.e., appraisals) that underlie a certain emotion.

Proceedings of the Fifth Workshop on Natural Language Processing and Computational Social Science (NLP+CSS), pages 25 - 32
November 7, 2022 ©2022 Association for Computational Linguistics

vided by appraisal interpretations, another novelty that we contribute to the emotion SRL panorama. Appraisal-based emotion representations capture entity-specific aspects that lead to an emotion, as they describe the subjective qualities that an individual sees in events.

We propose a method for experiencer-specific emotion and appraisal analysis that bridges emotion classification and semantic role labeling. Given texts that describe events and that include annotations for all participants, we assign an emotion and an appraisal vector to each potential emoter. Our proposal is computationally simpler than creating a full graph of relations between causes and entities, as is normally done in (emotion) SRL. Yet, its fine-grained focus on event participants is beneficial over traditional classification- and regression-based approaches: by predicting an emotion and scoring multiple appraisals for each entity, our model strongly outperforms text-level baselines. Thus, the results demonstrate that assigning one emotion to the entire instance, or multiple emotions without considering for whom they hold, is a simplification of the emotional import of the text.

2 Related Work

In natural language processing, emotions are usually represented as discrete names following theories of basic emotions (Ekman, 1992; Plutchik, 2001), or as values of valence and arousal (Russell and Mehrabian, 1977). Computational models based on such representations have been applied to many text sources, including Reddit comments (Demszky et al., 2020) and tales (Alm et al., 2005), but also to resources created as part of psychological research. An example is the ISEAR corpus. It consists of short reports collected in lab (Scherer and Wallbott, 1997), instructing participants to describe events that caused in them a certain emotion. A similar collection practice was adopted by Troiano et al. (2019). In their enISEAR, crowdworkers completed sentences like "I felt [EMOTION NAME] when ..." for seven emotion names.

The emotions of entities are considered in emotion SRL, whose goals comprise the recognition of emotion cue words, emotion experiencers/emoters and descriptions of emotion causes and targets (Mohammad et al., 2018; Bostan et al., 2020; Kim and Klinger, 2018; Campagnano et al., 2022, i.a.). Yet, most work focused on detecting causes (i.e., emotion-triggering events), and less on other semantic roles (Russo et al., 2011; Chen et al., 2018, 2010; Cheng et al., 2017, i.a.).

Emotion Class	# inst.	# exp.
anger	259	336
disgust	73	87
fear	173	220
joy, pride, contentment	181	265
no emotion	223	269
other, anticipation, hope, surprise, trust	102	117
sadness, disappointment, frustration	320	423
shame, guilt	282	325
total	720	1329

Table 1: Number of instances and experiencer spans annotated for each emotion. Non-bold emotion names are concepts in the x-enVENT data that we merge with bold emotion names in our experiments.

The gap between entity-specific emotion analysis and emotion SRL was partially filled in by Troiano et al. (2022). They aimed at better understanding the readers' attempts to interpret the experience of the texts' authors. They post-annotated instances from enISEAR with emotions and 22 appraisal concepts, both for the writer and all other event participants mentioned in the text. The appraisal variables include evaluations of events, as they were likely conducted by the event experiencers, including if authors felt responsible, if they needed to pay attention to the environment, whether they found themselves in control of the situation, and its pleasantness (see Table 1 in their paper for explanations of the variables). However, their work was limited to corpus creation and analysis, and did not provide any modeling of appraisals or emotions in an emotion experiencer-specific manner. Therefore, it is not clear whether a simplifying assumption that all entities experience the same emotion or an actual entity-specific model performs practically better. We address this concern and show that experiencer-specific modeling is beneficial.

Finally, our work is related to structured sentiment analysis (Barnes et al., 2021), in which opinion targets, their polarity, but also an opinion-holding (or expressing) entity is to be detected. Most studies focused on sentiment targets and aspects (Brauwers and Frasincar, 2021), but there are also some that aim at detecting the opinion holder (Kim and Hovy, 2006; Wiegand and Klakow, 2011; Seki, 2007; Wiegand and Klakow, 2012, i.a.).

Model	Input instance	Annotation: Emotion	Annotation: Appraisal
EXP	⟨exp⟩WRITER⟨/exp⟩ I felt bad ... for him	{guilt}	$(5, 1, 1, \ldots)$
	WRITER I felt bad ... for ⟨exp⟩him⟨/exp⟩	{sadness}	$(1, 3, 1, \ldots)$
TEXT	WRITER I felt bad ... for him	{guilt, sadness}	$(3, 2, 1, \ldots)$

Table 2: Example representation at training time for the EXP model and the TEXT baseline for the instance "WRITER I felt bad for not being there for him".

3 Methods and Experimental Setting

Model. We model the task of experiencer-specific emotion analysis as a classification of instances which consist of experiencers e in the context of a text $\mathbf{t}_e = (t_1, \ldots, t_n)$. There can be multiple experiencers in one text, therefore $\mathbf{t}_e = \mathbf{t}_{e'}$ is possible. Each experiencer consists of a corresponding token sequence $(t_i, \ldots, t_j)$ $(1 \leq i, j, \leq |\mathbf{t}_e|)$, a set of emotion labels $E_e \in \{\text{anger}, \text{fear}, \text{joy}, \ldots\}$, and a 22-dimensional appraisal vector $\mathbf{a}_e \in [1; 5]^{22}$.

To predict $\mathbf{a}_e$ and E_e for each experiencer e with the help of $\mathbf{t}_e$, we use as input a positional indicator-encoding of the experiencers in context (inspired by Zhou et al., 2016). The writer is encoded with an additional special token $t_o = \texttt{WRITER}$. We refer to this experiencer-specific model as EXP.

Baseline. We compare this model to a baseline in which we simplify the experiencer-specific classification as text-level classification. During training, we assign the text $\mathbf{t}$ the union of all emotion labels of all contained experiencers, namely $E_\mathbf{t} = \bigcup_{e, \mathbf{t}_e = \mathbf{t}} E_e$. Analogously, the aggregation of the appraisal vectors is the centroid of all experiencers in one text: $\mathbf{a}_\mathbf{t} = \frac{1}{|\{e|\mathbf{t}_e = \mathbf{t}\}|} \sum_{e, \mathbf{t}_e = \mathbf{t}} \mathbf{a}_e$. We refer to this baseline model as TEXT(-based prediction). Table 2 examplifies the input representations.

Data Preparation. We use the x-enVENT data set (Troiano et al., 2022) for our experiments. It consists of 720 event descriptions, mainly from the enISEAR corpus (Troiano et al., 2019), which we split into 612 instances for training and 108 instances for testing (stratified). Each text has been annotated by four annotators and adjudicated to span-based experiencer annotations with a multi-label emotion classification and an appraisal vector. We merge infrequent emotion classes from the original corpus. Table 1 shows the label distribution.

Emotion Class	TEXT P	TEXT R	TEXT F_1	EXP P	EXP R	EXP F_1	ΔF_1
anger	40	82	54	60	80	68	+14
disgust	50	93	65	60	80	69	+4
fear	44	86	58	53	71	61	+3
joy	55	70	62	61	77	68	+6
no emotion	29	80	42	51	80	62	+20
other	11	10	10	14	10	12	+2
sadness	47	90	62	62	93	74	+12
shame	34	89	49	48	85	61	+12
Macro avg.	39	75	51	51	72	60	+9
Micro avg.	40	79	53	55	78	64	+11

Table 3: Emotion classification results of the TEXT-based baseline which is not informed about experiencer-specific emotions with our emotion experiencer-specific model EXP.

Implementation. We fine-tune Distil-RoBERTa (Liu et al., 2019) based on the Hugging Face implementation (Wolf et al., 2020). For both the emotion classification and the appraisal regression tasks, we follow a multi-task learning scheme. All emotion categories are predicted jointly by one model with a multi-output classification head, analogously with a regression head for the appraisal vector. The appendix contains implementation details.[2]

Evaluation. We evaluate performance by calculating experiencer-specific F_1 scores for emotion classification and Spearman's ρ for appraisal regression. In the TEXT baseline, we project the decision for the text to each experiencer that it contains.

4 Results

Quantitative Evaluation. Tables 3 and 4 show the results. For emotion classification, we report precision, recall, and F_1 measures for the baseline TEXT and the experiencer-specific predictions by EXP in Table 3. EXP substantially outperforms TEXT in terms of F_1 score. This trend holds across all emotion categories, as a result of an increased precision, which is intuitively reasonable, because the EXP model learns to distribute the emotions that are contained in a text to individual experiencers, while the TEXT baseline distributes all emotions to all experiencers equally, leading to an increased recall. The most substantial improvements are observed for *anger* (+14), *sadness* (+12) and *shame* (+12) as well as for *no emotion* (+20). These results are in line with the corpus analysis by Troiano

[2]Our implementation is available at `https://www.ims.uni-stuttgart.de/data/appraisalemotion`.

Appraisal Dimension	TEXT ρ	EXP ρ	$\Delta\rho$
Suddenness	0.32	0.54	+0.22
Familiarity	0.17	0.37	+0.20
Pleasantness	0.34	0.60	+0.26
Understand	0.24	0.30	+0.06
Goal relevance	0.15	0.33	+0.18
Self responsibility	0.31	0.68	+0.37
Other responsibility	0.33	0.68	+0.35
Situational respons.	0.59	0.68	+0.09
Effort	0.33	0.54	+0.21
Exert	0.97	0.25	−0.72
Attend	0.27	0.41	+0.14
Consider	0.55	0.62	+0.07
Outcome probability	0.14	0.38	+0.24
Expect. discrepancy	0.43	0.54	+0.11
Goal conduciveness	0.47	0.65	+0.18
Urgency	0.20	0.25	+0.05
Self control	0.36	0.64	+0.28
Other control	0.41	0.69	+0.28
Situational control	0.63	0.67	+0.04
Adjustment check	0.39	0.56	+0.17
Internal check	0.47	0.58	+0.11
External check	0.66	0.54	−0.12
Avg.	0.44	0.54	+0.09

Table 4: Appraisal regression results of the TEXT-based baseline and the experiencer-specific model EXP. The average has been calculated via FisherZ-Transformation.

et al. (2022). They found that some emotions are often shared between different experiencers within one text, but others occur in common pairs, namely *guilt–anger*, *no emotion–sadness*, *guilt–sadness* and *shame–anger*. Noteworthy is the category *no emotion*, which commonly occurs with all other emotions (Troiano et al., 2022, Figure 4). The performance increase for *joy*, *fear* and *disgust* is less distinct: these emotions are likely shared by all event experiencers.

For the appraisal predictions, we report Spearman's ρ in Table 4. We observe an improved performance prediction across nearly all dimensions. Appraisals that distinguish between who caused the event and who had the power to influence it (*self* vs. *other*) show the most substantial improvement, namely *self responsibility* (+0.37) and *self control* (+0.28), as well as *other responsibility* (+0.35) and *other control* (+0.28). This is reasonable – the *self* and *other* are often mutually exclusive. This interaction of appraisals cannot be exploited by purely text-level prediction models. However, if an event is caused by external factors, like *situational responsibility* (+.09) and *situational control* (+.04), all experiencers are equally affected by it. The decrease in performance for *external check* (−0.12) might be explained by the fact that this dimension is often shared between experiencers, rendering the TEXT model sufficiently efficient.

Analysis. We show some examples in Table 5 that highlight the usefulness of EXP over TEXT. Next to the emotion classification annotations and predictions from both models, we show the appraisals of *self responsibility/other responsibility* and *self control/other control*. In each example, the writer is one emotion experiencer. All other experiencers are underlined.

We observe that the TEXT model has a tendency to predict the union of the emotions for all experiencers, but sometimes predicts more additional categories. This is a consequence of the tendency towards high recall predictions of this model. In Example 1, both EXP and TEXT correctly assign the emotions *anger*, *disgust* and *no emotion*, but only EXP distributes them correctly between "Writer" and "The owners" (*sadness* is wrongly detected by both models). In Example 2, *joy* is not predicted by TEXT, but correctly assigned to "a group of children" by EXP. EXP further distributes *shame* and *sadness* to the correct entities (with a mistake assigning *anger* and *no emotion* to "a group of children" as well as *anger* and *fear* to "another child"). In Example 3, EXP correctly assigns *sadness* and *shame* to "Writer" and *sadness* and *no emotion* to "my sister", while TEXT fails to detect *no emotion.* In Example 4, EXP's prediction of *anger* and *fear* (for "our children") could be accepted to be correct despite it not being in line with the gold annotation. EXP further predicts the correct emotions for "Writer" (but makes a mistake assigning *joy* to "my ex husband"). In Example 5, the emotions of "Writer" are correctly assigned; "my son" is wrongly assigned *joy* in addition to *no emotion* (TEXT mistakenly predicts *other* as well). However, the correctness of this annotation is debatable.

Maximal values for the gold appraisal values for self/other control and self/other responsibility are, in nearly all cases, mutually exclusive across experiencers. The TEXT model is not informed about that and distributes the values across all entities. The EXP model does indeed recover the individual values for the appraisals, but to varying degrees. In Examples 2, 3, and 4, nearly all experiencers receive appraisal values close to the gold annotations. Example 2 appears to be challenging: the writer has a high gold annotation value for *self responsibility* which is not automatically detected. Further, "a

ID	Text
1	I felt ... working in the street seeing faeces of dogs. The owners should take care of them but are being so lazy and neglected, that is terrible.
2	I felt ... when I remember being part of a group of children at school who verbally bullied another child.
3	I felt ... when I lost my sister's necklace that I had borrowed.
4	I felt ... when my ex husband was hateful towards our children.
5	I felt ... when my son was born.

(a) Example Texts

		Gold		TEXT		EXP	
ID	Experiencer Text	Emotion	Appraisal	Emotion	Appraisal	Emotion	Appraisal
1	Writer	a d		a d no sa		a d sa	
	The owners	no		a d no sa		no	
2	Writer	sh		a no sa sh		sh	
	a group of children	j sh		a no sa sh		a j no sh	
	another child	sa		a no sa sh		a f sa	
3	Writer	sa sh		sa sh		sa sh	
	my sister	sa no		sa sh		sa no	
4	Writer	a sa		a f j no sa sh		a sa	
	my ex husband	a sh		a f j no sa sh		a j sh	
	our children	sa		a f j no sa sh		a f sa	
5	Writer	j		j o no		j	
	my son	no		j o no		j no	

(b) Annotations

Table 5: Examples of EXP and TEXT predictions. a: anger, d: disgust, no: no emotion, o:other, sa: sadness, sh: shame, f: fear, j: joy. The boxes show the appraisal *self responsibility*, *other responsibility*, *self control*, *other control*, with values between □ and ■.

group of children" receives the same values for the four appraisals. Examples 1/5 are cases in which the appraisal prediction does not work as expected.

5 Discussion and Conclusion

We presented the first approach of experiencer-specific emotion classification and appraisal regression. Our evaluation on event descriptions shows the need for such methods, and that a text-instance level annotation is a simplification.

This work provides the foundation for future research focused on texts in which multiple emotion labels co-occur, including reader/writer combinations or turn-taking dialogues. We propose to integrate experiencer-specific emotion modeling within such settings, for instance in novels, or news articles. It can also enrich the work of emotion recognition in dialogues (Poria et al., 2019): Chains of emotions have been modeled, but not considering mentioned entities.

Our work focused on a corpus that has been annotated specifically for writers' and entities' emotions. There exist, however, also other corpora with experiencer-specific emotion annotations, namely emotion role labeling resources (Kim and Klinger, 2018; Bostan et al., 2020; Campagnano et al., 2022; Mohammad et al., 2014). In addition to other information, they also provide experiencer-specific emotion labels, though not in such an event-focused context. Still, modeling them following our method needs to be compared to more traditional approaches that aim at recovering the full role labeling graph.

Our approach to encoding the experiencer position in the classifier has been a straightforward choice. Other model architectures (including positional embeddings, Wang and Chen, 2020) might perform better. Another interesting methodological avenue is to model the predictions of multiple experiencers jointly to exploit their relations.

Finally, an open question is how to incorporate information from existing resources that are not labeled with experiencer-specific information. For instance, Troiano et al. (2023) provide appraisal and emotion annotations for many more instances that might be beneficial in a transfer-learning setup.

Acknowledgements

This research is funded by the German Research Council (DFG), project "Computational Event Analysis based on Appraisal Theories for Emotion Analysis" (CEAT, project number KL 2869/1-2).

References

Cecilia Ovesdotter Alm, Dan Roth, and Richard Sproat. 2005. Emotions from text: Machine learning for text-based emotion prediction. In *Proceedings of Human Language Technology Conference and Conference on Empirical Methods in Natural Language Processing*, pages 579–586, Vancouver, British Columbia, Canada. Association for Computational Linguistics.

Jeremy Barnes, Robin Kurtz, Stephan Oepen, Lilja Øvrelid, and Erik Velldal. 2021. Structured sentiment analysis as dependency graph parsing. In *Proceedings of the 59th Annual Meeting of the Association for Computational Linguistics and the 11th International Joint Conference on Natural Language Processing (Volume 1: Long Papers)*, pages 3387–3402, Online. Association for Computational Linguistics.

Laura Ana Maria Bostan, Evgeny Kim, and Roman Klinger. 2020. GoodNewsEveryone: A corpus of news headlines annotated with emotions, semantic roles, and reader perception. In *Proceedings of the 12th Language Resources and Evaluation Conference*, pages 1554–1566, Marseille, France. European Language Resources Association.

Gianni Brauwers and Flavius Frasincar. 2021. A survey on aspect-based sentiment classification. *ACM Comput. Surv.* Just Accepted.

Sven Buechel and Udo Hahn. 2017. Readers vs. writers vs. texts: Coping with different perspectives of text understanding in emotion annotation. In *Proceedings of the 11th Linguistic Annotation Workshop*, pages 1–12, Valencia, Spain. Association for Computational Linguistics.

Cesare Campagnano, Simone Conia, and Roberto Navigli. 2022. SRL4E – Semantic Role Labeling for Emotions: A unified evaluation framework. In *Proceedings of the 60th Annual Meeting of the Association for Computational Linguistics (Volume 1: Long Papers)*, pages 4586–4601, Dublin, Ireland. Association for Computational Linguistics.

Ying Chen, Wenjun Hou, Xiyao Cheng, and Shoushan Li. 2018. Joint learning for emotion classification and emotion cause detection. In *Proceedings of the 2018 Conference on Empirical Methods in Natural Language Processing*, pages 646–651, Brussels, Belgium. Association for Computational Linguistics.

Ying Chen, Sophia Yat Mei Lee, Shoushan Li, and Chu-Ren Huang. 2010. Emotion cause detection with linguistic constructions. In *Proceedings of the 23rd International Conference on Computational Linguistics (Coling 2010)*, pages 179–187, Beijing, China. Coling 2010 Organizing Committee.

Xiyao Cheng, Ying Chen, Bixiao Cheng, Shoushan Li, and Guodong Zhou. 2017. An emotion cause corpus for chinese microblogs with multiple-user structures. *ACM Trans. Asian Low-Resour. Lang. Inf. Process.*, 17(1).

Dorottya Demszky, Dana Movshovitz-Attias, Jeongwoo Ko, Alan Cowen, Gaurav Nemade, and Sujith Ravi. 2020. GoEmotions: A dataset of fine-grained emotions. In *Proceedings of the 58th Annual Meeting of the Association for Computational Linguistics*, pages 4040–4054, Online. Association for Computational Linguistics.

Paul Ekman. 1992. An argument for basic emotions. *Cognition & emotion*, 6(3-4):169–200.

Diman Ghazi, Diana Inkpen, and Stan Szpakowicz. 2015. Detecting emotion stimuli in emotion-bearing sentences. In *International Conference on Computational Linguistics and Intelligent Text Processing*, pages 152–165. Springer.

Daniel Gildea and Daniel Jurafsky. 2000. Automatic labeling of semantic roles. In *Proceedings of the 38th Annual Meeting of the Association for Computational Linguistics*, pages 512–520, Hong Kong. Association for Computational Linguistics.

Xavier Glorot and Yoshua Bengio. 2010. Understanding the difficulty of training deep feedforward neural networks. In *Proceedings of the Thirteenth International Conference on Artificial Intelligence and Statistics, AISTATS 2010, Chia Laguna Resort, Sardinia, Italy, May 13-15, 2010*, volume 9 of *JMLR Proceedings*, pages 249–256. JMLR.org.

Jan Hofmann, Enrica Troiano, Kai Sassenberg, and Roman Klinger. 2020. Appraisal theories for emotion classification in text. In *Proceedings of the 28th International Conference on Computational Linguistics*, pages 125–138, Barcelona, Spain (Online). International Committee on Computational Linguistics.

Evgeny Kim and Roman Klinger. 2018. Who feels what and why? annotation of a literature corpus with semantic roles of emotions. In *Proceedings of the 27th International Conference on Computational Linguistics*, pages 1345–1359, Santa Fe, New Mexico, USA. Association for Computational Linguistics.

Soo-Min Kim and Eduard Hovy. 2006. Extracting opinions, opinion holders, and topics expressed in online news media text. In *Proceedings of the Workshop on Sentiment and Subjectivity in Text*, pages 1–8, Sydney, Australia. Association for Computational Linguistics.

Diederik P. Kingma and Jimmy Ba. 2015. Adam: A method for stochastic optimization. In *3rd International Conference on Learning Representations, ICLR 2015, San Diego, CA, USA, May 7-9, 2015, Conference Track Proceedings*.

Yinhan Liu, Myle Ott, Naman Goyal, Jingfei Du, Mandar Joshi, Danqi Chen, Omer Levy, Mike Lewis, Luke Zettlemoyer, and Veselin Stoyanov. 2019. RoBERTa: A robustly optimized BERT pretraining approach. arXiv:1907.11692.

Saif Mohammad, Felipe Bravo-Marquez, Mohammad Salameh, and Svetlana Kiritchenko. 2018. SemEval-2018 task 1: Affect in tweets. In *Proceedings of The 12th International Workshop on Semantic Evaluation*, pages 1–17, New Orleans, Louisiana. Association for Computational Linguistics.

Saif Mohammad, Xiaodan Zhu, and Joel Martin. 2014. Semantic role labeling of emotions in tweets. In *Proceedings of the 5th Workshop on Computational Approaches to Subjectivity, Sentiment and Social Media Analysis*, pages 32–41, Baltimore, Maryland. Association for Computational Linguistics.

Robert Plutchik. 2001. The nature of emotions. *American Scientist*, 89(4):344–350.

Soujanya Poria, Navonil Majumder, Rada Mihalcea, and Eduard Hovy. 2019. Emotion recognition in conversation: Research challenges, datasets, and recent advances. *IEEE Access*, 7:100943–100953.

Jonathan Posner, James A. Russell, and Bradley S. Peterson. 2005. The circumplex model of affect: an integrative approach to affective neuroscience, cognitive development, and psychopathology. *Development and Psychopathology*, 17(3):715–734.

James A Russell and Albert Mehrabian. 1977. Evidence for a three-factor theory of emotions. *Journal of research in Personality*, 11(3):273–294.

Irene Russo, Tommaso Caselli, Francesco Rubino, Ester Boldrini, and Patricio Martínez-Barco. 2011. EMOCause: An easy-adaptable approach to extract emotion cause contexts. In *Proceedings of the 2nd Workshop on Computational Approaches to Subjectivity and Sentiment Analysis (WASSA 2.011)*, pages 153–160, Portland, Oregon. Association for Computational Linguistics.

Klaus R. Scherer. 2005. What are emotions? And how can they be measured? *Social Science Information*, 44(4):695–729.

Klaus R. Scherer and Harald G. Wallbott. 1997. The ISEAR questionnaire and codebook. Geneva Emotion Research Group.

Yohei Seki. 2007. Opinion holder extraction from author and authority viewpoints. In *Proceedings of the 30th Annual International ACM SIGIR Conference on Research and Development in Information Retrieval*, SIGIR '07, page 841–842, New York, NY, USA. Association for Computing Machinery.

Craig A Smith and Phoebe C Ellsworth. 1985. Patterns of cognitive appraisal in emotion. *Journal of personality and social psychology*, 48(4):186–209.

Carlo Strapparava and Rada Mihalcea. 2007. SemEval-2007 task 14: Affective text. In *Proceedings of the Fourth International Workshop on Semantic Evaluations (SemEval-2007)*, pages 70–74, Prague, Czech Republic. Association for Computational Linguistics.

Enrica Troiano, Laura Oberländer, and Roman Klinger. 2023. Dimensional modeling of emotions in text with appraisal theories: Corpus creation, annotation reliability, and prediction. *Computational Linguistics*, 49(1):1–71. In print.

Enrica Troiano, Laura Oberländer, Maximilian Wegge, and Roman Klinger. 2022. x-enVENT: A corpus of event descriptions with experiencer-specific emotion and appraisal annotations. In *Proceedings of The 13th Language Resources and Evaluation Conference*, Marseille, France. European Language Resources Association.

Enrica Troiano, Sebastian Padó, and Roman Klinger. 2019. Crowdsourcing and validating event-focused emotion corpora for German and English. In *Proceedings of the 57th Annual Meeting of the Association for Computational Linguistics*, pages 4005–4011, Florence, Italy. Association for Computational Linguistics.

Yu-An Wang and Yun-Nung Chen. 2020. What do position embeddings learn? an empirical study of pre-trained language model positional encoding. In *Proceedings of the 2020 Conference on Empirical Methods in Natural Language Processing (EMNLP)*, pages 6840–6849, Online. Association for Computational Linguistics.

Michael Wiegand and Dietrich Klakow. 2011. The role of predicates in opinion holder extraction. In *Proceedings of the RANLP 2011 Workshop on Information Extraction and Knowledge Acquisition*, pages 13–20, Hissar, Bulgaria. Association for Computational Linguistics.

Michael Wiegand and Dietrich Klakow. 2012. Generalization methods for in-domain and cross-domain opinion holder extraction. In *Proceedings of the 13th Conference of the European Chapter of the Association for Computational Linguistics*, pages 325–335, Avignon, France. Association for Computational Linguistics.

Thomas Wolf, Lysandre Debut, Victor Sanh, Julien Chaumond, Clement Delangue, Anthony Moi, Pierric Cistac, Tim Rault, Remi Louf, Morgan Funtowicz, Joe Davison, Sam Shleifer, Patrick von Platen, Clara Ma, Yacine Jernite, Julien Plu, Canwen Xu, Teven Le Scao, Sylvain Gugger, Mariama Drame, Quentin Lhoest, and Alexander Rush. 2020. Transformers: State-of-the-art natural language processing. In *Proceedings of the 2020 Conference on Empirical Methods in Natural Language Processing: System Demonstrations*, pages 38–45, Online. Association for Computational Linguistics.

Peng Zhou, Wei Shi, Jun Tian, Zhenyu Qi, Bingchen Li, Hongwei Hao, and Bo Xu. 2016. Attention-based bidirectional long short-term memory networks for relation classification. In *Proceedings of the 54th Annual Meeting of the Association for Computational Linguistics (Volume 2: Short Papers)*, pages 207–212, Berlin, Germany. Association for Computational Linguistics.

A Implementation Details.

We fine-tune Distil-RoBERTa (Liu et al., 2019) as implemented in the Hugging Face library[3] (Wolf et al., 2020) and leave default parameters unchanged. For both the emotion classification and the appraisal regression tasks, we follow a multi-task learning scheme. All emotion categories are predicted jointly by one model with a multi-output classification head, analogously with a regression head for the appraisal vector prediction. The classification head consists of a linear layer with dropout (0.5) and ReLU activation function, followed by a final linear layer with sigmoid activation. For the appraisal regression, the sigmoid activation function in the final layer is replaced by a linear activation. We use binary cross entropy loss in the emotion classifier and mean squared error loss in the appraisal regressor. Both models are trained for 10 epochs without early stopping. We use the Adam optimizer (Kingma and Ba, 2015) with weight decay (0.001) and a learning rate of $2 \cdot 10^{-5}$. The weights of each layer are initialized using the Xavier uniform initialization (Glorot and Bengio, 2010). The hyperparameters and architecture have been decided on via 10-fold cross validation on the training data.

[3] `https://huggingface.co/distilroberta-base`

Understanding Narratives from Demographic Survey Data: a Comparative Study with Multiple Neural Topic Models

Xiao Xu
NIDI-KNAW
University of Groningen
xu@nidi.nl

Gert Stulp
University of Groningen
g.stulp@rug.nl

Antal van den Bosch
Utrecht University
a.p.j.vandenbosch@uu.nl

Anne Gauthier
NIDI-KNAW
gauthier@rug.nl

Abstract

Fertility intentions as verbalized in surveys are a poor predictor of actual fertility outcomes, the number of children people have. This can partly be explained by the uncertainty people have in their intentions. Such uncertainties are hard to capture through traditional survey questions, although open-ended questions can be used to get insight into people's subjective narratives of the future that determine their intentions. Analyzing such answers to open-ended questions can be done through Natural Language Processing techniques. Traditional topic models (e.g., LSA and LDA), however, often fail to do since they rely on co-occurrences, which are often rare in short survey responses. The aim of this study was to apply and evaluate topic models on demographic survey data. In this study, we applied neural topic models (e.g. BERTopic, CombinedTM) based on language models to responses from Dutch women on their fertility plans, and compared the topics and their coherence scores from each model to expert judgments. Our results show that neural models produce topics more in line with human interpretation compared to LDA. However, the coherence score could only partly reflect on this, depending on the method and corpus used for calculation. This research is important because, first, it helps us develop more informed strategies on model selection and evaluation for topic modeling on survey data; and second, it shows that the field of demography has much to gain from adopting novel NLP methods.

1 Introduction

Demographers are interested in the number of children people have or will have, also referred to as fertility. In trying to understand future fertility, researchers have studied fertility intentions, i.e. plans to have children in the future. The usefulness of measurements of fertility intentions are often debated among demographers due to the gap between intentions and fertility outcomes (Brinton et al., 2018; Trinitapoli and Yeatman, 2018) and a large portion of respondents being uncertain about their intentions (Bhrolcháin and Beaujouan, 2019). It is proposed that this is because fertility intentions are contextual and largely depend on subjective narratives (Vignoli et al., 2020). Therefore, understanding these narratives might be the key for advancing theories on the fertility decision-making process.

Open-ended questions (OEQs) help researchers obtain "top-of-the-head" answers from respondents, and they have been employed in previous qualitative demographic studies (e.g., interviews with a small sample of respondents, sometime deliberately non-representative of the whole population) (Schatz and Williams, 2012; Staveteig et al., 2017). However, to expand the analysis to a larger and generalizable sample of the population, an automatic process of extracting and quantifying themes from responses is needed as an initial exploratory data analysis. This objective can be met with topic modeling methods.

Latent Dirichlet Allocation (LDA; Blei et al. (2003)) is one of the most popular topic modeling algorithms, which is based on co-occurrence of words. LDA's performance on short texts, such as online survey responses, may be compromised due to the small number of co-occurrences. To overcome this problem, many topic models that support incorporating prior language knowledge (e.g. word embeddings or language models) have been developed, such as *Sparse Contextual Hidden and Observed Language AutoencodeR* (SCHOLAR; (Card et al., 2017)). This model uses variational autoencoder (VAE) to incorporate word2vec (Mikolov et al., 2013) embeddings. A different example is Bidirectional Encoder Representations from Transformers (BERT, Devlin et al. (2018)), one of the most prominent language models, that has also been incorporated in topic modeling tasks, e.g. in Combined Topic Model (CombinedTM; Bianchi

Proceedings of the Fifth Workshop on Natural Language Processing and Computational Social Science (NLP+CSS), pages 33 - 38
November 7, 2022 ©2022 Association for Computational Linguistics

et al. (2020)) and BERTopic (Grootendorst, 2022).

In this paper, our first aim is to compare the performance of multiple topic modelling algorithms on responses to open questions. Such an analysis of survey responses is rare, and it is an open question how well these topic models do on short texts from relatively few respondents (400), a scale larger than usual qualitative studies. To achieve this, we implemented and evaluated four models (LDA, SCHOLAR, CombinedTM and BERTopic), trained on the fertility response dataset to provide unsupervised topics. We then compare metrics of quality across these diverse methods through comparable implementations. Building on the comparative study of Baumer et al. (2017), we further compare metrics and their difference to human annotations respectively.

Our study contributes to the literature by: 1) evaluating the performance of multiple topic models incorporating prior knowledge; 2) examining the correlation between metrics and human judgments; 3) modeling topics on Dutch texts of online survey responses and 4) bringing novel text analysis methods to the field of demography.

2 Data

The data used in this study is collected through the LISS (Longitudinal Internet Studies for the Social sciences) panel administered by CentERdata at Tilburg University, The Netherlands. The study is based on the second wave of survey *Social networks and fertility (in Dutch: Sociale relaties en kinderkeuzes onderzoek)* within the LISS panel in 2021, which was first fielded in 2018. The module's objective was to investigate fertility intentions and attitudes in relation to people's personal networks. For this round of our survey, 596 female participants were invited, and 464 women between the ages of 21 and 44 completed the questionnaire. The survey was conducted in Dutch. The open-ended questions (henceforth: OEQ) regarding fertility intentions are presented to respondents that are not currently pregnant (N=433). After removing 6 answers that were without information (e.g. "niets") or not in Dutch, there were in total 427 responses available.

The OEQ was placed directly after a standard closed questions on fertility intention ("Do you intend to have a/another child during the next three years?") from the Generations & Gender Surveys (GGS) (Gauthier et al., 2018). Respondents were presented with a text box, where they can input text answers. Two versions of the OEQ were tested:

- **Original** Can you tell us more about what makes you (un)certain about whether or not to have children?
- **Adaptive reminder** You answered the previous question "Do you plan to have a child in the next three years?" with [*[1]]. Can you tell us more about what makes you (un)certain about whether or not to have children?

The answers contain 32 words on average. Since answers to these two questions were similar on a suite of textual characteristics (e.g., sentence length, number of nouns), we did not differentiate between answers to these two questions in the subsequent analyses.

3 Evaluation

Each model was evaluated on three different metrics: topic coherence, topic diversity, and comparison to human-assigned labels.

Topic coherence measures how close the top n words (typically, $n = 10$) from a topic are to each other: if the words always co-occur in documents, they are considered "close" and the topic is considered *coherent*. It is calculated through non-negative point-wise mutual information (NPMI, Newman et al. (2010)), where w denotes a word:

$$\text{NPMI}(w_i) = \sum_{j}^{n-1} \frac{log \frac{P(w_i, w_j)}{P(w_i)P(w_j)}}{-logP(w_j, w_j)}$$

The calculation of topic coherence requires an external test corpus for calculating how frequently words in the topic occur together in real language usage Blair et al. (2020). The external corpus was crawled from the Viva forum, a Dutch online discussion board mainly aimed at women. We prepared two corpora for cross validation: first the "Child wish" corpus, which contains 436 threads and replies including the keyword "child wish[2]"; second the "Pregnancy[3]" corpus, containing 5507 comments under the "Pregnancy" board. Coherence scores were calculated on both corpora.

Topic diversity measures how different the top ten words from all topics are; i.e. if topics share

[1]definitely yes / probably yes / unsure / probably not / definitely not/ don't know

[2]In Dutch: *kinderwens*

[3]In Dutch: *Zwanger*

the same words. It is calculated through Inversed Rank-Biased Overlap (ρ; Webber et al. (2010)), where the top ten words are compared. The score ranges from 0 to 1, representing topics that contain exact same words to totally different topics.

The four authors of this paper intensively read on recent fertility trends and events in the Netherlands. The first and fourth authors read through the dataset to develop qualitative insights and proposed themes of discussions from respondents; as we coded the responses iteratively, although exact labels were not yet given to each response, six themes were summarized. Then, all authors interpreted lists of top words for each topic generated by models, and compared results with different number of topics K to develop the ideal K. Eventually, we have together determined the optimal number of topics to be $K = 9$ and established a verbal theme for each topic.

We ran grid search on each model for hyper-parameter tuning under the same number of topics $K = 9$; this did not apply to BERTopic as it used HDBSCAN algorithm and did not require a pre-defined K. We use COW word embedding (Tulkens et al., 2016) for SCHOLAR model, and we use RobBERT (Delobelle et al., 2020), a state-of-the-art Dutch BERT model for CombinedTM and BERTopic.

4 Results

In this section, we first present the themes from qualitative insights. These are then compared to results from the four topic models. Since human produced themes may correspond to more than one topic (Baumer et al., 2017), we calculate how many themes were accounted for and present them together with other metrics. The themes and corresponding topics are presented in Table 1. Each relevant topic has a human-assigned label, describing its perceived content; if there are multiple topics relevant to one theme, they are separated by the & symbol.

4.1 Qualitative insights

These insights were summarized by the authors of this paper through rounds of reading and discussion. Here, people talked about the issues and conditions about what made them feel uncertain about having kids. Age and family size were the most prominent themes, while various other personal circumstances and societal issues were also mentioned.

4.1.1 Age

Age is one of the most mentioned themes in the answers; in fact, some respondent only left one word "age" in their answer. Other more elaborated responses can be divided into two groups: "too young" (e.g. "I'm only 23 years old and still studying") and "too old" (e.g. "I'm already 43 and I do not have wish for child").

4.1.2 Number of kids

Many respondents who already have kids and are satisfied with their current family size. For example, "My family is complete, and we are satisfied with 2 kids".

4.1.3 Lifestyle

This theme concerns those who have other plans or want to do a lot of things before having children, e.g. studying, traveling, finding a part-time job. It sometimes co-occurs with young age. An example is, "I would really like to have children, but at the moment I am still at an age where I also want to have time with my boyfriend to make beautiful trips and have time for the two of us".

4.1.4 Pre-conditions

Having children may require a lot of pre-conditions and this is used as justification for not wanting to have (more) children, especially among younger respondents. Conditions that were mentioned including having a stable partner, a stable job, a property, or finishing studies. This is a typical response from a student: "I will finish my studies this year, after that I first want to be able to work full-time for a number of years in order to possibly also buy a house".

4.1.5 Health issues

In our study, the theme of health issues refers to cases where the respondent wanted to or had been trying to have kids, but failed to or refrain from getting pregnant due to infertility or other medical conditions. For example, one mentioned that "the risk of complications with myself is quite high. In addition, I take medicines that are not possible in combination with a pregnancy".

4.1.6 Dissatisfaction

There is a small set of responses that, instead of personal circumstances, talked about broader dissatisfaction with the world or society. Issues raised include environmental concerns ("The world is not a nice place now. Climate changes are becoming

Theme	LDA	SCHOLAR	CombinedTM	BERTopic
1. Age	**Yes**	No	**Yes** (too young & too old)	**Yes** (too old)
2. Number of kids	No	No	**Yes** (family complete)	**Yes** (family complete)
3. Lifestyle	No	**Yes** (sacrifice to make)	**Yes** (early stage of life)	**Yes** (freedom)
4. Pre-conditions	**Yes** (partner)	**Yes** (housing & relation)	**Yes** (studies & jobs)	**Yes** (partner & jobs)
5. Health issues	No	**Yes** (health & medicine)	**Yes** (infertile & illness)	**Yes** (postnatal)
6. Dissatisfaction	No	**Yes** (climate change)	**Yes** (general)	**Yes** (economy)
Themes covered	2	4	**6**	**6**
Topic coherence (internal)	0.055	**0.464**	0.110	0.134
Topic coherence (corpus "pregnancy")	0.134	0.050	0.096	**0.158**
Topic coherence (corpus "child wish")	0.110	0.052	0.098	**0.146**
Topic diversity	0.506	**1**	0.871	0.755

Table 1: Comparison of performance between the four topic models

more and more intense"), religion ("from a biblical perspective I think it is important that I have children and hopefully let them participate in the faith"), social media ("kids nowadays are easily influenced by social media, internet, etc."). Although the issues were different by themselves, these types of responses were unified by a general sense of dissatisfaction ("I think it is very difficult to raise children in this society and world in which we now live").

4.2 Comparing topic models

We describe and compare the performance of topics in terms of each model through two sets of criteria. First, we compare topics generated by the algorithm to human produced themes, and count the number of themes that are resonated with at least one topic; then, the above-mentioned three metrics are also calculated. All results are summarized in Table 1.

We note that the two topic models that are based on BERT (CombinedTM and BERTopic) matched all themes from qualitative insights, while LDA and SCHOLAR failed to do so. This suggests that their results are closer to human judgments. However, this is only partly reflected by metrics. The SCHOLAR model, based on autoencoder and word embeddings, scored far beyond others in internal topic coherence, while BERTopic scored better than the other models on external topic coherence. SCHOLAR topped the ranking of topic diversity, while LDA scored poorly at 0.506.

Overall, we found that neural topic models indeed brought improvements over LDA: all three other models exceeded LDA by most metrics, while BERTopic outperformed LDA by all criteria.

5 Discussion

Demographers have long been calling for empirical evidence on fertility intention uncertainty and narratives (Bhrolcháin and Beaujouan, 2019; Vignoli et al., 2020). With the results from this study, we showed that neural topic models were able to provide insights similar to human judgments, thus providing a powerful tool for future demographic studies.

Our results also demonstrated the significant improvement of performance that neural topic models brought to text analysis on short survey data. The prior knowledge of language, incorporated by language models such as BERT, enabled results of quality close to traditional qualitative analysis in social studies, while previously used models such as LDA failed to so. This may have a direct application in processing online open surveys or interview data, and enabling qualitative analysis on a larger scale.

The contrast between the ranking of scores in internal and external coherence revealed that the evaluation strategy on topic models may need to be reconsidered, especially in social science studies. Although topics generated by SCHOLAR showed an extremely high internal coherence, a closer look showed that it is mostly due to some topics consisting of words that were almost exclusively from one document (response), dragging coherence of that topic up to almost 1 (i.e. words would always co-occur). This also explained its unusually high topic diversity (at 1, which entails no repeated words at all across topics), as the topics consist of only unique words from the one document.

Our results remind us that some metrics for topic models may be misleading on a smaller, shorter dataset, and choosing the right, field-relevant corpus is a key step in correctly evaluating topic coherence. Moreover, using multiple criteria help us to avoid pitfalls and making more informed choices in selecting topic models for survey data.

Limitations

Due to limitations in time and resources, we did not conduct a thorough, full-scale grounded analysis on the corpus, as Baumer et al. (2017) did. Instead, a more lightweight approach to develop qualitative insights were chosen. Therefore, our qualitative insights and labels may still have space to improve, and the themes we proposed cannot be interpreted as a "gold standard" of model performance.

We only applied a few among many neural topic models in this study, based on easiness of implementation and availability of Dutch resources. There are several other neural topic models that are optimized for short texts, which are well summarized by Zhao et al. (2021). It would be interesting to add them for further comparisons in the future.

Ethics Statement

Ethical permission for the study was obtained from the ethical committee of sociology at the University of Groningen (ECS-201123). The dataset will be made available at `dataarchive.lissdata.nl`.

References

Eric PS Baumer, David Mimno, Shion Guha, Emily Quan, and Geri K Gay. 2017. Comparing grounded theory and topic modeling: Extreme divergence or unlikely convergence? *Journal of the Association for Information Science and Technology*, 68(6):1397–1410.

Máire Ní Bhrolcháin and Éva Beaujouan. 2019. Do people have reproductive goals? constructive preferences and the discovery of desired family size. In *Analytical family demography*, pages 27–56. Springer.

Federico Bianchi, Silvia Terragni, and Dirk Hovy. 2020. Pre-training is a hot topic: Contextualized document embeddings improve topic coherence. *arXiv preprint arXiv:2004.03974*.

Stuart J Blair, Yaxin Bi, and Maurice D Mulvenna. 2020. Aggregated topic models for increasing social media topic coherence. *Applied Intelligence*, 50(1):138–156.

David M Blei, Andrew Y Ng, and Michael I Jordan. 2003. Latent dirichlet allocation. *the Journal of machine Learning research*, 3:993–1022.

Mary C Brinton, Xiana Bueno, Livia Oláh, and Merete Hellum. 2018. Postindustrial fertility ideals, intentions, and gender inequality: A comparative qualitative analysis. *Population and Development Review*, 44(2):281–309.

Dallas Card, Chenhao Tan, and Noah A Smith. 2017. Neural models for documents with metadata. *arXiv preprint arXiv:1705.09296*.

Pieter Delobelle, Thomas Winters, and Bettina Berendt. 2020. RobBERT: a Dutch RoBERTa-based Language Model. In *Findings of the Association for Computational Linguistics: EMNLP 2020*, pages 3255–3265, Online. Association for Computational Linguistics.

Jacob Devlin, Ming-Wei Chang, Kenton Lee, and Kristina Toutanova. 2018. Bert: Pre-training of deep bidirectional transformers for language understanding. *arXiv preprint arXiv:1810.04805*.

Anne H Gauthier, Susana Laia Farinha Cabaço, and Tom Emery. 2018. Generations and gender survey study profile. *Longitudinal and Life course studies*, 9(4):456–465.

Maarten Grootendorst. 2022. Bertopic: Neural topic modeling with a class-based tf-idf procedure. *arXiv preprint arXiv:2203.05794*.

Tomas Mikolov, Kai Chen, Greg Corrado, and Jeffrey Dean. 2013. Efficient estimation of word representations in vector space. *arXiv preprint arXiv:1301.3781*.

David Newman, Jey Han Lau, Karl Grieser, and Timothy Baldwin. 2010. Automatic evaluation of topic coherence. In *Human language technologies: The 2010 annual conference of the North American chapter of the association for computational linguistics*, pages 100–108.

Enid Schatz and Jill Williams. 2012. Measuring gender and reproductive health in africa using demographic and health surveys: the need for mixed-methods research. *Culture, health & sexuality*, 14(7):811–826.

Sarah Staveteig, Richmond Aryeetey, Michael Anie-Ansah, Clement Ahiadeke, and Ladys Ortiz. 2017. Design and methodology of a mixed methods follow-up study to the 2014 ghana demographic and health survey. *Global health action*, 10(1):1274072.

Jenny Trinitapoli and Sara Yeatman. 2018. The flexibility of fertility preferences in a context of uncertainty. *Population and Development Review*, 44(1):87.

Stephan Tulkens, Chris Emmery, and Walter Daelemans. 2016. Evaluating unsupervised dutch word embeddings as a linguistic resource. In *Proceedings of the Tenth International Conference on Language Resources and Evaluation (LREC 2016)*, Paris, France. European Language Resources Association (ELRA).

Daniele Vignoli, Giacomo Bazzani, Raffaele Guetto, Alessandra Minello, and Elena Pirani. 2020. Uncertainty and narratives of the future: a theoretical framework for contemporary fertility. In *Analyzing contemporary fertility*, pages 25–47. Springer.

William Webber, Alistair Moffat, and Justin Zobel. 2010. A similarity measure for indefinite rankings. *ACM Transactions on Information Systems (TOIS)*, 28(4):1–38.

He Zhao, Dinh Phung, Viet Huynh, Yuan Jin, Lan Du, and Wray Buntine. 2021. Topic modelling meets deep neural networks: A survey. *arXiv preprint arXiv:2103.00498*.

To Prefer or to Choose? Generating Agency and Power Counterfactuals Jointly for Gender Bias Mitigation

Maja Stahl and **Max Spliethöver** and **Henning Wachsmuth**
Leibniz University Hannover, Hannover, Germany
Institute of Artificial Intelligence
{m.stahl, m.spliethoever, h.wachsmuth}@ai.uni-hannover.de

Abstract

Gender bias may emerge from an unequal representation of *agency* and *power*, for example, by portraying women frequently as passive and powerless ("She accepted her future") and men as proactive and powerful ("He chose his future"). When language models learn from respective texts, they may reproduce or even amplify the bias. An effective way to mitigate bias is to generate counterfactual sentences with opposite agency and power to the training. Recent work targeted agency-specific verbs from a lexicon to this end. We argue that this is insufficient, due to the interaction of agency and power and their dependence on context. In this paper, we thus develop a new rewriting model that identifies verbs with the desired agency and power in the context of the given sentence. The verbs' probability is then boosted to encourage the model to rewrite both connotations jointly. According to automatic metrics, our model effectively controls for power while being competitive in agency to the state of the art. In our evaluation, human annotators favored its counterfactuals in terms of both connotations, also deeming its meaning preservation better.

1 Introduction

Gender bias refers to the conscious or unconscious unequal treatment of people because of being male, female, or diverse. In natural language text, it manifests in various ways, including the explicit expression of stereotypes and discrimination as well as implicit prejudicial or generalized representations of genders (Hitti et al., 2019; Doughman et al., 2021). Language models that learn from such text may reproduce or even amplify the bias (Hovy and Spruit, 2016). An effective approach to mitigate this behavior is to reduce bias in the training data (Hitti et al., 2019). In particular, augmenting the data with counterfactuals has been shown to effectively reduce bias in language models (Zmigrod et al., 2019; Lu et al., 2020). Generating counterfactuals that change the depiction of people through the choice of words is the focus of our research.

Several works have analyzed gender bias in the subliminal messages transmitted by the framing of people's actions (Sap et al., 2017; Field et al., 2019; Field and Tsvetkov, 2019; Park et al., 2021). They suggest that the framing of an action influences how the reader perceives the acting person behind. The verb choice can therefore weaken or strengthen the person under consideration (Rashkin et al., 2016; Sap et al., 2017), as in the following example:

1. "She *desires* to get paid." (weakening) vs.
2. "She *demands* to get paid." (strengthening)

To study bias in verb choice, the connotational dimensions of *agency* and *power* as well as their interactions are particularly important (Sap et al., 2017). Agency describes how active a person is portrayed:

3. "X *chooses* their future." (high agency) vs.
4. "X *accepts* their future." (low agency)

Power, on the other hand, describes how much control a person has with respect to a given setting:

5. "X *demands* mercy from their opponent." (high power) vs.
6. "X *begs* their opponent for mercy." (low pow.)

Analyses along these dimensions showed differences between women and men, reflecting gender stereotypes, as detailed in Section 2. For agency-related bias, Ma et al. (2020) created a model that rewrites sentences into a desired agency using the connotation frame lexicon of Sap et al. (2017). We argue that an agency lexicon is not enough to generate counterfactuals, due to the interaction of agency and power and their dependence on context. Especially, power remains untackled so far.

In this paper, we study how to generate counterfactuals for gender bias mitigation by rewriting sentences jointly in terms of both agency and power—while preserving meaning as much as possible. We hypothesize that simply extending an

Proceedings of the Fifth Workshop on Natural Language Processing and Computational Social Science (NLP+CSS), pages 39 - 51
November 7, 2022

agency rewriting model by the power connotation is insufficient to successfully change both connotations of input sentences. Instead, we propose a new model that refines the rewriting process in two ways: First, we determine verbs that are not only similar to the original verb but also have the desired target connotations, by classifying their agency and power within the context of the input sentence. We expect that this results in verbs that allow for a more cohesive sentence rewriting. Second, we boost the generation probability of these verbs for both connotations, encouraging the model to achieve the desired agency and power jointly.

To include verbs indicative of agency and power from diverse contexts, we train the classifiers on sentences from the datasets of Kiesel et al. (2017), Pungas (2017), and Wang et al. (2018). In experiments on the movie summary dataset of Bamman et al. (2013), we then compare our rewriting model against the state-of-the-art for agency (Ma et al., 2020). Concretely, we assess the rewritten sentences in terms of their compliance with target agency, target power, and meaning preservation.

Our automatic pre-evaluation indicates that the new model is competitive in controlling for agency, while outperforming Ma et al. (2020) in terms of power compliance and meaning preservation. In our manual evaluation, human annotators favor our model in terms of all three criteria.

Contributions In summary, our main contributions are:[1]

1. A rewriting model for joint agency and power adaptation on the sentence level.
2. Classifiers for assessing the agency and power of verbs in a given sentence context.
3. Empirical evidence for the importance of joint agency and power control to generate counterfactuals for gender bias mitigation.

Ethical Consideration The methods developed in this paper aim to mitigate gender bias in natural language sentences. As such, we expect primarily positive ethical consequences from the contributions of this paper. However, we point out a significant risk emanating from applying the developed methods: By adjusting the agency and power levels, the meaning of a sentence may likely be changed to some degree. This can have negative implications when facts are distorted. An example of this is misrepresenting a victim as a perpetrator by portraying that person with more agency and/or power. In case our methods are used for modifying language that humans perceive, the methods should thus be used in a semi-automated environment with human supervision. Further ethical implications of this work are discussed in Section 9.

2 Related Work

Unequal communication towards social groups, for example in the form of texts, can be the origin of social bias and is one of the main reasons why individuals, their characteristics, and their actions are not perceived correctly. Instead, people's perceptions are often overshadowed and distorted by prejudiced beliefs, resulting in potentially unfair treatment (Steele et al., 2004). Different types of social bias have been studied in NLP research recently (Nangia et al., 2020; Sap et al., 2020; Spliethöver and Wachsmuth, 2020). We focus on one of the most prevailing types, *gender bias*. For comparability with prior work, we use existing datasets in our experiments, limiting them to binary gender instead of considering further social and linguistic gender categories (Cao and Daumé III, 2020).

Previous work analyzed implicit forms of gender bias conveyed through language, often reflected by imbalances in *connotation frames* that capture subjective roles and relations conveyed by a predicate (Rashkin et al., 2016). Connotation frames were introduced by Rashkin et al. (2016), who studied the sentiment and presuppositions of predicates. Sap et al. (2017) extended their notion by explicitly modeling agency and power. The authors created a connotation frame lexicon of common verbs, 2146 of which were manually assigned an agency level, 1737 a power level (positive, equal, or negative). They used the lexicon to compare movie characters, finding that males are generally portrayed with more agency and power. Field et al. (2019) and Field and Tsvetkov (2019) found power imbalances in media articles. For example, female politicians are often portrayed as less powerful than their actual role in society compared to males. Instead of *identifying* gender bias, we focus on *mitigating* it.

Bias mitigation has been addressed at the preprocessing, the training, and the postprocessing level (Feldman and Peake, 2021). One preprocessing approach is to balance gender occurrences in training data. For example, Alhafni et al. (2020) and Sun

[1]Our code is published at `https://github.com/webis-de/NLPANDCSS-22`.

et al. (2021) learned on parallel corpora to change the gender of sentences across languages. Park et al. (2018) augmented data with gendered sentences to reduce bias in word embeddings, and Zmigrod et al. (2019) aimed to convert between masculine and feminine inflected sentences without parallel data. At the training level, Dinan et al. (2020) adapted the training process and applied bias controlled training to generative dialogue models to make them generate an equal number of gendered words for both genders considered. Lastly, Bolukbasi et al. (2016), Zhao et al. (2019) and Liang et al. (2020) postprocessed pre-trained word embeddings to remove encoded gender information.

To debias text through the lens of agency connotations, Ma et al. (2020) formalized a new rewriting task called *controllable debiasing* that seeks to correct implicit bias in textual portrayals. Unlike its name (PowerTransformer) suggests, their approach aims to change the *agency* connotation of an input sentence (not power). Using the agency lexicon of Sap et al. (2017), Ma et al. (2020) provide information about agency connotations to the model using self-supervision on a reconstruction task and auxiliary supervision on a paraphrasing task. Inspired by Ghosh et al. (2017), they performed vocabulary boosting at each decoding step based on the agency lexicon to further enhance the agency change.

In this paper, we build on the rewriting model of Ma et al. (2020), but we extend it to jointly control for agency and power. Moreover, we substantially refine the rewriting process by using classifiers to determine which verbs to boost in the given context. Existing classifiers rely on logistic and kernel ridge regression for agency and power, based on decontextualized ELMo (Peters et al., 2018) and BERT (Devlin et al., 2019) embeddings of a verb (Field et al., 2019; Field and Tsvetkov, 2019; Park et al., 2021). In contrast, we use the whole sentence context as input and perform classification, improving the state of the art in our experiments.

3 Approach

This section presents our approach to generating counterfactuals for gender bias mitigation. Based on the contextual classification of verbs, it rewrites sentences jointly in terms of agency and power.

Overview Figure 1 depicts the two parts of the approach: (1) Given a sentence, we identify candidate verbs for its rewritten version. To foster meaning preservation, we filter verbs similar to the original verb. The agency and power of these verbs are then classified in the context of the masked sentence. (2) To rewrite the sentence based on the target connotations, a transformer computes the next-word probability logits. The logits of verbs with target agency and power are boosted to foster connotation change in the output sentence.

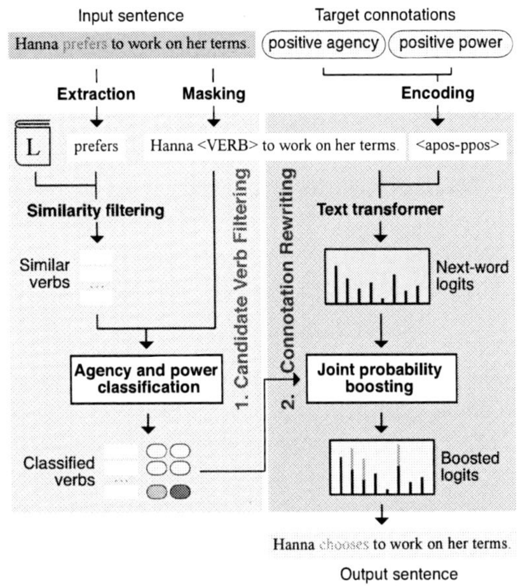

Figure 1: Proposed approach: After masking the verb in the input sentence, all similar verbs from a lexicon L are classified for agency and power in the sentence context. A transformer then rewrites the sentence. At each decoding step, the unnormalized token probabilities (logits) of verbs with target agency and power are increased.

3.1 Candidate Verb Filtering in Context

We seek to find verbs that have a meaning similar to the original verb of a given input sentence s and fit the given target agency and power. As candidates, we consider all verbs from a verb lexicon L.

Similarity Filtering First, we retrieve all verbs from L whose similarity to the original verb in s lies above a threshold γ. Concretely, we employ cosine similarity of the verbs' GloVe representations (Pennington et al., 2014) as a measure.

Agency and Power Classification The next task is to determine the agency and power connotation of all similar verbs. Unlike the lexicon-based connotation filtering of Ma et al. (2020), we classify a verb's agency and power in the context of the masked sentence. In contrast to existing connotation classifiers (Field et al., 2019; Field and

Tsvetkov, 2019), we fine-tune a pre-trained language model based on full sentences. We hypothesize that these changes improve both the identification of the correct agency and power and the resulting cohesiveness of the rewritten sentences.

To emphasize the verb while having the rest of the sentence as context, we separate the verb and the masked sentence with a special token, *[sep]*. The verb is replaced inside the sentence by *[verb]*:

verb [sep] masked_sentence

The resulting sequence is passed to a BERT model (Devlin et al., 2019). As target value, we provide the verb's agency or power connotation as given in the lexicon of Sap et al. (2017). Possible connotation values are *positive*, *equal*, and *negative*.

3.2 Joint Connotation Rewriting

Given a sentence with original agency and power connotations, the task is to rewrite it to express a target agency and power while preserving the meaning as much as possible.

Text Transformer Analog to Ma et al. (2020), we fine-tune a GPT transformer model (Radford et al., 2018) on two tasks: (1) Reconstructing partially masked sentences and (2) paraphrasing sentences. Training for the respective loss functions is done in an alternating manner. For lack of parallel data, the model is trained using self-supervision during reconstruction and auxiliary supervision during paraphrasing. During training, the target agency and power are provided as control tokens, which guide the output connotation during inference. Each control token is composed as follows, where *a* refers to agency and *p* to power, each followed by the respective target value:

<a (pos | equal | neg) – p (pos | equal | neg)>

During reconstruction, the model learns to restore the masked verbs of sentences. Let s be a sentence represented as the sequence of $n \geq 1$ tokens, $s = (t_1, \ldots, t_n)$. The connotations of s are encoded as a control token, t_c. t_c is given to the model as target connotation, along with the masked sentence $\hat{s}$, in which the main verb is replaced by *[verb]*. The target output is the original sentence s. As Ma et al. (2020), we minimize the cross entropy of the target output sentence given the inputs:

$$\mathcal{L}_{recon} = -\frac{1}{n}\sum_{i=1}^{n} \log P(t_i \mid t_1, \ldots, t_{i-1}; \hat{s}; t_c)$$

To enable the model to perform edits that go beyond exchanging verbs, we extend the paraphrasing objective of Ma et al. (2020) whose goal is to achieve coherent, meaningful rewriting. While the verbs in the input sentences are masked as before, t_c now reflects the agency and power connotation of a matching paraphrase $\tilde{s} = (\tilde{t}_1, \ldots, \tilde{t}_m), m \geq 1$. The target output is the paraphrase, $\tilde{s}$. In this way, the control token always represents the connotations of the target output. As with reconstruction, we minimize the cross entropy:

$$\mathcal{L}_{para} = -\frac{1}{m}\sum_{i=1}^{m} \log P(\tilde{t}_i \mid \tilde{t}_1, \ldots, \tilde{t}_{i-1}; \hat{s}; t_c)$$

Joint Probability Boosting At generation time, we boost the probability of verbs with target agency and power to foster the model to change the connotation of a sentence. In this process, the unnormalized probabilities produced by the rewriting model for the next token, called logits $l_i \in \mathbb{R}^{|V|}$ (where V is the vocabulary), are rescaled at each decoding step i to increase the likelihood of generating verbs with the target agency and power. This process is referred to as *boosting*. The boosted logits are then used to compute the next token probabilities:

$$P(t_i|\tilde{t}_1, \ldots, \tilde{t}_{i-1}; s; t_c) \propto softmax(l_i + \beta \cdot A \cdot w)$$

Here, A is a $\mathbb{R}^{V \times 9}$ matrix with a 9-dimensional *{apos-ppos, ..., aneg-pneg}* agency-power embedding for each token in the vocabulary V, w is a $\mathbb{R}^9$ one-hot vector encoding of the control token and $\beta \geq 1$ is a scalar hyperparameter representing the boosting strength. Instead of using the connotation frame lexicon as Ma et al. (2020), we encode in A the candidate verbs with target connotations determined by the contextual classification.

4 Data

As part of our experiments, we employ data for two purposes: First, to train the agency and power classifiers, we require sentences that include verbs from the given connotation frame lexicon in a variety of contexts. We therefore combine sentences from three corpora, as detailed below. In our subsequent rewriting experiments, we then use a corpus of movie summaries for the reconstruction objective as well as a parallel paraphrase corpus for the paraphrasing objective. The paraphrase corpus is only used during training, whereas the movie summaries also serve to validate and test rewriting models.

4.1 Data for Agency and Power Classification

We extract all plain-text sentences, which contain any verb indicating agency or power according to the lexicon of Sap et al. (2017),[2] from three existing corpora, covering different contexts and domains:

- Wikipedia biography texts (Wang et al., 2018)
- Plain-text jokes (Pungas, 2017)
- English simple sentences (Kiesel et al., 2017)

As the agency and power labels in the connotation frame lexicon are imbalanced, we undersample the data by removing sentences containing verbs of the majority labels *positive* agency and *positive* power pseudo-randomly. This results in 109,136 sentences labeled for agency and 97,098 for power. A random sample of 20% of the lexicon verbs and the respective sentences are reserved for testing.

4.2 Data for Connotation Rewriting

For our rewriting experiments, we use the movie summary corpus of Bamman et al. (2013). Besides the plain-text plot summaries, the corpus also contains metadata about the movie characters. We use the characters' names and coreferences to perform entity linking. This ensures that each sentence we aim to rewrite contains a character with known agency and power levels. Next, we identify agency and power of each sentence based on its main verb, using the lexicon of Sap et al. (2017). As the main verb, we consider the highest verb in the dependency parse tree of a sentence given by CoreNLP (Manning et al., 2014) that is also the head of a nominal subject dependency with a character mention being the dependent. Finally, we select 25k sentences per gender pseudo-randomly to balance gender occurrences and avoid an underrepresentation of female forms. The total of 50k sentences is then divided into training, validation, and test set using a ratio of 7:2:1.

For the paraphrasing objective, we follow Ma et al. (2020) in taking the parallel corpus by Creutz (2018). For both sentences of each paraphrase pair, we determine the agency and power levels based on the main verb and its associated lexicon entry. The resulting 33,122 pairs are used for training only.

5 Evaluation

This section reports experiments on agency and power classification and on the generation counterfactuals for gender bias mitigation. The main goal is to evaluate our joint agency-power approach to sentence rewriting in light of the state of the art.

5.1 Agency and Power Classification

We tackle the determination of agency and power of a sentence as a three-class tasks each (positive, equal, negative), comparing our contextual classification approach against two baselines:

Approach We trained one BERT model (Base-uncased, 110M parameters) each for agency (*bert-agency*) and power (*bert-power*), using the transformer library of Wolf et al. (2020). We chose to train two separate models, since the correlation between agency and power levels in the lexicon of Sap et al. (2017) is rather low (Kendall's $\tau = 0.30$). We fine-tuned the models in 5-fold cross-validation on the training data from Section 4. To prevent data leakage, we ensured that each verb was included in one fold only. In hyperparameter search, we tested batch sizes from 5 to 35 in increments of 5, learning rates from 10^{-5} to 10^{-9}, and numbers of epochs from 3 to 20. Our final models have been trained using AdamW optimizer (Loshchilov and Hutter, 2019) for 12 epochs with learning rate 10^{-8} and batch size 20, which was the best setting in cross-validation in terms of macro F_1-score.[3]

Baselines We compare our approach to simple majority classifiers (*majority-agency*, *majority-power*) as well as to the state-of-the-art token-level agency and power prediction approach of Field et al. (2019), trained on the given data. We call the latter *log-reg-agency* and *log-reg-power*, since they use logistic regression models for prediction. As input, they employ averaged, and thereby decontextualized, ELMo embeddings of verbs as they appear in training sentences. As ground-truth labels, they also rely on the lexicon of Sap et al. (2017).

Results Table 1 shows the classification results. Our approach achieves the best macro-F_1 scores (0.507 and 0.532 respectively) as well as the highest scores for neutral and negative agency and power. They also reach a more balanced performance across the classes for both target connotations compared to the log-reg baselines.

The confusion matrices in Figure 2 reveal that, if any, our classifiers mostly confuse *positive* or *negative* with *equal* rather than with the opposite class.

[2]The verbs in the sentences are identified using the flair library (Akbik et al., 2019).

[3]All our models were trained on one NVIDIA A100 GPU. Training took about half an hour per epoch for the classifiers.

Model	Positive	Neutral	Negative	Macro
majority-agency	**0.875**	0.000	0.000	0.292
log-reg-agency	0.832	0.146	0.417	0.465
bert-agency (ours)	0.841	**0.252**	**0.430**	**0.507**
majority-power	0.822	0.000	0.000	0.274
log-reg-power	**0.847**	0.272	0.389	0.503
bert-power (ours)	0.805	**0.373**	**0.417**	**0.532**

Table 1: Agency and power classification: Test set macro F_1-scores of our BERT-based classifiers and the baselines, along with the F_1-scores for all three classes.

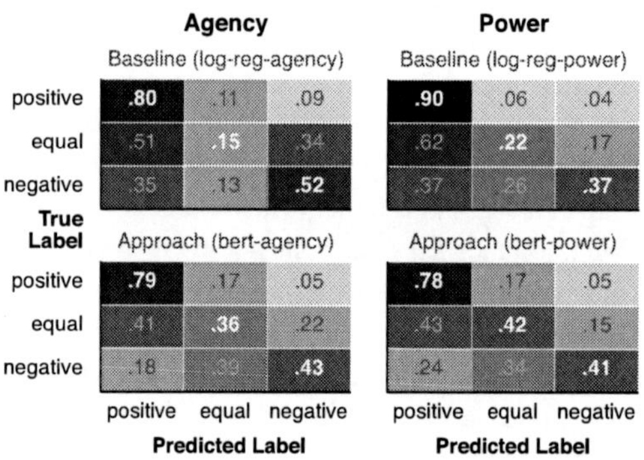

Figure 2: Confusion matrices of the evaluated baseline and our approach for agency and power classification. Our approach avoids strong misclassification notably better, such as classifying negative agency as positive.

In contrast, the log-reg baselines exhibit these more serious errors more often, for example, classifying 37% of the cases with negative power as positive. These results support our hypothesis that sentence context and the pre-trained language understanding of BERT helps differentiate the connotation levels.

5.2 Connotation Rewriting

Next, we test the hypothesis that boosting the candidate verbs found with similarity filtering and contextual classification helps to change both sentence connotations while preserving meaning. To this end, we evaluate the output of rewriting manually.

Approach As Ma et al. (2020), we fine-tuned a pre-trained GPT for 10 epochs on the combined reconstruction and paraphrasing objective. However, we extended the control tokens to also include power (see Section 3). We replicated the training setting of Ma et al. (2020), using AdamW optimizer (Loshchilov and Hutter, 2019) with a learning rate of 10^{-5}, a batch size of 4, and top-$p = 0.4$ nucleus sampling (Holtzman et al., 2020) for decoding. To increase the chance of finding suitable candidates, we employed a bigger lexicon than Ma et al. (2020), containing 8,751 verbs.[4] We compared boosting strengths β from 1 to 12 and similarity thresholds γ from 0.2 to 0.5. We found that $\beta = 10$ and $\gamma = 0.5$ effectively control the generation towards the target connotation while minimizing token repetitions.[5]

We also tested a variation of our approach (*Appr. w/o class.*) where we used the lexicon-based connotation filtering of Ma et al. (2020), in combination with our similarity filtering and controlled jointly for agency and power. Here, the boosting strength $\beta = 8$ led to the most promising results.

Baseline We compare our approach to the agency rewriting approach of Ma et al. (2020), trained using the authors' code and settings on the ROC stories corpus (Mostafazadeh et al., 2016) as well as on the paraphrase dataset that we also use to train our model. As previously mentioned, we chose a bigger dataset from a similar domain to train our approach on reconstruction. We hypothesize that this improves the models ability to generate sentences with the desired connotations.

Pre-Evaluation To compare to Ma et al. (2020), we evaluated the approaches first using four of the automatic metrics the authors suggested:[6]

1. *Agency/Power.* Accuracy of changing agency and power, comparing the target connotations to the achieved output connotations according to the lexicon of Sap et al. (2017);[7]
2. *Meaning preservation.* BERTScore F_1 (Zhang et al., 2020), measuring the semantic similarity of input and output sentences;
3. *Fluency.* Perplexity (PPL) of 1000 random output sentences measured using GPT;
4. *Repetition.* The fraction of output sentences containing at least one bigram repetition.

Results Table 2 presents the results of the pre-evaluation. We see that the state-of-the-art baseline performs best in terms of agency change (0.544) and perplexity (134.2). However, its low power accuracy (0.353) reveals that a change in agency

[4]Ma et al. (2020) used the lexicon of Sap et al. (2017) with 2,155 verbs. The list of 8,751 verbs was provided by Ma et al. (2020) for experiments, but did not make it into their model.

[5]Training took about one hour per epoch.

[6]We omitted the fifth measure, uniqueness, as it provides little insight for the scope of this paper.

[7]As the baseline does not control for power separately, we assume target power to equals target agency for its accuracy.

	Agency	Power	Meaning	Fluency	Repetit.
Model	Acc. ↑	Acc. ↑	BScore ↑	PPL ↓	$Rep_{\geq 2}$ ↓
Ma et al. (2020)	**0.544**	0.353	0.908	**134.2**	0.189
Appr. w/o class.	0.464	**0.495**	**0.931**	161.5	**0.127**
Approach	0.448	0.484	**0.931**	158.2	0.132

Table 2: Automatic pre-evaluation of rewriting quality: Performance of our approach (and its variation without classifiers) on the test set in comparison to the baseline.

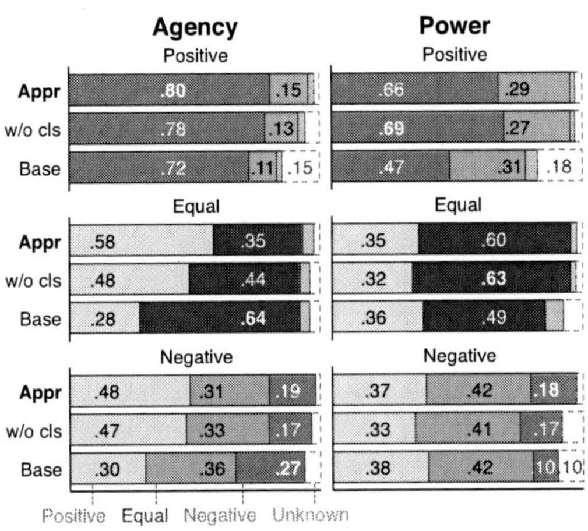

Figure 3: Accuracy of the baseline (*Base*) and both approach variations (*Appr*, Appr *w/o class*) in creating sentences with a specific agency (left) and power (right). The dark-colored bar segment (with white text) in each of the six cases indicates a correct result, the others a wrong one. We beat the baseline in all but two cases.

does not always imply a change in power, stressing the need to control for both connotations. Accordingly, our approach and its variation achieve a much higher power accuracy and similar results on most other metrics. They also preserve the meaning better (BERTScore of 93.1 each) and produce fewer bigram repetitions, resulting in less gibberish sentences that consist of few often repeated tokens.

To understand the models' behavior, Figure 3 shows the agency and power accuracy per target agency and power. Our approach variations perform best on positive agency (.80) and all power levels. Note that this evaluation is unable to assess outputs that do not contain a lexicon verb, including gibberish sentences (shown as *Unknown*).

Main Evaluation The automatic pre-evaluation only roughly approximates quality, especially since it can assess agency and power connotations of lexicon verbs only. We therefore also conducted a user study where six annotators manually evaluated the agency and power change as well as the meaning preservation. All annotators have academic degrees, advanced English skills, and equally represent both genders (no author of this paper).

We selected 450 sentences from the test set randomly, 50 for each of the nine control tokens, that is, for each combination of agency and power connotation. To reduce the workload while remaining able to assess annotation reliability, we divided the sentences into two sets of 225 and let three annotators each evaluate all sentences from one set. We asked all annotators to rank the output sentences by three criteria: *target agency compliance*, *target power compliance*, and *meaning preservation* (annotation guidelines can be found in Appendix A). The average pairwise inter-annotator agreement in terms of Kendall's τ was 0.41 for agency, 0.42 for power, and 0.58 for meaning preservation.

Results Table 3 shows that our *approach* outperforms both other models in terms of all three evaluation criteria. As in the pre-evaluation, it performs similarly to the variation without classifiers on meaning preservation (mean rank 1.69 and 1.73), beating the state of the art of Ma et al. (2020) (2.15). For power and agency, our approach is best with mean rank 1.67 and 1.69 respectively, outperforming Ma et al. (2020) (1.96 and 1.99) again.

The difference to the pre-evaluation in the two latter criteria may be caused by the fact that not all sentences could be evaluated there due to the limitations of the connotation frame lexicon. This speaks for a successful boosting of verbs in general. Another reason lies in the subjectivity of agency and power assessment. While we provided annotators with the same notions of agency and power as previous work, their assessment might still differ from the one encoded in the lexicon.

Ablation Study For further insights, we analyzed the impact of the different parts of our approach on the results. In particular, we compared our full approach to using only the connotation frame lexicon instead of the bigger lexicon for boosting (*No big lex.*), to omitting the similarity filtering (*No sim. filter.*), and to their combination (*Neither*). The results in Table 4 suggest that the connotation frame lexicon would benefit agency and power accuracy. This is expected, since the automatic metrics can only assess those verbs. Omitting similarity filtering seems to worsen the meaning preservation. Our full model scores comparably good for repetition.

	Agency Compliance				Power Compliance				Meaning Preservation			
Model	Rank 1	Rank 2	Rank 3	Mean	Rank 1	Rank 2	Rank 3	Mean	Rank 1	Rank 2	Rank 3	Mean
Ma et al. (2020)	33.5%	36.9%	29.6%	1.96	33.4%	34.4%	32.2%	1.99	23.9%	36.8%	39.3%	2.15
Appr. w/o class.	40.8%	44.4%	14.8%	*1.74	39.8%	43.6%	16.6%	*1.77	44.4%	37.9%	17.8%	*1.73
Approach	**48.7%**	35.0%	16.2%	***1.67**	**46.1%**	39.2%	14.7%	***1.69**	**46.7%**	37.6%	15.7%	***1.69**

Table 3: Manual main evaluation of rewriting quality: Proportion of rewritten sentences with Rank 1, 2, and 3 as well as mean rank per evaluated approach for agency compliance, power compliance, and meaning preservation. Significant gains over Ma et al. (2020) are marked with * (computed using Wilcoxon Signed-Rank Test at $p < .05$).

	Agency	Power	Meaning	Fluency	Repetit.
Model	Acc.$\uparrow$	Acc.$\uparrow$	B.Sc.$\uparrow$	PPL$\downarrow$	Rep$_{\geq 2}\downarrow$
No big lex.	**0.452**	0.488	**0.933**	167.0	**0.129**
No sim. filter.	0.407	0.459	0.903	129.8	0.168
Neither	0.445	**0.504**	0.916	**128.4**	0.154
Full model	0.448	0.484	0.931	158.2	0.132

Table 4: Ablation study: Automatic evaluation of rewriting quality for different variations of our approach.

Error Analysis To better understand the differences between the models, we manually inspected some examples from the annotation study. Exemplarily, Table 5 compares three outputs of the models. Matching the automatic results, our approach and its variation generate fewer gibberish sentences with n-gram repetitions than the baseline (see Example 3). Failures in paraphrasing of the latter additionally leads to a reduced meaning preservation (see Example 1). A reason might be the smaller reconstruction dataset, since the paraphrase corpus has the same size. In most cases, the biggest difference between the output sentences is the choice of words (see Example 2), which tends to be best for our approach, according to the annotators.

Lexicon Expansion Lastly, we use our agency and power classifiers to identify potential new verbs for the connotation frame lexicon from the bigger lexicon. Table 6 shows the verbs that are classified to express high or low agency or power with the highest confidence. Most of these partly quite specific verbs match the intuitions of agency and power well. A few classifications may be debatable, though, such as the low agency for "thrive".

6 Conclusion

In this work, we have studied how to rewrite sentences to adjust the agency and power of their subjects jointly. To this end, we have developed a new candidate verb identification method that fosters a meaning-preserving adaptation of both connotations in transformer-based generation. By employing classifiers for agency and power, our rewriting approach can handle any given verb in the current sentence context, unlike previous approaches.

Our experiments have stressed the importance of addressing agency and power jointly. In automatic evaluation, the proposed approach has turned out competitive in agency to the previous state of the art, while effectively controlling for power for the first time. In manual evaluation, human annotators favored the sentences rewritten by our approach in terms of all relevant dimensions: target agency, target power, and meaning preservation.

We thus conclude that our approach contributes towards the generation of counterfactuals that can be used for gender bias mitigation, as shown in previous work. Yet, the results leave room for improvements regarding both connotations, which should be addressed in future work. For a refined evaluation, more extensive agency and power lexicons may be needed. To facilitate the lexicon creation process, the classifiers may be used to suggest labels prior to human post-checking.

7 Acknowledgments

We thank the anonymous reviewers, particularly for their valuable comments on potential ethical concerns. Moreover, we thank Malena Brinkmann, Niklas Hahn, Eileen Köllmann, Rica Nieland, Jonas Rieskamp and Niclas Stahl for their feedback. This work has been partially funded by the German Research Foundation (DFG) within the project ArgSchool, project number 453073654.

8 Limitations

The study of counterfactual generation carried out in this paper has a number of limitations, the most important of which we discuss in the following.

First, for a clear paper focus, we decided to leave out any experiments on the impact of the generated counterfactuals on actual gender bias mitigation. While previous research has already shown that the

#	Input Sentence	Target	Model	Output Sentence
1	Johnny, enraged with the way Joe and Jake treat Ginny, *[verb]* them.	apos-ppos	Ma et al. (2020)	pos hurt ginny, hurting them.
			Appr. w/o cls.	johnny, enraged with the way joe and jake treat ginny, attacks them.
			Approach	johnny, enraged with the way joe and jake treat ginny, defend them.
2	After some time Tristan is *[verb]* to flee to Cornwall.	aneg-pequal	Ma et al. (2020)	tristan is forced to flee to cornwall after a period of time.
			Appr. w/o cls.	tristan is seen to flee to cornwall after a period of time.
			Approach	tristan is sensed to flee to cornwall after a period of time.
3	Enraged, Roopa *[verb]* to commit suicide by jumping into a waterfall as she finds it better to kill herself rather than be a mistress.	aequal-ppos	Ma et al. (2020)	pos decided to commit suicide by jumping into a waterfall as she becomes a mistress better to kill herself better to kill herself better to kill herself better to kill herself better to kill herself better to kill herself better to kill kill kill kill kill kill kill kill kill kill kill kill ...
			Appr. w/o cls.	enraged, roopa resolves to commit suicide by jumping into a waterfall as she finds it better to kill herself rather than be a mistress
			Approach	enraged, roopa seeks to commit suicide by jumping into a waterfall as she finds it better to kill herself rather than be a mistress.

Table 5: Output sentences generated by the three rewriting models for the given masked input sentences and target connotations: (1) The baseline (Ma et al., 2020) attempts to paraphrase. Both approach variations generate similar output; (2) our approach matches the target connotation; (3) the baseline starts promising but ends with gibberish.

	Agency-related Verbs			Power-related Verbs		
high	inflate	gun	instate	ionize	ambush	damn
	bridge	reset	distance	recycle	augment	indict
	extort	maim	reanimate	fracture	reset	auction
low	bloom	reside	succumb	repent	revere	venerate
	thrive	average	yearn	profess	elate	mediate
	aspire	crave	slumber	rejoice	yearn	heed

Table 6: New candidate verbs for the connotation frame lexicon, selected based on the classification and confidence level of our agency and power classifiers.

intended use of counterfactuals helps in this regard, we therefore can ultimately not make assertions on the practical benefit of our method compared to others. Future work should investigate upon the use of our method in downstream tasks.

Furthermore, the unequal portrayal of people in terms of their agency and power represents only one of different ways of how gender bias manifests in language. As a matter of fact, even if our method was perfectly effective, it would not suffice alone to mitigate gender bias to the full extent. Moreover, despite the evidence we found that the proposed method improves over the state of the art in terms of agency and power rewriting, its effectiveness still shows notable room for improvement. It is noteworthy, though, that our experiments suggest that the method rarely modifies agency and power in the opposite direction, implying that additional harm caused by the method is unlikely.

Finally, the data used in our experiments restricts the generalizability of our results to some extent. In particular, we analyzed the effectiveness of our method on English movie summaries only. Other genres as well as other languages may lead to different behavior, although we do not see an immediate reason why it should not work there. As far as the availablity of data will permit, we plan to do further experiments in other settings in the future.

9 Ethical Statement

The intended use of the methods developed in this paper is to mitigate gender bias in natural language sentences. The goal of applying these methods is to obtain linguistic data that allows for a more equal representation of genders (e.g., for the training of embedding models). As such, we predominantly expect positive ethical consequences of the contributions of this paper. However, we see two noteworthy risks that emanate from an availability of the developed methods:

First, due to the methods' non-perfect effectiveness and to the general complexity of natural language, the bias mitigation may come with possibly unintended changes of meaning of the sentences being rewritten. This may lead to a misrepresentation of genders or specific representatives of the genders. The effects of applying the methods should therefore be observed carefully. Where possible, it should ideally be in a semi-automatic setting with human post-checking.

Second, as with any other text generation technology, the methods may be misused for an application they are not meant for, for example, to picture an individual or a group of people in a misleading way. We cannot prevent such usage, but the still limited effectiveness of the methods makes a purposeful deceptive usage in our view impractical.

Aside from the risks, we would like to state explicitly again that the consideration of gender as a binary dimension, as done in this paper, is a simplification of reality. The only reason why we restrict our view exclusively to men and women is the lack of data for studying tasks as the given one more properly with respect to gender diversity.

Finally, we point out that no personal information has been collected from any participant of our annotation study; there is no way to match the created annotations to their identities. The participants came from the surroundings of authors of this paper. Participation was not paid for, but more done in terms of a friendly turn. It was fully voluntary.

References

Alan Akbik, Tanja Bergmann, Duncan Blythe, Kashif Rasul, Stefan Schweter, and Roland Vollgraf. 2019. Flair: An easy-to-use framework for state-of-the-art nlp. In *NAACL 2019, 2019 Annual Conference of the North American Chapter of the Association for Computational Linguistics (Demonstrations)*, pages 54–59.

Bashar Alhafni, Nizar Habash, and Houda Bouamor. 2020. Gender-aware reinflection using linguistically enhanced neural models. In *Proceedings of the Second Workshop on Gender Bias in Natural Language Processing*, pages 139–150, Barcelona, Spain (Online). Association for Computational Linguistics.

David Bamman, Brendan O'Connor, and Noah A. Smith. 2013. Learning latent personas of film characters. In *Proceedings of the 51st Annual Meeting of the Association for Computational Linguistics (Volume 1: Long Papers)*, pages 352–361, Sofia, Bulgaria. Association for Computational Linguistics.

Tolga Bolukbasi, Kai-Wei Chang, James Y Zou, Venkatesh Saligrama, and Adam T Kalai. 2016. Man is to Computer Programmer as Woman is to Homemaker? Debiasing Word Embeddings. In *Advances in Neural Information Processing Systems*, volume 29, pages 4349–4357, Barcelona Spain. Curran Associates, Inc.

Yang Trista Cao and Hal Daumé III. 2020. Toward Gender-Inclusive Coreference Resolution. In *Proceedings of the 58th Annual Meeting of the Association for Computational Linguistics*, pages 4568–4595, Online. Association for Computational Linguistics.

Mathias Creutz. 2018. Open subtitles paraphrase corpus for six languages. In *Proceedings of the Eleventh International Conference on Language Resources and Evaluation (LREC 2018)*, Miyazaki, Japan. European Language Resources Association (ELRA).

Jacob Devlin, Ming-Wei Chang, Kenton Lee, and Kristina Toutanova. 2019. BERT: pre-training of deep bidirectional transformers for language understanding. In *Proceedings of the 2019 Conference of the North American Chapter of the Association for Computational Linguistics: Human Language Technologies, NAACL-HLT 2019, Minneapolis, MN, USA, June 2-7, 2019, Volume 1 (Long and Short Papers)*, pages 4171–4186. Association for Computational Linguistics.

Emily Dinan, Angela Fan, Adina Williams, Jack Urbanek, Douwe Kiela, and Jason Weston. 2020. Queens are powerful too: Mitigating gender bias in dialogue generation. In *Proceedings of the 2020 Conference on Empirical Methods in Natural Language Processing (EMNLP)*, pages 8173–8188, Online. Association for Computational Linguistics.

Jad Doughman, Wael Khreich, Maya El Gharib, Maha Wiss, and Zahraa Berjawi. 2021. Gender bias in text: Origin, taxonomy, and implications. In *Proceedings of the 3rd Workshop on Gender Bias in Natural Language Processing*, pages 34–44, Online. Association for Computational Linguistics.

Tal Feldman and Ashley Peake. 2021. End-To-End Bias Mitigation: Removing Gender Bias in Deep Learning. *arXiv:2104.02532 [cs]*. http://arxiv.org/abs/2104.02532.

Anjalie Field, Gayatri Bhat, and Yulia Tsvetkov. 2019. Contextual affective analysis: A case study of people portrayals in online #metoo stories. *Proceedings of the International AAAI Conference on Web and Social Media*, 13(01):158–169.

Anjalie Field and Yulia Tsvetkov. 2019. Entity-centric contextual affective analysis. In *Proceedings of the 57th Annual Meeting of the Association for Computational Linguistics*, pages 2550–2560, Florence, Italy. Association for Computational Linguistics.

Sayan Ghosh, Mathieu Chollet, Eugene Laksana, Louis-Philippe Morency, and Stefan Scherer. 2017. Affect-LM: A neural language model for customizable affective text generation. In *Proceedings of the 55th Annual Meeting of the Association for Computational Linguistics (Volume 1: Long Papers)*, pages 634–642, Vancouver, Canada. Association for Computational Linguistics.

Yasmeen Hitti, Eunbee Jang, Ines Moreno, and Carolyne Pelletier. 2019. Proposed taxonomy for gender bias in text; a filtering methodology for the gender generalization subtype. In *Proceedings of the First Workshop on Gender Bias in Natural Language Processing*, pages 8–17, Florence, Italy. Association for Computational Linguistics.

Ari Holtzman, Jan Buys, Li Du, Maxwell Forbes, and Yejin Choi. 2020. The curious case of neural text degeneration. In *8th International Conference on Learning Representations, ICLR 2020, Addis Ababa, Ethiopia, April 26-30, 2020*. OpenReview.net.

Dirk Hovy and Shannon L. Spruit. 2016. The social impact of natural language processing. In *Proceedings of the 54th Annual Meeting of the Association for Computational Linguistics (Volume 2: Short Papers)*, pages 591–598, Berlin, Germany. Association for Computational Linguistics.

Johannes Kiesel, Benno Stein, and Stefan Lucks. 2017. A large-scale analysis of the mnemonic password advice. In *24th Annual Network and Distributed System Security Symposium, NDSS 2017, San Diego, California, USA, February 26 - March 1, 2017*. The Internet Society.

Paul Pu Liang, Irene Mengze Li, Emily Zheng, Yao Chong Lim, Ruslan Salakhutdinov, and Louis-Philippe Morency. 2020. Towards Debiasing Sentence Representations. In *Proceedings of the 58th Annual Meeting of the Association for Computational Linguistics*, pages 5502–5515, Online. Association for Computational Linguistics.

Ilya Loshchilov and Frank Hutter. 2019. Decoupled weight decay regularization. In *7th International Conference on Learning Representations, ICLR 2019, New Orleans, LA, USA, May 6-9, 2019*. OpenReview.net.

Kaiji Lu, Piotr Mardziel, Fangjing Wu, Preetam Amancharla, and Anupam Datta. 2020. *Gender Bias in Neural Natural Language Processing*, pages 189–202. Springer International Publishing, Cham.

Xinyao Ma, Maarten Sap, Hannah Rashkin, and Yejin Choi. 2020. PowerTransformer: Unsupervised controllable revision for biased language correction. In *Proceedings of the 2020 Conference on Empirical Methods in Natural Language Processing (EMNLP)*, pages 7426–7441, Online. Association for Computational Linguistics.

Christopher Manning, Mihai Surdeanu, John Bauer, Jenny Finkel, Steven Bethard, and David McClosky. 2014. The Stanford CoreNLP natural language processing toolkit. In *Proceedings of 52nd Annual Meeting of the Association for Computational Linguistics: System Demonstrations*, pages 55–60, Baltimore, Maryland. Association for Computational Linguistics.

Nasrin Mostafazadeh, Nathanael Chambers, Xiaodong He, Devi Parikh, Dhruv Batra, Lucy Vanderwende, Pushmeet Kohli, and James Allen. 2016. A corpus and cloze evaluation for deeper understanding of commonsense stories. In *Proceedings of the 2016 Conference of the North American Chapter of the Association for Computational Linguistics: Human Language Technologies*, pages 839–849, San Diego, California. Association for Computational Linguistics.

Nikita Nangia, Clara Vania, Rasika Bhalerao, and Samuel R. Bowman. 2020. CrowS-pairs: A challenge dataset for measuring social biases in masked language models. In *Proceedings of the 2020 Conference on Empirical Methods in Natural Language Processing (EMNLP)*, pages 1953–1967, Online. Association for Computational Linguistics.

Chan Young Park, Xinru Yan, Anjalie Field, and Yulia Tsvetkov. 2021. Multilingual contextual affective analysis of LGBT people portrayals in wikipedia. In *Proceedings of the Fifteenth International AAAI Conference on Web and Social Media, ICWSM 2021, held virtually, June 7-10, 2021*, pages 479–490. AAAI Press.

Ji Ho Park, Jamin Shin, and Pascale Fung. 2018. Reducing Gender Bias in Abusive Language Detection. In *Proceedings of the 2018 Conference on Empirical Methods in Natural Language Processing*, pages 2799–2804, Brussels, Belgium. Association for Computational Linguistics.

Jeffrey Pennington, Richard Socher, and Christopher Manning. 2014. GloVe: Global vectors for word representation. In *Proceedings of the 2014 Conference on Empirical Methods in Natural Language Processing (EMNLP)*, pages 1532–1543, Doha, Qatar. Association for Computational Linguistics.

Matthew E. Peters, Mark Neumann, Mohit Iyyer, Matt Gardner, Christopher Clark, Kenton Lee, and Luke Zettlemoyer. 2018. Deep contextualized word representations. In *Proceedings of the 2018 Conference of the North American Chapter of the Association for Computational Linguistics: Human Language Technologies, NAACL-HLT 2018, New Orleans, Louisiana, USA, June 1-6, 2018, Volume 1 (Long Papers)*, pages 2227–2237. Association for Computational Linguistics.

Taivo Pungas. 2017. A dataset of English plaintext jokes.

Alec Radford, Karthik Narasimhan, Tim Salimans, and Ilya Sutskever. 2018. Improving Language Understanding by Generative Pre-Training.

Hannah Rashkin, Sameer Singh, and Yejin Choi. 2016. Connotation frames: A data-driven investigation. In *Proceedings of the 54th Annual Meeting of the Association for Computational Linguistics (Volume 1: Long Papers)*, pages 311–321, Berlin, Germany. Association for Computational Linguistics.

Maarten Sap, Saadia Gabriel, Lianhui Qin, Dan Jurafsky, Noah A. Smith, and Yejin Choi. 2020. Social bias frames: Reasoning about social and power implications of language. In *Proceedings of the 58th Annual Meeting of the Association for Computational Linguistics*, pages 5477–5490, Online. Association for Computational Linguistics.

Maarten Sap, Marcella Cindy Prasettio, Ari Holtzman, Hannah Rashkin, and Yejin Choi. 2017. Connotation frames of power and agency in modern films.

In *Proceedings of the 2017 Conference on Empirical Methods in Natural Language Processing*, pages 2329–2334, Copenhagen, Denmark. Association for Computational Linguistics.

Maximilian Spliethöver and Henning Wachsmuth. 2020. Argument from old man's view: Assessing social bias in argumentation. In *Proceedings of the 7th Workshop on Argument Mining*, pages 76–87, Online. Association for Computational Linguistics.

Jennifer Steele, Y. Susan Choi, and Nalini Ambady. 2004. Stereotyping, Prejudice, and Discrimination. In Theresa A. Thorkildsen and Herbert J. Walberg, editors, *Nurturing Morality*, Issues in Children's and Families' Lives, pages 77–97. Springer, Boston, MA.

Tony Sun, Kellie Webster, Apurva Shah, William Yang Wang, and Melvin Johnson. 2021. They, them, theirs: Rewriting with gender-neutral english. *CoRR*, abs/2102.06788.

Qingyun Wang, Xiaoman Pan, Lifu Huang, Boliang Zhang, Zhiying Jiang, Heng Ji, and Kevin Knight. 2018. Describing a knowledge base. In *Proceedings of the 11th International Conference on Natural Language Generation*, pages 10–21, Tilburg University, The Netherlands. Association for Computational Linguistics.

Thomas Wolf, Lysandre Debut, Victor Sanh, Julien Chaumond, Clement Delangue, Anthony Moi, Pierric Cistac, Tim Rault, Remi Louf, Morgan Funtowicz, Joe Davison, Sam Shleifer, Patrick von Platen, Clara Ma, Yacine Jernite, Julien Plu, Canwen Xu, Teven Le Scao, Sylvain Gugger, Mariama Drame, Quentin Lhoest, and Alexander Rush. 2020. Transformers: State-of-the-art natural language processing. In *Proceedings of the 2020 Conference on Empirical Methods in Natural Language Processing: System Demonstrations*, pages 38–45, Online. Association for Computational Linguistics.

Tianyi Zhang, Varsha Kishore, Felix Wu, Kilian Q. Weinberger, and Yoav Artzi. 2020. Bertscore: Evaluating text generation with BERT. In *8th International Conference on Learning Representations, ICLR 2020, Addis Ababa, Ethiopia, April 26-30, 2020*. OpenReview.net.

Jieyu Zhao, Tianlu Wang, Mark Yatskar, Ryan Cotterell, Vicente Ordonez, and Kai-Wei Chang. 2019. Gender Bias in Contextualized Word Embeddings. In *Proceedings of the 2019 Conference of the North American Chapter of the Association for Computational Linguistics: Human Language Technologies, Volume 1 (Long and Short Papers)*, pages 629–634, Minneapolis, Minnesota. Association for Computational Linguistics.

Ran Zmigrod, Sabrina J. Mielke, Hanna Wallach, and Ryan Cotterell. 2019. Counterfactual data augmentation for mitigating gender stereotypes in languages with rich morphology. In *Proceedings of the 57th Annual Meeting of the Association for Computational Linguistics*, pages 1651–1661, Florence, Italy. Association for Computational Linguistics.

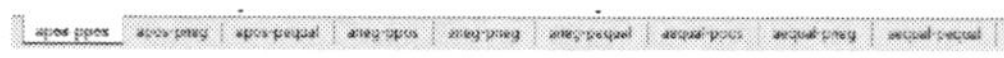

Figure 4: Sheets in the annotation file. You can switch between sheets at the bottom of the window.

A Human Annotation Guidelines

A.1 Introduction

This document contains instructions for the annotation study that is being conducted in the course of our research. Additionally, the concepts relevant to performing the tasks are explained. The goal of this annotation study is to rank the output sentences generated by three different models.

These models were developed with the goal of rewriting input sentences so that they subsequently express the target agency and target power, which will be explained in the following sections. At the same time, the meaning of the input sentences should remain the same as far as possible.

A.2 What is Agency?

The agency level of a sentence describes how **active**, **decisive** or **energetic** the main person of the sentence is portrayed as. High agency stands for activity, while low agency stands for passivity. In the example in Table 7, the name "X" and neutral pronouns were chosen to avoid triggering gender bias.

A.3 What is Power?

The power level of a sentence describes how **powerful**, **strong** or **influential** the main person of the sentence is portrayed as. A distinction is made between whether the main person has power over the theme (high power) or whether the theme has power over the main person (low power).

As can be seen from the example "He begged his opponent for mercy." (see Table 8) a sentence can express different levels of agency and power simultaneously, but this need not be the case.

A.4 Instructions

Your task will be to **rank** the agency, power and meaning preservation of three **generated sentences** per one original sentence. You will receive an Excel file containing the sentences that should be annotated. This file will contain nine sheets with different sentences (see Figure 4)

Example	Agency	Explanation
X *chose* their future.	high	X is actively choosing and taking charge of their future.
X *begged* their opponent for mercy.	high	X is actively trying to invoke mercy.
X *demanded* mercy from their opponent	high	X is actively trying to invoke mercy.
X *accepted* their future.	low	X passively agrees to what is happening.
X *survived* the crash.	low	X is portrayed as not having active influence on their survival.
X used to *fear* dogs.	low	X's fear was not actively influenceable.

Table 7: Agency examples.

Example	Power	Explanation
X *demanded* mercy from their opponent	high	X tells the opponent what to do and has therefore power over them.
X *chose* their future.	high	X has power over their future because they shape the future themself.
X *hugs* their father.	high	X is portrayed as influencing the interaction with their father.
X *begged* their opponent for mercy.	low	The opponent is portrayed as having power over them.
X *admitted* their mistake.	low	The mistake influences X's actions.
X used to *fear* dogs.	low	Dogs have power over X instead of the other way around.

Table 8: Power examples.

Figure 5: Header and first example in sheet "apos-ppos".

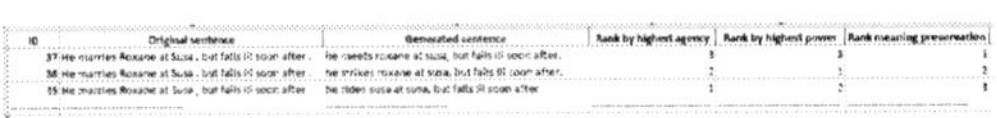

Figure 6: Possible annotations for the first example.

Figure 7: Possible annotations for another example, in which two generated sentences are equal.

All nine sheets should be filled in. Figure 5 shows an example on the first sheet "apos-ppos" of how the header and the first example might look like.

The ID column can be ignored. The first relevant column contains the original sentence, which should be used as reference to rate the meaning preservation. For each group of three generated sentences, the original sentence will be the same. Next, the three generated sentences are displayed. Those should be read carefully to then **rank the agency, the power and the meaning preservation from 1-3 comparing the generated sentences with each other**. In this example, the sentence with the highest agency should get rank 1, the sentence with the next highest agency rank 2 and the remaining one rank 3. Same goes for power and meaning preservation (see Figure 6).

On each sheet, the agency and power assessment tasks are slightly different. The possible variations are:

1. Rank by **highest** agency / power
2. Rank by **most neutral** agency / power
3. Rank by **lowest** agency / power

As the instructions suggest, for "the most neutral" the sentence with the most neutral agency/power should get rank 1. The same goes for "lowest", where the sentence with the lowest agency/power should be ranked 1.

In case you feel like two or more sentences should have the **same ranking in one or more category**, because the agency, power and/or meaning preservation is the same, feel free to give them the same score. In the following example, two models created the same sentence, which leads to the same annotation for them. But it could also be different sentences for which you feel like the agency, power or meaning preservation are equal (see Figure 7).

Conspiracy Narratives in the Protest Movement Against COVID-19 Restrictions in Germany. A Long-term Content Analysis of Telegram Chat Groups.

Manuel Weigand
Goethe University Frankfurt
weigand.mnl@gmail.com

Maximilian Weber
Goethe University Frankfurt
m.weber@soz.uni-frankfurt.de

Johannes Gruber
Vrije Universiteit Amsterdam
j.b.gruber@vu.nl

Abstract

From the start of the COVID-19 pandemic in Germany, different groups have been protesting measures implemented by different government bodies in Germany to control the pandemic. It was widely claimed that many of the offline and online protests were driven by conspiracy narratives disseminated through groups and channels on the messenger app Telegram. We investigate this claim by measuring the frequency of conspiracy narratives in messages from open Telegram chat groups of the *Querdenken* movement, set up to organize protests against COVID-19 restrictions in Germany. We furthermore explore the content of these messages using topic modelling. To this end, we collected 822k text messages sent between April 2020 and May 2022 in 34 chat groups. By fine-tuning a Distilbert model, using self-annotated data, we find that 8.24% of the sent messages contain signs of conspiracy narratives. This number is not static, however, as the share of conspiracy messages grew while the overall number of messages shows a downward trend since its peak at the end of 2020. We further find a mix of known conspiracy narratives make up the topics in our topic model. Our findings suggest that the *Querdenken* movement is getting smaller over time, but its remaining members focus even more on conspiracy narratives.

1 Introduction

Conspiracy narratives already existed way before the rise of social networks or messenger services (see Goertzel, 1994), but their spread was generally modest. In the last decade, however, there have been recurrent debates about the rise of conspiracy narratives in public and media discourse. Two factors in particular are made responsible for this: first, social networks have allowed so-called alternative news media to emerge, exposing the visibility of the widespread existence of conspiracy narratives in society; and second, the COVID-19 pandemic was a catalyst for misinformation, conspiracy narratives, and populist protest (Boberg et al., 2020) over the last two years. Research in the past has shown that conspiracy narratives emerge more likely when people feel loss of control and uncertainty (Goertzel, 1994; Lamberty, 2020). It was, therefore, not surprising that conspiracy narratives began to circulate relatively quickly at the onset of the COVID-19 pandemic.

In Germany, several demonstrations against measures of the government to control the COVID-19 pandemic began to take place in the middle of 2020. In the context of this movement, criticism of government measures often merged with the belief that conspiratorial secret organizations ultimately determine the actions of governments during the pandemic. Over time, the so-called *Querdenken* (transl. to "lateral thinking") movement emerged as the main collective that organised many of the protests and connected groups scattered throughout Germany. In particular, the Stuttgart initiative *Querdenken 711* was a role model for many smaller initiatives in numerous regions of Germany. At the movement's demonstrations, the prevalence of common conspiracy narratives could not be missed. As Lamberty et al. (2022) have suggested, the messenger service Telegram played a major role in the mobilization and organization of the protests in Germany. Furthermore, Simon et al. (2022) suggest that the affordances of Telegram as a platform with lenient content guidelines led to networks forming around more radical content and the spread of conspiracy narratives in Dutch-language public Telegram channels discussing developments in the COVID-19 pandemic.

In this short contribution, we analyze conspiracy narratives in Telegram groups in the specific context of the *Querdenken* movement using supervised and unsupervised machine learning approaches for a systematic automated content analysis. We attempt to focus on conspiracy narratives, following

Proceedings of the Fifth Workshop on Natural Language Processing and Computational Social Science (NLP+CSS), pages 52 - 58
November 7, 2022

a relatively basic operationalization: conspiracy narratives are beliefs and convictions that attempt to interpret historical and contemporary events and general societal changes as a conspiracy and/or secret plan by a group of powerful actors (Pigden, 1995; Keeley, 1999). Scholars have pointed out that the prevalence of conspiracy narratives could be one key indicator of radicalization (Schulze et al., 2022), as it could act as "radicalization catalysts" (Lamberty, 2020). We, therefore, address important concerns for social cohesion with our two research questions:

RQ1: How prevalent are conspiracy narratives in Telegram groups that set out to organize protest against COVID-19 measures in Germany over time?

RQ2: What kind of conspiracy narratives make up the discussion in these groups?

Additionally, we want to know how to automatically detect conspiracy narratives from a technical standpoint in order to pave the way for broader scope research on the topic.

2 Data

We use data from *Querdenken* Telegram chat groups that are publicly viewable without joining the groups (see Appendix A for selection process and list of groups). There are also info channels where only selected people can post, while in the open chat groups anyone who joins can post. To protect the privacy of message senders, we only use the time and text of a sent message. We use all public chat groups that are advertised on a page of the main initiative.

2.1 Dataset

We crawled over one million messages sent between 29.04.2020 and 29.05.2022. Since we focus on text messages, messages that contain only a video, an image or a link have been removed with regular expressions. Resulting in a corpus of 821,903 messages that were exchanged in 34 groups. In the beginning, the *Querdenken* initiative was primarily active in Southern Germany. In Eastern Germany, the *Querdenken* movement never established a foothold as other groups already occupied the same ideological space. However, we decided to focus on the *Querdenken* groups because of their supposed appeal on a wider part of society.

2.2 Annotation

We use expert annotations to manually code a sample of the messages. Four experts labeled 4,863 messages. In addition, to compare intercoder reliability, each expert also labeled the same 100 randomly selected messages. The κ agreement is 0.82. The guidelines for annotating differentiates between two classes. A message is annotated as showing signs of conspiracy (annotated as 1) if it clearly indicates signs of conspiracy narratives (see Appendix B for details). A message is annotated as not showing signs of conspiracy (annotated as 0), if no terminology related to know conspiracy is used or the coder cannot determine if the message contains signs of conspiracy narratives.

3 Methods

The manually labeled data is used to train different supervised machine learning models. The best performing model is a fine-tuned distilbert model (Sanh et al., 2019). To evaluate the performance of the models, we use 5-fold cross-validation. We fine-tune an already fine-tuned model for German toxic comment classification – "distilbert-base-german-cased-toxic-comments" (ML6 Team, 2022). Our model classifies the messages in a 2-way classification (message shows signs of conspiracy / does not show signs of conspiracy). The average macro F1-Score for this model is 0.851 and therefore outperforms other experiments (e.g. SVM, Naive Bayes). However, the SVM had an F1-Score of 0.69 for the class "signs of conspiracy" (compared to 0.76 for the best performing model) while being less computationally expensive. The best performing method, the fine-tuned distilbert model is trained on all annotated data to get the final model, which we use to automatically label the remaining 822k messages.

To analyze trends in the data, we perform a frequency analysis. In addition, we analyze the topics of messages showing signs of conspiracy by using a Structural Topic Model (STM).

	F1	SD	Recall	Precision
no signs of conspiracy	0.946	0.006	0.966	0.927
signs of conspiracy	0.757	0.017	0.692	0.837
macro avg	0.851	0.012	0.829	0.882

Table 1: F1-Scores for the different labels and Macro F1-Score. Mean and standard deviation over 5 runs with different test and dev sets

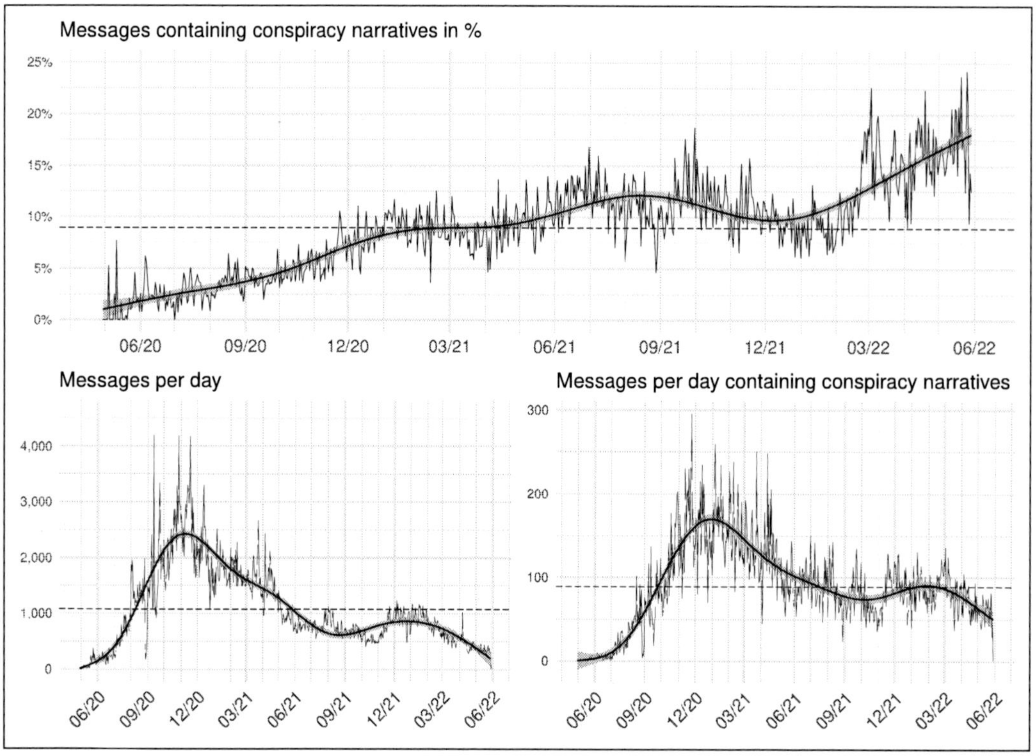

Figure 1: Trend curves. Ratio of messages that include signs of conspiracy over time (top graph). Frequency of messages sent in the chat groups (bottom left) and frequency of messages containing signs of conspiracy over time (bottom right)

4 Temporal analysis

Over a period of more than two years, users in the groups we analyzed sent an average of 1080 messages per day. The number of messages, and thus the activity of the groups, had its peak towards the end of 2020. Since then and especially the mid of 2021, the participation has been on a downward trend and the groups of the *Querdenken* movement were no longer active by the same degree. In April 2022, the monitored groups averaged around 457 messages per day.

Concerning the prevalence of conspiracy narratives (**RQ1**), our trained model identified 67,698 messages containing characteristics of conspiracy narratives, representing 8.24% of the total corpus. Over the two years, the average was 89 messages per day. With regard to the distribution of all messages in the corpus, the identified messages containing conspiracy narratives follow a similar trend. The prevalence of classified messages is highly correlated with the total message volume, and peaked at the end of 2020 and has been on a downward trend since then, although not quite as steep as the total message volume. However, we found an increasing uptrend in the proportion of messages containing conspiracy narratives to the whole corpus. A look at these numbers confirms this impression: The share of messages containing signs of conspiracy narratives is increasing over time and is still ongoing. In particular, a further increase has been noticeable since February 2022 peaking at values around 20%.

5 Topic Model

We chose an STM model with 10 topics after following the approach outlined by Roberts et al. (2019) to decide on an optimal number of k (see Appendix C for details). Table 2 shows the five words with the highest β-probability and the highest FREX value (Airoldi and Bischof, 2016) respectively.

What we find is that most of the topics describe different categories of common conspiracy narratives (**RQ2**). The most prevalent topics describe how the "Altparteien" (old parties) would control the media to stay in power (T5), how the govern-

Table 2: STM Topics

Topic (prevalence)		Terms
T5 (21.8%)	prob	germany, government, politics, state, land
	FREX	afd, antifa, querdenker, vote, the left
T3 (12.8%)	prob	vaccination, virus, dr, pandemic, vaccine
	FREX	study, pcr-test, infection, tested, rki
T9 (12.8%)	prob	people, children, life, fear, world
	FREX	humanity, nature, old, suffering, earth
T7 (10.1%)	prob	__, t.me, channel, video, media
	FREX	t.me, subscribe, stuttgart basic law protests, kenjebsen, wearemore
T1 (9.1%)	prob	reset, great, money, world, million
	FREX	reset, ikb, great, partner, donate
T6 (9.1%)	prob	usa, the, gates, ukraine, russia
	FREX	ukraine, russia, putin, biden, nato
T4 (9.1%)	prob	freedom, people, police, resistance, berlin
	FREX	stage, restoration, streets, rally, peaceful
T10 (6.9%)	prob	merkel, measures, lockdown, germany, federal government
	FREX	chancellor, bundestag, chancellor, angela, autumn
T8 (5.4%)	prob	telegram, o'clock, compulsory vaccination, flag:German, think
	FREX	1k, news, flag:Austrian, @faktenfriedenfreiheit, web
T2 (2.8%)	prob	health, masks, mask, work, phone
	FREX	phone, ministry, social, integration, nothing

[a] Some Unicode characters were replaced (e.g., flag:German used to be a flag emoji)
[b] German words were translated, see original version of the table in Appendic C)
[c] German compound words have been separated in the translation

ment and other elites would conceal how damaging the corona vaccine is and use allegedly fake PCR-tests to convince people they are sick (T3), and that the vaccination campaign and mandatory vaccination laws are illegal and constitute crimes against humanity that are supposedly already fought in several court cases (T9). Two topics tie in with a collection of larger global-scale conspiracies narratives like the *"Great Reset"* (T1) and narratives in which Bill Gates, Barack Obama, Joe Biden or the *"Deep State"* secretly control the pandemic, the vaccine as well as other crises in the world (T6). Interestingly, Russia's war on Ukraine is lumped in here and the US or the aforementioned actors are made responsible for it — essentially repeating some of the claims spread by Russian news. Consequently, T6's prevalence increases massively, after the start of the invasion on 24 February 2022 — which is the only noteworthy shift in prevalence for a topic over time (see details in Appendix C). In the less prevalent topics we see narratives talking about the obligation of "awake" citizens to resist against the elites who try to use Corona to control the "sleeping" mainstream public of Germany (T4); how the measures against the pandemic would secretly constitute a power grab similar to the "Ermächtigungsgesetz von 1933" (Enabling Act of 1933) (T10); and narratives surrounding the alleged negative and harmful impact of masks (T2).

Overall, we are able to directly link most of the topics to known conspiracy narratives. The two exceptions are T8 and T7 which inform about future protest events and advertise alternative news content, often with a reference to censorship and how the content was already removed from YouTube or archives of TV-stations, allegedly because it contains the truth.

6 Conclusion

In this paper, we explored conspiracy narratives in German Telegram chat groups in which people organize protest against restrictions introduced due to the COVID-19 pandemic (i.e. the *Querdenken* movement). Using an automated machine learning approach, we were able to analyze 822k text messages sent in open chat groups. Despite the decrease in overall activity in the Telegram groups since late 2020, we found an upward trend in the relative share of messages containing conspiracy narratives. The topic model maps the different types of conspiracy narratives that we encountered in the dataset and that play a role in the group discussions. Moreover, the fact that almost all themes can be clearly linked to a conspiracy narrative shows the robustness of our approach to automatically detect conspiracy narratives despite remaining uncertainty in the Distilbert model.

Our analysis suggests that the remaining core of people in the *Querdenken* Telegram groups is increasingly immersed in conspiracy narratives, which appear to become the ideological reference point of the movement after many of the measures implemented to control the pandemic in Germany have been lifted. This might be a meaningful issue considering that beliefs in conspiracy narratives are a key element of radicalization dynamics (Schulze et al., 2022). Moreover, because the affinity for conspiracy narratives, or the individual "conspiracy mentality", as social psychologists (Imhoff and Bruder, 2014; Lamberty et al., 2022) refer to it, could lead the remaining core of the movement to shift to other topics, which are suitable for conspiracy ideological mobilization. We observe, for example, that much news regarding the Russian invasion in Ukraine are made sense of in the groups by falling back on previously common narratives of international cabals, predominantly from the US, who allegedly control crises in the world for their own gains. In the future, this increasing detachment from reality could bring with it the potential for further disintegration of social cohesion in Germany.

We acknowledge the limitation that our study excluded most protest groups from East Germany, as some of these do not operate under the label of the *Querdenken* movement, even if they share some of the same goals and ideologies.

7 Ethical Considerations

All data we use in the analysis is publicly available through the official Telegram API, or in the Telegram App itself, and joining the public groups we queried is not necessary to gain access (see Appendix A for details on the groups). We did not collect or store any user data, such as telephone numbers, names or user handles of group members. The metadata for each message consists only of the group URL and timestamp. When we show individual messages as examples, we do not disclose the time of posting or the group name, to minimize any remaining impact on the anonymous authors of the message. Therefore, we do not expect any negative impact on the authors of the messages we examine. We follow the Terms of Service of the Telegram API: https://core.telegram.org/api/terms.

References

Edoardo M. Airoldi and Jonathan M. Bischof. 2016. Improving and Evaluating Topic Models and Other Models of Text. *Journal of the American Statistical Association*, 111(516):1381–1403.

Svenja Boberg, Thorsten Quandt, Tim Schatto-Eckrodt, and Lena Frischlich. 2020. Pandemic Populism: Facebook Pages of Alternative News Media and the Corona Crisis – A Computational Content Analysis.

Ted Goertzel. 1994. Belief in conspiracy theories. *Political Psychology*, 15(4):731–742.

Roland Imhoff and Martin Bruder. 2014. Speaking (un–)truth to power: Conspiracy mentality as a generalised political attitude. *European Journal of Personality*, 28(1):25–43.

Brian L. Keeley. 1999. Of conspiracy theories. *The Journal of Philosophy*, 96(3):109–126.

Pia Lamberty. 2020. CIA, HIV und BRD GmbH: die Psychologie der Verschwörungstheorie. In Jonas Knäble, editor, *Verschwörungstheorien im Diskurs*, pages 32–56. Beltz Juventa.

Pia Lamberty, Josef Holnburger, and Maheba Goedeke Tort. 2022. Zwischen „Spaziergängen“ und Aufmärschen: Das Protestpotential während der COVID-19-Pandemie.

David Mimno, Hanna Wallach, Edmund Talley, Miriam Leenders, and Andrew McCallum. 2011. Optimizing semantic coherence in topic models. *Proceedings of the 2011 conference on empirical methods in natural language processing*, pages 262–272.

ML6 Team. 2022. ml6team/distilbert-base-german-cased-toxic-comments · Hugging Face.

Charles Pigden. 1995. Popper revisited, or what is wrong with conspiracy theories? *Philosophy of the Social Sciences*, 25(1):3–34.

Margaret E. Roberts, Brandon M. Stewart, and Dustin Tingley. 2019. stm: An *R* Package for Structural Topic Models. *Journal of Statistical Software*, 91(2).

Margaret E. Roberts, Brandon M. Stewart, Dustin Tingley, Christopher Lucas, Jetson Leder-Luis, Shana Kushner Gadarian, Bethany Albertson, and David G. Rand. 2014. Structural Topic Models for Open-Ended Survey Responses. *American Journal of Political Science*, 58(4):1064–1082.

Victor Sanh, Lysandre Debut, Julien Chaumond, and Thomas Wolf. 2019. Distilbert, a distilled version of bert: smaller, faster, cheaper and lighter. *arXiv preprint arXiv:1910.01108*.

Heidi Schulze, Julian Hohner, Simon Greipl, Maximilian Girgnhuber, Isabell Desta, and Diana Rieger. 2022. Far-right conspiracy groups on fringe platforms: a longitudinal analysis of radicalization dynamics on telegram. *Convergence*, 0(0):1–24.

Mónika Simon, Kasper Welbers, Anne C. Kroon, and Damian Trilling. 2022. Linked in the dark: A network approach to understanding information flows within the Dutch Telegramsphere. *Information, Communication & Society*, pages 1–25.

Appendix

A Data

We use all public chat groups of the local *Querdenken* initiatives linked on the initiative's directory on May 1, 2022 at https://app.querdenken-711.de/initiatives-directory. The groups add parts of the local area telephone code to their name. The telegram groups are named accordingly: "https://t.me/querdenken[number]". List of the groups: 201, 215, 234, 235, 238, 242, 284, 30, 351, 381, 441, 511, 53, 6051, 615, 6201, 621, 69, 713, 7141, 7171, 718, 7192, 721, 751, 762, 763, 775, 791, 793, 8331, 8341, 89m, 911. All publicly available Telegram posts were collected via Python and the Telethon library, which is built on top of the official Telegram API.

B Coding Guidelines

Read the guidelines for annotating conspiracy narratives carefully

Definition of conspiracy narratives

- The belief and conviction in narratives which try to interpret historical and present events and general social change as a conspiracy and secret plan of a group of powerful actors.

Guiding Questions

- There are secret organizations that have great influence on political decisions
- Politicians and other leaders are just puppets of the powerful actors behind them
- The government uses COVID-19 to monitor and control the people
- The government conceals the truth from the population
- COVID-19 is orchestrated by (evil) actors

General Rules

- Do not take links (urls) into account when annotating
- Emojis, if easily interpretable, can be taken into account
- When annotating use the scheme: contains no signs of conspiracy narratives: 0, contains signs of conspiracy narratives: 1

- A message is annotated as **not showing signs of conspiracy (annotated as 0)**, when at least one of the following is true:
    1. The message contains no signs of conspiracy narratives
    2. The message contains terminology related to known topics of conspiracy narratives
    3. It cannot be determined, whether the message contains signs of conspiracy narratives (e.g., since referenced information is missing or unknown)

- A message is annotated as **showing signs of conspiracy (annotated as 1)**, when:
    1. The message clearly indicates signs of conspiracy narratives
    2. One of the guiding questions applies

Examples

Example messages that should be considered as showing signs of conspiracy:

- "Ist auch nichts anderes als in Deutschland. Das ist ein vom Deep State finanzierte Radiosender." [*"It's no different than in Germany. It's a Deep State-funded radio station."*]
- "[...] wie der Krieg jetzt mit der Plandemie zusammenhängt [...]" [*[...] how the war is now connected with the plandemy [...]*]
- "Die Verbrecher sind erst zufrieden, wenn sie ihre Agenda vom Great Reset durchgeknüppelt haben. Dazu muss der Bürger mit aller Macht gezwungen werden. Da spielen menschliche Opfer keine Rolle." [*"The criminals will not be satisfied until they have bludgeoned through their agenda of the Great Reset. The citizen must be forced to do this with all his might. Human sacrifice doesn't matter."*]
- "[...] das gelingt bei vielen die masse schaut auf den virus und der wef kann im hintergrund mit hilfe der regierungsmarionetten das system umwandeln wie auch immer das dann aussehen soll" [*"[...] this succeeds with many the masses look at the virus and the wmf can transform the system in the background with the help of the government puppets however that should look then"*]

- "[...] ihr ziel durch zwangsimpfungen die zahl der toten zu maximieren wird in seiner ganzen skrupellosigkeit erkennbar [...]" [*"[...] their goal of maximizing the number of deaths through compulsory vaccination becomes apparent in all its unscrupulousness [...]"*]
- "Das interessiert Merkel nicht, auch nicht die pharmaindustrie(Bill gates). Die Diktatur hat gestern begonnen, als Merkel sagte, nicht geimpfte werden vom Leben ausgeschlossen. Sie hat damit einen Buerger Krieg angezettelt." [*"Merkel doesn't care, neither does the pharma industry(Bill gates). The dictatorship started yesterday when Merkel said unvaccinated will be excluded from life. She started a civil war with that."*]

C Details on the topic modelling with STM

As suggested by Roberts et al. (2019), we ran STM models with the same parameters ($\alpha = 50/k$, $\eta = 0.01$) but varying k from 5 to 15 topics. We then calculate semantic coherence (Mimno et al., 2011) and exclusivity for each topic in each model. As (Roberts et al., 2014) note, high semantic coherence can be obtained by choosing a low number for k. However, exclusivity usually increases with k, meaning that one can evaluate an optimal number of topics by considering the trade-off between the two. In Figure 2, we see that 10 appears to be a good choice for a k as there is a local peak for the mean semantic coherence while exclusivity still grows from 9 to 10 topics.

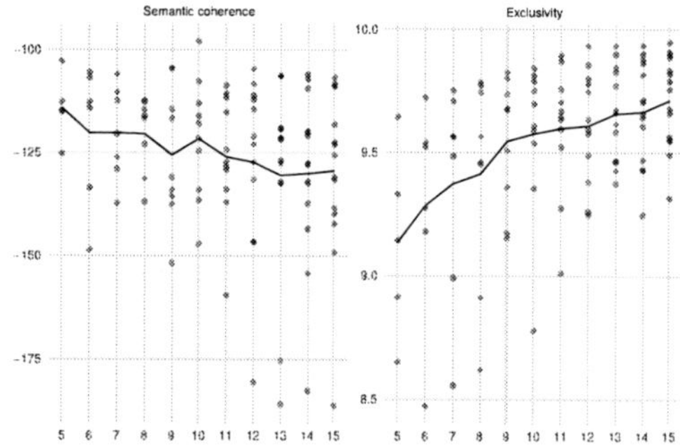

Figure 2: Model diagnostics by number of topics

Table 3: STM Topics, German original

Topic (prevalence)		Terms
T5 (21.8%)	prob	deutschland, regierung, politik, staat, land
	FREX	afd, antifa, querdenker, wählen, linken
T3 (12.8%)	prob	impfung, virus, dr, pandemie, impfstoff
	FREX	studie, pcr-test, infektion, getestet, rki
T9 (12.8%)	prob	menschen, kinder, leben, angst, welt
	FREX	menschlichkeit, natur, alten, leiden, erde
T7 (10.1%)	prob	__, t.me, kanal, video, medien
	FREX	t.me, abonnieren, stuttgartgrundgesetzdemos, kenjebsen, wirsindvielmehr
T1 (9.1%)	prob	reset, great, geld, welt, millionen
	FREX	reset, ikb, great, partner, spenden
T6 (9.1%)	prob	usa, the, gates, ukraine, russia
	FREX	ukraine, russia, putin, biden, nato
T4 (9.1%)	prob	freiheit, menschen, polizei, widerstand, berlin
	FREX	bühne, wiederherstellung, straßen, kundgebung, friedlich
T10 (6.9%)	prob	merkel, maßnahmen, lockdown, deutschland, bundesregierung
	FREX	kanzlerin, bundestag, bundeskanzlerin, angela, herbst
T8 (5.4%)	prob	telegram, uhr, impfpflicht, flag:German, denkt
	FREX	1k, news, flag:Austrian, @faktenfriedenfreiheit, web
T2 (2.8%)	prob	gesundheit, masken, maske, arbeit, telefon
	FREX	telefon, ministerium, soziales, integration, nix

[a] Some Unicode characters were replaced (e.g., flag:German used to be a flag emoji)

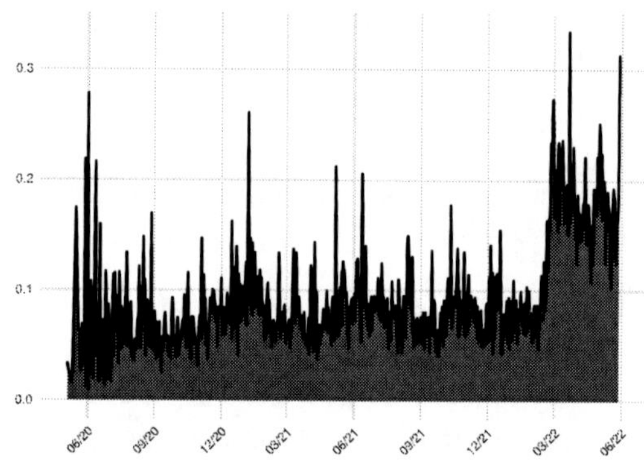

Figure 3: Topic prevalence (mean γ) over time for T6

Table 3 shows the original German version of Table 2. Figure 3 displays the change in prevalence over time for Topic 6.

Conditional Language Models for Community-Level Linguistic Variation

Bill Noble and **Jean-Philippe Bernardy**
Centre for Linguistic Theory and Studies in Probability (CLASP)
Dept. of Philosophy, Linguistics and Theory of Science
University of Gothenburg
{bill.noble@, jean.philippe.bernardy@}.gu.se

Abstract

Community-level linguistic variation is a core concept in sociolinguistics. In this paper, we use conditioned neural language models to learn vector representations for 510 online communities. We use these representations to measure linguistic variation between communities and investigate the degree to which linguistic variation corresponds with social connections between communities. We find that our sociolinguistic embeddings are highly correlated with a social network-based representation that does not use any linguistic input.

1 Introduction

Linguistic communication requires that speakers share certain linguistic conventions, such as syntactic structure, word meanings, and patterns of interaction. Speakers assume that these conventions are *common ground* among their interlocutors, based on joint membership in a community (Stalnaker, 2002; Clark, 1996). Such *speech communities* (Gumperz, 1972) range in size from the very small, like members of a friend group, to the very large, like speakers of English. However, as Eckert and McConnell-Ginet (1992) point out, it is *communities of practice*—defined by mutual social engagement in a common activity—that are the primary locus of linguistic variation.

Variation is an important object of study in sociolinguistics, and is naturally amenable to computational analysis (Nguyen et al., 2016). Most previous computational work on linguistic variation has considered variation at the level of macro-social categories, such as gender (Burger et al., 2011; Ciot et al., 2013; Bamman et al., 2014b), age (Nguyen et al., 2013), and geographic location (Eisenstein et al., 2010; Bamman et al., 2014a).In the present work, however, we investigate linguistic variation across online communities in the social media website Reddit.

For this purpose, we introduce (section 2) various Community-Conditioned Language Models (CCLMs for short). These models are conditioned on a vector representation (or embedding), which varies by community. Hence, they learn *community embeddings*. We report which architectures make best use of the community information (section 3), however our our primary purpose is not to improve language models in terms of perplexity, but rather to extract community embeddings that capture linguistic similarities between communities and test how the resulting embeddings correspond to the social structure of subreddits. To that end, we test the how well the community embeddings correlate with a social network-based representation of communities (section 4).

The contributions of this work are twofold. First, we develop a language model-based community embedding that we show is correlated with (but still different from) an embedding based on community membership alone. Second, the method we describe for testing the correlation between two embeddings from different models is, to our knowledge, novel to computational linguistics.

2 Community-conditioned language models (CCLMs)

We experiment with two kinds of model architecture: simple unidirectional LSTM (Hochreiter and Schmidhuber, 1997) and a masked Transformer (Vaswani et al., 2017). Although Transformer-based language models are considered state-of-the-art, they achieve dominance partly thanks to the availability of very large data sets (e.g., Devlin et al., 2019; Brown et al., 2020), which are not available to us.[1] Thus the LSTM is a worthy

[1] Fine-tuning existing models is not compatible with our methodology, because we fundamentally change the structure of the network by concatenating community embeddings with hidden states at various levels.

Proceedings of the Fifth Workshop on Natural Language Processing and Computational Social Science (NLP+CSS), pages 59 - 78
November 7, 2022

model to test for us.

In either case, the model is organised as a standard 3-layer neural sequence encoder, where the input for the tth timestep of the $n+1$st layer is the tth hidden state of the nth layer. As usual, the input to the first layer, is a sequence of tokens, encoded with a trainable embedding layer over a predetermined vocabulary. At the other end, word tokens are predicted using a softmax projection layer. What we have described so far does not take community into account and as such we call them *unconditioned models*, but the same encoder architecture also forms the core of our conditioned models.

In the CCLMs, we add a *community embedding* parameter, which varies depending on the community of origin of the input sample. This parameter is concatenated (at each time step) with the hidden layer of the sequence encoder, at some layer $l_c \leq n$, and passed through a linear layer which projects the resulting vector back to the original hidden layer size. For $l_c = n$, the output of this linear layer is passed directly to the softmax function, just as the final hidden layer of the sequence encoder is in other models. For $l_c = 0$, the community embedding is concatenated with the token embedding. For this reason, we set the hidden size of the sequence encoder and the size of the token embedding to be equal for all models.

2.1 Data sets

We investigate linguistic variation across various communities from the social media website Reddit.[2] Reddit is divided into forums called *subreddits*, which are typically organised around a topic of interest. Users create *posts*, which consist of a link, image, or text, along with a *comment* section. Comments are threaded: a comment can be made directly on a post, or appear as a reply to another comment. Hereafter we refer to such comments as "messages", matching our convention in mathematical formulas: the letter c stands for a community, and m stands for a message.

Our dataset includes messages from 510 subreddits, the set of all subreddits with at least 5000 messages per month for each month of the year 2015. Ignoring empty and deleted comments, we randomly sampled 42 000 messages from 2015 for each community. We reserved 1000 messages from each community for development and testing, leaving a total of 20.4M messages for training.

Using `langid.py` (Lui and Baldwin, 2012), we observe that a majority of the overall messages are classified as English (95% of the test set) and 498 of 510 communities have more than half of their messages classified as English. Given the small amount of non-English data, we decided that the bias introduced by attempting to filter message by language outweighted the potential benefits.[3]

Messages were preprocessed as follows: we excluded the content of block quotes, code blocks, and tables and removed markup (formatting) commands, extracting only rendered text. Messages were tokenized using the default English model for the SpaCy tokenizer Version 2.2.3 (Honnibal and Montani, 2017).

2.2 Training scheme

Models used a vocabulary of 40 000 tokens (including a special out-of-vocabulary token), consisting of the most frequent tokens across all communities.

We trained the models on a simple autoregressive language modeling task with cross-entropy loss. Because the Transformer operates on all tokens in the sequence at once, the inputs to the model were masked and incrementally unmasked. We used the AdamW (Loshchilov and Hutter, 2019) optimisation algorithm, with an initial learning rate of 0.001 and no extra control on the decay of learning rate. The batch size was 256 and the maximum sequence length set to 64 tokens, truncating longer messages (16.8% of messages were longer than 64 tokens). During training, a dropout rate of 0.1 was applied between encoder layers and after each linear layer.

All experiments use models with 3 encoder layers, each with hidden (and token embedding) size of 256. The Transformer models had 8 attention heads per layer.[4] The conditional models were given a community embedding with 16 dimensions. We experimented with every possible value for l_c, the depth of the community embedding, in a three-layer model ($l_c \in \{0, 1, 2, 3\}$).

We trained the models until the validation loss stopped decreasing for two epochs in a row, and used the weights from the epoch with the small-

[2]Comments were obtained from the archive at `https://pushshift.io/`. (Baumgartner et al., 2020). Code for reproducing our dataset, as well as our pre-trained community embeddings are available at URL.

[3]See section 7 for futher discussion.

[4]This number of attention heads was chosen to give the LSTM and Transformer models a comparable number of parameters (22 171 203 and 21 779 523, respectively).

est validation loss for testing. Each training epoch took approximately 1.5 hours of GPU time.

3 CCLM Performance

In this section, we report the performance of the conditioned and un-conditioned models on the held out test set. First, we define two performance metrics: perplexity and information gain. In the following, we use M to refer to messages in the combined test set, and M_j for the partition of the test set originating from community c_j.

3.1 Perplexity

For a given model, let $H(m)$ be the model's cross-entropy loss, averaged over tokens in m. We define the perplexity on a set of messages, M, to be the exponential of the model's average cross-entropy loss:

$$\mathsf{Ppl}_M = e^{\text{average}_{m \in M} H(m)}$$

CCLM Information Gain We also consider the average information gain per token of the CCLM over its baseline un-conditioned counterpart, with the same sequence encoder architecture. For a given message, information gain is defined as the difference between the cross-entropy of the unconditioned model and the conditioned model:

$$H_{\text{LM}}(m) - H_{\text{CCLM}}(m)$$

For a set of messages, M, we consider the average information gain in exponential space (as a ratio of perplexities):

$$\mathsf{IG}_M = \frac{e^{\text{average}_{m \in M}(H_{\text{LM}}(m))}}{e^{\text{average}_{m \in M}(H_{\text{CCLM}}(m))}}$$

$$\mathsf{IG}_M = e^{\text{average}_{m \in M}(H_{\text{LM}}(m) - H_{\text{CCLM}}(m))}$$

Unsurprisingly, the conditioned models mostly have lower perplexity than their respective unconditioned baseline models, (i.e., $\mathsf{IG}_M > 1$, table 1). While the absolute performance (Ppl_M) of the LSTM models is better, the best Transformer models have somewhat higher information gain than their LSTM counterparts.

The effect of l_c, the depth of the community embedding, is also different across architectures. For the LSTM encoder, the best model concatenates the community embedding after the first encoder layer ($l_c = 1$), but all of the conditioned models perform similarly well. For the Transformer, the best model incorporates the community information first, concatenating it directly to the word vectors ($l_c = 0$). It performs similarly to the model that only integrates the community information after all all the Transformer layers ($l_c = 3$), but the two middle-layer models actually perform worse than the unconditioned model (with $\mathsf{IG}_M < 1$).

	l_c	test epoch	Ppl_M	IG_M
LSTM	-	12	68.74	-
	0	13	66.16	1.039
	1	7	**66.01**	**1.041**
	2	4	66.19	1.039
	3	4	66.35	1.036
Transformer	-	4	79.13	-
	0	4	**75.66**	**1.046**
	1	4	82.12	0.964
	2	7	83.53	0.947
	3	3	75.90	1.043

Table 1: Performance of baseline (first row for each encoder architecture) and CCLM models. The scope of perplexity and information gain (M) is the entire test set, i.e. 5000×510 messages; 5000 for each community.

We also consider performance stratified by community; that is, Ppl_{M_j} and IG_{M_j}, where M_j is the set of messages originating from community c_j (fig. 1). We observe a lot of variation in baseline perplexity across communities, with Ppl_{M_j} ranging from 3.67 to 93.58 for the best conditional LSTM model (fig. 1; also see appendix B for detailed community-level results). The conditioned models also perform differently across different communities — even among the best models, some communities have $\mathsf{IG}_{M_j} < 1$, meaning that the CCLM performs worse than the unconditioned baseline for messages from that community. For other communities IG_{M_j} is much higher, meaning that the CCLM performs better (fig. 1).[5]

We observe that across all the models we tested, communities where conditioning has the least effect tend to be organised around more general interest topics, such as `/r/relationships` and `/r/advice`, where the subject matter is rele-

[5]Some of the communities with consistently high IG_{M_j} across all models are primarily non-English, but surprisingly, not the three most extreme outliers. There are `/r/counting`, `/r/friendsafari`, and `/r/Fireteams`, the later two of which are places where people coordinate to play video games together. The messages in these communites adhere to highly regular formats, which are presumably conventional to the community.

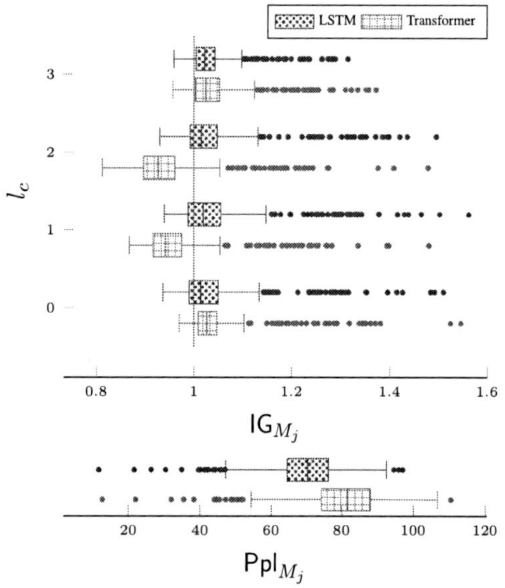

Figure 1: Average model performance by community. The boxes indicate upper and lower quartiles, while the whiskers are placed at the upper and lower maximum, with communities more than $1.5 \times IQR$ (inter-quartile range) above the upper quartile considered outliers (represented as dots). The three most extreme outliers are excluded from this view.

vant to a broad range of people. Conditioning the model on community appears to have the most benefit for narrower special-interest subreddits, such as those organised around a certain videogame, sports team, or subculture. These empirical observations corroborate the idea that communities of practice are the primary locus of linguistic variation.

4 Comparison of CCLM community embeddings with a social network embedding

In this section we investigate the degree to which CCLM community embeddings correlate with the social network structure of Reddit.

To this end, we compare the CCLM-learned community embeddings[6] with the community embedding created by Kumar et al. (2018),[7] which were generated using using a negative-sampling optimization algorithm, with the author-community co-occurrence matrix as ground truth, using data from January 2014 to April 2017. We refer the reader to Kumar et al. (2018) for details, but the important point is that no linguistic information is used to create these embeddings: they only reflect the social relationship between communities via community membership. In contrast, CCLM community embeddings depend in no way on which user is the author of any given message: we only use the contents of messages, not authorship data.

4.1 Comparing embeddings: cosine similarities

When comparing social embeddings and linguistic embeddings, a difficulty is that they range over completely unrelated spaces. Thus one cannot use the usual cosine similarity metric *between* these spaces. One can, however, use cosine similarity between *pairs* of communities, and verify that the similarities are correlated between linguistic and social embeddings. This gives a way of characterizing the differences between the two kinds of community representation. To get a more concrete sense of what this method yields, we first survey some of the most salient community pairs. We stress that this survey is not meant as a rigorous statistical analysis, as we shall see. Rather it is meant to give a flavor of discrepancies and similarities existing between linguistic and social relations.

We consider communities from three different selection criteria: Those with high linguistic *and* social similarity (where the sum of the two is highest), those with high linguistic and low social similarity (where social similarity is below the median and linguistic similarity is highest), and those with low linguistic and high social similarity (where linguistic similarity is below these median and linguistic similarity is highest).[8][9] We do not consider pairs of communities that are different in both ways, since these don't offer much in the way of understanding the respective embeddings.

Unsuprisingly, the first category (fig. 2, left) yields communities that are qualitatively very similar. The `/r/SSBPM` and `/r/darksouls` communities are focused around discussion of a par-

[6]In this section, we only consider the embeddings from the *best* (highest information gain) CCLM from each architecture family; that is, the LSTM with $l_c = 1$ and the Transformer with $l_c = 0$, however we observed similar results for other values of l_c.

[7]Available at `https://snap.stanford.edu/data/web-RedditEmbeddings.html`

[8]We use the LSTM ($l_c = 1$) community vectors for these purposes, but results attain with the best Transformer model.

[9]Median similarity among pairs of communities was 0.177 for the social embedding and 0.010 and 0.012 for the LSTM and Transformer linguistic embeddings, respectively.

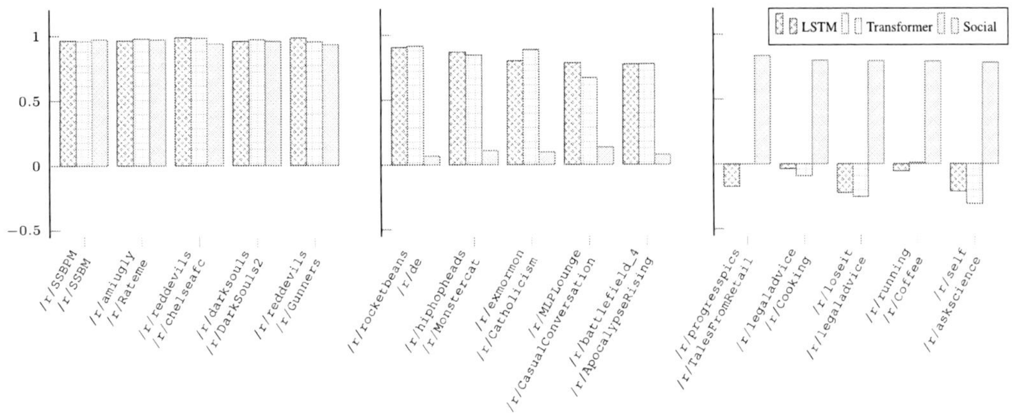

Figure 2: Cosine similarity between pairs of communities, computed for vectors from the best CCLM embeddings (LSTM: $l_c = 1$, Transformer: $l_c = 0$) and the social embedding from Kumar et al. (2018). Communities with high linguistic and social similarity **(left)**, high linguistic but low social similarity **(center)**, and low linguistic but high social similarity **(right)**. See text for details on the selection criteria.

ticular videogame, and are paired with communities that discuss a variation of the same game. The /r/amiugly and /r/Rateme communities are both forums where the posts are selfies and the comments are mostly comments on the person's appearance. The two communities paired with /r/reddevils are likewise comprised of fans of a particular English football club.

Communities with similar linguistic embeddings but dissimilar social embeddings (fig. 2, left) tend to share a similar topic, mode of interaction, or language variety, but in all cases we looked at, there is some reason to expect that they might nevertheless attract different members. For example, /r/hiphopheads and /r/Monstercat are both topically related to music, but the music genres are different, and the later has a more geographically local focus (Monstercat is an independent electronic music label based in Vancouver). The interactions in both /r/MLPLounge and /r/CasualConversation could be described as casual conversation, the former is intended specifically for members of a niche internet sub-culture. The /r/exmormon and /r/Catholicism communities discuss the Mormon and Catholic churches, although their members have different relationships towards those organizations — the former is intended for former members of the church, whereas the later is geared towards practicing Catholics. Finally, both /r/rocketbeans and /r/de are primarily German-language subreddits, but the former is comprised of fans of a computer gaming YouTube channel, while the later is more general-interest.

Differences at the other end of the spectrum (fig. 2, right) are somewhat harder to interpret. It is mostly easy to see why these communities would have different linguistic embeddings — in all cases the topics are quite different. The reason they have similar social embeddings is less obvious, but we can discern some trends in how the communities are premised. The /r/progresspics and /r/TalesFromRetail are premised, in part, on seeking support from other people with similar experiences; /r/legaladvice, /r/Cooking, and /r/loseit all involve sharing knowledge on a particular topic; /r/running and /r/Coffee are hobby-focused; and /r/self (often) and /r/askscience (by premise) are places people ask and answer questions. It may be that there are different patterns in the *social function* that people attribute to this particular social media website — people who use Reddit in one way are more likely to belong to communities that are premised on the same kind of social function, even if the topics (and indeed language) of those communities are quite different. Testing this hypothesis would require a more focused study design and ideally consider communities from multiple social networks (online or otherwise).

In sum, empirical observation simultaneously reveals examples of high and low correlation between social and linguistic embeddings. To quantify correlation and extract the general trends, we must resort to statistical tools, as we do below.

A straightforward (but ultimately flawed) way to measure how similar the two spaces are would be to generalise the above method, by consider each pair of communities (i, j), and compute the correlation between the cosine similarities of both embeddings.

That is, we can compute the Pearson correlation factor of the data set:

$$C = \{(x = L_i \cdot L_j, y = S_i \cdot S_j) \text{ for } i, j \in [1, 510]\}$$

where L_i and S_i are the linguistic and social embeddings for community i. (Thus L is the matrix of (normed) linguistic embeddings and S the matrix of (normed) social embeddings.)

The analysis shows positive correlation for both the LSTM ($r = 0.438$) and Transformer ($r = 0.452$) linguistic embeddings.[10] The correlations are significant with $p < 0.001$ in all cases. However, we note that the number of pairs grows with the square of the number of communities (with 510 communities, we have 129795) pairs), meaning that standard statistical tests on Pearson correlation will assure us of statistical significance in all but the weakest of correlations. A further flaw is that the data points in C are *not* distributed independently—far from it in fact, since each data point is generated from 2 of 510 independent variables. We consider this last flaw fatal, and take a different approach for computing the correlation between community embeddings in the next section.

4.2 Comparing embeddings: Procrustes method

In this section, we propose a systematic approach with which we can quantify the correlation between social proximity and linguistic proximity, and measure its statistical significance.

Instead of comparing embedding pairs, as in section 4.1, we will compare embeddings community by community. A naive approach would be to calculate the distance between two embeddings index-wise, which is equal to the Frobenius distance between L and S:

$$||L - S||_F = \sum_i (L_i - S_i)$$

The problem with the above metric is that even if several dimensions of L and S are correlated, they will not coincide in the *representation* of embeddings. That is, re-aligning the embeddings by applying a simple rotation (orthogonal transformation) on either matrix widely changes the $||L - S||_F$ correlation metric.

To make the metric independent of the representation (up to orthogonal transformations, which preserve cosine similarities), we compute the *minimum* distance between L_i and S_i, for any orthogonal matrix Ω applied to L:

$$d(L, S) = \mathsf{argmin}_\Omega ||\Omega L - S||_F$$

Here, the orthogonal matrix Ω gives a map from linguistic embeddings to social embeddings. The problem of computing $d(L, S)$ is known as the orthogonal Procrustes problem (Gower and Dijksterhuis, 2004).[11] The solution is

$$d(L, S) = n - \mathsf{Tr}(\Sigma)$$

where the matrix Σ is obtained by the singular value decomposition (SVD) $U^T \Sigma V = LS^T$. The vectors of U and V give the directions of correlation respectively of L and S. That is, each singular value σ_i (the elements of the diagonal matrix Σ), gives a measure of how much correlation there is between the directions U_i and V_i.

As is common when doing SVD, we arrange U, V and Σ such that $\sigma_i > \sigma_j$ iff $i < j$. Doing so, the largest singular value σ_0 corresponds to the principal directions of correlation (U_0, V_0), σ_1 to the second principal direction, etc.

The $d(L, S)$ metric ranges from 0 (corresponding to perfect correlation, obtained for example if $L = S$) to n (corresponding to perfect orthogonality), where $n = 510$ is the number of communities considered.

Now, to test if $d(L, S)$ corresponds to a significant correlation, it suffices to check if its value is significantly larger than the same value for random linguistic embeddings L'. The distribution of $d(L', S)$ for random embeddings is difficult to compute analytically, but we can instead evaluate it using a Monte Carlo method.

Doing so, we observed that $d(L', S)$ exhibits a mean of $\mu_d = 431.39$ and a (Bessel's-corrected) standard deviation $s_d = 2.90$ in their distance from the social embedding, S.

Thus if the real $d(L, S)$ is below the mean by several standard deviations, we can safely assume

[10]By comparison, the correlation between the two linguistic embeddings is 0.759.

[11]This approach has also been used to compare word embeddings across representations (e.g., Hamilton et al., 2016).

		LSTM	Transformer
l_c	0	254.06 (61.21)	239.41 (66.79)
	1	245.14 (64.29)	**232.18** (68.54)
	2	249.17 (62.90)	233.47 (68.32)
	3	**241.13** (65.67)	237.74 (66.84)

Table 2: Distance between CCLM embeddings and the social network-based embedding of Kumar et al. (2018), as measured by $d(L, S)$. In parentheses is the number of standard deviations from the mean distance of our random embedding samples.

that there is statistically significant correlation between L and S. A 4-sigma difference has less than one percent chance of occurring randomly. In our case, we observe a difference of between 61 and 68 standard deviations (table 2). This definitely indicates a significant correlation. Furthermore, by coming back to the definition of $d(L, S)$, we know that, on average, the cosine similarity between ΩL and S is $0.45 = (510 - 232.18/510)$. It further means that if we obtain a linguistic embedding L_k for a new community k, we can estimate its social embedding by ΩL_k, and the cosine similarity with its true social embedding S_k is expected to be $0.39 = (431.39 - 232.18)/510$ — accounting for over-fitting effects by taking the average distance rather than the maximum. In sum, it is clear that the CCLM embeddings predict some aspect the social-network embeddings — but far from all of it.

To finish, we also give a sense of *how* the correlation is manifested overall, by analysis of the two principal components of correlation in the linguistic embeddings, U_0 and U_1. To do so we plot the projection of each embedding along their first two principle components which, together with the corresponding singular values, gives an idea of how much and in what way they differ (see fig. 4).

5 Related work

We have presented results using conditional neural language models to model variation between speech communities. The architecture of these models concatenates a vector representation of the conditioned variable to the input of the sequence model. This approach has been applied in various conditioned text generation domains such as image captioning (Vinyals et al., 2015), machine translation (Kalchbrenner and Blunsom, 2013), but it has not, to our knowledge, been used extensively to study linguistic variation.

There are, however, related applications of conditional neural language models. Lau et al. (2017) presents a neural language model that jointly learns to predict words on the sentence-level and represent topics on the document level. The topic representation is then fed back into the language model, improving its performance on next word prediction. This is similar to how our model experiences improved performance by learning community representations. Unlike our model, topics are inferred in an unsupervised way, raising the question of whether communities could be identified from unlabeled data as well.

A piece of work with similar goals as ours is that of O'Connor et al. (2010), which uses a Bayesian generative model to infer communities from variation in text data. In contrast to our work, this model treats words as independent events, ignoring the structure (and variation) in the construction of sequences. It does further suggest, however, that community-level variation can be modeled in an unsupervised way.

Del Tredici and Fernández (2017), use a modified skip-gram model to community-level linguistic variation. They show that lexical semantic variation occurs even across different communities organised around the same topic. Their approach does not result in community level representations, however.

There are several other recent studies that aim to measure *linguistic distinctiveness* at the level of speech community (O'Connor et al., 2010; Zhang et al., 2017; Lucy and Bamman, 2021). Distinctiveness is one possible interpretation of the community-stratified information gain of the CCLM over its unconditioned counterpart (section 3.1). Whereas the metrics in previous work are based on lexical frequency (and in the case of Lucy and Bamman (2021), word sense distributions), CCLM information gain is capable of capturing distinctiveness at multiple levels of linguistic analysis. However, further work is needed to investigate exactly what kinds of variation are captured.

While the focus of this paper is sociolinguistic aspects, computational models of variation can also support robust, equitable language technology. Previous work has shown that speaker demographics can improve performance on standard NLP tasks (Hovy, 2015; Yang and Eisenstein,

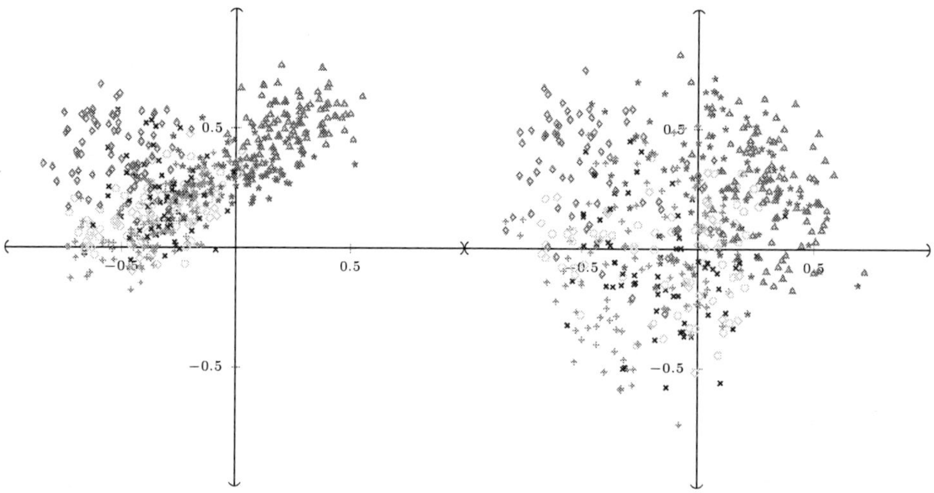

Figure 3: First two components of the aligned social (left) and linguistic (right) embeddings, where the lingusitic embedding is taken from the LTSM with $l_c = 1$. Correlation between these directions is given by $\sigma_0 = 53.4$ and $\sigma_1 = 35.6$. Colors are assigned by k-means clustering of the social embedding. This figure is reproduced in the supplementary materials with a legend that helps to characterise the clusters.

2017).

6 Discussion and Conclusion

To sum up our findings, we have defined community-conditioned language models (CCLMs). These models are generally able to attune to community-specific language, as witnessed by the information gain that they exhibit over baseline unconditioned models.

We find that the layer depth of the community embedding (l_c) has a weak effect on the information gain and the perplexity of the CCLMs.

For LSTM models, the perplexity per word, averaged over messages from all communities, was between 66.01 and 66.35 (with 68.74 for the unconditioned model). For Transformer models, it varies a bit more, between 75.66 and 83.53, but this seems to be mainly due to the poor performance of the models where the community embedding is inserted between Transformer layers ($l_c = 2$ and 3 both test above the unconditioned Transformer's average perplexity of 79.13).

The pattern of information gain by community is similar across architectures; communities that benefit most from the conditioned model behave that way for both the LSTM and Transformer. However, there are some differences. For example, many of the communities with the biggest difference in information gain between the $l_c = 0$ and $l_c = 3$ LSTMs are organised around trading collectables or organising virtual meetups (e.g., `/r/Pokemongiveaway`, `/r/ACTrade`, and `/r/SVExchange`). These communities tended to have highly conventionalized ways negotiating trades and coordinating meetups. It would be interesting to investigate these differences further in future work, since it could reveal differences in the kind of linguistic variation the different model architectures capture.

Our main result is that community representations learned by CCLMs are positively correlation with user co-occurrence patterns. Even though such *homophilic* correlation is a core hypothesis of sociolinguistics (see Kovacs and Kleinbaum (2020), for example), we believe that this study is the first to test it at the level of communities of practice using computational methods. Furthermore, it appears that our method (correlating linguistic embeddings and social embeddings) is novel. Indeed, even though the Procrustes method has been used to correlate two sets of linguistic embeddings *for the same model*, we find no evidence of the method being applied to embeddings for widely different models, as we have done.

7 Ethical considerations

Data privacy Our work uses publicly available data from Reddit, collected from the API made available by Baumgartner et al. (2020). Additional considerations apply, however (see Gliniecka et al.

(2021) for discussion). Reddit users are not, in general, aware of the possibility that their data will be used for research purposes, and deleted posts can persist in archive formats. We do not release any data, since the it is already publicly available and duplicating the dataset increases the likelihood that deleted posts will persist.

The paper does not include any text that could be linked back to personally identifiable information. We do release our trained community embeddings, but they have low dimensionality and pose a low risk for exposing personally identifiable information.

Language identification As mentioned in section section 2.1, we decided not to filter our data for non-English comments. Although our focus in this paper is intra-language variation, language identification has the potential to introduce bias by reinforcing hegemonic language classes and the boundaries between them. In our case, filtering out messages classified as non-English would introduce bias by disproportionately removing messages in non-standard and code-switched language varieties, which are of interest in the current work.

Nevertheless, the representations learned by our model are (necessarily) relative to the other communities in the dataset. Thus the learned representations for non-English communities tend to be more similar to each other than to other communities that use mostly English, even if their predominant language is not the same. This would probably not be the case if the distribution of messages was more varied across hegemonic language classes; our work cannot be used to conclude, for example, that there is more variation within English than between Dutch and German.

Subjective analysis In the qualitative discussion offered in section 4.1, our comparative characterization of the topic, mode of interaction, and language varieties used in the pairs of communities were formed by reading comments from the data our language models were trained on. This included Googling words and phrases that were unfamiliar. Where we make claims about the how the community is "premised" or what kinds of members it is "geared towards" or "intended for", these are based on the text of the sidebar on the community's Reddit page. While we believe this methodology, aggregated over many pairs of communities, is appropriate for making a qualitative comparison of the community features encoded by different representations, to make conclusions about *particular* communities based on such an analysis would be dubious and potentially harmful.

Acknowledgements

This work was supported by grant 2014-39 from the Swedish Research Council (VR) for the establishment of the Centre for Linguistic Theory and Studies in Probability (CLASP) at the University of Gothenburg.

References

David Bamman, Chris Dyer, and Noah A. Smith. 2014a. Distributed Representations of Geographically Situated Language. In *Proceedings of the 52nd Annual Meeting of the Association for Computational Linguistics (Volume 2: Short Papers)*, pages 828–834, Baltimore, Maryland. Association for Computational Linguistics.

David Bamman, Jacob Eisenstein, and Tyler Schnoebelen. 2014b. Gender identity and lexical variation in social media. *Journal of Sociolinguistics*, 18(2):135–160.

Jason Baumgartner, Savvas Zannettou, Brian Keegan, Megan Squire, and Jeremy Blackburn. 2020. The Pushshift Reddit Dataset. *arXiv:2001.08435 [cs]*.

Tom B. Brown, Benjamin Mann, Nick Ryder, Melanie Subbiah, Jared Kaplan, Prafulla Dhariwal, Arvind Neelakantan, Pranav Shyam, Girish Sastry, Amanda Askell, Sandhini Agarwal, Ariel Herbert-Voss, Gretchen Krueger, Tom Henighan, Rewon Child, Aditya Ramesh, Daniel M. Ziegler, Jeffrey Wu, Clemens Winter, Christopher Hesse, Mark Chen, Eric Sigler, Mateusz Litwin, Scott Gray, Benjamin Chess, Jack Clark, Christopher Berner, Sam McCandlish, Alec Radford, Ilya Sutskever, and Dario Amodei. 2020. Language Models are Few-Shot Learners. *arXiv:2005.14165 [cs]*.

John D. Burger, John Henderson, George Kim, and Guido Zarrella. 2011. Discriminating Gender on Twitter. In *Proceedings of the 2011 Conference on Empirical Methods in Natural Language Processing*, pages 1301–1309, Edinburgh, Scotland, UK. Association for Computational Linguistics.

Morgane Ciot, Morgan Sonderegger, and Derek Ruths. 2013. Gender Inference of Twitter Users in Non-English Contexts. In *Proceedings of the 2013 Conference on Empirical Methods in Natural Language Processing*, pages 1136–1145, Seattle, Washington, USA. Association for Computational Linguistics.

Herbert H. Clark. 1996. *Using Language*. Cambridge University Press.

Marco Del Tredici and Raquel Fernández. 2017. Semantic Variation in Online Communities of Practice. In *IWCS 2017 - 12th International Conference on Computational Semantics - Long Papers*.

Jacob Devlin, Ming-Wei Chang, Kenton Lee, and Kristina Toutanova. 2019. BERT: Pre-training of Deep Bidirectional Transformers for Language Understanding. In *Proceedings of the 2019 Conference of the North American Chapter of the Association for Computational Linguistics: Human Language Technologies, Volume 1 (Long and Short Papers)*, pages 4171–4186, Minneapolis, Minnesota. Association for Computational Linguistics.

Penelope Eckert and Sally McConnell-Ginet. 1992. Communities of practice: Where language, gender, and power all live. *Locating Power, Proceedings of the 1992 Berkeley Women and Language Conference*, pages 89–99.

Jacob Eisenstein, Brendan O'Connor, Noah A. Smith, and Eric P. Xing. 2010. A Latent Variable Model for Geographic Lexical Variation. In *Proceedings of the 2010 Conference on Empirical Methods in Natural Language Processing*, pages 1277–1287, Cambridge, MA. Association for Computational Linguistics.

Martyna Gliniecka, Joseph Reagle, Nicholas Proferes, Casey Fiesler, Sarah Gilbert, Naiyan Jones, Michael Zimmer, Huichuan Xia, Connie Moon Sehat, Tarunima Prabhakar, and Aleksei Kaminski. 2021. AoIR ethics panel 2: Platform challenges. *AoIR Selected Papers of Internet Research*.

J. C. Gower and Garmt B. Dijksterhuis. 2004. *Procrustes Problems*. Number 30 in Oxford Statistical Science Series. Oxford University Press, Oxford ; New York.

J Gumperz. 1972. The Speech Community. In Pier Paolo Giglioli, editor, *Language and Social Context: Selected Readings*. Harmondsworth : Penguin.

William L. Hamilton, Jure Leskovec, and Dan Jurafsky. 2016. Diachronic Word Embeddings Reveal Statistical Laws of Semantic Change. In *Proceedings of the 54th Annual Meeting of the Association for Computational Linguistics (Volume 1: Long Papers)*, pages 1489–1501, Berlin, Germany. Association for Computational Linguistics.

Sepp Hochreiter and Jürgen Schmidhuber. 1997. Long Short-Term Memory. *Neural Computation*, 9(8):1735–1780.

Matthew Honnibal and Ines Montani. 2017. spaCy 2: Natural language understanding with Bloom embeddings, convolutional neural networks and incremental parsing. Explosion.

Dirk Hovy. 2015. Demographic Factors Improve Classification Performance. In *Proceedings of the 53rd Annual Meeting of the Association for Computational Linguistics and the 7th International Joint Conference on Natural Language Processing (Volume 1: Long Papers)*, pages 752–762, Beijing, China. Association for Computational Linguistics.

Nal Kalchbrenner and Phil Blunsom. 2013. Recurrent Continuous Translation Models. In *Proceedings of the 2013 Conference on Empirical Methods in Natural Language Processing*, page 10, Seattle, Washington.

Balazs Kovacs and Adam M. Kleinbaum. 2020. Language-Style Similarity and Social Networks. *Psychological Science*, 31(2):202–213.

Srijan Kumar, William L. Hamilton, Jure Leskovec, and Dan Jurafsky. 2018. Community Interaction and Conflict on the Web. In *Proceedings of the 2018 World Wide Web Conference on World Wide Web - WWW '18*, pages 933–943, Lyon, France. ACM Press.

Jey Han Lau, Timothy Baldwin, and Trevor Cohn. 2017. Topically Driven Neural Language Model. In *Proceedings of the 55th Annual Meeting of the Association for Computational Linguistics (Volume 1: Long Papers)*, pages 355–365, Vancouver, Canada. Association for Computational Linguistics.

Ilya Loshchilov and Frank Hutter. 2019. Decoupled Weight Decay Regularization. *arXiv:1711.05101 [cs, math]*.

Li Lucy and David Bamman. 2021. Characterizing English Variation across Social Media Communities with BERT. *Transactions of the Association for Computational Linguistics*, 9:538–556.

Marco Lui and Timothy Baldwin. 2012. Langid.py: An Off-the-shelf Language Identification Tool. In *Proceedings of the ACL 2012 System Demonstrations*, pages 25–30, Jeju Island, Korea. Association for Computational Linguistics.

Dong Nguyen, A. Seza Doğruöz, Carolyn P. Rosé, and Franciska de Jong. 2016. Computational Sociolinguistics: A Survey. *Computational Linguistics*, 42(3):537–593.

Dong Nguyen, Rilana Gravel, Dolf Trieschnigg, and Theo Meder. 2013. How Old Do You Think I Am?: A Study of Language and Age in Twitter. In *Proceedings of the Seventh International AAAI Conference on Weblogs and Social Media*, page 10.

Brendan O'Connor, Jacob Eisenstein, Eric P Xing, and Noah A Smith. 2010. A mixture model of demographic lexical variation. In *In Proceedings of NIPS Workshop on Machine Learning for Social Computing*, page 6, Vancouver, BC, Canada. 2010.

Robert Stalnaker. 2002. Common Ground. *Linguistics and Philosophy*, 25(5-6):701–721.

Ashish Vaswani, Noam Shazeer, Niki Parmar, Jakob Uszkoreit, Llion Jones, Aidan N. Gomez, Lukasz Kaiser, and Illia Polosukhin. 2017. Attention Is All You Need. *arXiv:1706.03762 [cs].*

Oriol Vinyals, Alexander Toshev, Samy Bengio, and Dumitru Erhan. 2015. Show and Tell: A Neural Image Caption Generator. *arXiv:1411.4555 [cs].*

Yi Yang and Jacob Eisenstein. 2017. Overcoming Language Variation in Sentiment Analysis with Social Attention. *Transactions of the Association for Computational Linguistics*, 5:295–307.

Justine Zhang, William L Hamilton, Cristian Danescu-Niculescu-Mizil, Dan Jurafsky, and Jure Leskovec. 2017. Community Identity and User Engagement in a Multi-Community Landscape. In *Proceedings of the International AAAI Conference on Weblogs and Social Media*, pages 377–386. International AAAI Conference on Weblogs and Social Media.

A Projection of aligned embeddings

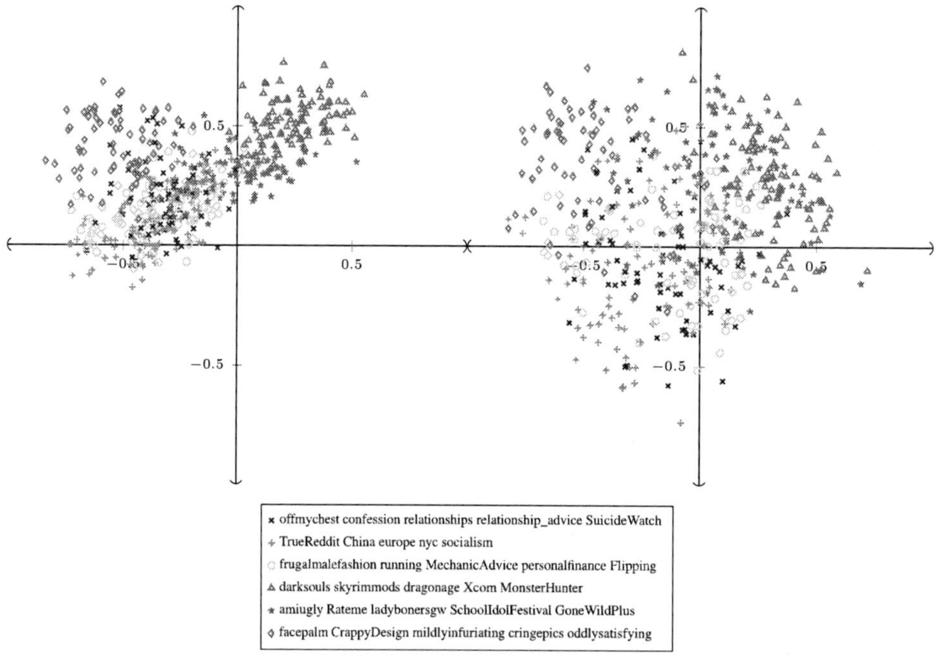

Figure 4: First two components of the aligned social (top) and linguistic (bottom) embeddings, where the lingusitic embedding is taken from the LTSM with $l_c = 1$. Correlation between these directions is given by $\sigma_0 = 53.4$ and $\sigma_1 = 35.6$. Colors are assigned by k-means clustering of the social embedding. The legend shows the closest 5 communites to each cluster centroid. The legend shows the closest 5 communites to each cluster centroid. The cluster of each community is also available in appendix B

B Community-level results

The following table shows results at the community level. The baseline Ppl_{M_j} is computed from the unconditioned LSTM and the CCLM results (Ppl_{M_j}, IG_{M_j}, and Ind_{M_j} use the LSTM with $l_c = 1$). "Social cluster" is determined by k-means clustering of the social embedding.

Subredddit	baseline Ppl_{M_j}	CCLM Ppl_{M_j}	IG_{M_j}	Ind_{M_j}	Social embed. cluster
ukraina	21.74	15.19	1.43	0.006	4
france	68.34	50.85	1.34	0.008	1
brasil	64.13	57.68	1.11	0.008	1
podemos	55.71	42.89	1.3	0.008	4
Denmark	64.2	54.56	1.18	0.009	1
de	71.06	54.49	1.3	0.01	1
rocketbeans	95.95	74.17	1.29	0.011	4
thenetherlands	69.16	53.61	1.29	0.011	1
italy	59.56	44.62	1.33	0.011	1
argentina	70.14	53.01	1.32	0.012	4
Romania	58.34	43.84	1.33	0.012	1
sweden	53.21	43.12	1.23	0.013	1
friendsafari	26.55	9.76	2.72	0.026	4
Fireteams	43.85	20.01	2.19	0.039	4
SVExchange	44.44	30.88	1.44	0.062	4
summonerschool	83.28	75.35	1.11	0.082	4
EDH	76.55	58.21	1.32	0.085	3
buildapcforme	74.75	69.45	1.08	0.098	3
Pokemongiveaway	47.1	32.12	1.47	0.099	4
summonerswar	90.06	81.71	1.1	0.108	4
ACTrade	47.82	33.77	1.42	0.121	4
makeupexchange	53.03	40.85	1.3	0.136	4
SkincareAddiction	58.2	56.43	1.03	0.153	0
listentothis	35	32.07	1.09	0.157	5
pokemontrades	52.37	41.69	1.26	0.175	4
AsianBeauty	70.35	67.43	1.04	0.177	4
MechanicAdvice	82.64	78.14	1.06	0.179	2
amiugly	49.01	43.24	1.13	0.179	0
ClashOfClans	78.73	71.12	1.11	0.184	2
dndnext	94.53	91.07	1.04	0.186	3
Homebrewing	79.8	74.67	1.07	0.187	2
fountainpens	66.31	64.16	1.03	0.19	2
buildapc	66.77	62.5	1.07	0.192	3
Pathfinder_RPG	97.05	93.58	1.04	0.196	3
Rateme	60.74	45.41	1.34	0.199	0
Coffee	70.76	66.47	1.06	0.201	2
MakeupAddiction	69.2	64.46	1.07	0.213	0
Vaping	73.15	66.63	1.1	0.216	2
makinghiphop	70.47	62.22	1.13	0.218	2
SSBM	84.02	77.93	1.08	0.218	3
PuzzleAndDragons	79.77	74.57	1.07	0.222	4
Aquariums	68.74	63.47	1.08	0.232	2
gameswap	69.99	50.77	1.38	0.236	3
dogs	67.25	65.98	1.02	0.247	2
bodyweightfitness	72.5	71.38	1.02	0.247	2
Indiemakeupandmore	73.19	69.11	1.06	0.257	4
vaporents	69.66	64.79	1.08	0.264	2
churning	75.02	72.01	1.04	0.264	2
Animesuggest	75.84	72.22	1.05	0.272	3
HomeImprovement	78.86	76.24	1.03	0.275	2
edmproduction	70.49	67.59	1.04	0.28	0
poker	80.61	74.09	1.09	0.289	2
learnprogramming	68.05	66.95	1.02	0.29	2
yugioh	90.35	83.49	1.08	0.292	3
eu4	81.78	77.56	1.05	0.292	3
femalefashionadvice	66.48	65.45	1.02	0.292	0
beyondthebump	69.56	68.34	1.02	0.294	4
Watches	61.97	58.26	1.06	0.297	2
DebateReligion	76.39	76.91	0.99	0.298	0
3Dprinting	73.61	69.77	1.06	0.299	2
headphones	65.24	61.43	1.06	0.301	2

Subredddit	baseline Ppl_{M_j}	CCLM Ppl_{M_j}	IG_{M_j}	Ind_{M_j}	Social embed. cluster
frugalmalefashion	68.61	62.57	1.1	0.305	2
ecigclassifieds	51.95	40.7	1.28	0.316	4
Multicopter	73.95	69.85	1.06	0.316	2
goodyearwelt	66.06	63.71	1.04	0.324	2
steroids	78.23	73.67	1.06	0.326	4
WeAreTheMusicMakers	70.03	68.65	1.02	0.326	0
bravefrontier	86.87	80.39	1.08	0.328	4
techsupport	69.66	66.14	1.05	0.33	3
xxfitness	70.02	70.48	0.99	0.331	0
math	75.52	73.93	1.02	0.335	2
rawdenim	72.29	69.83	1.04	0.335	2
weddingplanning	66.62	64.88	1.03	0.34	0
Guitar	73.45	71.53	1.03	0.34	0
worldpowers	50.61	46.38	1.09	0.342	4
jailbreak	60.47	54.55	1.11	0.345	4
csgobetting	80.89	66.01	1.23	0.346	4
DnD	87.77	87.84	1	0.35	3
networking	81.33	79.74	1.02	0.35	2
keto	68.32	66.66	1.02	0.354	0
counting	11.77	3.67	3.21	0.355	5
hardwareswap	57.3	43.39	1.32	0.355	3
electronic_cigarette	66.98	62.44	1.07	0.357	2
magicTCG	81.65	74.11	1.1	0.36	3
hearthstone	78.36	74.29	1.05	0.361	3
pathofexile	91	85.54	1.06	0.367	3
photography	69.07	68.28	1.01	0.368	2
MMORPG	79.01	77.84	1.02	0.369	3
randomactsofcsgo	41.37	26.47	1.56	0.369	4
Boxing	73.85	69.41	1.06	0.37	1
malefashionadvice	68.62	65.47	1.05	0.377	2
Cooking	82.3	77.61	1.06	0.378	2
Diablo	85.14	81.71	1.04	0.379	3
askscience	40.25	35.11	1.15	0.381	5
relationship_advice	53.94	54.56	0.99	0.382	0
loseit	59.5	59.16	1.01	0.384	0
skyrimmods	75.03	71.98	1.04	0.386	3
SSBPM	81.88	77.59	1.06	0.386	3
golf	77.53	74.76	1.04	0.387	2
ar15	73.38	70.38	1.04	0.387	5
investing	81.32	80.7	1.01	0.387	2
supremeclothing	85.59	67.65	1.27	0.388	4
ADHD	62.9	64.03	0.98	0.39	0
Fitness	64.81	64.27	1.01	0.39	2
chelseafc	69.95	64.93	1.08	0.39	1
Xcom	92.33	89.68	1.03	0.392	3
DeadBedrooms	62.03	63.7	0.97	0.392	0
millionairemakers	42.31	35.32	1.2	0.392	5
heroesofthestorm	80.23	78.53	1.02	0.398	3
photoshopbattles	30.56	26.92	1.14	0.404	5
BabyBumps	67.72	67.66	1	0.404	4
DarkSouls2	78.64	75	1.05	0.405	3
NHLHUT	60.6	53.07	1.14	0.406	4
buildapcsales	66.81	63.34	1.05	0.409	3
reddevils	72.75	67.73	1.07	0.409	1
woodworking	73.29	70.82	1.03	0.41	2
MechanicalKeyboards	65.95	61.4	1.07	0.41	3
civ	87.7	84.83	1.03	0.411	3
discgolf	76.52	74.18	1.03	0.412	5
LSD	68.01	65.36	1.04	0.412	0
progresspics	51.02	46.98	1.09	0.415	0
stopdrinking	55.44	53.91	1.03	0.418	0
dbz	70.71	69.7	1.01	0.419	3
Twitch	66.02	64.59	1.02	0.419	3
Sneakers	72.98	63.04	1.16	0.421	4
beer	71.65	68.97	1.04	0.421	2
Surface	70.56	69.52	1.01	0.423	2
CrusaderKings	76.55	74.28	1.03	0.426	3
Gunners	68.4	64.23	1.06	0.428	1

Subredddit	baseline Ppl_{M_j}	CCLM Ppl_{M_j}	IG_{M_j}	Ind_{M_j}	Social embed. cluster
WorldofTanks	82.8	81.15	1.02	0.429	3
personalfinance	61.2	62.06	0.99	0.429	2
Bitcoin	75.17	73.26	1.03	0.429	1
LiverpoolFC	72.85	68.22	1.07	0.43	1
webdev	73.46	72.34	1.02	0.432	2
Smite	84.11	79.08	1.06	0.433	4
running	74	75.24	0.98	0.433	2
feedthebeast	81.55	77.04	1.06	0.433	3
windowsphone	77.28	74.32	1.04	0.434	2
elderscrollsonline	80.75	79.12	1.02	0.436	3
cscareerquestions	69.79	70.57	0.99	0.436	2
GoneWildPlus	61.76	47.5	1.3	0.441	4
rpg	87.28	88.46	0.99	0.443	3
Naruto	66.46	63.63	1.04	0.446	3
smashbros	78.81	73.38	1.07	0.447	3
philosophy	71.98	73.55	0.98	0.448	1
RandomActsOfGaming	39.71	26.4	1.5	0.448	3
FIFA	65.16	61.11	1.07	0.451	4
eagles	69.93	66.27	1.06	0.454	1
programming	85.82	84.6	1.01	0.457	1
bjj	74.59	74.23	1	0.457	4
vinyl	69.04	67.42	1.02	0.46	2
subaru	72.5	67.33	1.08	0.461	2
MaddenUltimateTeam	72.05	63.72	1.13	0.462	4
asktrp	70.4	71.31	0.99	0.464	0
linux	79.71	77.57	1.03	0.466	1
SchoolIdolFestival	77.47	72.93	1.06	0.468	4
longboarding	75.86	69.68	1.09	0.468	2
darksouls	74.81	72.79	1.03	0.468	3
socialism	76.18	77.14	0.99	0.469	1
zen	71.52	68.15	1.05	0.47	0
gonewild	62.73	50.47	1.24	0.47	4
starbucks	78.55	77.12	1.02	0.471	0
wiiu	69.32	67.77	1.02	0.472	3
gonewildcurvy	61.23	48.92	1.25	0.473	4
vita	71.64	71.51	1	0.474	3
wow	86.05	84.34	1.02	0.475	3
Drugs	64.08	64.16	1	0.476	0
CCW	69.49	70.23	0.99	0.477	5
OnePiece	70.44	68.17	1.03	0.477	3
PoliticalDiscussion	79.6	82.62	0.96	0.478	1
PurplePillDebate	75.96	77.38	0.98	0.479	0
nintendo	73.99	71.66	1.03	0.48	3
gonewildaudio	59.05	51.82	1.14	0.481	4
MonsterHunter	80.89	80.07	1.01	0.485	3
Warthunder	85.85	84.04	1.02	0.486	3
streetwear	78.19	65.36	1.2	0.487	4
relationships	53.37	54.64	0.98	0.488	0
KerbalSpaceProgram	74.81	72.6	1.03	0.489	3
CanadaPolitics	81.79	83.99	0.97	0.49	1
Warhammer40k	86.64	85.07	1.02	0.49	3
iphone	69	66.68	1.03	0.492	2
Economics	90.45	91.44	0.99	0.492	1
coys	67.54	64.03	1.05	0.493	1
vegan	68.74	68.82	1	0.493	0
manga	72.97	69.65	1.05	0.495	4
Metal	75.65	73.47	1.03	0.495	4
leagueoflegends	76.76	72.42	1.06	0.495	4
islam	69.7	69.48	1	0.496	1
Christianity	72.59	73.29	0.99	0.496	1
depression	47.83	49.21	0.97	0.497	0
knifeclub	60.88	58.21	1.05	0.499	4
Music	67.94	65.58	1.04	0.502	5
playrust	78.58	74.51	1.05	0.504	3
SuicideWatch	41.51	42.05	0.99	0.505	0
serialpodcast	71.76	72.58	0.99	0.505	1
NoFap	62.15	61.51	1.01	0.505	0
jobs	55.59	56.72	0.98	0.505	2

Subredddit	baseline Ppl_{M_j}	CCLM Ppl_{M_j}	IG_{M_j}	Ind_{M_j}	Social embed. cluster
russia	74.41	73.52	1.01	0.505	1
cars	67.48	66.17	1.02	0.506	2
Philippines	78.73	74.85	1.05	0.506	1
Parenting	67.68	69.58	0.97	0.51	2
Bad_Cop_No_Donut	78.04	77.35	1.01	0.511	1
syriancivilwar	77.33	77.4	1	0.512	1
h1z1	77.21	73.44	1.05	0.513	3
seduction	61.67	62.26	0.99	0.517	0
truegaming	73.32	75.89	0.97	0.517	3
3DS	68	67.06	1.01	0.518	3
flying	77.44	77.61	1	0.522	2
apple	74.05	73.43	1.01	0.523	2
exmuslim	74	74.63	0.99	0.523	1
swtor	80.56	81.2	0.99	0.524	3
ffxiv	79.74	80.22	0.99	0.525	3
whowouldwin	89.85	88	1.02	0.525	4
OutreachHPG	85.19	84.9	1	0.526	4
Fantasy	69.35	69.73	0.99	0.527	1
halo	75.8	75.12	1.01	0.528	3
WritingPrompts	46.13	41.44	1.11	0.528	0
ladybonersgw	55.83	44.16	1.26	0.529	4
sex	56.07	58.34	0.96	0.53	0
airsoft	71.09	68.82	1.03	0.53	3
Warframe	87.6	85.95	1.02	0.53	3
nfl	75.86	71.07	1.07	0.533	1
ukpolitics	79.49	80.44	0.99	0.533	1
DCcomics	73.92	73.51	1.01	0.535	1
rugbyunion	83.39	79.28	1.05	0.535	1
motorcycles	74.3	73.9	1.01	0.536	2
CoDCompetitive	76.44	71.77	1.07	0.536	4
indieheads	84.46	82.78	1.02	0.537	1
cordcutters	74.68	73.6	1.01	0.538	2
paradoxplaza	75.21	74.63	1.01	0.54	3
Android	76.03	74.05	1.03	0.541	2
letsplay	68.08	68.02	1	0.544	3
Guildwars2	81.19	80.72	1.01	0.544	3
sto	83.26	84.11	0.99	0.545	3
Cricket	89.17	82.26	1.08	0.545	1
Anarcho_Capitalism	83.27	84.21	0.99	0.545	1
bodybuilding	77.16	74.22	1.04	0.546	2
minnesotavikings	71.49	69.89	1.02	0.546	1
hiphopheads	78.14	71.33	1.1	0.547	1
soccer	74.33	71.16	1.04	0.547	1
guns	68.94	67.21	1.03	0.549	5
DestinyTheGame	81.85	81.09	1.01	0.55	3
boardgames	73.89	74.86	0.99	0.551	3
formula1	75.47	72.7	1.04	0.551	1
kpop	72.65	69.91	1.04	0.553	4
sysadmin	80.94	81.57	0.99	0.554	2
AskHistorians	53.96	52.75	1.02	0.556	0
horror	73.1	72.75	1	0.556	1
Justrolledintotheshop	82.13	78.16	1.05	0.559	5
bicycling	72.55	71.81	1.01	0.559	2
cats	59.55	55.74	1.07	0.561	5
politics	83.72	84.83	0.99	0.561	1
Flipping	70.57	69.43	1.02	0.561	2
MMA	69.95	66.04	1.06	0.562	1
Libertarian	77.87	78.87	0.99	0.563	1
neopets	67.31	64.27	1.05	0.564	4
Marvel	77.97	76.78	1.02	0.57	1
DotA2	84.24	79.15	1.06	0.573	4
survivor	66.58	64.4	1.03	0.573	4
Games	65.99	67.57	0.98	0.574	3
Catholicism	75.28	78.56	0.96	0.577	1
battlefield_4	75.42	73.96	1.02	0.577	3
DarkNetMarkets	72.35	69.67	1.04	0.578	0
marvelstudios	77.5	76.66	1.01	0.579	1
breakingmom	68.42	69.76	0.98	0.582	4

Subredddit	baseline Ppl_{M_j}	CCLM Ppl_{M_j}	IG_{M_j}	Ind_{M_j}	Social embed. cluster
EliteDangerous	82.32	82.86	0.99	0.584	3
dragonage	73.97	76.41	0.97	0.584	3
raisedbynarcissists	61.4	63.01	0.97	0.585	0
starcraft	79.73	77.33	1.03	0.585	3
opiates	69.82	68.43	1.02	0.586	0
amiibo	67.55	63.9	1.06	0.588	4
space	54.14	51.6	1.05	0.588	1
gamedev	72.03	73.98	0.97	0.589	3
EDC	67.23	66.72	1.01	0.589	5
comicbooks	78.94	78.29	1.01	0.589	1
legaladvice	63.01	62.68	1.01	0.592	0
nba	74.9	69.47	1.08	0.592	1
Patriots	70.71	69.9	1.01	0.593	1
worldpolitics	82.57	83.91	0.98	0.593	1
changemyview	74.27	78.29	0.95	0.594	0
Planetside	80.3	79.45	1.01	0.595	3
MensRights	74.53	76.96	0.97	0.596	1
dayz	69.58	68.07	1.02	0.597	3
asktransgender	60.84	63.19	0.96	0.597	0
runescape	73.83	71.15	1.04	0.598	4
books	65.13	66.44	0.98	0.598	1
GameDeals	63.24	62.81	1.01	0.6	3
travel	61.46	61.99	0.99	0.601	2
oculus	81.27	82.68	0.98	0.603	3
DIY	63.8	63.71	1	0.604	2
battlestations	63.3	60.03	1.05	0.605	3
worldbuilding	83.56	85.48	0.98	0.607	0
TheRedPill	74.87	77.57	0.97	0.608	0
anime	71.45	69.63	1.03	0.608	3
bindingofisaac	77.83	73.4	1.06	0.609	3
aviation	72.42	71.11	1.02	0.61	1
osugame	68.02	60.33	1.13	0.612	4
Minecraft	71.11	67.91	1.05	0.613	3
Conservative	65.03	65.92	0.99	0.615	1
pcgaming	73.15	74.15	0.99	0.616	3
Advice	53.12	55.05	0.97	0.617	0
MLS	75.07	72.32	1.04	0.618	1
writing	70.1	73.25	0.96	0.619	0
Filmmakers	66.7	67.55	0.99	0.619	2
xboxone	69.04	68.37	1.01	0.619	3
2007scape	74.44	69.96	1.06	0.621	4
TrueReddit	80.07	82.89	0.97	0.629	1
Monstercat	70.18	62.12	1.13	0.631	4
skyrim	71.84	70.53	1.02	0.633	3
Eve	84.15	80	1.05	0.635	3
rupaulsdragrace	73.74	69.88	1.06	0.635	4
europe	81.43	83.28	0.98	0.637	1
GlobalOffensive	73.65	69.85	1.05	0.637	4
PS4	67.45	67.75	1	0.64	3
tf2	76.61	73.79	1.04	0.646	3
fatlogic	70.99	72.33	0.98	0.646	0
Scotland	82.95	84.4	0.98	0.647	1
asoiaf	65.9	65.32	1.01	0.65	1
paydaytheheist	77.23	76.49	1.01	0.651	3
Anarchism	77.17	78.87	0.98	0.651	1
pcmasterrace	63.58	62.29	1.02	0.651	3
AskScienceFiction	88.54	90.24	0.98	0.653	0
food	65.9	59.79	1.1	0.653	5
atheism	72.62	75.05	0.97	0.654	5
science	45.72	43.24	1.06	0.655	1
ForeverAlone	55.78	58.2	0.96	0.656	0
Silverbugs	69.6	69.52	1	0.66	4
NASCAR	70.72	67.28	1.05	0.66	1
history	59.83	59.44	1.01	0.66	1
cigars	65.73	63.86	1.03	0.661	4
askgaybros	59.77	62.74	0.95	0.664	0
fireemblem	67.02	65.25	1.03	0.664	3
ProgrammerHumor	73.31	69.89	1.05	0.665	5

Subredddit	baseline Ppl_{M_j}	CCLM Ppl_{M_j}	IG_{M_j}	Ind_{M_j}	Social embed. cluster
harrypotter	65.42	66.1	0.99	0.668	5
Shitty_Car_Mods	70.04	65.03	1.08	0.668	5
scifi	72.28	72.43	1	0.669	1
gadgets	63.79	64.06	1	0.669	1
starcitizen	82.51	83.11	0.99	0.67	3
gameofthrones	58.92	57.41	1.03	0.67	5
Weakpots	74.45	70.04	1.06	0.671	4
Steam	70.07	69.55	1.01	0.671	3
confession	51.66	54.61	0.95	0.673	0
offmychest	51.86	54.5	0.95	0.675	0
lego	68.43	67.66	1.01	0.675	5
baseball	70.74	68.4	1.03	0.675	1
CFB	71.18	71.17	1	0.676	1
startrek	71.6	70.55	1.01	0.678	5
TheBluePill	72.1	74.67	0.97	0.681	1
StarWars	66.21	67.48	0.98	0.684	5
SquaredCircle	77.05	75.25	1.02	0.685	4
shittyfoodporn	68.5	60.2	1.14	0.687	5
ApocalypseRising	71.35	62.46	1.14	0.689	4
canada	75.02	77.62	0.97	0.69	1
opieandanthony	73.76	70.47	1.05	0.694	4
Futurology	77.87	78.86	0.99	0.695	1
worldnews	77.54	79.36	0.98	0.696	1
Entrepreneur	65.54	66.72	0.98	0.696	2
TwoXChromosomes	56.24	58.87	0.96	0.698	0
pokemon	63.22	61.43	1.03	0.701	3
hockey	67.11	64.73	1.04	0.702	1
fakeid	63.34	56.86	1.11	0.709	4
Frugal	70.53	72.71	0.97	0.713	2
masseffect	69.64	72.89	0.96	0.717	3
unitedkingdom	80.59	81.94	0.98	0.719	1
movies	71.46	72.31	0.99	0.719	1
news	72.41	74.2	0.98	0.725	1
exmormon	75.92	79.35	0.96	0.726	4
actuallesbians	57.76	59.88	0.96	0.731	0
ShitRedditSays	66.5	65.84	1.01	0.733	1
sports	65.9	65.08	1.01	0.733	1
AskMen	65.65	68.32	0.96	0.735	0
MapPorn	77.93	77.93	1	0.738	1
television	69.36	70.26	0.99	0.74	1
australia	90.21	91.61	0.98	0.741	1
AskWomen	62.65	65.26	0.96	0.743	0
circlejerk	53.48	41.55	1.29	0.743	5
Kappa	74.12	67.21	1.1	0.744	4
vancouver	77.54	79.82	0.97	0.744	1
nsfw	42.5	38.8	1.1	0.744	4
fivenightsatfreddys	60.84	55.88	1.09	0.746	4
aww	63.96	59.87	1.07	0.746	5
conspiracy	78.47	80.21	0.98	0.747	1
ultrahardcore	64.64	55.47	1.17	0.754	4
childfree	65	67.36	0.97	0.756	0
lewronggeneration	74.67	70.38	1.06	0.756	5
GamerGhazi	76.13	77.3	0.98	0.758	1
KotakuInAction	78.84	80.99	0.97	0.76	1
GetMotivated	53.69	54.68	0.98	0.761	2
boston	75.07	77.55	0.97	0.762	2
Seattle	81.3	83.34	0.98	0.764	2
Celebs	48.89	45.1	1.08	0.764	1
washingtondc	74.04	76.07	0.97	0.765	2
technology	76.7	78.91	0.97	0.766	1
GrandTheftAutoV	66.58	65.53	1.02	0.768	3
Civcraft	72.82	68.39	1.06	0.772	4
RealGirls	52.95	47.56	1.11	0.774	4
AirForce	74.36	75.44	0.99	0.774	2
gamegrumps	64.74	63.05	1.03	0.779	3
Fallout	71.83	71.08	1.01	0.783	3
rage	58.16	59.24	0.98	0.785	5
exjw	75.12	79.59	0.94	0.786	4

Subredddit	baseline Ppl_{M_j}	CCLM Ppl_{M_j}	IG_{M_j}	Ind_{M_j}	Social embed. cluster
OkCupid	65.09	66.74	0.98	0.787	0
JusticePorn	57.81	57.62	1	0.788	5
Tinder	66.8	62.91	1.06	0.789	5
nyc	74.19	75.98	0.98	0.79	1
China	80.86	82.35	0.98	0.791	1
EarthPorn	48.93	47.65	1.03	0.791	5
ProtectAndServe	68.97	71.76	0.96	0.791	2
TumblrInAction	72.39	73.72	0.98	0.792	5
chicago	70.98	72.54	0.98	0.794	2
Denver	74.52	76.23	0.98	0.795	2
talesfromtechsupport	74.42	74.99	0.99	0.8	5
forwardsfromgrandma	71.97	71.87	1	0.8	5
gaming	67.38	67.86	0.99	0.803	3
trees	72.34	69.43	1.04	0.803	0
Documentaries	65.16	67.01	0.97	0.803	1
metalgearsolid	73.5	74.33	0.99	0.804	3
PublicFreakout	64.42	64.08	1.01	0.804	5
offbeat	73.4	76.73	0.96	0.804	1
TwoBestFriendsPlay	77.9	78.3	0.99	0.805	3
LosAngeles	72.9	74.73	0.98	0.806	2
explainlikeimfive	73.28	76.26	0.96	0.807	5
whatisthisthing	61.1	59.35	1.03	0.808	5
nottheonion	67.33	68.82	0.98	0.812	5
Austin	78.35	81.43	0.96	0.812	2
army	74.93	75.26	1	0.814	2
SubredditDrama	69.59	70.97	0.98	0.815	1
weekendgunnit	67.8	60.63	1.12	0.816	4
HistoryPorn	59.95	59.49	1.01	0.816	1
toronto	72.25	74.51	0.97	0.817	1
dataisbeautiful	67.53	69.83	0.97	0.817	1
polandball	76.38	74.13	1.03	0.818	4
philadelphia	74.4	76.32	0.97	0.819	2
ireland	81.86	82.64	0.99	0.82	1
london	78.96	79.78	0.99	0.82	1
Whatcouldgowrong	65.73	63.96	1.03	0.82	5
india	82.2	81.55	1.01	0.824	1
TrollXChromosomes	62.66	65.22	0.96	0.825	0
furry	68.32	67.13	1.02	0.827	4
sydney	79.44	80.22	0.99	0.828	2
Random_Acts_Of_Amazon	58.85	56.22	1.05	0.828	4
ottawa	70.3	71.88	0.98	0.828	1
watchpeopledie	61.89	60.44	1.02	0.829	5
trashy	61.95	59.75	1.04	0.829	5
BlackPeopleTwitter	68.08	63.08	1.08	0.831	5
Art	47.23	47.1	1	0.831	1
Portland	79.22	81.43	0.97	0.831	2
Atlanta	68.99	70.68	0.98	0.833	2
Calgary	77.45	80.48	0.96	0.834	2
houston	75.12	76.18	0.99	0.834	2
creepyPMs	53.32	53.87	0.99	0.835	0
TalesFromRetail	61.27	63.24	0.97	0.838	0
justneckbeardthings	68.51	66.51	1.03	0.839	5
bestof	55.58	56.8	0.98	0.842	5
Military	73.37	74.32	0.99	0.843	1
self	60.25	63.57	0.95	0.843	0
tipofmytongue	56.53	52.54	1.08	0.843	5
shittyaskscience	80.42	79.24	1.01	0.845	5
cringepics	53.84	53.22	1.01	0.848	5
cringe	57.16	56.38	1.01	0.848	5
Wishlist	55.21	52.58	1.05	0.853	4
4chan	68.54	61.32	1.12	0.854	5
OldSchoolCool	58.75	57.78	1.02	0.856	5
roosterteeth	63.23	63.99	0.99	0.856	3
UpliftingNews	58.52	60.32	0.97	0.861	1
iamverysmart	66.58	66.41	1	0.862	5
teenagers	67.5	65.1	1.04	0.862	4
fireemblemcasual	64.14	62.75	1.02	0.865	4
melbourne	75.59	76.25	0.99	0.868	2

Subredddit	baseline Ppl_{M_j}	CCLM Ppl_{M_j}	IG_{M_j}	Ind_{M_j}	Social embed. cluster
newzealand	79.58	82.61	0.96	0.868	1
thatHappened	69.04	68.48	1.01	0.868	5
ImGoingToHellForThis	56.18	53.73	1.05	0.868	5
gaybros	71.02	75.55	0.94	0.872	0
RWBY	69.44	70.03	0.99	0.874	4
LifeProTips	64.54	65.85	0.98	0.875	5
OutOfTheLoop	60.83	64.38	0.94	0.875	5
WTF	69.05	67.8	1.02	0.876	5
AMA	61.41	63.51	0.97	0.876	0
Unexpected	59.3	57.25	1.04	0.876	5
nosleep	57.84	58	1	0.876	0
facepalm	64.59	65.56	0.99	0.877	5
todayilearned	77.6	78.75	0.99	0.878	5
rva	68.82	71.47	0.96	0.879	2
CasualConversation	62.58	64.02	0.98	0.88	0
tifu	64.84	65.06	1	0.88	5
oddlysatisfying	62.89	60.87	1.03	0.882	5
mylittlepony	64.29	63.91	1.01	0.883	4
videos	63.11	63.56	0.99	0.884	5
woahdude	63.53	61.9	1.03	0.885	5
gifs	63.96	62.03	1.03	0.886	5
creepy	61.21	59.49	1.03	0.886	5
Jokes	62.37	58.55	1.07	0.889	5
AdviceAnimals	66.09	69.02	0.96	0.89	5
mildlyinteresting	69.17	67.41	1.03	0.891	5
casualiama	60.5	62.03	0.98	0.891	0
NoStupidQuestions	66.89	69.53	0.96	0.893	0
interestingasfuck	63.16	61.9	1.02	0.897	5
CrappyDesign	66.41	66.1	1	0.901	5
pics	65.78	65.55	1	0.901	5
britishproblems	76.34	77.55	0.98	0.902	5
funny	62.25	61.28	1.02	0.902	5
mildlyinfuriating	67.46	67.37	1	0.906	5
CFBOffTopic	70.55	72.98	0.97	0.908	1
reactiongifs	54.47	54.14	1.01	0.909	5
singapore	81.94	85.02	0.96	0.912	2
AskReddit	74.3	75.72	0.98	0.913	5
MLPLounge	54.02	51.92	1.04	0.913	4
InternetIsBeautiful	64.82	65.13	1	0.914	1
Showerthoughts	71.29	69.45	1.03	0.918	5
IAmA	65.06	68.55	0.95	0.919	5

Understanding Interpersonal Conflict Types and their Impact on Perception Classification

Charles Welch †‡ and **Joan Plepi** † and **Béla Neuendorf** † and **Lucie Flek** †‡
† Conversational AI and Social Analytics (CAISA) Lab
Department of Mathematics and Computer Science, University of Marburg
‡ The Hessian Center for Artificial Intelligence (Hessian.AI)
{welchc,plepi,neuendob,lucie.flek}@uni-marburg.de

Abstract

Studies on interpersonal conflict have a long history and contain many suggestions for conflict typology. We use this as the basis of a novel annotation scheme and release a new dataset of situations and conflict aspect annotations. We then build a classifier to predict whether someone will perceive the actions of one individual as right or wrong in a given situation. Our analyses include conflict aspects, but also generated clusters, which are human validated, and show differences in conflict content based on the relationship of participants to the author. Our findings have important implications for understanding conflict and social norms.

1 Introduction

Understanding social norms is critical to understanding people's actions and intents, not only for humans, but also for artificial agents. The inability for artificial agents to take these norms into account may serve as a barrier to their ability to interact with humans (Pereira et al., 2016). However, perceptions of what is socially acceptable behavior vary and issues are often divisive (Lourie et al., 2021). It is critical to model these differences both to build higher performing systems and better understand people (Flek, 2020; Ovesdotter Alm, 2011).

In this work we classify an individual's assessment of conflict situations using the Reddit community `r/amitheasshole` (AITA). Previous work has examined the classification of social situations involving conflict at both the individual level, and community level (for the AITA subreddit). However, it does not consider the types of conflict situations from the perspective of existing conflict-focused literature.

We explore methods of clustering descriptions of social situations involving interpersonal conflict and perform a human evaluation and analysis. After proposing a novel annotation scheme, we annotate a set of 500 conflicts with six aspects of conflict. Aspects and clusters are then used to provide an analysis of our model performance.

We address the task of predicting whether someone will perceive the actions of one individual as right or wrong in a given situation. We hypothesize that, for the prediction model, (1) higher emotional intensity will make predicting the perception of conflict more difficult, (2) when more people are involved, conflict will be harder to assess, (3) the strength of disagreement will not affect prediction difficulty, and (4) that conflict over a longer duration, involving more interference, and that are more manifest than perceived, will be easier to predict, as the additional information gives a clearer picture of the situation and points of discussion.

2 Related Work

Many classification tasks are subjective in nature. While in some cases it may help to resolve differences between annotators (Hagerer et al., 2021), it is often insightful to acknowledge and explore the subjectivity of labels assigned by people or groups (Leonardelli et al., 2021; Sap et al., 2022a). A dataset with labels from individuals, termed *descriptive* annotations, will help us build models to better understand differences in people's views of socially acceptable behavior (Röttger et al., 2022).

Lourie et al. (2021) first examined AITA, suggesting that the descriptive ethics contained in people's judgements could serve as a valuable resource for developing machines that can appropriately and safely interact with people. Forbes et al. (2020) further attempted to derive rules-of-thumb from AITA to guide ethical reasoning. In contrast, our work classifies how individuals interpret these situations.

Several recent works have attempted to classify comments, or the judgement that individuals assign in their replies to posts. Efstathiadis et al. (2021) examined the classification of both posts and com-

Proceedings of the Fifth Workshop on Natural Language Processing and Computational Social Science (NLP+CSS), pages 79 - 88
November 7, 2022

ments on AITA, finding that posts were more difficult to classify. De Candia (2021) found that the subreddits where a user has previously posted can help predict how they will assign judgements and manually classified posts into five categories: family, friendship, work, society, and romantic relationships. More recently, Botzer et al. (2022) constructed a comment classifier and used it to study the behavior of users in different subreddits. Several of these works have examined characteristics of posts and authors and the judgements they receive, including passive voice, framing, gender, and age (Zhou et al., 2021; De Candia, 2021; Botzer et al., 2022).

Interpersonal Conflict. Distinctions between conflicts can be made based on who is involved. Intrapersonal occurs within oneself, while interpersonal occurs between individuals. Conflict with more people can occur within or across groups or organizations. Much research on the topic has focused on work goals and differentiates between task-related issues and those that result from differences in personality, values, or style (Pinkley, 1990). This work has found it useful to distinguish between conflicts concerning interpersonal incompatibilities and those that arise from the content of a task being performed (Jehn, 1995). Further types have been introduced, though meta-analyses have found these types to be highly correlated and thus researchers have called for improvements to how conflict is conceptualized and measured (Jehn, 1997; Korsgaard et al., 2008; Bendersky et al., 2014).

Barki and Hartwick (2004) surveyed work on interpersonal conflict and noted that studies focused on three common attributes: disagreement, negative emotion, and interference, which correspond to cognitions, emotions, and behaviors respectively. They suggest that these aspects vary across situations and that it is important to specify the target of the conflict. They define interpersonal conflict as "a dynamic process that occurs between interdependent parties as they experience negative emotional reactions to perceived disagreements and interference with the attainment of their goals." As this suggests, *conflict is about perception* (Hussein and Al-Mamary, 2019).

Korsgaard et al. (2008) referred to Barki and Hartwick (2004)'s three attributes as the experience of incompatibility, and suggested two additional considerations; differences in desired outcomes, behaviors, values, or beliefs, and the conflict between and among groups. Bendersky et al. (2014) further suggested clarifying the intensity of opposition (e.g. fight versus disagreement), specifying conflict duration, and distinguishing between perceived and manifest representations of conflict. These suggestions provided the basis of our annotation scheme described in §4.

To our knowledge, no study has yet examined computational approaches to classifying the perception of social situations from the perspective of previous work on interpersonal conflict.

3 Data

We collected data from Reddit, an online platform with many separate, focused communities called subreddits. In particular, we use data from the AITA subreddit, where members post a description of a social situation involving an interpersonal conflict and ask other members of the subreddit if they think the author of the post is the wrongdoer in the situation or not. Others will respond saying "you're the asshole" (YTA), or "not the asshole" (NTA). As an initial source to crawl the comments, we use the posts from Forbes et al. (2020). We crawl the post title together with its full text, and all the comments that contain a verdict (YTA or NTA, extracted with a list of variations). Our dataset contains 21K posts, and 364K verdicts (254K NTA, 110K YTA) written in English. To analyze the types of conflicts, we further group posts into distinct categories as described in §5.

4 Annotation of Conflict Aspects

Given the history of the typology of conflict, discussed in §2, we decided to measure six aspects of conflict; (1) strength of disagreement, (2) intensity of negative emotion, (3) degree of interference, (4) duration of conflict, (5) manifestation of conflict, and (6) how many people are involved. Aspects 1-3 correspond to the three attributes outlined by Barki and Hartwick (2004), but with the view of measuring their intensity. Bendersky et al. (2014)'s suggestions directly inspired aspects 4 and 5 and Korsgaard et al. (2008)'s suggestions about groups led to aspect 6.

The authors then annotated a sample of 25 conflicts in order to refine our task. This process made evident how previous conflict scales were not well-equipped for our data. Our conflict situations do not always take place in work settings. The nuance of scales like Jehn (1995) seemed unnecessary, as conflict is assumed in our setting and as a third party, levels of intensity are less clear (e.g. how to differentiate between degrees of friction, tension, emotional conflict, and personality conflict). Longitudinal aspects also cannot often be directly determined.

With these insights we refined our annotation questions, which are provided in Appendix A. A subset of 500 posts corresponding to 1,653 comments from the test set were provided to annotators. Matthews correlation coefficient (MCC, Matthews (1975)) was used to measure agreement between annotators for 100 posts and is shown in Table 1. We find moderate to strong agreement for most aspects with the exception of the degree of interference and whether the conflict is primarily manifest or perceived. For the non-binary aspects, we condensed labels (denoted by $\rightarrow$) and treat all labels as binary in subsequent analyses. Merged labels and label distributions are given in Appendix D.

Conflict Aspect	MCC
Disagreement Strength	0.39 $\rightarrow$ 0.49
Emotion Intensity	0.33 $\rightarrow$ 0.41
Interference Degree	0.13 $\rightarrow$ 0.20
Conflict Duration	0.39
Manifestation or Perception	0.10
Number of People	0.40

Table 1: Annotator agreement using Matthews correlation coefficient for all six aspects. For non-binary aspects, the improvement after merging labels is shown to the right of the $\rightarrow$.

5 Clustering

Before we acquired any annotated data, we performed an exploratory analysis to determine if there was a natural way of grouping conflicts into different types that would be useful for our analysis. We used two representations to perform clustering: situations and all text from the post (full text). Situations, as referred to in Forbes et al. (2020), come from the title of a Reddit post and serve as a summary of the situation described in the full post. The posts usually start with "AITA for", which we omit.

We cluster posts using Louvain clustering, which maximizes the modularity of our graph (Blondel et al., 2008). We create a weighted graph based on each criterion, using situations or full texts as nodes. Their embeddings are obtained with Sentence-BERT (SBERT; Reimers and Gurevych (2019)), and use the cosine similarity, normalized to $[0, 1]$ between each pair of nodes as weighted edges, resulting in two fully-connected graphs. The graphs are pruned by dropping the N% lowest edge weights determined by the adjusted Rand index between graphs with a 10% difference in the number of dropped edges in order to find a persistent clustering. This yields N=40% for situations and 30% for full texts. After clustering each had 3 clusters (see Appendix B).

Manually inspecting the clusters revealed that the groups differ from each other by the social relation of the author to the others in the situation, or how close the author is to others in the situation. For manual verification but also in an effort to explore possible modifications to the groupings, a subset of 100 posts were manually clustered by two of the authors, who intended to form a small number of groups based on the post title and content. While considering other possible groupings both came to the conclusion that it appears most natural to group the posts based on social relation. The events that occur in a conflict, understandably, appear strongly dependent on the relation between participants. Upon manual inspection and discussion between annotators, we find that differences arise from two sources. The first is boundaries between social relations. For instance, one annotator grouped family, romantic relationships, and best friends into one cluster, and put all other friends in a second cluster, while the other annotator put family in one cluster and all romantic relationships and friendships in a second. The second source of disagreement comes from perception of who is involved in the conflict. For instance, in one post, a person borrows an object from a family member's friend and although the family member is upset, we do not know if the friend is upset. One annotator saw this as a family conflict, while the other saw it as involving someone more distant. The ARI was 0.33 between humans, 0.38 and 0.15 between full text and humans, and 0.31 and 0.13 between humans and situations. We refer to the *Family* cluster and the clusters containing *Close* or more *Distant* individuals in subsequent analyses. Examples from each cluster type are shown in Appendix E.

6 Hypotheses

After choosing the six conflict types, we developed hypotheses about which values would be associated with conflicts whose verdicts would be most difficult for our model to predict. We hypothesized

Diff.	Disagreement $p < 0.002$ Mild	Strong	Emotion $p < 0.02$ Mild	Strong	Interference $p < 0.3$ Weak	Strong	Duration $p < 0.04$ Once	Longer	Manifestation $p < 0.04$ Perc.	Mani.	Num. People $p < 0.007$ One	More
Acc%	89.5	88.3	88.3	84.0	84.7	86.3	82.7	86.5	81.8	86.4	86.1	80.0
Micro F1%	70.8	69.5	70.0	69.6	56.4	85.5	68.2	70.7	51.9	73.7	73.1	42.5
Macro F1%	78.0	76.4	77.8	76.6	74.5	85.5	71.7	82.0	73.2	78.9	78.5	72.7

Table 2: Performance across conflict aspects (described in §4 and Table 1) for our model using the full text stratification, showing accuracy (Acc) and F1-score. Significance values for differences in model performance between each dyad are shown above, calculated with one-sided unpaired permutation tests.

that higher emotional intensity would be more difficult, as different people may empathize differently and the classification of emotions is known to be a challenging task in itself. When more people are involved in a conflict, we hypothesized that this would be harder for our model to predict. With more involved parties, coreference resolution becomes more challenging and the interaction of more parties may make interpretation of the situational context more complex. However, we thought that the classifier would perform similarly for both mild and strong disagreements, as we did not see why this aspect by itself would make the task more or less challenging.

We predicted that it will be easier for the model to predict conflicts that occur over a longer duration, that involve more interference, and that are more manifest than perceived. First, longer duration conflicts may mean that there has been more time to accumulate information about the conflict. In our observations, it also often means that someone is repeating an action. These repeated actions and additional information may give a clearer signal of what facts will lead to a verdict. Similarly, with interference, the action is much clearer when interference is high (e.g. someone taking something away from someone, or preventing people from seeing each other). Lastly, when conflict is manifest, it means that an annotator decided the conflict was more manifest than perceived by the author. When the conflict is more perceived, the reader has to infer more from the text. For example, the author may think they did something wrong (e.g. not moving in with friend) but the author does not seem to know how the other person feels.

7 Perception Experiments

We classify the perception of individuals based on their comments to posts. We concatenate the situation (post title) and comment text after filtering out any labels (e.g. YTA). As our base model, we fine-tune SBERT on the binary task of predicting the perception of the author, given by a verdict (YTA or NTA). We also tried using this model to encode the full text to use as additional features, though we found no difference in performance over using only the comment text and situation, which often succinctly captures the event.

		Full Text F1%	Full Text Acc%	Situation F1%	Situation Acc%
Botzer et al. (2022)	All	72.7	84.9	70.1	83.2
	Family	74.9	86.8	73.3	85.4
	Close	72.2	84.4	67.8	82.2
	Distant	71.2	82.2	68.5	80.8
Our Approach	All	77.2	87.0	77.4	87.2
	Family	79.0	88.3	78.7	88.4
	Close	76.7	86.9	77.4	86.9
	Distant	75.9	85.0	75.6	85.4

Table 3: Comparison between Botzer et al. (2022) and our approach with accuracy (Acc) and macro F1-score. Results are broken down by cluster (labels from §5).

We compare our model to the recent work of Botzer et al. (2022) JudgeBERT, which is a BERT-base (Devlin et al., 2019) model fine-tuned on our dataset, which is extended with a dropout layer and classification layer. JudgeBERT was evaluated in the work from Botzer et al. (2022) using a dataset with collections of posts submitted between January 1, 2017, and August 31, 2019, over different subreddits. For the purpose of this work, we re-implemented JudgeBERT in order to evaluate it on our dataset. The main difference between the two models is the encoder layer, where one uses a BERT-base model, and the other one a SBERT model. We train both models for 10 epochs, using the Adam optimizer, learning rate of $1e-4$ and focal loss (Lin et al., 2017) to cope with class imbalance. We split our dataset into 70-20-10 for training, validation, and test, respectively. We stratify in two ways, for each clustering method.

The results are reported in Table 3 for both models and splits. We see that our model significantly outperforms previous work on all data,[1] with a 5 point improvement on full text F1 (macro averaged over posts, which may have multiple verdicts from different users) and 7 points on situations.

We further break down our results by conflict aspects in Table 2. We find significant differences in our model's ability to predict perception of conflicts between each aspect dyad with the exception of interference, which had a label distribution least similar to the other conditions (see Appendix C). We correctly hypothesized that situations with more negative emotion would be more difficult for our classifier, though we also found this to be the case for disagreements. Further work is needed to understand the relation between disagreement strength and perception classification. We also correctly hypothesized that conflicts involving more people are more difficult for our classifier, and that stronger interference, longer duration, and primarily manifest conflicts were easier to classify, though the improvement for interference was not significant.

8 Discussion

Overall, our model outperforms previous work for our full data and for each cluster. As noted in §2, it is important to understand the subject of the conflict, though in our work we found that this was highly coupled with the type of relation between participants. Future work may consider ways of separating these concepts.

If one considers the Family cluster as the most close social relationship, we find an indirect relationship between the closeness of participants in a conflict and the difficulty in classifying perceptions of that conflict.

The closeness of relation to conflict participants, strength of negative emotions and opposition, duration of the conflict, manifestation, and the number of people involved all impact on our classifier's ability to classify people's perception of social norms. These findings pertain to the understanding of conflict, behavior, and personal narratives, but may prove useful for other tasks such as argumentation, framing detection, and understanding offensive speech.

9 Conclusions

We developed a novel annotation scheme for aspects of conflict and built a classifier to predict individual people's perception of right and wrong. Our analysis with the aspects and generated clusters showed that the closeness in social relation between people in conflict, strength of disagreement and negative emotion, conflict duration, manifestation, and the number of people involved all impact the difficulty of predicting personal perceptions. Future work on language understanding and social norms should consider the impact of these aspects. Our code and dataset containing 21K posts, 364K comments, two sets of cluster labels, and our 500 posts labeled with the six conflict aspects, corresponding to 1,653 verdicts is available on our GitHub.[2]

Limitations

Our experiments were performed using only English data from one subreddit discussing interpersonal conflicts. The data source conveniently provided annotated data for our application, but our findings may not fully generalize to other data sources or languages. Demographics of Reddit users are skewed toward certain populations. Similarly, we did not collect demographics of the crowd annotators, which has been shown to explain disagreements in annotation (Sap et al., 2022b).

There are many modeling decisions that could lead to better performing methods. Although we explored different clustering methods and parameters in preliminary experiments, it is possible other methods and interpretation by different human annotators would lead to different cluster themes.

Our novel annotation scheme has not been thoroughly validated, and agreement for some aspects is low. The scheme and annotation instructions could be refined in future work which may lead to higher agreement, particularly for assessing interference and the manifestation of conflict.

Ethics Statement

Better understanding social norms is important both for humans and artificial agents. Acknowledging that artificial agents could benefit from understanding that different people have different perspectives could lead to a type of author profiling task, where a model is used to predict someone's opinion of a conflict or type of conflict (Rangel et al., 2013). This could potentially be harmful in applications regardless of intention. We recommend against using such a model in applications

[1] Permutation test for full text and situations, $p < 0.0001$.

[2] `https://github.com/caisa-lab/interpersonal-conflict-types`

where the user is unaware of data being collected about them and the purpose of collection. Even with user consent, models that misclassify user's perceptions may lead to undesired outcomes depending on the application.

Acknowledgements

This work has been supported by the German Federal Ministry of Education and Research (BMBF) as a part of the Junior AI Scientists program under the reference 01-S20060, the Alexander von Humboldt Foundation, and by Hessian.AI. Any opinions, findings, conclusions, or recommendations in this material are those of the authors and do not necessarily reflect the views of the BMBF, Alexander von Humboldt Foundation, or Hessian.AI.

References

Henri Barki and Jon Hartwick. 2004. Conceptualizing the construct of interpersonal conflict. *International journal of conflict management.*

Corinne Bendersky, Julia Bear, Kristin Behfar, Laurie R Weingart, Gergana Todorova, and Karen A Jehn. 2014. Identifying gaps between the conceptualization of conflict and its measurement. In *Handbook of conflict management research.* Edward Elgar Publishing.

Vincent D Blondel, Jean-Loup Guillaume, Renaud Lambiotte, and Etienne Lefebvre. 2008. Fast unfolding of communities in large networks. *Journal of statistical mechanics: theory and experiment*, 2008(10).

Nicholas Botzer, Shawn Gu, and Tim Weninger. 2022. Analysis of moral judgement on reddit. IEEE Transactions on Computational Social Sciences.

Sara De Candia. 2021. Modeling the boundaries of social norms online. Master's thesis.

Jacob Devlin, Ming-Wei Chang, Kenton Lee, and Kristina Toutanova. 2019. BERT: Pre-training of deep bidirectional transformers for language understanding. In *Proceedings of the 2019 Conference of the North American Chapter of the Association for Computational Linguistics: Human Language Technologies, Volume 1 (Long and Short Papers)*, Minneapolis, Minnesota.

Ion Stagkos Efstathiadis, Guilherme Paulino-Passos, and Francesca Toni. 2021. Explainable patterns for distinction and prediction of moral judgement on reddit. In *Proceedings of the 1st Workshop on Human and Machine Decisions (WHMD 2021)*. Conference on Neural Information Processing Systems (NeurIPS).

Lucie Flek. 2020. Returning the N to NLP: Towards contextually personalized classification models. In *Proceedings of the 58th Annual Meeting of the Association for Computational Linguistics*, Online.

Maxwell Forbes, Jena D. Hwang, Vered Shwartz, Maarten Sap, and Yejin Choi. 2020. Social chemistry 101: Learning to reason about social and moral norms. In *Proceedings of the 2020 Conference on Empirical Methods in Natural Language Processing (EMNLP)*, Online.

Gerhard Hagerer, David Szabo, Andreas Koch, Maria Luisa Ripoll Dominguez, Christian Widmer, Maximilian Wich, Hannah Danner, and Georg Groh. 2021. End-to-end annotator bias approximation on crowdsourced single-label sentiment analysis. In *Proceedings of The Fourth International Conference on Natural Language and Speech Processing (ICNLSP 2021)*, Trento, Italy.

Abdul Fattah Farea Hussein and Yaser Hasan Salem Al-Mamary. 2019. Conflicts: Their types, and their negative and positive effects on organizations. *International Journal of Scientific & Technology Research*, 8(8).

Karen A Jehn. 1995. A multimethod examination of the benefits and detriments of intragroup conflict. *Administrative science quarterly.*

Karen A Jehn. 1997. A qualitative analysis of conflict types and dimensions in organizational groups. *Administrative science quarterly.*

M Audrey Korsgaard, Sophia Soyoung Jeong, Douglas M Mahony, and Adrian H Pitariu. 2008. A multilevel view of intragroup conflict. *Journal of management*, 34(6).

Elisa Leonardelli, Stefano Menini, Alessio Palmero Aprosio, Marco Guerini, and Sara Tonelli. 2021. Agreeing to disagree: Annotating offensive language datasets with annotators' disagreement. In *Proceedings of the 2021 Conference on Empirical Methods in Natural Language Processing*, Online and Punta Cana, Dominican Republic.

Tsung-Yi Lin, Priya Goyal, Ross B. Girshick, Kaiming He, and Piotr Dollár. 2017. Focal loss for dense object detection. In *IEEE International Conference on Computer Vision, ICCV 2017, Venice, Italy, October 22-29, 2017*. IEEE Computer Society.

Nicholas Lourie, Ronan Le Bras, and Yejin Choi. 2021. Scruples: A corpus of community ethical judgments on 32,000 real-life anecdotes. In *Proceedings of the AAAI Conference on Artificial Intelligence*, volume 35.

Brian W Matthews. 1975. Comparison of the predicted and observed secondary structure of t4 phage lysozyme. *Biochimica et Biophysica Acta (BBA)-Protein Structure*, 405(2):442–451.

Cecilia Ovesdotter Alm. 2011. Subjective natural language problems: Motivations, applications, characterizations, and implications. In *Proceedings of the 49th Annual Meeting of the Association for Computational Linguistics: Human Language Technologies*, Portland, Oregon, USA.

Gonçalo Pereira, Rui Prada, and Pedro A Santos. 2016. Integrating social power into the decision-making of cognitive agents. *Artificial Intelligence*, 241.

Robin L Pinkley. 1990. Dimensions of conflict frame: Disputant interpretations of conflict. *Journal of applied psychology*, 75(2).

Francisco Rangel, Paolo Rosso, Moshe Koppel, Efstathios Stamatatos, and Giacomo Inches. 2013. Overview of the author profiling task at pan 2013. In *CLEF Conference on Multilingual and Multimodal Information Access Evaluation*. CELCT.

Nils Reimers and Iryna Gurevych. 2019. Sentence-BERT: Sentence embeddings using Siamese BERT-networks. In *Proceedings of the 2019 Conference on Empirical Methods in Natural Language Processing and the 9th International Joint Conference on Natural Language Processing (EMNLP-IJCNLP)*, Hong Kong, China.

Paul Röttger, Bertie Vidgen, Dirk Hovy, and Janet B Pierrehumbert. 2022. Two contrasting data annotation paradigms for subjective NLP tasks. In *Proceedings of the 2022 Conference of the North American Chapter of the Association for Computational Linguistics: Human Language Technologies*.

Maarten Sap, Swabha Swayamdipta, Laura Vianna, Xuhui Zhou, Yejin Choi, and Noah A Smith. 2022a. Annotators with attitudes: How annotator beliefs and identities bias toxic language detection. In *Proceedings of the 2022 Conference of the North American Chapter of the Association for Computational Linguistics: Human Language Technologies*.

Maarten Sap, Swabha Swayamdipta, Laura Vianna, Xuhui Zhou, Yejin Choi, and Noah A. Smith. 2022b. Annotators with attitudes: How annotator beliefs and identities bias toxic language detection. In *Proceedings of the 2022 Conference of the North American Chapter of the Association for Computational Linguistics: Human Language Technologies*, pages 5884–5906, Seattle, United States. Association for Computational Linguistics.

Karen Zhou, Ana Smith, and Lillian Lee. 2021. Assessing cognitive linguistic influences in the assignment of blame. In *Proceedings of the Ninth International Workshop on Natural Language Processing for Social Media*, Online.

A Annotation Task

We recruited annotators from the crowdsourcing platform Prolific,[3] as well as asking researchers at our university to help annotate as part of their paid working time. There were 14 annotators in total and all were required to have English fluency. All surveys included two attention check questions that provided the same options as the disagreement strength and negative emotion questions, but asked "How should you answer this question? You should answer", followed by one of the three options. All annotators passed all attention checks. Annotators were asked the following six questions for each Reddit post and additional details on how the labels should be used:

1. How strong is the disagreement or opposition? **Labels:** (Mild, Strong, Intense) with Strong and Intense merged. **Additional details:** You should consider how significant the event seems to the author. For example, a conflict over who should clean the dishes may seem mild, whereas a conflict over divorce may seem intense. However, if the author describes the conflict over dishes as a fight that is causing irreparable damage to the relationship, it may be strong or intense.

2. How intense are the negative emotions? **Labels:** (Mild, Strong, Intense) with Strong and Intense merged. **Additional details:** Use the mild label when emotions are weaker, or it is not clear if they are there at all. Use the strong and intense labels to differentiate between situations where you perceive stronger emotions from the participants.

3. How much is one person interfering with what another wants to or can do? **Labels:** (Not at all, Somewhat, Strongly) with Not at all and Somewhat merged. **Additional Details:** If someone clearly cannot do what they would like and that is the subject of the conflict, then the interference is strong. If there is a disagreement, but parties can still take whichever action they desire, then there is no interference (e.g. telling someone not to do their homework but not stopping them from doing it). If there are alternatives or possibility for some degree of compromise then there is some interference (e.g. a tenant is upset that they cannot pay rent in two parts, landlord gives several alternatives), but if the restricted party is clearly opposed to all options then the interference is still strong (e.g. daughter is not allowed to go to boyfriends house).

[3] `https://www.prolific.co/`

Cutoff %	0	10	20	30	40	50	60	70	80	90
Number of Situation Clusters	4	3	4	3	3	4	4	4	4	4
Situation ARI	-	0.44	0.47	0.46	0.93	0.57	0.45	0.49	0.91	0.85
Number of Fulltext Clusters	3	3	3	4	3	5	8	18	49	165
Full Text ARI	-	0.60	0.92	0.91	0.75	0.72	0.74	0.89	0.81	0.65

Table 4: The resulting number of clusters using Louvain for different graph representations, and cutoff percentages. ARI denotes the adjusted rand index between the listed cutoff percentage and 10% less.

Disagreement		Emotion		Interference		Duration		Manifestation		Num. People	
Mild	Strong	Mild	Strong	Weak	Strong	Once	Longer	Perc.	Mani.	One	More
33.0	67.0	35.7	64.3	35.3	64.7	48.3	51.7	33.7	66.3	72.0	28.0

Table 5: Label distribution for merged label values resulting from human annotation of 500 posts.

4. What is the duration of the conflict? **Labels:** (One-time incident, Longer) **Additional Details:** Additional Details: If someone describes a specific incident that occurred at one point in time then it is a one-time incident (e.g. posting something rude one time on Facebook, not wanting sibling to take over a family vacation with her plans). If the author explicitly states that something is an ongoing conflict over multiple days (or longer), or if it can be reasonably inferred that a conflict spans multiple days (e.g. "every time I talk to my parents we have this problem"), then the conflict is longer term.

5. Has the conflict primarily manifested in what someone has said or done, or is the conflict primarily perceived by the author? **Labels:** (Manifest, Perceived) **Additional Details:** Additional Details: A conflict can become manifest, for example, in the form of fights, arguments, telling someone something, or taking something, whereas the perception of conflict happens inside someone's head (e.g. someone thinks of themselves as rude/mean/unfair, but we do not know if another party has this same perception because we do not know what they have said or done or if they are aware of or have engaged in the same events as the author). For example, the author feels bad for not texting his parents back quickly. If we have no evidence that this is causing problems between them or that the parents have a problem with this then it is perceived. Sometimes there are small manifestations, but the conflict is still mostly perceived. For instance, the author is blocked on Facebook for not inviting a friend to a party, but the author does not seem to engage with the other person or understand why this is a conflict. In this case it is primarily perceived by the other person.

6. Who else is directly in conflict with the author? **Labels:** (One person, Multiple people) **Additional Details:** Additional Details: A conflict with multiple people should only count people engaging with or contributing to the conflict. For example, if A tells B to shave their beard and C gets mad at B for doing so, B and C are in conflict but as long as A does not engage, they should not be considered to be part of the conflict and so this would be a one person conflict.

B Clustering

When clustering, we first determined how many edges from our fully-connected graphs to drop. This was determined using the adjusted rand index between 10% differences. Further threshold values, ARI, and resulting cluster numbers are provided in 4. Although we do use a cutoff of 30% for full texts, which has 4 clusters, one of these clusters contained only 25 posts, so we removed it. We experimented with K-means in preliminary experiments but found that it had lower agreement with human clusters and clusters seemed less clear.

C Judgements Across Aspects

We also find that the types of judgements in our sample vary significantly across each aspect of conflict. The difference in the distribution of NTA and YTA labels between each dyad shown in Table 2 is statistically significant using Fisher's exact test. In the difference for disagreement ($p < 0.004$),

Strong contains an 11% higher ratio of YTA/NTA judgements. For emotion ($p < 0.02$), this difference was 9%. Interference ($p < 0.001$) had the highest difference of 78%, with more YTA judgements when the degree was *Strong*. For duration ($p < 0.001$), *One-time incidents* had a 13% higher ratio. Manifestation of conflict ($p < 0.0003$) showed a 13% higher ratio when conflict was more manifest than perceived. Lastly, when only one person was involved ($p < 0.03$), the ratio of YTA/NTA was 11% higher. All ratios skew toward more NTA, as this is the overall bias of the dataset, and all differences in ratio are calculated as absolute differences of YTA/NTA between values of an aspect.

D Label Merging and Distribution

As discussed in §4, we merged labels for aspects that had more than two labels. The *strong* and *intense* labels for the negative emotion and disagreement aspects were merged into one *strong* category. The *lesser* and *none* labels for the degree of interference were merged into *mild*. Other labels were already binary and were unchanged. The resulting distribution is shown in Table 5.

E Cluster Examples

Two examples of posts belonging to each of the clusters are shown in Table 6. Clusters were obtained using the full text.

Family
Situation: Helping my sister take my parents cat **Full Text:** Some context: my sister raised a litter of kittens from 4 days old, and my parents decided to keep one of them. We'll call him F. F wasn't learning to stay off counters, so my mother put a shock collar on him. My sister learned of on her birthday, and is vehemently against it, saying that it's cruel, and that cats don't learn like dogs do. Last night, I helped my sister sneak him out of the house, to her college dorm. AITA? **Situation:** Not watching horror films with my husband **Full Text:** I really don't like horror movies. I dislike gore and loud noise out of nowhere shock tactics especially, but I also have a tendency to get nightmares from movies that don't have those issues. I don't enjoy being scared. Plot holes also stick out like a sure thumb in horror to me. I will try movies on occasion if he really wants me to see them and he says it isn't a gore/shock tactic movie, but it takes a lot of pleading on his part. I almost never enjoy them and generally my reaction is that it was okay/fine, wouldn't watch it again. I watch things I want to see but he wouldn't enjoy separately. I ask him to watch things that I think he will actually like sometimes and he always does. He often watches horror after I go to bed. The things we watch together are things we are both agreeable to. We watch at home. I only wonder if I'm the asshole because it seems common for couples to trade off who picks movies.
Close Relationships
Situation: Feeling abandoned by all my friends after a break up **Full Text:** Well, long story short , i had no friends until I met this girl which I dates for about a year, she included me in his close circle of friends, and I thought they like me for who I was, not only because we were dating. Oh, well, I was wrong. we break up, and now none of my supposed friends talk to me, no one wants to hang out, and when I pointed that out to the one of them that I feel the more trust via text message, he just call me an asshole, but whatever, that doesn't change the facts that I'm now as alone as I started. Roast me reddit **Situation:** Not attending my friend's debut **Full Text:** She already placed me on a list where they call people up to give gifts ad stuff without eve asking beforehand if I'll be able to attend. I feel like a real asshole right now because 18th birthdays only happen once in a lifetime ad I wasn't there to celebrate with her when she was expecting me because I needed to attend a birthday for my uncle who was released out of prison. On the other hand, I do feel a bit angry that she listed me before asking. Now everyone has cards with my name on them, ad whoever is attending will expect me to join as well. I feel some conflict. She didn't even tell me the address, she just told me that I'm invited and my name is on the card and I need to give her a gift. She seemed really disappointed days ago when I told her that i could't attend. Stopped talking to me. Didn't even look at me. Tried texting my other friends who were invited but didn't respond. Too busy partying. I have a feeling that people will think of me as a shitty friend and that I'm no good. So, AITA?
Distant Relationships
Situation: Leaving low tips **Full Text:** So there was an event at a bar/club I bought a ticket for online, *pre-paid* - but when I got there, even though I had a ticket, they were unable to let me in due to "max capacity". I mean, normally I don't take it to heart and either wait or find somewhere else, but this was something that I paid for, so I figured it's not fair since I technically paid to be part of that 'capacity'. There were a few others in the same boat as me who they had to do that to who were also frustrated. Eventually I got in, but I was super aggravated because I ended up missing over an hour of the event because of this, and while I was able to eventually enjoy my night I found myself leaving low tips, since I was quite livid (and felt I lost some of my money's worth). Later on I felt kind of bad because I realized it's probably not the bartenders' faults. AITA though? **Situation:** Getting mad at an elderly co-worker for always getting my name wrong **Full Text:** Ok, so i work for a store and one of the employees is this elderly man, about 71 or so. Now, he always gets my name wrong. He always greets me as "Eddie". My name is nowhere close to Eddie. There is no Eddie anywhere in the store. I'm the only one he calls by the wrong name. "How goes it, Eddie?" "Eddie, why are you stacking those like that?" "Eddie, that's not how you use the coffee machine!" At first, i let it slide because i just figured he was senile and didn't know who i was. I corrected him, he called me by my name for about a day. The next day, he kept calling me Eddie. TBH i wouldn't mind it, this guy is kind of a prick. He isn't above me in terms of position, we hold the same position. He's not a manager or anything. But he corrects me on every little thing. Even though i'm doing it the way the boss told me. My first day stocking shelves, i was apparently putting the stuff up wrong. I was putting top shelf items on the bottom shelf. The manager corrected me. While the manager is trying to show me the right way, he shouts across the room. "Now Eddie! I know you got more sense then that! Put that stuff on the bottom shelf where it belongs!" The manager was already telling me how, but he chose to embarrass me in front of the entire store. He makes fun of me for being on a diet. I got a salad for lunch and he started mocking me "Hell, Eddie, that's not enough to even keep a damn bird alive!" So, i finally snapped. I shouted at him that my name wasn't Eddie. "My God, My name's not Eddie! Jesus, if you're gonna act like you run this place, at least get my fucking name right!" Everyone in the store was staring at me and i feel kind of guilty. But was i truly the a-hole in this situation?

Table 6: Two examples of post situations and full text for each of the three clusters (manually labeled, but automatically clustered using the full text).

Examining Political Rhetoric with Epistemic Stance Detection

Ankita Gupta[◇] **Su Lin Blodgett**[♡] **Justin H Gross**[◇] **Brendan O'Connor**[◇]

[◇]University of Massachusetts Amherst, [♡]Microsoft Research
{ankitagupta,jhgross,brenocon}@umass.edu
sublodge@microsoft.com

Abstract

Participants in political discourse employ rhetorical strategies—such as hedging, attributions, or denials—to display varying degrees of belief commitments to claims proposed by themselves or others. Traditionally, political scientists have studied these epistemic phenomena through labor-intensive manual content analysis. We propose to help automate such work through epistemic stance prediction, drawn from research in computational semantics, to distinguish at the clausal level what is asserted, denied, or only ambivalently suggested by the author or other mentioned entities (*belief holders*). We first develop a simple RoBERTa-based model for multi-source stance predictions that outperforms more complex state-of-the-art modeling. Then we demonstrate its novel application to political science by conducting a large-scale analysis of the Mass Market Manifestos corpus of U.S. political opinion books, where we characterize trends in cited belief holders—respected allies and opposed bogeymen—across U.S. political ideologies.

1 Introduction

Political argumentation is rich with assertions, hypotheticals and disputes over opponent's claims. While making these arguments, political actors often employ several rhetorical strategies to display varying degrees of commitments to their claims. For instance, political scientists have studied the *footing-shift* strategy, where actors convey their own beliefs while claiming that they belong to someone else (Goffman, 1981; Clayman, 1992). Sometimes they may attribute their beliefs to a majority of the population via *argument from popular opinion* (Walton et al., 2008). Actors can also resort to *hedging*, stating their own beliefs, but qualified with a partial degree of certainty (Fraser, 2010; Lakoff, 1975; Hyland, 1996) or express simple *political disagreements*, contradicting claims made by their opponents (Jang, 2009; Klofstad et al., 2013; Frances, 2014; Christensen, 2009).

Traditionally, political scientists and other scholars have manually analyzed the impact of such strategies and argumentation on audience perception (Clayman, 1992; Fraser, 2010). Recent advances in natural language processing (NLP) and digital repositories of political texts have enabled researchers to conduct large-scale analyses of political arguments using methods such as subjectivity analysis (Liu, 2012; Pang and Lee, 2008), argument mining (Trautmann et al., 2020; Toulmin, 1958; Walton, 1996), and opinion mining (Wiebe et al., 2005; Bethard et al., 2004; Kim and Hovy, 2004; Choi et al., 2005). While these approaches primarily concern argument structure and normative attitudes, we propose a complementary approach to analyze sources' *epistemic* attitudes towards assertions (Langacker, 2009; Anderson, 1986; Arrese, 2009)—what they believe to be true and the extent to which they commit to these beliefs.

Consider an example shown in Figure 1, where the author of the text (s1) quotes a speculation from the Congressional Quarterly (s2) about what Mitch McConnell (s3) said concerning Obama (s4). In this example, while the author of the text believes that the Congressional Quarterly hinted something about McConnell (thus, exhibiting a *certainly positive* (*CT+*) stance towards the event (e1), she remains *uncommitted* (*Uu*) about the quoted event (e3) that McConnell describes (edge omitted for visual clarity). Of course, this event is asserted as *certainly negative* (*CT-*) by McConnell, the speaker of the quote. The Congressional Quarterly suggests that Mitch McConnell made a statement (a *probably positive* (*PR+*) stance towards e2) while remaining *uncommitted* towards what he said. Finally, *Obama*'s own beliefs about whether he paid attention to Republican ideas are not expressed in this sentence; thus, s4 (Obama) has a *non-epistemic* label toward the listening event (e3).

To address this challenging problem of epistemological analysis, researchers within the NLP community have created several datasets and models

Proceedings of the Fifth Workshop on Natural Language Processing and Computational Social Science (NLP+CSS), pages 89 - 104
November 7, 2022

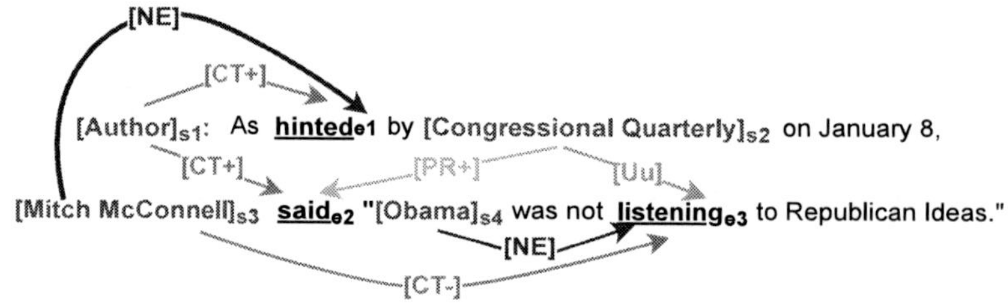

Figure 1: Illustrative example, simplified and adapted from a sentence in the Mass Market Manifestos corpus. There are four sources (s1–s4) and three events (e1–e3) with $4 \times 3 = 12$ labels between them; all epistemic stances are shown, but most non-epistemic (NE) labels are hidden for clarity. §1 and §3 describe the labels.

in various domains (Minard et al., 2016; Rambow et al., 2016; Rudinger et al., 2018b; Lee et al., 2015; Stanovsky et al., 2017; White et al., 2016; de Marneffe et al., 2012), often motivated directly by the interesting challenges of these linguistic semantic phenomena. However, there is a great potential to use an epistemic stance framework to analyze social relations (Soni et al., 2014; Prabhakaran et al., 2015; Swamy et al., 2017), motivating us to further advance this framework to support analysis of common rhetorical strategies and argumentation styles used in political discourse.

In this paper, we seek to further how *epistemic stance* analysis can help computationally investigate the use of *rhetorical strategies* employed in political discourse. In particular, we use the theory, structure and annotations of FactBank (Saurí and Pustejovsky, 2009), an expert-annotated corpus drawn from English news articles, which distinguishes different types of epistemic stances expressed in text. FactBank features annotations not just for the author, but also other sources (entities) mentioned in the text. Such multi-source annotations allow us to disambiguate the author's own beliefs from the beliefs they attribute to others.

Our main contributions in this work are:

- We conduct a literature review connecting ideas related to epistemic stance as studied across several disconnected scholarly areas of linguistics, NLP, and political science (§2).
- We develop a fine-tuned RoBERTa model (Liu et al., 2019) for multi-source epistemic stance prediction (§4), whose simplicity makes it accessible to social scientist users,[1] while performing at par with a more complex state-of-the-art model (Qian et al., 2018).
- We use our model to identify the most frequent *belief holders* which are epistemic sources whose views or statements are expressed by the author. Identifying belief holders is an essential first step in analyzing rhetorical strategies and arguments. We conduct this study on the Mass-Market Manifestos (MMM) Corpus, a collection of 370 contemporary English-language political books authored by an ideologically diverse group of U.S. political opinion leaders. We compare results to traditional named entity recognition. Finally, we analyze differences in what belief holders tend to be cited by left-wing versus right-wing authors, revealing interesting avenues for future work in the study of U.S. political opinion (§5).
- In the appendix, we additionally validate our model by replicating an existing manual case study comparing the commitment levels of different political leaders (§D, Jalilifar and Alavi, 2011), and give further analysis of the model's behavior with negative polarity items and different types of belief holders (§E).

2 Epistemic Stance from Different Perspectives

The notion of epistemic stances has been studied under several scholarly areas, including linguistics, political science and NLP. In this section, we discuss various notions of epistemic stances and how they have been utilized in these different areas.

2.1 Epistemic Stance in Linguistics

A speaker's *epistemic stance* is their positioning about their knowledge of, or veracity of, communicated events and assertions (Biber and Finegan, 1989; Palmer, 2001; Langacker, 2009). Epistemic stance relates to the concept of *modality*, which deals with the degree of certainty of situations in

[1]All resources accompanying this project are added to our project page: `https://github.com/slanglab/ExPRES`

the world, and has been extensively studied under linguistics (Kiefer, 1987; Palmer, 2001; Lyons, 1977; Chafe, 1986) and logic (Horn, 1972; Hintikka, 1962; Hoek, 1990; Holliday, 2018). From a cognitivist perspective, epistemic stance concerns the pragmatic relation between speakers and their knowledge regarding assertions (Biber and Finegan, 1989; Mushin, 2001; Martin and White, 2005).

2.2 Epistemic Stance in Political Science

The use of epistemic stances is widespread in political communication and persuasive language, to describe assertions when attempting to influence the reader's view (Chilton, 2004; Arrese, 2009). For instance, Chilton (2004) studies use of epistemic stances by speakers/writers for legitimisation and coercion; Arrese (2009) examines epistemic stances taken by speakers to reveal their ideologies. In these studies, a speaker's communicated stance may follow what they believe due to their experiences, inferences, and mental state (Anderson, 1986). From a psychological perspective, Shaffer (1981) employs balance theory (Heider, 1946)—the cognitive effect of knowing an entity's stance towards an issue—in explaining public perceptions of presidential candidates' issue positions.

2.3 Epistemic Stance in NLP

In the NLP literature, epistemic stances—typically of authors, and sometimes of mentioned textual entities—have been studied under the related concepts of *factuality* (Saurí and Pustejovsky, 2012; Rudinger et al., 2018a; Lee et al., 2015; Stanovsky et al., 2017; Minard et al., 2016; Soni et al., 2014) and *belief commitments* (Prabhakaran et al., 2015; Diab et al., 2009). de Marneffe et al. (2012) prefers the term *veridicality* to study the reader's, not author's, perspective.

We use the term *epistemic stance* to avoid confusion with at least two more recent subliteratures that use *factuality* differently from the above. In misinformation detection, factuality refers to a proposition's objective truth (Rashkin et al., 2017; Mihaylova et al., 2018; Thorne et al., 2018; Vlachos and Riedel, 2014). By contrast, we follow the epistemic stance approach in not assuming any objective reality—we simply model whatever subjective reality that agents assert. Furthermore, text generation work has studied whether text summaries conform to a source text's asserted propositions—termed the factuality or "factual correctness" of a summary (Maynez et al., 2020; Wiseman et al., 2017; Kryscinski et al., 2019; Dhingra et al., 2019).

Type	Dataset	Perspective	Genre	Label
Factuality	FactBank (Saurí and Pustejovsky, 2012)	Multi	News	Disc (8)
	Stanovsky et al., 2017	Author	News	Cont [-3, 3]
	MEANTIME (Minard et al., 2016)	Multi	News (Italian)	Disc (3)
	Lee et al., 2015	Author	News	Cont [-3, 3]
	UDS-IH2 (Rudinger et al., 2018b)	Author	Open	Disc (2) & Conf [0,4]
	Yao et al., 2021	Multi	News	Disc (6)
	Vigus et al., 2019	Multi	Open	Disc (6)
Indirect Reporting	Soni et al., 2014	Reader	Twitter	Likert (5)
Pragmatic Veridicality	PragBank (de Marneffe et al., 2012)	Reader	News	Disc (7)
Beliefs	Diab et al., 2009	Author	Open	Disc (3)
	Prabhakaran et al., 2015	Author	Forums	Disc (4)

Table 1: Summary of epistemic stance annotated datasets. *Perspective*: which sources are considered for annotation? Stance *Label* may be discrete with the given number of categories (where many or all are ordered), or continuous with a bounded range.[2] All datasets except MEANTIME consist of English text.

Several researchers in NLP have explored interesting social science applications in multiple settings such as organizational interactions (Prabhakaran et al., 2010), Supreme Court hearings (Danescu-Niculescu-Mizil et al., 2012), discussion (Bracewell et al., 2012; Swayamdipta and Rambow, 2012) and online forums (Biran et al., 2012; Rosenthal, 2014). In particular, Prabhakaran et al. (2010) use epistemic stances to analyse power relations in organizational interactions. These studies demonstrate the potential of using epistemic stance analysis for social science applications. Motivated by these advances, we use epistemic stance framework to analyze political rhetoric, a genre that has not been explored earlier.

Existing Datasets Several existing datasets (Rudinger et al., 2018b; Lee et al., 2015; Prabhakaran et al., 2015; Diab et al., 2009; Stanovsky et al., 2017) have successfully driven the progress of epistemic stance analysis in NLP, but have largely focused on author-only analysis. Soni et al. (2014) and de Marneffe et al. (2012) examine epistemic stances from the reader's (not author's) perspective. Table 1 summarizes these datasets.[2]

Political discourse is a particularly interesting because the multiple sources discussed can have diverse stances towards the same event. Among all existing datasets, FactBank (Saurí and Pustejovsky, 2012) and MEANTIME (Minard et al., 2016) explore multi-source analysis in the news domain.

[2]UDS-IH2 collects a binary category and a confidence score. Yao et al. (2021) and Vigus et al. (2019) extend multi-source annotations as dependency graphs with additional edge types.

Algorithm	Features/Model	Perspective	Systems
Rule-Based	Predicate Lexicons	Author	Nairn et al., 2006 Lotan et al., 2013 (TruthTeller)
		Multiple	Saurí and Pustejovsky, 2012 (DeFacto)
Feature-Based Supervised Machine Learning	Lexico-Syntactic	Author	Diab et al., 2009, Lee et al., 2015 Prabhakaran et al., 2015
		Reader	de Marneffe et al., 2012 Soni et al., 2014
		Multiple	Qian et al., 2015
	Output of Rule System	Author	Stanovsky et al., 2017
		Multiple	Saurí and Pustejovsky, 2012
Neural Networks (NN)	LSTM	Author	Rudinger et al., 2018b
	GAN	Multiple	Qian et al., 2018
	Graph NN	Author	Pouran Ben Veyseh et al., 2019
Neural Pretrained	BERT	Author	Jiang and de Marneffe, 2021
		Multiple	This work

Table 2: Epistemic stance prediction models.

While MEANTIME has helped advance epistemic stance analysis in Italian, FactBank—built on English news text—is closest to our goal.

Existing Models Several computational models have been developed for epistemic stance prediction as explicated in Table 2. Early models proposed deterministic algorithms based on hand-engineered implicative signatures for predicate lexicons (Lotan et al., 2013; Nairn et al., 2006; Saurí and Pustejovsky, 2012). A number of systems used lexico-syntactic features with supervised machine learning models, such as SVMs or CRFs (Diab et al., 2009; Prabhakaran et al., 2010; Lee et al., 2015; Saurí and Pustejovsky, 2012; Stanovsky et al., 2017). Lately, there has been a growing interest in using neural models for epistemic stance prediction (Rudinger et al., 2018b; Pouran Ben Veyseh et al., 2019), though sometimes with complex, task-specific network architectures (e.g. GANs; Qian et al. (2018)), which raise questions about generalization and replicability for practical use by experts from other fields. Recently, Jiang and de Marneffe (2021) explore fine-tuning pre-trained language models (LM), such as BERT, for author-only epistemic stance prediction by adding a simple task-specific layer. We take this more robust approach, extending it to multiple sources.

General Stance Detection in NLP Recently, there has been a growing interest in analyzing stance, including a broad spectrum of stance-takers (speaker/writer), the objects of stances, and their relationship. While our work also examines the stance relationship between a source (stance-taker) and an event (object), we differ from the existing literature in several ways. For instance, unlike our work where a stance-taker is the author or a mentioned source in the text, Mohtarami et al. (2018), Pomerleau and Rao (2017) and Zubiaga et al. (2016) consider the entire document/message to be a stance-taker. Similarly, the object of the stance could be a target entity (such as a person, organization, movement, controversial topic, etc.) that may or may not be explicitly mentioned in the input document (Mohammad et al., 2016). On the contrary, in this work, event propositions (object) are always embedded within the text.

Finally, we can also analyze the kind of stance relationship exhibited by the stance-taker towards an object from two linguistic perspectives: affect and epistemic. Affect involves the expression of a broad range of personal attitudes, including emotions, feelings, moods, and general dispositions (Ochs and Schieffelin, 1989), and has been explored in Mohammad et al. (2016). On the other hand, epistemic—this work's focus—refers to the speaker's expressed attitudes towards knowledge of events and her degree of commitment to the validity of the communicated information (Chafe, 1986; Biber and Finegan, 1989; Palmer, 2001). The analysis explored in Mohtarami et al. (2018), Pomerleau and Rao (2017) and Zubiaga et al. (2016) seems to be epistemic as they implicitly incorporate the knowledge or claims expressed in the evidence document and hence their stances towards them, although such distinctions are not made explicitly in their work. While the stance literature discussed in this section has not been connected to epistemic stance literature in NLP, we think interesting future work can be done to establish this relationship.

3 An Epistemic Stance Framework for Analyzing Political Rhetoric

This section formally introduces the task of epistemic stance detection and describes the details of the FactBank dataset. We then explain how the epistemic stance framework relates to several rhetorical strategies often used in political discourse.

3.1 Epistemic Stances

We define an epistemic stance tuple as a triple of *(source, event, label)* within a sentence, where the label is the value of the source's epistemic stance (or a non-epistemic relation) toward the event. The triples can be viewed as a fully connected graph among all sources and events in the sentence (Figure 1). We use the structure and theory of FactBank (Saurí and Pustejovsky, 2012) to identify sources, events and the stance labels.

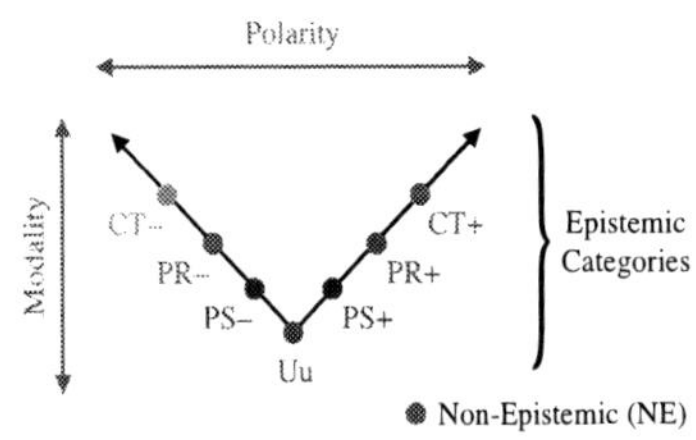

Figure 2: Stance labels used in this work, ordered along two linguistic dimensions, as well as a separate non-epistemic category.

Sources and Events A *source* is an entity—either the text's author, or an entity mentioned in the sentence—which can hold beliefs. FactBank contains annotations for sources that are subjects of source-introducing predicates (SIPs), a manually curated lexicon of verbs about report and belief such as *claim, doubt, feel, know, say, think.* Annotations of these embedded sources allow us to analyze the author's depiction of the embedded source's beliefs towards an event. The special *Author* source is additionally included to analyze the author's own beliefs. FactBank's definition of *events* includes a broad array of textually described eventualities, processes, states, situations, propositions, facts, and possibilities. FactBank identifies its event tokens as those marked in the highly precise, manually annotated TimeBank and AQUAINT TimeML[3] corpora.

Epistemic Stance Label FactBank characterizes epistemic stances along two axes, polarity and modality. The polarity is binary, with the values positive and negative—the event did (not) happen or the proposition is (not) true. The modality constitutes a continuum ranging from uncertain to absolutely certain, discretely categorized as *possible (PS), probable (PR)* and *certain (CT).* An additional *underspecified or uncommitted stance (Uu)* is added along both axes to account for cases such as attribution to another source (non-commitment of the source) or when the stance of the source is unknown. The epistemic stance is then characterized as a pair *(modality, polarity)* containing a modality and a polarity value (e.g., *CT+*) (Figure 2).

FactBank gives epistemic stance labels between certain pairs of sources and events only, based on structural syntactic relationships. However, for raw text we may not have reliable access to syntactic structures, and sources and events must be automatically identified, which may not be completely accurate. We use a simple solution by always assuming edges among the cross-product of all sources and events within a sentence, and to predict a separate *Non-Epistemic (NE)* category for the large majority of pairs. This accounts for any spurious event-source pairs, structurally invalid configurations such as an embedded source's stance towards an event outside their factive context (Figure 1: (s4,e2)), or a source that cannot be described as a belief holder (and thus, all its stances are *NE*).

Given that a variety of datasets have been collected for tasks related to epistemic stance (§2), Stanovsky et al. (2017) argues to combine them for modeling. However, some datasets address different epistemic questions (e.g., the reader's perspective), and they follow very different annotation guidelines and annotation strategies, risking ambiguity in labels' meaning. In preliminary work we attempted to crowdsource new annotations but found the resulting labels to be very different than FactBank, which was created by a small group of expert, highly trained annotators. Thus we decided to exclusively use FactBank for modeling.

3.2 Connections between Epistemic Stances and Rhetorical Strategies

Some epistemic stances in FactBank's framework can be mapped to a common political rhetorical strategy. For instance, a source utilizing *certainly positive/negative* (*CT+/CT-*) stances more frequently can be associated with displaying higher commitment levels. The *CT+/CT-* stances can also help analyze *political disagreements* by identifying two sources with opposite stances towards an event, i.e., a source asserting an event (*CT+*) and a source refuting the same event (*CT-*). A source may exhibit a *probable/possible* (*PR/PS*) stance to indicate that the event could have happened, abstaining from expressing strong commitments towards this event, which can be useful to analyze *hedging*. Finally, *underspecified/uncommitted* (*Uu*) stances can help identify the embedded sources whose beliefs are mentioned by the author while remaining uncommitted, a strategy related to *footing-shift* in political discourse. Use of *Uu* stances is also helpful to identify *belief holders*—entities described as having epistemic stances (§5)—since sometimes the author remains uncommitted while reporting the embedded source's stance.

4 Model

We present a simple and reproducible RoBERTa-based neural model for epistemic stance classifica-

[3]https://web.archive.org/web/20070721130754/http://www.timeml.org/site/publications/specs.html

Model	CT+	CT-	PR+	PS+	Uu	NE	Macro Avg (Non-NE)	Macro Avg (All)
DeFacto (Saurí and Pustejovsky, 2012)	85.0	75.0	46.0	59.0	75.0	-	70.0	-
SVM (Saurí and Pustejovsky, 2012; Prabhakaran et al., 2010)	90.0	61.0	29.0	39.0	66.0	-	59.0	-
BiLSTM (Qian et al., 2018)	85.2	74.0	58.2	61.3	73.3	-	70.4	-
AC-GAN (Qian et al., 2018)	85.5	74.1	63.1	65.4	75.1	-	72.6	-
BERT (Jiang and de Marneffe, 2021)	89.7	69.8	45.0	46.7	82.8	97.9	66.8	72.0
RoBERTa (this work)	90.7	78.4	51.4	62.7	84.8	97.8	73.6	77.6

Table 3: F1 scores for our RoBERTa based epistemic stance classifier and all baseline models.

tion using a standard fine-tuning approach.[4] BERT fine-tuning is effective for many NLP tasks (Devlin et al., 2019), and recent work on pre-trained language models such as BERT (Shi et al., 2016; Belinkov, 2018; Tenney et al., 2019a,b; Rogers et al., 2020) shows such models encode syntactic and semantic dependencies within a sentence, which is highly related to the epistemic stance task.

Recently, Jiang and de Marneffe (2021) use a fine-tuned BERT model for author-only epistemic stance prediction, obtaining strong performance on several datasets. We extend their approach, developing a BERT model (using the RoBERTa (Liu et al., 2019) pre-training variant) for the structurally more complex multi-source task, and give the first full comparison to the foundational multi-source system, DeFacto (Saurí and Pustejovsky, 2012). We leave the exploration of other advanced transformer-based models (Brown et al., 2020; Raffel et al., 2020) for further performance gains as future work.

To develop a model suitable for multi-source predictions, we follow Tenney et al. (2019b) and Rudinger et al. (2018a)'s architecture for semantic (proto-role) labeling, which they formulate as predicting labels for pairs of input embeddings. To predict the epistemic stance for an event-source pair (e, s) in a sentence, we first compute contextual embeddings for the sentence's tokens, $[h_1^L, h_1^L, ..., h_n^L]$, from a BERT encoder's last (L^{th}) layer. We concatenate the source (h_s^L) and event (h_e^L) token embeddings (each averaged over BERT's sub-token embeddings), and use a single linear layer to parameterize a final softmax prediction $\hat{f} \in [0, 1]^C$ over the $C = 6$ epistemic stance classes,[5] which is trained with cross entropy loss over all tuples in the training set. We apply inverse frequency class weighting to encourage accurate modeling for comparatively rare classes like the *CT-, PR+ and PS+* class. Finally, to cleanly analyze the author source in the same manner as other mentioned sources, we augment the sentence with the prefix "Author: " (following a dialogue-like formatting),[6] and use its index and embedding for inferences about the author source.

Table 3 shows the performance of our RoBERTa based epistemic stance classifier. We compare our model against several baselines, including rule-based methods (DeFacto; Saurí and Pustejovsky (2012)), machine learning classifiers (SVM Saurí and Pustejovsky (2012); Prabhakaran et al. (2010)), and neural network based methods (BiLSTM and AC-GAN by Qian et al. (2018)) as described in §2.3.[7] We also extend the author-only BERT model by Jiang and de Marneffe (2021) to support multi-source predictions in line with our modeling approach. The RoBERTa model performs the best obtaining a macro-averaged F1 score of 77.6±0.011 on all six epistemic labels and an F1 score of 73.6±0.031 on the original five epistemic labels (excluding the *Non-Epistemic* label). Although the RoBERTa model has a much simpler architecture, it performs the same or better than AC-GAN. All pairwise significance tests resulted in p-values $<$ 0.01. Details of implementations and statistical testing is provided in Appendix §A.1 and §A.2.

The above epistemic stance classifier, like most previous modeling approaches (Qian et al., 2015; Saurí and Pustejovsky, 2012), requires pre-identified sources and events, which do not exist in real-world text. We use Qian et al. (2018)'s two-step approach to first identify sources and events in the input text and then determine stances for every recognized (source, event) pair. Source and event identification is through two RoBERTa-based token classifiers, using a linear logistic layer for binary classification of whether a token is a source (or event), fine-tuned on the same training corpus.

Our source and event identification models

[4]We intentionally keep the modeling simple to make it more accessible to political scientists and users with less computational experience. We further simplify by augmenting BERT with a single task-specific layer, as opposed to a new task-specific model architecture proposed in Pouran Ben Veyseh et al. (2019); Qian et al. (2018); Rudinger et al. (2018b).

[5]CT+, CT-, PR+, PS+, Uu, NE; Saurí and Pustejovsky (2012) additionally define probably/possibly negative (PR-/PS-) stances. However, these stances are rare in the corpus, making modeling and evaluation problematic. Following Qian et al. (2015, 2018), we omit them in this study.

[6]With and without the trailing colon gave same results.

[7]Since the DeFacto implementation is not available, we compare our model's predictions on the FactBank test set against evaluation statistics derived from the test set confusion matrix reported by Saurí and Pustejovsky. We use implementation provided at `https://github.com/qz011/ef_ac_gan` for SVM, BiLSTM and AC-GAN baselines.

achieve a macro-averaged F1 score of 81.8 ± 0.019 and 85.78 ± 0.007, respectively, slightly improving upon the only existing prior work of Qian et al. (2018) by 1.85% and 1.29% respectively, with pairwise significance tests resulting in p-values < 0.01. We also experimented with a joint model to identify sources and events; however, individual classifiers gave us better performance (Appendix §B.1).

5 Case Study: Belief Holder Identification

Political discourse involves agreement and contention between the author and other belief-holding sources they cite. As a first step, we extract major belief holders mentioned in a text to allow analysis of ideological trends in U.S. political discourse.

5.1 Corpus Description

We conduct our case study on the new Mass-Market Manifestos (MMM) corpus, a curated collection of political nonfiction authored by U.S. politicians, media activists, and opinion elites in English, published from 1993-2020. It subsumes and more than triples the size of Contemporary American Ideological Books (Sim et al., 2013). The corpus contains 370 books (31.9 million tokens) spanning various U.S. political ideologies. Human coders identified 133 books as liberal or left-wing, 226 as conservative or right-wing, and 11 as explicitly centrist or independent. Since ideological opponents often draw from a shared set of concepts—sometimes stating perceived facts and sometimes dismissing others' claims—this presents us with a perfect challenge for detection of epistemic stance.

5.2 Belief Holder Identification

A *belief holder* is defined as a non-author source that holds at least one epistemic stance toward some event. We identify belief holders by using our best-performing model (fine-tuned RoBERTa, predictions averaged over 5 random restarts) to infer epistemic stances for all source-event pairs identified in the 370 books in the MMM corpus. For the problem of identifying sources that are belief holders as per this definition, we obtain 77.3 precision and 79.4 recall on FactBank's evaluation corpus.

For aggregate analysis (§5.4), especially for named entity sources, a longer span is more interpretable and less ambiguous. Thus, when a source token is recognized as part of a traditional named entity (via spaCy v3.0.6; Honnibal and Johnson (2015)), the belief holder is defined as the full NER span; otherwise, simply the source token is used.

5.3 Comparison to Named Entity Recognition

Instead of using epistemic stance-based belief holder identification, an alternative approach is to exclusively rely on named entity recognition (NER) from a set of predefined types. NER has been used in opinion holder identification (Kim and Hovy, 2004) and within belief evaluation in the TAC KBP Belief/Sentiment track (TAC-KBP, 2016). By contrast, our model can instead find *any* entity as a belief holder, as long as it holds epistemic stances, without a type restriction. To illustrate this, we compare our belief holder identifier to a standard NER implementation from spaCy v3.0.6 (Honnibal and Johnson, 2015),[8] trained on English web corpus of OntoNotes 5.0 (Hovy et al., 2006). We use entities identified as one of OntoNotes' 11 non-numeric named entity types.[9] Aggregating among all books in the corpus, the set of belief holders identified by our model has only a 0.198 Jaccard similarity with the set of NER-detected entities (Appendix §E.2 Table 9 provides qualitative examples from one conservative book).[10]

Is it reasonable to define a set of named entity types to identify belief holders? We calculate each named entity type's *belief score*, which is the average proportion of named entities of that type that are described as holding an epistemic stance.[11] As shown in Figure 3, while the Organization, NORP, Person and GPE types have significantly higher belief score than others, there is a wide range of variation, including non-obvious types such as Work of Art (e.g., The Bible), suggesting that a NER type whitelists undercover or overcover possible belief holders. We provide a further linguistic breakdown of identified belief holders in Appendix §E.3.

5.4 Political Analysis of Belief Holders

The MMM corpus, including both left and right-wing authors, gives an opportunity to study the belief holder citation practices for each U.S. political ideology. Using our epistemic stance and entity aggregation postprocessing (§5.2), we count the number of books each belief holder is mentioned in. There are 1269 sources mentioned as a belief

[8] CPU optimized version of `en_core_web_lg`. Stanza's (Qi et al., 2020) performance-optimized NER system gave broadly similar results.

[9] *Event, Facility, GPE, Language, Law, Location, NORP, Organization, Person, Product, Work_of_Art*

[10] An entity is defined as a belief holder if it is the source for at least one epistemic tuple; similarly, it is a named entity if at least one occurrence is identified as part of an NER span.

[11] For each source instance with same NER type, we find the proportion of epistemic (non-NE) stances among events in its sentence, then average these values across the corpus.

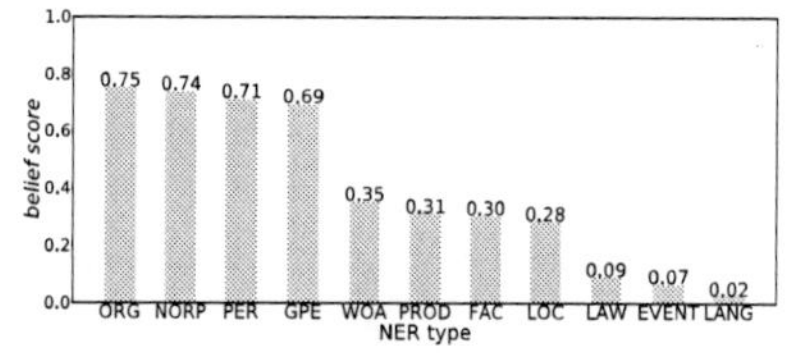

Figure 3: Imperfect correlation between belief scores and OntoNotes NER types. (WOA: Work of Art, PROD: Product, PER: Person, ORG: Organization, LOC: Location, NORP: Nationalities or Religious or Political Groups, FAC: Facility, LANG: Language, GPE: Geo-Political Entity)

Highly Cited by Left-wing Authors		Highly Cited by Right-wing Authors	
Belief Holder	View	Belief Holder	View
Tom Delay	Opposed	Paul Johnson	Respected
Martin Gilens	Respected	Marvin Olasky	Respected
Michelle Alexander	Respected	Saul Alinsky	Opposed
Grover Norquist	Opposed	Robert Rector	Respected
Jane Mayer	Respected	Thomas Sowell	Respected
Albert Camus	Respected	The Tax Foundation	Respected
Consumers	Respected	Soviets	Opposed
Thomas Edsall	Respected	George Soros	Opposed
Jacob Hacker	Respected	Pew Research	Respected
James Baldwin	Respected	John Edwards	Opposed
Jeffrey Sachs	Respected	George Stephanopoulos	Opposed
Michele Bachmann	Opposed	John Stossel	Respected
Ben Bernanke	Unclear	Thomas Sowell	Respected
Chris Hedges	Respected	Nicholas Eberstadt	Respected
Lobbyists	Opposed	James Wilson	Respected
Bill Moyers	Respected	Iran	Opposed
Daniel Bell	Respected	Hollywood	Opposed
David Cay Johnston	Respected	George Gilder	Respected
Instructor	Generic	Dennis Prager	Respected
Moderator	Generic	Arthur Brooks	Respected

Table 4: Top 20 most frequently mentioned belief holders per author ideology (left vs. right), among belief holders mentioned in ≥ 8 books in the MMM corpus.

holder in ≥ 8 books. For each belief holder, we calculate its left-right citation ratio: the proportion of left-wing books it is mentioned in, versus the proportion of right-wing books (proportions are calculated using a book pseudocount of 1 to avoid dividing by zero). Belief holders with a ratio ~ 1.0 include some generic (*team, organization, official*) and anaphoric (*anyone, many*) examples.

Table 4 shows the top 20 belief holders for both left and right, as ranked by this ratio, yielding a rich set of politicians (Delay, Edwards), journalists (Mayer, Stephanopoulos), activists (Norquist, Alinsky), and many social scientists and scholars (Gilens, Johnson). Most of these belief holders were recognized by an expert (political scientist coauthor) as being respected or opposed from the citing ideological perspective. Based on prior knowledge of U.S. politics it was straightforward to immediately give such judgments for most entries; for a few unclear ones, we checked individual sentences mentioning the belief holder. A common strategy is to describe an opponent's views or statements—the use of a rhetorical bogeyman.

Repeating the analysis for widely cited belief holders appearing in ≥ 100 books, yields more general, and again politically meaningful, entities (Table 5). Some well-known patterns are clearly visible, such as liberals' respect for technocratic authority (*economists, scientists, research*), and conservative respect for the semi-mythical *founders* alongside derision for the *media*. Both sides frequently cite the opposition (L: *Republicans*, R: *Democrats*), though interestingly the right cites both conservatives and liberals (relatively more frequently than the left). Figure 4 shows examples of *founders*, with the most skewed ratio ($0.308 \approx 3.2^{-1}$) among this set of entities. Overall, our automated belief holder identification yields a politically significant entity list, laying the groundwork for more systematic manual and computational analysis (e.g., network or targeted sentiment analysis).

Left-cited		Right-cited	
Economists	Studies	Founders	Democrats
Woman	Research	Media	Officials
Polls	Republicans	Poll	President
Scientists	Group	Obama	Conservatives
Groups	Friend	Government	Liberals

Table 5: Top 10 most frequently mentioned belief holders per author ideology, among belief holders mentioned in at least 100 books.

- We know that most of the **[Founders]**$_s$ regarded slavery as a wrong that would have to be addressed. *Chuck Norris, Black Belt Patriotism (R)*
- Sometimes, whether against gator or human predator, you're on your own, as the frontier-expanding **[Founders]**$_s$ well knew. *Charlie Kirk, The MAGA Doctrine (R)*
- This is not to say the **[founders]**$_s$ believed that only religious individuals could possess good character. *William Bennett, America the Strong (R)*
- The **[founders]**$_s$, however, had quite another idea, based on their experience in the colonies over the decades before, where actual religious freedom had existed. *Eric Metaxas, If You Can Keep It (R)*
- The **[Founders]**$_s$ recognized that there were seeds of anarchy in the idea of individual freedom [..], for if everybody is truly free, without the constraints of birth or rank or an inherited social order [..] then how can we ever hope to form a society that coheres? *Barack Obama, The Audacity of Hope (L)*

Figure 4: Examples of *founders* as a belief holder.

6 Conclusion

Semantic modeling has exciting potential to deepen the NLP analysis of political discourse. In this work, we analyze the epistemic stance of various sources toward events, by developing a RoBERTa-based model, and using it for identifying major belief holders mentioned by political authors. We conduct a large-scale analysis of the Mass Market Manifestos corpus of U.S. political opinion books, where we characterize trends in cited belief holders across U.S. political ideologies. In future, we hope to use this framework to help construct a database of beliefs, belief holders, and their patterns of agreement and disagreement in contentious domains.

Acknowledgements

We are thankful for the feedback and comments from the reviewers. We are grateful to Philip Resnik, Michael Colaresi, Arthur Spirling, Katherine Keith, Geraud Nangue Tasse, Kalpesh Krishna, Marzena Karpinska, and the UMass NLP group for valuable discussions during the course of the project. This work was supported by National Science Foundation grants 1814955 and 1845576. Any opinions, findings, conclusions or recommendations expressed in this material are those of the authors and do not necessarily reflect the views of the National Science Foundation.

References

Kareem Abdul-Jabbar and Raymond Obstfeld. 2016. *Writings on the wall: Searching for a new equality beyond Black and White*. Time Inc. Books.

Lloyd B. Anderson. 1986. Evidentials, paths of change, and mental maps: Typologically regular asymmetries. In Wallace L. Chafe and Johanna Nichols, editors, *Evidentiality: The Linguistic Coding of Epistemology*, pages 273–312. Ablex.

Juana I Marín Arrese. 2009. Effective vs. epistemic stance, and subjectivity/intersubjectivity in political discourse. a case study. *Studies on English modality in honour of Frank Palmer. Linguistic Insights*, 111:23–131.

Glenn Beck. 2018. *Addicted to Outrage: How Thinking Like a Recovering Addict Can Heal the Country*. Threshold Editions.

Yonatan Belinkov. 2018. *On internal language representations in Deep Learning: An analysis of Machine Translation and Speech Recognition*. Ph.D. thesis, Massachusetts Institute of Technology, Cambridge, USA.

Taylor Berg-Kirkpatrick, David Burkett, and Dan Klein. 2012. An empirical investigation of statistical significance in NLP. In *Proceedings of the 2012 Joint Conference on Empirical Methods in Natural Language Processing and Computational Natural Language Learning*, pages 995–1005, Jeju Island, Korea. Association for Computational Linguistics.

Steven Bethard, Hong Yu, Ashley Thornton, Vasileios Hatzivassiloglou, and Dan Jurafsky. 2004. Automatic extraction of opinion propositions and their holders. In *Proceedings of the AAAI Spring Symposium on Exploring Attitude and Affect in Text: Theories and Applications*, volume 2224.

Douglas Biber and Edward Finegan. 1989. Styles of stance in english: Lexical and grammatical marking of evidentiality and affect. *Text-Interdisciplinary Journal for the study of Discourse*, 9(1):93–124.

Or Biran, Sara Rosenthal, Jacob Andreas, Kathleen McKeown, and Owen Rambow. 2012. Detecting influencers in written online conversations.

David B Bracewell, Marc Tomlinson, and Hui Wang. 2012. A motif approach for identifying pursuits of power in social discourse. In *2012 IEEE Sixth International Conference on Semantic Computing*, pages 1–8. IEEE.

Tom Brown, Benjamin Mann, Nick Ryder, Melanie Subbiah, Jared D Kaplan, Prafulla Dhariwal, Arvind Neelakantan, Pranav Shyam, Girish Sastry, Amanda Askell, Sandhini Agarwal, Ariel Herbert-Voss, Gretchen Krueger, Tom Henighan, Rewon Child, Aditya Ramesh, Daniel Ziegler, Jeffrey Wu, Clemens Winter, Chris Hesse, Mark Chen, Eric Sigler, Mateusz Litwin, Scott Gray, Benjamin Chess, Jack Clark, Christopher Berner, Sam McCandlish, Alec Radford, Ilya Sutskever, and Dario Amodei. 2020. Language models are few-shot learners. In *Advances in Neural Information Processing Systems*, volume 33, pages 1877–1901. Curran Associates, Inc.

Pat Buchanan. 1999. A republic, not an empire: Reclaiming america's destiny.

Wallace Chafe. 1986. Evidentiality in english conversation and academic writing. *W. Chafe, & J. Nichols (Eds.), Evidentiality: The Linguistic Coding of Epistemology (pp. 261-272). Norwood, NJ: Ablex Publishing Corp.*

Paul Chilton. 2004. *Analysing Political Discourse: Theory and Practice*. London: Routledge.

Yejin Choi, Claire Cardie, Ellen Riloff, and Siddharth Patwardhan. 2005. Identifying sources of opinions with Conditional Random Fields and extraction patterns. In *Proceedings of the Conference on Human Language Technology and Empirical Methods in Natural Language Processing*, HLT '05, page 355–362, USA. Association for Computational Linguistics.

David Christensen. 2009. Disagreement as evidence: The epistemology of controversy. *Philosophy Compass*, 4(5):756–767.

Steven E Clayman. 1992. Footing in the achievement of neutrality: The case of news interview discourse. *Talk at work: Interaction in institutional settings*, 163:198.

Ann H Coulter. 2009. Guilty: Liberal" victims" and their assault on america. Crown Forum.

Cristian Danescu-Niculescu-Mizil, Lillian Lee, Bo Pang, and Jon Kleinberg. 2012. Echoes of power: Language effects and power differences in social interaction. In *Proceedings of the 21st international conference on World Wide Web*, pages 699–708.

Marie-Catherine de Marneffe, Christopher D. Manning, and Christopher Potts. 2012. Did it happen? the pragmatic complexity of veridicality assessment. *Computational Linguistics*, 38(2):301–333.

Jacob Devlin, Ming-Wei Chang, Kenton Lee, and Kristina Toutanova. 2019. BERT: Pre-training of deep bidirectional transformers for language understanding. In *Proceedings of the 2019 Conference of the North American Chapter of the Association for Computational Linguistics: Human Language Technologies, Volume 1 (Long and Short Papers)*, pages 4171–4186, Minneapolis, Minnesota. Association for Computational Linguistics.

Bhuwan Dhingra, Manaal Faruqui, Ankur Parikh, Ming-Wei Chang, Dipanjan Das, and William Cohen. 2019. Handling divergent reference texts when evaluating table-to-text generation. In *Proceedings of the 57th Annual Meeting of the Association for Computational Linguistics*, pages 4884–4895, Florence, Italy. Association for Computational Linguistics.

Mona Diab, Lori Levin, Teruko Mitamura, Owen Rambow, Vinodkumar Prabhakaran, and Weiwei Guo. 2009. Committed belief annotation and tagging. In *Proceedings of the Third Linguistic Annotation Workshop (LAW III)*, pages 68–73, Suntec, Singapore. Association for Computational Linguistics.

Jesse Dodge, Gabriel Ilharco, Roy Schwartz, Ali Farhadi, Hannaneh Hajishirzi, and Noah A. Smith. 2020. Fine-tuning pretrained language models: Weight initializations, data orders, and early stopping. *Computing Research Repository*, arXiv:2002.06305.

Rod Dreher. 2018. *The Benedict option: A strategy for Christians in a post-Christian nation.* Penguin.

Steve Forbes and Elizabeth Ames. 2012. *Freedom Manifesto: Why Free Markets Are Moral and Big Government Isn't.* Currency.

Bryan Frances. 2014. *Disagreement.* John Wiley & Sons.

Bruce Fraser. 2010. Hedging in political discourse. *OKULSKA, U., CAP, P., Perspectives in Politics and Discourse, Capitolo*, 8.

Matt Gardner, Joel Grus, Mark Neumann, Oyvind Tafjord, Pradeep Dasigi, Nelson F. Liu, Matthew Peters, Michael Schmitz, and Luke Zettlemoyer. 2018. AllenNLP: A deep semantic natural language processing platform. In *Proceedings of Workshop for NLP Open Source Software (NLP-OSS)*, pages 1–6, Melbourne, Australia. Association for Computational Linguistics.

Erving Goffman. 1981. *Forms of talk.* University of Pennsylvania Press.

Fritz Heider. 1946. Attitudes and cognitive organization. *The Journal of psychology*, 21(1):107–112.

Kaarlo Jaakko Juhani Hintikka. 1962. Knowledge and belief: An introduction to the logic of the two notions.

Wiebe van der Hoek. 1990. Systems for knowledge and beliefs. In *European Workshop on Logics in Artificial Intelligence*, pages 267–281. Springer.

Wesley H Holliday. 2018. Epistemic logic and epistemology. In *Introduction to formal philosophy*, pages 351–369. Springer.

Matthew Honnibal and Mark Johnson. 2015. An improved non-monotonic transition system for dependency parsing. In *Proceedings of the 2015 Conference on Empirical Methods in Natural Language Processing*, pages 1373–1378, Lisbon, Portugal. Association for Computational Linguistics.

Laurence Robert Horn. 1972. *On the semantic properties of logical operators in English.* University of California, Los Angeles.

Eduard Hovy, Mitchell Marcus, Martha Palmer, Lance Ramshaw, and Ralph Weischedel. 2006. OntoNotes: The 90% solution. In *Proceedings of the Human Language Technology Conference of the NAACL, Companion Volume: Short Papers*, pages 57–60, New York City, USA. Association for Computational Linguistics.

Ken Hyland. 1996. Writing without conviction? hedging in science research articles. *Applied linguistics*, 17(4):433–454.

Ali Reza Jalilifar and Maryam Alavi. 2011. Power and politics of language use: A survey of hedging devices in political interviews. *Journal of Teaching Language Skills*, 30(3):43–66.

Seung-Jin Jang. 2009. Are diverse political networks always bad for participatory democracy? indifference, alienation, and political disagreements. *American Politics Research*, 37(5):879–898.

Nanjiang Jiang and Marie-Catherine de Marneffe. 2021. He thinks he knows better than the doctors: BERT for event factuality fails on pragmatics. *CoRR*, cs.CL/2107.00807v1.

Ferenc Kiefer. 1987. On defining modality.

Soo-Min Kim and Eduard Hovy. 2004. Determining the sentiment of opinions. In *COLING 2004: Proceedings of the 20th International Conference on Computational Linguistics*, pages 1367–1373, Geneva, Switzerland. COLING.

Diederik P. Kingma and Jimmy Ba. 2015. Adam: A method for stochastic optimization. In *3rd International Conference on Learning Representations, ICLR 2015, San Diego, CA, USA, May 7-9, 2015, Conference Track Proceedings.*

Casey A Klofstad, Anand Edward Sokhey, and Scott D McClurg. 2013. Disagreeing about disagreement: How conflict in social networks affects political behavior. *American Journal of Political Science*, 57(1):120–134.

Wojciech Kryscinski, Nitish Shirish Keskar, Bryan McCann, Caiming Xiong, and Richard Socher. 2019. Neural text summarization: A critical evaluation. In *Proceedings of the 2019 Conference on Empirical*

Methods in Natural Language Processing and the 9th International Joint Conference on Natural Language Processing (EMNLP-IJCNLP), pages 540–551, Hong Kong, China. Association for Computational Linguistics.

George Lakoff. 1975. Hedges: A study in meaning criteria and the logic of fuzzy concepts. In *Contemporary research in philosophical logic and linguistic semantics*, pages 221–271. Springer.

Ronald W. Langacker. 2009. *Investigations in Cognitive Grammar*. De Gruyter Mouton.

Kenton Lee, Yoav Artzi, Yejin Choi, and Luke Zettlemoyer. 2015. Event detection and factuality assessment with non-expert supervision. In *Proceedings of the 2015 Conference on Empirical Methods in Natural Language Processing*, pages 1643–1648, Lisbon, Portugal. Association for Computational Linguistics.

Bing Liu. 2012. Sentiment analysis and opinion mining. *Synthesis lectures on Human Language Technologies*, 5(1):1–167.

Yinhan Liu, Myle Ott, Naman Goyal, Jingfei Du, Mandar Joshi, Danqi Chen, Omer Levy, Mike Lewis, Luke Zettlemoyer, and Veselin Stoyanov. 2019. Roberta: A robustly optimized bert pretraining approach. *arXiv preprint arXiv:1907.11692*.

Amnon Lotan, Asher Stern, and Ido Dagan. 2013. TruthTeller: Annotating predicate truth. In *Proceedings of the 2013 Conference of the North American Chapter of the Association for Computational Linguistics: Human Language Technologies*, pages 752–757, Atlanta, Georgia. Association for Computational Linguistics.

John Lyons. 1977. Semantics cambridge university press. *Cambridge, UK*, 1.

James G MacKinnon. 2009. Bootstrap hypothesis testing. *Handbook of computational econometrics*, 183:213.

James R Martin and Peter RR White. 2005. Appraisal in English. *The language of evaluation*.

Joshua Maynez, Shashi Narayan, Bernd Bohnet, and Ryan McDonald. 2020. On faithfulness and factuality in abstractive summarization. In *Proceedings of the 58th Annual Meeting of the Association for Computational Linguistics*, pages 1906–1919, Online. Association for Computational Linguistics.

Tsvetomila Mihaylova, Preslav Nakov, Lluís Màrquez, Alberto Barrón-Cedeño, Mitra Mohtarami, Georgi Karadzhov, and James Glass. 2018. Fact checking in community forums. *Proceedings of the AAAI Conference on Artificial Intelligence*, 32(1).

Anne-Lyse Minard, Manuela Speranza, Ruben Urizar, Begoña Altuna, Marieke van Erp, Anneleen Schoen, and Chantal van Son. 2016. MEANTIME, the NewsReader multilingual event and time corpus. In *Proceedings of the Tenth International Conference on Language Resources and Evaluation (LREC'16)*, pages 4417–4422, Portorož, Slovenia. European Language Resources Association (ELRA).

Saif Mohammad, Svetlana Kiritchenko, Parinaz Sobhani, Xiaodan Zhu, and Colin Cherry. 2016. SemEval-2016 task 6: Detecting stance in tweets. In *Proceedings of the 10th International Workshop on Semantic Evaluation (SemEval-2016)*, pages 31–41, San Diego, California. Association for Computational Linguistics.

Mitra Mohtarami, Ramy Baly, James Glass, Preslav Nakov, Lluís Màrquez, and Alessandro Moschitti. 2018. Automatic stance detection using end-to-end memory networks. In *Proceedings of the 2018 Conference of the North American Chapter of the Association for Computational Linguistics: Human Language Technologies, Volume 1 (Long Papers)*, pages 767–776, New Orleans, Louisiana. Association for Computational Linguistics.

Marius Mosbach, Maksym Andriushchenko, and Dietrich Klakow. 2021. On the stability of fine-tuning BERT: Misconceptions, explanations, and strong baselines. In *International Conference on Learning Representations*.

Ilana Mushin. 2001. Evidentiality and epistemological stance. *Narrative retelling*.

Rowan Nairn, Cleo Condoravdi, and Lauri Karttunen. 2006. Computing relative polarity for textual inference. In *Proceedings of the Fifth International Workshop on Inference in Computational Semantics (ICoS-5)*.

Elinor Ochs and Bambi Schieffelin. 1989. Language has a heart:. *Text - Interdisciplinary Journal for the Study of Discourse*, 9(1):7–26.

Frank Robert Palmer. 2001. *Mood and modality*. Cambridge university press.

Bo Pang and Lillian Lee. 2008. Opinion mining and sentiment analysis. *Foundations and Trends in Information Retrieval*, 2(1-2):1–135.

Adam Paszke, Sam Gross, Soumith Chintala, Gregory Chanan, Edward Yang, Zachary DeVito, Zeming Lin, Alban Desmaison, Luca Antiga, and Adam Lerer. 2017. Automatic Differentiation in PyTorch. In *NIPS 2017 Workshop on Autodiff*.

Susan U Philips. 1985. William m. o'barr, linguistic evidence: Language. power, and strategy in the courtroom.(studies on law and social control.) new york: Academic, 1982. pp. xv+ 192. *Language in Society*, 14(1):113–117.

Dean Pomerleau and Delip Rao. 2017. The Fake News Challenge: Exploring how Artificial Intelligence technologies could be leveraged to combat Fake News. *Fake News Challenge*.

Amir Pouran Ben Veyseh, Thien Huu Nguyen, and Dejing Dou. 2019. Graph based neural networks for event factuality prediction using syntactic and semantic structures. In *Proceedings of the 57th Annual Meeting of the Association for Computational Linguistics*, pages 4393–4399, Florence, Italy. Association for Computational Linguistics.

Vinodkumar Prabhakaran, Tomas By, Julia Hirschberg, Owen Rambow, Samira Shaikh, Tomek Strzalkowski, Jennifer Tracey, Michael Arrigo, Rupayan Basu, Micah Clark, Adam Dalton, Mona Diab, Louise Guthrie, Anna Prokofieva, Stephanie Strassel, Gregory Werner, Yorick Wilks, and Janyce Wiebe. 2015. A new dataset and evaluation for belief/factuality. In *Proceedings of the Fourth Joint Conference on Lexical and Computational Semantics*, pages 82–91, Denver, Colorado. Association for Computational Linguistics.

Vinodkumar Prabhakaran, Owen Rambow, and Mona Diab. 2010. Automatic committed belief tagging. In *Coling 2010: Posters*, pages 1014–1022, Beijing, China. Coling 2010 Organizing Committee.

Peng Qi, Yuhao Zhang, Yuhui Zhang, Jason Bolton, and Christopher D Manning. 2020. Stanza: A Python Natural Language Processing toolkit for many human languages. *arXiv preprint arXiv:2003.07082*.

Zhong Qian, Peifeng Li, Yue Zhang, Guodong Zhou, and Qiaoming Zhu. 2018. Event factuality identification via generative adversarial networks with auxiliary classification. In *Proceedings of the Twenty-Seventh International Joint Conference on Artificial Intelligence, IJCAI-18*, pages 4293–4300. International Joint Conferences on Artificial Intelligence Organization.

Zhong Qian, Peifeng Li, and Qiaoming Zhu. 2015. A two-step approach for event factuality identification. In *2015 International Conference on Asian Language Processing (IALP)*, pages 103–106.

Colin Raffel, Noam Shazeer, Adam Roberts, Katherine Lee, Sharan Narang, Michael Matena, Yanqi Zhou, Wei Li, and Peter J. Liu. 2020. Exploring the limits of transfer learning with a unified text-to-text transformer. *Journal of Machine Learning Research*, 21(140):1–67.

Owen Rambow, Daniel Bauer, Axinia Radeva, Meenakshi Alagesan, Gregorios A. Katsios, Tomek Strzalkowski, Claire Cardie, Mona T. Diab, Michael Arrigo, Jennifer Tracey, Adam Dalton, and Greg Dubbin. 2016. The 2016 TAC KBP BeSt evaluation. In *Text Analysis Conference*. NIST.

Hannah Rashkin, Eunsol Choi, Jin Yea Jang, Svitlana Volkova, and Yejin Choi. 2017. Truth of varying shades: Analyzing language in fake news and political fact-checking. In *Proceedings of the 2017 Conference on Empirical Methods in Natural Language Processing*, pages 2931–2937, Copenhagen, Denmark. Association for Computational Linguistics.

Robert B Reich. 2005. *Reason: Why liberals will win the battle for America*. Vintage.

Anna Rogers, Olga Kovaleva, and Anna Rumshisky. 2020. A primer in BERTology: What we know about how BERT works. *Transactions of the Association for Computational Linguistics*, 8:842–866.

Sara Rosenthal. 2014. Detecting influencers in social media discussions. *XRDS: Crossroads, The ACM Magazine for Students*, 21(1):40–45.

Rachel Rudinger, Adam Teichert, Ryan Culkin, Sheng Zhang, and Benjamin Van Durme. 2018a. Neural-Davidsonian Semantic Proto-Role labeling. In *Proceedings of the 2018 Conference on Empirical Methods in Natural Language Processing*, pages 944–955, Brussels, Belgium. Association for Computational Linguistics.

Rachel Rudinger, Aaron Steven White, and Benjamin Van Durme. 2018b. Neural models of factuality. In *Proceedings of the 2018 Conference of the North American Chapter of the Association for Computational Linguistics: Human Language Technologies, Volume 1 (Long Papers)*, pages 731–744, New Orleans, Louisiana. Association for Computational Linguistics.

Roser Saurí and James Pustejovsky. 2009. FactBank: a corpus annotated with event factuality. *Language resources and evaluation*, 43(3).

Roser Saurí and James Pustejovsky. 2012. Are you sure that this happened? Assessing the factuality degree of events in text. *Computational Linguistics*, 38(2):261–299.

Stephen D Shaffer. 1981. Balance theory and political cognitions. *American Politics Quarterly*, 9(3):291–320.

Ben Shapiro. 2019. *Facts don't care about your feelings*. Creators Publishing.

Xing Shi, Inkit Padhi, and Kevin Knight. 2016. Does string-based neural MT learn source syntax? In *Proceedings of the 2016 Conference on Empirical Methods in Natural Language Processing*, pages 1526–1534, Austin, Texas. Association for Computational Linguistics.

Yanchuan Sim, Brice D. L. Acree, Justin H. Gross, and Noah A. Smith. 2013. Measuring ideological proportions in political speeches. In *Proceedings of the 2013 Conference on Empirical Methods in Natural Language Processing*, pages 91–101, Seattle, Washington, USA. Association for Computational Linguistics.

Sandeep Soni, Tanushree Mitra, Eric Gilbert, and Jacob Eisenstein. 2014. Modeling factuality judgments in social media text. In *Proceedings of the 52nd Annual Meeting of the Association for Computational Linguistics (Volume 2: Short Papers)*, pages 415–420, Baltimore, Maryland. Association for Computational Linguistics.

Gabriel Stanovsky, Judith Eckle-Kohler, Yevgeniy Puzikov, Ido Dagan, and Iryna Gurevych. 2017. Integrating deep linguistic features in factuality prediction over unified datasets. In *Proceedings of the 55th Annual Meeting of the Association for Computational Linguistics (Volume 2: Short Papers)*, pages 352–357, Vancouver, Canada. Association for Computational Linguistics.

Sandesh Swamy, Alan Ritter, and Marie-Catherine de Marneffe. 2017. " i have a feeling trump will win..................": Forecasting winners and losers from user predictions on twitter. *arXiv preprint arXiv:1707.07212*.

Swabha Swayamdipta and Owen Rambow. 2012. The pursuit of power and its manifestation in written dialog. In *2012 IEEE Sixth International Conference on Semantic Computing*, pages 22–29. IEEE.

TAC-KBP. 2016. Task description for source/target belief and sentiment evaluation (best) at tac 2016. `http://www.cs.columbia.edu/~rambow/best-eval-2016/task-spec-v2.4.pdf`.

Ian Tenney, Dipanjan Das, and Ellie Pavlick. 2019a. BERT rediscovers the classical NLP pipeline. In *Proceedings of the 57th Annual Meeting of the Association for Computational Linguistics*, pages 4593–4601, Florence, Italy. Association for Computational Linguistics.

Ian Tenney, Patrick Xia, Berlin Chen, Alex Wang, Adam Poliak, R Thomas McCoy, Najoung Kim, Benjamin Van Durme, Sam Bowman, Dipanjan Das, and Ellie Pavlick. 2019b. What do you learn from context? Probing for sentence structure in contextualized word representations. In *International Conference on Learning Representations*.

James Thorne, Andreas Vlachos, Christos Christodoulopoulos, and Arpit Mittal. 2018. FEVER: a large-scale dataset for fact extraction and verification. *CoRR*, abs/1803.05355.

Stephen E. Toulmin. 1958. *The Uses of Argument*. Cambridge University Press.

Dietrich Trautmann, Johannes Daxenberger, Christian Stab, Hinrich Schütze, and Iryna Gurevych. 2020. Fine-grained argument unit recognition and classification. In *The Thirty-Fourth AAAI Conference on Artificial Intelligence, AAAI 2020, The Thirty-Second Innovative Applications of Artificial Intelligence Conference, IAAI 2020, The Tenth AAAI Symposium on Educational Advances in Artificial Intelligence, EAAI 2020, New York, NY, USA, February 7-12, 2020*, pages 9048–9056. AAAI Press.

Meagan Vigus, Jens E. L. Van Gysel, and William Croft. 2019. A dependency structure annotation for modality. In *Proceedings of the First International Workshop on Designing Meaning Representations*, pages 182–198, Florence, Italy. Association for Computational Linguistics.

Andreas Vlachos and Sebastian Riedel. 2014. Fact Checking: Task definition and dataset construction. In *Proceedings of the ACL 2014 Workshop on Language Technologies and Computational Social Science*, pages 18–22, Baltimore, MD, USA. Association for Computational Linguistics.

Hanna Wallach. 2014. Big data, machine learning, and the social sciences: Fairness, accountability, and transparency. Talk at NIPS 2014 Workshop on Fairness, Accountability, and Transparency in Machine Learning.

Douglas Walton, Christopher Reed, and Fabrizio Macagno. 2008. *Argumentation schemes*. Cambridge University Press.

Douglas N Walton. 1996. *Argumentation schemes for presumptive reasoning*. Psychology Press.

Larry Wasserman. 2004. *All of statistics: a concise course in statistical inference*, volume 26. Springer.

Aaron Steven White, Drew Reisinger, Keisuke Sakaguchi, Tim Vieira, Sheng Zhang, Rachel Rudinger, Kyle Rawlins, and Benjamin Van Durme. 2016. Universal decompositional semantics on Universal Dependencies. In *Proceedings of the 2016 Conference on Empirical Methods in Natural Language Processing*, pages 1713–1723, Austin, Texas. Association for Computational Linguistics.

Janyce Wiebe, Theresa Wilson, and Claire Cardie. 2005. Annotating expressions of opinions and emotions in language. *Language Resources and Evaluation*, 39(2):165–210.

Sam Wiseman, Stuart Shieber, and Alexander Rush. 2017. Challenges in data-to-document generation. In *Proceedings of the 2017 Conference on Empirical Methods in Natural Language Processing*, pages 2253–2263, Copenhagen, Denmark. Association for Computational Linguistics.

Jiarui Yao, Haoling Qiu, Jin Zhao, Bonan Min, and Nianwen Xue. 2021. Factuality assessment as modal dependency parsing. In *Proceedings of the 59th Annual Meeting of the Association for Computational Linguistics and the 11th International Joint Conference on Natural Language Processing, ACL/IJCNLP 2021, (Volume 1: Long Papers), Virtual Event, August 1-6, 2021*, pages 1540–1550. Association for Computational Linguistics.

Tianyi Zhang, Felix Wu, Arzoo Katiyar, Kilian Q Weinberger, and Yoav Artzi. 2021. Revisiting few-sample BERT fine-tuning. In *International Conference on Learning Representations*.

Arkaitz Zubiaga, Elena Kochkina, Maria Liakata, Rob Procter, and Michal Lukasik. 2016. Stance classification in rumours as a sequential task exploiting the tree structure of social media conversations. In *Proceedings of COLING 2016, the 26th International Conference on Computational Linguistics: Technical Papers*, pages 2438–2448, Osaka, Japan. The COLING 2016 Organizing Committee.

Appendices

A Experimental Details

A.1 Implementation Details

All our models are implemented with PyTorch 1.9, using `roberta-large` (with 1024-dimensional embeddings) accessed from AllenNLP 2.5.1 (Paszke et al., 2017; Gardner et al., 2018). We train the models with the Adam optimizer (Kingma and Ba, 2015), using at most 20 epochs, batch size 16, and learning rate 5×10^{-6}, following Zhang et al. (2021) and Mosbach et al. (2021)'s training guidelines. We use an early stopping rule if the validation loss does not reduce for more than two epochs; this typically ends training in $5-6$ epochs. We report macro-averaged precision, recall, and F1 over the original train-test set splits of FactBank. Since fine-tuning BERT (and its variants) can be unstable on small datasets (Dodge et al., 2020), we report average performance over five random restarts for each model. To fine-tune BERT and RoBERTa models, we start with the pre-trained language model, updating both the task-specific layer and all parameters of the language model.

A.2 Significance Testing

We use a nonparametric bootstrap (Wasserman, 2004, ch. 8) to infer confidence intervals for an individual model's performance metric (precision, recall, F1) and hypothesis testing between pairs of models. We utilize 10^4 bootstrap samples of sentences for source and event identification models and 10^4 bootstrap samples of epistemic stance tuples for stance classifier in FactBank's test set to report 95% bootstrap confidence intervals (CI), via the normal interval method (Wasserman, 2004, ch. 8.3), and compare models with a bootstrap two-sided hypothesis test to calculate a p-value for the null hypothesis of two models having an equal macro-averaged F1 score (MacKinnon, 2009).[12]

B Performance of Source and Event Identification Models

B.1 Source and Event Identification

Table 6 mentions performance scores of the source and event identification models.

[12]MacKinnon's bootstrap hypothesis test has subtle differences from Berg-Kirkpatrick et al. (2012)'s in the NLP litearture; we find MacKinnon's theoretical justification clearer.

Model	Event			Source		
	Prec	Recall	F1	Prec	Recall	F1
CNN (Qian et al., 2018)	86.6	82.8	84.6	80.7	77.4	78.9
RoBERTa (Joint)	84.4	87.6	86.0	81.4	62.7	70.8
RoBERTa (Individual)	84.1	87.2	85.6	79.7	81.2	80.5

Table 6: Performance of the source and event identification models. Individual classifiers perform better than a combined classifier.

B.2 Error Analysis: Correlation with the events denoted by verb *"say"*

We conducted an error analysis of our source identification model. We tested the model to examine whether the model understands the notion of source or merely associates the notion of source with presence of vents denoted by verb "say" in a given sentence. Table 7 demonstrates that the model does not merely rely on presence or absence of such events.

"Say"	**F1**	**Precision**	**Recall**	**#sentences**
Present	84.6	86.4	82.9	147
Absent	65.2	58.4	73.8	269

Table 7: Source Error Analysis

C Performance of Epistemic Stance Classifier

C.1 Error Analysis: Negative Polarity Items

The *CT-* class is the most rare in FactBank, and it is useful to identify for a possible future use case of finding disagreements in text. For corpus exploration, an alternative to our model could be to simply view sentences with explicit negative polarity items (NPIs); such sentences[13] indeed contain a large majority (88.2%) of FactBank's gold standard *CT-* tuples. They are still uncommon within NPI-containing sentences (13.5% of such tuples are *CT-*), and quite rare within sentences without NPIs (0.33% of such tuples are *CT-*). For this challenging CT- class, the model attains a F1 score of 78.4%. To examine the model performance on CT- class in political domain, we qualitatively analyzed correct classifications. We observe that the model exhibits ability to deal with complex connections between negation-bearing constructions like *Unable to*, *refuse*, etc. (Table 8).

D External Validity: A Case Study on Hedging and power

Jalilifar and Alavi (2011) examine the relationship between an author's perceived political power and their expressed commitment to their beliefs. While

[13]Using an NPI list of: *no, not, n't, never, nobody, none*

• **[Author]**$_s$: Unable to **reach**$_e$ Russo in the era before cell phones, the House Speaker, Jim Wright, kept the vote open for some twenty minutes while an aide coaxed a member to change his vote to yes.
• Author: **[John Boehner]**$_s$, the Speaker of the House, refused to **address**$_e$ immigration reform in 2013.
• Author: **[People]**$_s$ are beginning to move worlds apart and find it increasingly difficult to **establish**$_e$ common ground.
• **[Author]**$_s$: Although still incapable of actually **cutting**$_e$ spending, except for needed defense, conservative leaders imply our national crisis is merely some budgeting blunder remediable through a balanced budget amendment to the Constitution.

Table 8: Examples of *CT-* epistemic stances, in sentences without explicit NPIs in PoliBelief, that BERT correctly predicts; sources are highlighted in bold, and events are underlined.

hedging and hesitations have been utilized to measure lack of commitment (Philips, 1985), political discourse can feature many more strategies beyond a simple lexicon of hedge words, such as indirect speech acts, hypothetical if-then clauses, or framing claims as questions (Fraser, 2010). Thus, analyzing hedging requires understanding of syntactic contexts within which claims are expressed, which our model can tackle. We establish the external validity of our proposed epistemic stance framework by computationally replicating the findings of Jalilifar and Alavi (2011)'s manual content analysis. To ensure the external validity of our proposed epistemic stance framework, we computationally replicate the findings of Jalilifar and Alavi (2011)'s manual content analysis.

The study examines transcripts of topically similar television interviews of three political figures, George W. Bush (at the time, incumbent U.S. president), Jimmy Carter (former U.S. president), and David Coltart (founding member of Zimbabwe's main opposition party).[14] For each interview transcript, we employ our epistemic stance classifier to predict the stance of the political figure (author source) towards all extracted events, and calculate each author's uncertainty level as the fraction of events with a *PR+* or *PS+* epistemic stance.

We find the same ordering of commitment as the previous work: Bush using the fewest uncertain *PR+/PS+* stances (5.41%), with progressively more for Carter (8.32%) and Coltart (12.2%). This follows Jalilifar and Alavi's interpretation of commitment being correlated to power (Bush being the highest status, for example).

E Case Study: Belief Holder Identification

E.1 Details of MMM Corpus

The MMM, maintained by one of the authors (*anon. for review*), is an example of a researcher-curated "artisanal data" (Wallach, 2014) collection, common in political science and communication research. Books were chosen according to a number of selection criteria and not as a representative sample of any presumed population of publications. Nominees for consideration include books appearing on best-seller lists from a number of politically-oriented Amazon book categories, mostly under the heading "Politics & Government—Ideologies & Doctrines." Additionally, all presidential primary candidates authoring a book during this period were considered, as were other officials (e.g. governors, sheriffs, senators) and ideologues attaining public prominence. Over the course of several years, scholars of American ideology have been invited to nominate additional authors for consideration, as the long-term goal is to maintain as comprehensive as possible a corpus of mass-marketed ideologically-oriented manuscripts. Among nominees, books that were more memoir than manifesto were eliminated, as were books too narrowly focused on a particular policy area.

Books in the MMM were published from 1993 through 2020, with a majority during the Obama presidential administration (233 in 2009-2016), as well as 57 from the George W. Bush presidency (2001-2008) and 80 during the Trump presidency (2017-2020).

E.2 Comparison with NER: Qualitative Examples

Table 9 describes whether the book's belief holders are recognized as named entities—three of ten are not.

Belief Holder	Detected by NER?	Belief Holder	Detected by NER?
Media	Yes	Bernie Sanders	No
Democrats	Yes	Right	Yes
Donald Trump	Yes	Republicans	No
Left	No	Courts	Yes
Conservatives	Yes	Joe Biden	Yes

Table 9: Top 10 sources detected as belief holders in Ben Shapiro's *Facts Don't Care About Your Feelings.*

E.3 Linguistic Analysis of Belief Holders

We identify two interesting linguistic phenomena among belief holders mentions.

[14]Authors also analyzed interviews by U.S. politician Sarah Palin, but we these transcripts were not available at the provided URL.

Common and Collective Nouns Many belief holders can also be described by common nouns, such as a plural form referring to classes of people (or other agents), or collective nouns denoting aggregate entities, including informally defined ones. We show several examples, along with an event toward which they have an epistemic stance.

(1) A recent survey of studies published in peer-reviewed scientific journals found that 97 percent of actively publishing climate **[scientists]**$_s$ agree that global warming has been **caused**$_e$ by human activity. (Abdul-Jabbar and Obstfeld, 2016)

(2) The **[Left]**$_s$ properly pointed out the widespread problems of racism and sexism in American society in the 1950s — and their diagnosis was to **destroy**$_e$ the system utterly. (Shapiro, 2019)

(3) The agents seized rosewood and ebony that the **[government]**$_s$ believed was illegally **imported**$_e$. (Forbes and Ames, 2012)

(4) The **[media]**$_s$ simply asserted that Clinton was **beloved**$_e$ across the land — despite never being able to get 50 percent of the country to vote for him, even before the country knew about Monica Lewinsky. (Coulter, 2009)

(5) Maybe American **[society]**$_s$ concluded, at some deep level of collective unconsciousness, that it had to **reject**$_e$ the previous generation 's model of strict fathering in favor of nurturing mothering. (Reich, 2005)

Word Sense Disambiguation If an entity is described as a belief holder, that can help disambiguate its word sense or entity type. Our model distinguishes agentive versus non-agentive versions of a geographical locations. In the following two examples, the locations or ideas "Europe" and "Silicon Valley" are belief holders with opinions toward various future scenarios (all with uncommitted *Uu* stances, which FactBank uses for all conditionals and hypotheticals). These location entities are treated as agents with political desires and intentions, perhaps more like an organizational or geopolitical NER type, despite the fact that these instances do not represent formally defined or even universally agreed-upon entities.

(6) **[Europe]**$_s$ sees it [NATO expansion] as a scheme for permanent U.S. hegemony and has decided that if the Americans want to play Romans, let Americans **pay**$_e$ the costs and **take**$_e$ the risks. (Buchanan, 1999)

(7) "Currently **[Silicon Valley]**$_s$ is in the midst of a love affair with BMI, arguing that when robots **come**$_e$ to **take**$_e$ all of our jobs, we're going to **need**$_e$ stronger redistributive policies to **help**$_e$ **keep**$_e$ families afloat," Annie Lowrey, who has a book on the subject coming July 10, wrote in New York magazine. (Beck, 2018)

By contrast, "Europe" and "Iowa" below have no epistemic stances (all edges toward sentence events are *NE*), and the entities are used simply to describe geographic locations.

(8) Napoleon was the dictator of a French state so anticlerical that many in **[Europe]**$_s$ speculated that he was the Antichrist. (Dreher, 2018)

(9) While reporters waited outside in the **[Iowa]**$_s$ cold amid a mix-up at one of Trump's rallies [...] (Abdul-Jabbar and Obstfeld, 2016)

Linguistic Elements of Engaging Customer Service Discourse on Social Media

Sonam Singh[1] **and Anthony Rios**[2]
[1]Department of Marketing
[2]Department of Information Systems and Cyber Security
University of Texas at San Antonio
{sonam.singh, anthony.rios}@utsa

Abstract

Customers are rapidly turning to social media for customer support. While brand agents on these platforms are motivated and well-intentioned to help and engage with customers, their efforts are often ignored if their initial response to the customer does not match a specific tone, style, or topic the customer is aiming to receive. The length of a conversation can reflect the effort and quality of the initial response made by a brand toward collaborating and helping consumers, even when the overall sentiment of the conversation might not be very positive. Thus, through this study, we aim to bridge this critical gap in the existing literature by analyzing language's content and stylistic aspects such as expressed empathy, psycho-linguistic features, dialogue tags, and metrics for quantifying personalization of the utterances that can influence the engagement of an interaction. This paper demonstrates that we can predict engagement using initial customer and brand posts.

1 Introduction

Providing quality customer service on social media has become a priority for most companies (brands) today. A simple customer-brand interaction started by a moment of annoyance can be relieved when the brand resolves the issue in a public display of exceptional customer service. According to Forbes, companies that use Twitter as a social care channel have seen a 19 percent increase in customer satisfaction (Forbes, 2018). Furthermore, customers are rapidly turning to social media for customer support; Research from JD Power finds that approximately 67 percent of consumers now tap networks like Twitter and Facebook for customer service (Power, 2013). While providing timely and stellar service has its advantages, engaging in a collaborative dialogue with its customers also leads to mutual trust and transparency according to social customer relations management (SCRM) theories (Yahav et al., 2020). SCRM has been documented as a core business strategy (Woodcock et al., 2011). SCRM refers to "*a philosophy and a business strategy, supported by a technology platform, business rules, processes, and social characteristics, designed to engage the customer in a collaborative conversation to provide mutually beneficial value in a trusted and transparent business environment*" (Greenberg, 2010). While brand agents on social platforms are typically motivated and well-intentioned to help engage with customers, their efforts are often ignored if their initial response to the customer does not match a specific tone, style, or topic the customer is aiming to receive. Hence, we explore what textual elements of a brand's response are predictive of customer engagement.

While there has been substantial research on customer service on social platforms, a majority has predominantly addressed issues such as timely response (Xu et al., 2017), timely transfer from a bot to human (Liu et al., 2020), improving bot performance (Adam et al., 2020; Følstad and Taylor, 2019; Xu et al., 2017; Hu et al., 2018), improving dialogue act prediction (Oraby et al., 2017; Bhuiyan et al., 2018), and managing customer sentiment of users on the platform (Mousavi et al., 2020). A few studies have also examined the tone and emotional content of the customer service chats (Hu et al., 2018; Herzig et al., 2016; Oraby et al., 2017). However, more subtle and integral stylistic aspects of language, such as expressed empathy, psycho-linguistic features (e.g., time orientation), and the level of personalization of the responses, have received little attention, particularly when analyzed for engagement metrics. For the few studies that have looked at subtle stylistic aspects of language in customer service settings (Clark et al., 2013; Wieseke et al., 2012), the studies were more lab-based in synchronous, face-to-face, or call settings and may not translate to asynchronous, text-based contexts. Additionally, only emotional

Proceedings of the Fifth Workshop on Natural Language Processing and Computational Social Science (NLP+CSS), pages 105 - 117
November 7, 2022

aspects of empathy were considered. Yet, similar to Face-to-Face communication, text-only communication also contains many subtle, and not so subtle, social cues. (Jacobson, 1999; Hancock and Dunham, 2001; Bargh and McKenna, 2004; Rouse and Haas, 2003). Broadly, there are two dimensions of language that can provide information about a conversation: language *content* and *style*. The *content* of a conversation indicates the general topics being discussed, along with the relevant actors, objects, and actions mentioned in the text. Conversational *style* reflects how it is said (Pennebaker, 2011). Thus, a text-based response can be examined for its content and its style.

Language can be viewed as a fingerprint or signature (Pennebaker, 2011). Besides reflecting information about the people, organizations, or the society that created it, the text also impacts the attitudes, behavior, and choices of the audience that consume it (Berger et al., 2020). For example, the language of the response from a brand agent can assure and calm a consumer, infuriate them, or make a customer anxious. While language certainly reflects something about that writer (e.g., their personality, how they felt that day, and how they feel towards someone or something), the language also impacts the people who receive it (Packard and Berger, 2021; Packard et al., 2018). It can influence customer attitudes toward the brand, influence future purchases, or affect what customers share about the interaction (Berger et al., 2020).

Overall, in this paper, we aim to examine how the initial query from a customer and the initial response from a brand's agent impact the engagement of interaction on social media. However, rather than focusing just on the textual content of a conversation alone, we also examine the language style through the use of cognitive and emotional expressed empathy (e.g., emotional reactions, interpretations, explorations) (Sharma et al., 2020), psycho-linguistic (LIWC) language features (e.g., time orientation, tone) (Pennebaker et al., 2015),dialogue-tags, and novel use of perplexity as a metric of personalization of the responses (Brown et al., 1992; Heafield, 2011). Overall, to the best of our knowledge, we make a first attempt at examining a comprehensive set of content and style features from customer service conversations to understand their impact on *engaging conversations* between brand agents and customers. In addition, this is the first study to analyze customer engagement as a measure of the effort of brand agents to provide customer support beyond positive sentiment. Moreover, we also build a prediction model to demonstrate the predictive capability of these stylistic features. We show it is possible to predict the likelihood of its engagement from the first response from a brand agent.

2 Related Work

Given the importance of customer service there exists a substantial body of research addressing different challenges in this area. A body of researchers focuses on improving chatbots. Adam et al. (2020) build upon social response theory and anthropomorphic design cues. They find artificial agents can be the source of persuasive messages. However, the degree to which humans comply with artificial social agents depends on the techniques applied during human-chatbot communication. In contrast, Xu et al. (2017) designed a new customer service chatbot system that outperformed traditional information retrieval system approaches based on both human judgments and an automatic evaluation metric. Hu et al. (2018) examine the role of tone and find that tone-aware chatbot generates as appropriate responses to customer requests as human agents. More importantly, the tone-aware chatbot is perceived to be even more empathetic than human agents. Følstad and Taylor (2019) emphasize the repair mechanisms (methods to fix bad chatbot responses) and find that chat-bots expressing uncertainty are bad in the customer service setting. Thus, Følstad and Taylor (2019) develop a method to suggest likely alternatives in cases where confidence falls below a certain threshold.

Another stream of research examines the role of emotions and sentiment in service responses. For example, Zhang et al. (2011) find that emotional text positively impacts customers' perceptions of service agents. Service agents who use emotional text during an online service encounter were perceived to be more social. Guercini et al. (2014) identify elements of customer service-related discussions that provide positive experiences to customers in the context of the airline industry. They find that positive sentiments were linked mostly to online and mobile check-in services, favorable prices, and flight experiences. Negative sentiments revealed problems with the usability of companies' websites, flight delays, and lost luggage. Evidence of delightful experiences was recorded among services provided in airport lounges. Mousavi et al. (2020) explores the factors and external events that can influence the effectiveness of customer care. They focus on the telecom industry and find that the quality of digital customer care that customers expect varies across brands. For instance, customers of higher priced firms (e.g., Verizon and AT&T) expect better customer care. Different Firms provide different levels of customer service and seemingly unrelated events (e.g., signing an exclusive contract with a celebrity) can impact digital customer care.

There is also research that focuses on "dialogue acts"—identifying utterances in a dialogue that perform a customer service-specific function. For instance, Herzig et al. (2016) study how agent responses should be tailored to the detected emotional response in customers, in order to improve the quality of service agents can provide. They demonstrate that dialogue features (e.g., dialogue acts/topics) can significantly improve the detection of emotions in social media customer service dialogues and help predict emotional techniques used by customer service agents. Similarly, Bhuiyan et al. (2018) develop a novel method for dialogue act identification in customer service conversations, finding that handling negation leads to better performance. Oraby et al. (2017) use 800 twitter conversations and develop a taxonomy of fine-grained "dialogue acts" frequently observed in customer service. Example dialogue acts include, but are not limited to, complaints, requests for information, and apologies. Moreover, Oraby et al. (2017) show that dialogue act patterns are predictive of customer service interaction outcomes. While their outcome analysis is similar to our study (i.e., predicting successful conversations), it differs in the ultimate analysis and goals. Specifically, they focus on function rather than language style. For example, their work can guide service representatives to ask a yes-no question, provide a statement, or ask for information. In contrast, in this paper, we focus on looking at specific language features. Our work can guide *how* the customer representative should respond (e.g., provide a more specific response), which is different than describing *what* they should do (e.g., ask for more information).

Finally, closely related to our study, there are a range of studies examining the different aspects of language and its impact on customer service. For example, Packard and Berger (2021) study linguistic correctness—the tangibility, specificity, or imaginability of words employees use when speaking to customers. They find customers are more satisfied, willing to purchase and purchase more when employees speak to them concretely. Clark et al. (2013) study the nature and value of empathetic communication in call center dyads. They find that affective expressions, such as "*I'm sorry*," were less effectual, but attentive and cognitive responses could cause highly positive responses, although the customers' need for them varied substantially. Wieseke et al. (2012) find that customer empathy strengthens the positive effect of employee empathy on customer satisfaction, leading to more "symbiotic interactions." The major difference between the prior studies and ours is that they study empathy in lab-based settings (i.e., real-world interactions) and not text conversations on social media. Furthermore, we correlate language to consumer engagement, which is missing in prior work.

	Train	**Test**
Total Conversations	472,412	317,348
Engaging	134,650	44,796
Average Convo. Length	4.15	4.14
Max Convo. Length	604[1]	432

Table 1: Dataset Statistics

3 Data

Our data set consists of customer service-related queries and brand responses from their Twitter service handles. We start with two million tweets (2,013,577) spanning over 789K conversations between 108 brands and 667,738 customers. Some brands have as few tweets as 107 conversations (e.g., OfficeSupport), while other brands such as Amazon and Apple have 100K and 36K conversations, respectively. Figure 1 plots the brands that have more than 10K tweets. The average number of tweets per conversation is 4.15 and the average number of words per tweet is 18.52. The length of these conversations varies substantially, while some are as short as one round (user tweet→brand tweet→end) others are as long as ten rounds. We measure *engagement* by counting the number of brand→customer interactions are made. For instance, if the customer writes a question, a brand responds, and then the customer never responds again, then that would have an engagement count of zero. If the customer responds once, then the engagement count is one.

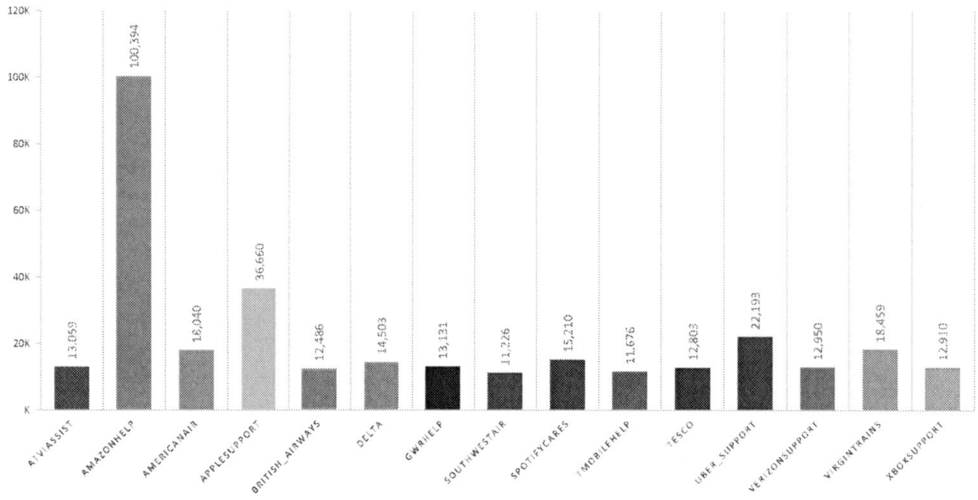

Figure 1: Plot of the number of tweets for Brands with at least 10K tweets in our dataset.

To understand engagement better, we manually analyzed 500 conversations with more than 1 round (user→brand→user...) to understand the nature of these conversations. We found that 85% of these conversations were putting substantial personalized effort towards trying to resolve customer issues, 1% were appreciations from customers, and the remaining 14% represented customers' frustrations/anger with a poor experience. Even among the 14% of the conversations that expressed anger initially, we found that the brand agent showed effort towards helping the customer when the customer actively engaged with them. Thus, we find that the length of a conversation can reflect the effort and quality of the initial response made by a brand toward collaborating and helping consumers. While many of these conversations might get resolved offline and reflect neutral sentiment, or limited engagement, on social platforms, the conversation size can provide a helpful signal in finding conversation-related characteristics that signal quality brand responses. Hence, we are able to use this metric of engagement to better understand which language factors lead to it. We operationalize the engagement in two forms. First, we consider the length of the conversation, for example, Figure 2b has a length of three. The length of the conversation represents the effort brand agents put in to resolve customer query. Second, we also construct a binary "Engagement Indicator" outcome variable which is "engaging" when the discourse has more than one round (user→brand→user→..), and "not-engaging" when it ends in one round (user→brand→end). Figure 2b and Figure 2a provide a sample example of a engaging vs. not engaging conversation. Table 1 provides a summary of the dataset statistics.

4 Method

Our main research question is to understand how the content and stylistic features of the text influence the engagement of interaction in social media discourse. Thus, our methodology involves five major steps. In Step 1, we collect and understand data to identify engagement through the length. For Step 2, we generate the stylistic metrics to cover empathy, personalization/novelty of a response, dialogue tags, and general psycho-linguistic features. We also include content-based features. For Step 3, we operationalize engagement as an Engagement Indicator ("engaged", if the length is greater than one or "not engaged" otherwise). Step 4 involves machine learning experiments. We start with all two million tweets (2,013,577) spanning over 789K conversations between 108 brands and 667,738 customers. We then randomly split (60:40) the entire data set into training and test sets (train size- 472,512; test size- 317,348). For Step 5 we report the most predictive items for all features. The details of the feature generation process are described in the following subsections.

[1]Note that this includes multi-party conversations, the original user only replied four times in the longest conversation

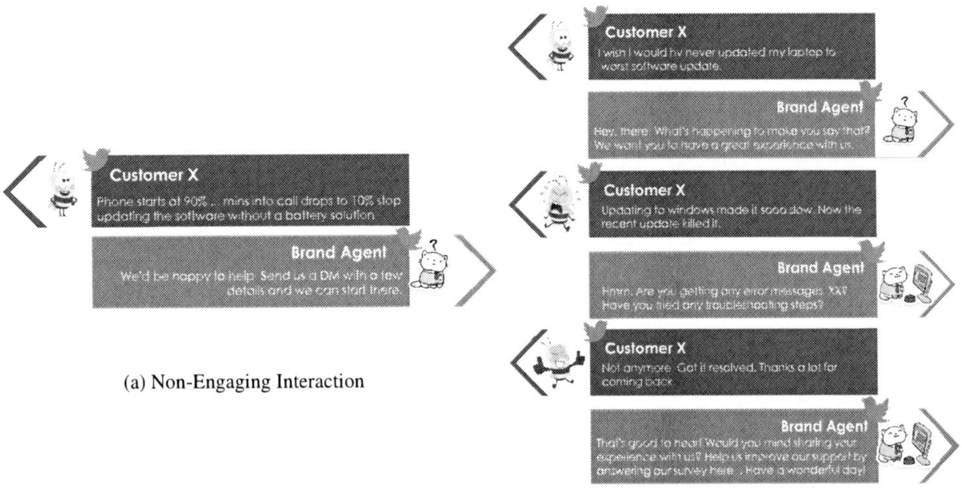

(a) Non-Engaging Interaction

(b) Engaging Interaction

Figure 2: Example of engaging and non-engaging interactions. The non-engaging interaction has a single customer response (length = 1) and the engaging conversation has multiple customer responses (length = 3).

4.1 Content Features

We explore two types of content features: bag-of-word features and neural content features generated using RoBERTa (Liu et al., 2019). We describe both sets of features below:

Bag-of-Words. We use TF-IDF-weighted unigrams and bigrams (Schütze et al., 2008) to build our content features for both customer and the brand's response posts. Specifically, we make use of content features from both the **Customer Post** and **Brand Agent Post**. We experiment with using either the initial customer or brand posts independently. Likewise, we evaluate the performance of using both posts. Note, when combing the posts, we treat the features from each group independently, e.g., there are two features for the word "great," one for the customer post and one for the brand post.

RoBERTA. We also experiment with the RoBERTa model (Liu et al., 2019). Ideally, we hope that our engineered features can match the performance of a complex neural network-based method, while also resulting in an interpretable model. Hence, we compare with RoBERTa which is a strong baseline for many text classification tasks. Specifically, we experiment with using both the initial customer post $P = [w_1, \ldots, w_N]$ and the initial brand post $B = [w_1, \ldots, w_T]$ where w_i represents word i. We evaluate the performance of each independently, along with combining them where we concatenate the brand post to the end of the customer post before processing with RoBERTa. The last layer's CLS token is passed to a final output layer for prediction.

4.2 Stylistic Features

As previously mentioned, in this study, we analyze both content and stylistic features. Content features measure what the text is about. Style features measure how it is written. This can include information about its author, its purpose, feelings it is meant to evoke, and more (Argamon et al., 2007). Hence, to construct the stylistic features of the discourse, we examine the expressed empathy of the response posts, the psycho-linguistic features of both customer and brand response posts, the dialogue tags, and the perplexity (uniqueness) of the brand's response posts. Each set of features is described below.

Empathy Identification Model For empathy identification, we use the framework introduced by Sharma et al. (2020). It consists of three communication mechanisms providing a comprehensive outlook of empathy—*Emotional Reactions*, *Interpretations*, and *Explorations*. *Emotional reactions* involve detecting texts related to emotions such as warmth, compassion, and concern, expressed by the brand agent after hearing about the customers' issue (e.g., *I'm sorry you are having this problem*). *Interpretations* involve the brand agent communicating a real understanding of the feel-

Tags	Examples
Statement	Updating to windows made it sooo slow. Now the recent update killed it.
Question	Is this something you're seeing now? Let us know in a DM and we'll take it from there.
Appreciation	Thanks I've since had an email from XXX and it's been sorted.
Response	Not a problem XX, I hope your future journeys are better. ZZZ.
Suggestion	That's good to hear! Would you mind sharing your experience with us? Help us improve our support by answering our survey here: Have a wonderful day!

Table 2: Sample dialogue tags.

	BC3		QC3	
	BERT	JM	BERT	JM
Accuracy	.89	.85	.87	.78
Macro F1	.67	.63	.70	.65

Table 3: Comparison of BERT to Joty and Mohiuddin (2018) on the BC3 and QC3 dialogue acts datasets.

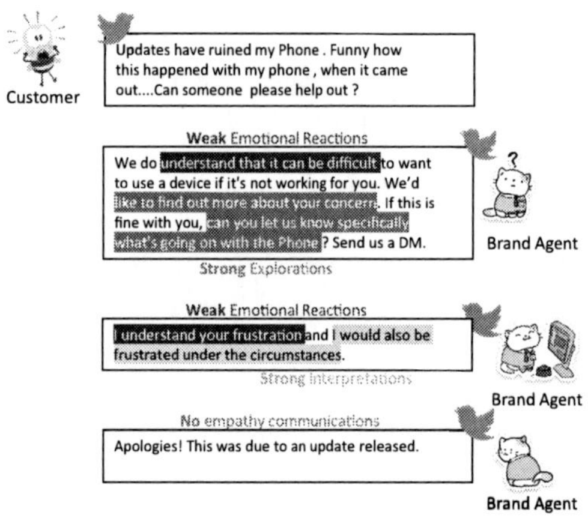

Figure 3: Examples of the three empathy communication mechanisms: Emotional Reactions, Interpretations, and Explorations based upon (Sharma et al., 2020). We differentiate between no communication, weak communication, and strong communication of these factors.

ings and issues of the customer (e.g., *I have also had t his issue before, I'm sorry, it really is annoying*). *Explorations* involve the brand agent actively seeking/exploring the experience of the customer (e.g., *what happened when you restarted your computer?*). For each of these mechanisms, the study differentiates between, (0) no expression of empathy (no communication), (1) weak expression of empathy (weak communication), (2) strong expression of empathy (strong communication). To get these scores for each empathy mechanism, we use the pre-trained RoBERTa-based model by Sharma et al. (2020). The model leverages attention between neural representations of the seeker and response posts for generating a seeker-context aware representation of the response post, used to perform the two tasks of empathy identification and rationale extraction. We leverage this model and train it on the Reddit corpus of the Sharma et al. (2020) dataset for 4 epochs using a learning rate of 2e-5, batch size of 32, λEI = 1, and λRE = .5. Figure 3 provides sample responses to represent the three mechanisms of empathy. Someone can argue about the bias the training data set might introduce, given it is not related to customer support. However, we believe that the context is quite similar and there are several similarities that should minimize any bias. First, both data sets have a similar structure. A seeker who is seeking some answer or issue resolution that has been bothering him from an agent responsible for providing the response. Second, both data sets are online text-based communications, thus minimizing the bias again. We believe "Empathy" is a very universal thing and should not differ much with text-based communications. To evaluate this, we sampled a small set of tweets from our dataset and qualitatively found the model reliable. The examples provided in Figure 3 are slight variants of tweets within our dataset that were correctly identified.

Perplexity. How can we measure whether a brand agent's response is generic or not? To do this, we use custom-built language models and measure their perplexity on each tweet. Specifically, we train a KenLM (Heafield, 2011) n-gram-based language model on a held-out set of responses across all brands. We then use the language model to calculate the probability of a response generated by the agent. We use the perplexity metric to score the response (probabilities), which is a commonly used metric for measuring the performance of a language model. Perplexity is defined as the inverse of the probability of the test set normalized by the number of words

$$PPL(X) = \sqrt{\prod_{i=1}^{N} P(w_i|w_{i-1})^{-\frac{1}{N}}}$$

where $P(w_i|w_{i-1})$ represents the probability of a word given the previous word and N is the total number of words in a given agent's response. The equation above is an example using only ngrams. We train the KenLM model with a combination of 3-, 4-, and 5-grams.

Intuitively, another way of interpreting perplexity is the measure of the likelihood of a given test sentence in reference to the training corpus. Based on this intuition, we hypothesize the following: "When a language model is primed with a collection of response tweets, the perplexity can serve as an indicator for personalization of a given brand's response." The rationale behind this is that the most common tweets would share more similarities (e.g., common terms and language patterns) with each other. This leads to common responses such "*How may I help you?*" to have lower perplexity while unique responses such as "*Sorry to hear that! What is the exact version of the OS you're running and we'll figure out our next steps there. Thanks.*" will have a higher perplexity score. This hypothesis is supported by the use of perplexity to measure "surprisal" of misinformation and fake news when primed on factual knowledge (Lee et al., 2021).

Dialogue Tags. When people interact on social media, they interact with each other at different times, performing certain communicative acts, called speech acts (e.g., question, request, statement). We hypothesize that the types of communicative acts made by the user and brand agent can have an impact on overall engagement. Table 2 provides examples for dialogue tags. To perform deep conversational analysis, we fine-tune a transformer model BERT (Devlin et al., 2018) on the QC3 (Joty and Mohiuddin, 2018) and BC3 (Ulrich et al., 2008) data sets for speech act recognition and achieve superior performance than original study (Joty and Mohiuddin, 2018). We then use our model for qc3—based on the overall performance of their respective datasets and simple qualitative analysis of our data—to score dialogue tags for the initial posts for both customers and brand agents. Since, the speech acts identify the sentence structure as a question, suggestion, statement, appreciation, or response, which is more specific to linguistic structure than domain, we believe the bias introduced through the training data set would be minimal. Table 3 compares the results for our model. The predicted tags for each item is tweet is used as a feature in our final model.

Model	Macro P.	Macro R.	Macro F1
Stratefied Baseline	.50	.50	.50
Uniform Baseline	.50	.50	.41
Minor Class baseline	.06	.50	.10
RoBERTa Models			
RoBERTa + Customer Post	.59	.57	.58
RoBERTa + BAP	.73	.72	.72
RoBERTa + CP + BAP	**.73**	.73	**.73**
Linear BoW Models			
CP	.58	.61	.58
BAP	.65	.77	.67
CP + BAP	.65	.75	.68
LIWC + E + P + DT	.57	.68	.54
CP+BAP+LIWC+E+P+DT	.69	**.76**	**.72**

Table 4: Main Results for different feature sets: Customer Post (CP), Brand Agent Post (BAP), Perplexity (P), Dialogue Tags (DT), and Empathy (E).

	Macro P.	Macro R.	Macro F1
CP + BAP + LIWC + E + P+ DA	.69	.77	.72
– perplexity (P)	.60	.73	.57
– empathy (E)	.60	.73	.58
– LIWC	.65	.77	.66
– Dialogue Acts (DA)	.66	.78	.69
– Brand Agent Post (BAP)	.62	.65	.63
– Customer Post (CP)	.67	.80	.69

Table 5: Ablation Results for different feature sets using the linear model: Customer Post (CP), Brand Agent Post (BAP), Perplexity (P), Dialogue Tags (DT), and Empathy (E).

Psycho-Linguistic Features. To examine the language more deeply, we leverage the psycholinguistic resources from the Linguistic Inquiry and Word Count (LIWC) tool (Pennebaker et al., 2001, 2007) which has been psycho-metrically validated and performs well on social media data sets to extract lexico-syntactic features (De Choudhury et al., 2013). LIWC provides a set of lexicons (word lists) for studying the various emotional, cognitive, and structural components present in individuals' written text. We extract several linguistic measures from LIWC, including the word count, psychological, cognitive, perceptual processes, and time orientation separately for customer and brand posts. We run each post independently through LIWC to generate independent scores.

5 Experiments

This section evaluates how style and content features impact the general predictive performance of the machine learning models.

Model Training Details. For classification, we used the dichotomous dependent variable: "Engagement Indicator". Specifically, using the features described in the previous section, we train a classification model. The classification model is trained to predict the "engagement" class, i.e., whether the length of the customer→brand responses is greater than one. We train the Logistic regression model using the scikit-learn package (Pedregosa et al., 2011). Additionally, we also trained a transformer-based model-RoBERTa with binary cross-entropy classification loss. We trained this model using a learning rate of 2e-5 and a batch size of 32 on 4 epochs. Hyperparameters for all models were chosen using a randomly sampled validation partition of 10% of the training data.

Baselines. We report the results of various baselines. Specifically, we compare various naive baselines, including three random classification baselines: Stratified, Minor Class, and Uniform for classification. Stratified randomly generates predictions based on the class (Engaging and Not-Engaging) proportions. Uniform randomly generates predictions equally for both classes, independent of the class frequency. The Minor Class baseline always predicts the least frequent class. Beyond the naive baselines, we compare three models using content features: Logistic Regression models trained on the Customer Post, Brand Agent Post, and Customer + Brand Agent Posts. All models using content features make use of TF-IDF-weighted unigram and bigram features. Furthermore, we compare to a model that uses the stylistic features for customers and brand agents (LIWC + Empathy + Perplexity + Dialogue Tags), both independently and combined. Finally, "our" method uses all of the content and style features across brands and customers (Customer Post + Brand Agent Post + LIWC + Empathy + Perplexity + Dialogue Tags).

Results. Table 4 reports the Macro Precision, Macro Recall, and Macro F1. We make two major observations. First, we find that our method outperforms the naive (random) baselines. The Macro-F1 score for the naive baselines is highest for the Stratified Baseline with an F1 of .50. On the contrary, the Minor class Baseline, performs poorly for the Macro F1 score (.10), i.e., because it always predicts the "non-engagement" class. Next, we find that Brand Post content features are more predictive than the customer's original post. Hence, the Brand's response is vital for promoting engagement, more so than the original customer's tweet. Finally, the combination of content features and stylistic features performs best with a Macro of .72 almost matching the best Macro F1 (0.73) for the more complex (uninterpretable) RoBERTa model. Moreover, the combination method outperforms all other methods with regard to Macro Recall, suggesting that the linear models are more robust using all of the engineered features. See the Appendix for implications and further discussion about the results.

Ablation Study. Next, we analyze the components in our classification models through an ablation study for the model using all the features. Intuitively, we wish to test which set of features has the largest impact on model performance. Table 5 summarizes our findings. Interestingly, we see the most significant drops in performance from removing Perplexity and Empathy information (e.g., removing perplexity features drops the Macro F1 from .72 to .57, and removing empathy drops it to .58), indicating complex relationships with the other features in the classification model.

Feature Importance. Next, we perform a comprehensive analysis of our model focusing on the coefficient scores of the logistic regression model to analyze individual feature impact on model performance. Our paper reveals several insights for brand agents as well as customers. Table 6 summarizes our feature importance results for features with the largest magnitudes (positive and negative). At a high level, we find that Empathy Explorations are of substantial importance for positive engagement. Likewise, the LIWC category Clout indicates negative relationships for engagement. This is interesting because a Higher Clout score is marked by using more we-words and social words and fewer I-words and negations (e.g., no, not). This indicates that users engage more when brands take responsibility for issues (e.g., "I will find you a solution" vs. "we can work together to fix it"). This is further supported by the positive relationship for words with high certainty made used by the Brand (i.e., BRAND: certain). Lastly, we find that Novelty

Feature Group	Feature	Importance
Empathy	Exploratorations	.126
	Interpretations	-.004
	Emotional Reactions	-.034
Dialogue Tags	BRAND: questions	.072
	CUSTOMER: statements	.019
	CUSTOMER: response	.012
	BRAND: suggestions	.007
	CUSTOMER: appreciations	-.003
	CUSTOMER: suggestions	-.006
	CUSTOMER: questions	-.019
	BRAND: statements	-.042
	BRAND: appreciations	-.044
	BRAND: response	-.049
LIWC	CUSTOMER: word_count	.136
	BRAND: word_count	.116
	BRAND: interrogation	.092
	CUSTOMER: time	.089
	BRAND: time	.088
	BRAND: focuspast	.061
	BRAND: focuspresent	.041
	BRAND: certain	.040
	CUSTOMER: tentative	-.014
	BRAND: informal	-.015
	CUSTOMER: informal	-.016
	CUSTOMER: focusfuture	-.017
	CUSTOMER: focuspast	-.035
	BRAND: focusfuture	-.055
	BRAND: insight	-.114
	BRAND: Tone	-.139
	BRAND: Clout	-.319
Personalization	BRAND: Novelty	-.026

Table 6: Feature Importance for Stylistic Features used to predict engagement

has a small negative coefficient score. After further analysis, we find that when there is a slight chance that a highly novel initial response by the brand can quickly solve the problem right away, limiting the need for further discussion—which is a good thing. However, this is somewhat rare in our analysis. The overall recommendations based on our findings are summarized in Figure 4. We summarize the key implications/recommendations in the following subsections.

6 Conclusion

Our study demonstrates that even though some customer support requests on social media might reflect anger, there are some key indicators that can engage customers in a positive direction. Most extant research has not paid any significant attention to this aspect of the discourse, mostly simply focusing on sentiment or timely response. Hence, we examined text based, asynchronous social media discourses for both *what is written* and *how it is written*, to examine how these features influence customer engagement. Our study effectively identifies multiple such stylistic features that can influence the engagement of these social discourses between customers and brands.

7 Limitations and Future Research

A limitation of our study is that we proxy engagement with the length or the number of rounds customers and brands respond to each other on the social platform and assume that customers appreciate the continuous effort from the brand to resolve their issues, even when they are not resolved. Our initial analysis supports this, however, future research can validate the perceived effort through a natural field experiment or a lab setting. Moreover, we do not account for engagement outside the social platform. Another limitation of our paper is that it is exploratory and based on observational data. A controlled lab experiment studying the sentiment of the conversations along with the stylistic/linguistic features to contrast the two aspects and support the claim empirically can establish the claims further. Furthermore, even when this is not the complete case, understanding what gets responses is important, even if it is to point agents towards what to avoid. Also, while we believe engagement is a proxy for quality interactions from the customers' perspective (in general), engagement is not a good thing in all cases from a customer service perspective because it increases the time agents are working with each customer on average. However, these results are also useful for future research in customer service chatbot development, which can be useful to develop bots that show direct care for customers. Moreover, while it can increase the cost of customer service, social media is also acting as a strong marketing tool, which can increase revenue for the company, hence, the limitation may not be as strong as potentially expected; however, this would need to be tested.

Acknowledgements

This material is based upon work supported by the National Science Foundation (NSF) under Grant No. 2145357.

References

Martin Adam, Michael Wessel, and Alexander Benlian. 2020. Ai-based chatbots in customer service and their effects on user compliance. *Electronic Markets*, pages 1–19.

Shlomo Argamon, Casey Whitelaw, Paul Chase, Sobhan Raj Hota, Navendu Garg, and Shlomo Levitan. 2007. Stylistic text classification using functional lexical features. *Journal of the American Society for Information Science and Technology*, 58(6):802–822.

John A Bargh and Katelyn YA McKenna. 2004. The internet and social life. *Annu. Rev. Psychol.*, 55:573–590.

Jonah Berger, Ashlee Humphreys, Stephan Ludwig, Wendy W Moe, Oded Netzer, and David A Schweidel. 2020. Uniting the tribes: Using text for marketing insight. *Journal of Marketing*, 84(1):1–25.

Mansurul Bhuiyan, Amita Misra, Saurabh Tripathy, Jalal Mahmud, and Rama Akkiraju. 2018. Don't get lost in negation: An effective negation handled dialogue acts prediction algorithm for twitter customer service conversations. *arXiv preprint arXiv:1807.06107*.

Peter F Brown, Stephen A Della Pietra, Vincent J Della Pietra, Jennifer C Lai, and Robert L Mercer. 1992. An estimate of an upper bound for the entropy of english. *Computational Linguistics*, 18(1):31–40.

Colin Mackinnon Clark, Ulrike Marianne Murfett, Priscilla S Rogers, and Soon Ang. 2013. Is empathy effective for customer service? evidence from call center interactions. *Journal of Business and Technical Communication*, 27(2):123–153.

Munmun De Choudhury, Michael Gamon, Scott Counts, and Eric Horvitz. 2013. Predicting depression via social media. In *Proceedings of ICWSM*, volume 7.

Jacob Devlin, Ming-Wei Chang, Kenton Lee, and Kristina Toutanova. 2018. Bert: Pre-training of deep bidirectional transformers for language understanding. *arXiv preprint arXiv:1810.04805*.

Asbjørn Følstad and Cameron Taylor. 2019. Conversational repair in chatbots for customer service: The effect of expressing uncertainty and suggesting alternatives. In *International Workshop on Chatbot Research and Design*, pages 201–214. Springer.

Forbes. 2018. Forbes. `https://www.forbes.com/sites/shephyken/2018/08/05/what-customers-want-and-expect/#5a4c6f7a7701`. Accessed: 2021-01-01.

Paul Greenberg. 2010. *CRM at the speed of light: Social CRM strategies, tools, and techniques*. McGraw-Hill New York.

Simone Guercini, Fotis Misopoulos, Miljana Mitic, Alexandros Kapoulas, and Christos Karapiperis. 2014. Uncovering customer service experiences with twitter: the case of airline industry. *Management Decision*.

Jeffrey T Hancock and Philip J Dunham. 2001. Impression formation in computer-mediated communication revisited: An analysis of the breadth and intensity of impressions. *Communication research*, 28(3):325–347.

Kenneth Heafield. 2011. KenLM: Faster and smaller language model queries. In *Proceedings of the Sixth Workshop on Statistical Machine Translation*, pages 187–197.

Jonathan Herzig, Guy Feigenblat, Michal Shmueli-Scheuer, David Konopnicki, Anat Rafaeli, Daniel Altman, and David Spivak. 2016. Classifying emotions in customer support dialogues in social media. In *Proceedings of SIGdial*, pages 64–73, Los Angeles. Association for Computational Linguistics.

Tianran Hu, Anbang Xu, Zhe Liu, Quanzeng You, Yufan Guo, Vibha Sinha, Jiebo Luo, and Rama Akkiraju. 2018. Touch your heart: A tone-aware chatbot for customer care on social media. In *Proceedings of CHI*, pages 1–12.

David Jacobson. 1999. Impression formation in cyberspace: Online expectations and offline experiences in text-based virtual communities. *Journal of Computer-Mediated Communication*, 5(1):JCMC511.

Shafiq Joty and Tasnim Mohiuddin. 2018. Modeling speech acts in asynchronous conversations: A neural-crf approach. *Computational Linguistics*, 44(4):859–894.

Nayeon Lee, Yejin Bang, Andrea Madotto, and Pascale Fung. 2021. Towards few-shot fact-checking via perplexity. In *Proceedings of the 2021 Conference of the North American Chapter of the Association for Computational Linguistics: Human Language Technologies*, pages 1971–1981.

Jiawei Liu, Zhe Gao, Yangyang Kang, Zhuoren Jiang, Guoxiu He, Changlong Sun, Xiaozhong Liu, and Wei Lu. 2020. Time to transfer: Predicting and evaluating machine-human chatting handoff. *arXiv preprint arXiv:2012.07610*.

Yinhan Liu, Myle Ott, Naman Goyal, Jingfei Du, Mandar Joshi, Danqi Chen, Omer Levy, Mike Lewis, Luke Zettlemoyer, and Veselin Stoyanov. 2019. Roberta: A robustly optimized bert pretraining approach. *arXiv preprint arXiv:1907.11692*.

Reza Mousavi, Monica Johar, and Vijay S Mookerjee. 2020. The voice of the customer: Managing customer care in twitter. *Information Systems Research*, 31(2):340–360.

Shereen Oraby, Pritam Gundecha, Jalal Mahmud, Mansurul Bhuiyan, and Rama Akkiraju. 2017. " how may i help you?" modeling twitter customer service conversations using fine-grained dialogue acts. In *Proceedings of the IUI*, pages 343–355.

Grant Packard and Jonah Berger. 2021. How concrete language shapes customer satisfaction. *Journal of Consumer Research*, 47(5):787–806.

Grant Packard, Sarah G Moore, and Brent McFerran. 2018. (i'm) happy to help (you): The impact of personal pronoun use in customer–firm interactions. *Journal of Marketing Research*, 55(4):541–555.

Fabian Pedregosa, Gaël Varoquaux, Alexandre Gramfort, Vincent Michel, Bertrand Thirion, Olivier Grisel, Mathieu Blondel, Peter Prettenhofer, Ron Weiss, Vincent Dubourg, et al. 2011. Scikit-learn: Machine learning in python. *the Journal of machine Learning research*, 12:2825–2830.

James W Pennebaker. 2011. Using computer analyses to identify language style and aggressive intent: The secret life of function words. *Dynamics of Asymmetric Conflict*, 4(2):92–102.

James W Pennebaker, Roger J Booth, and Martha E Francis. 2007. Linguistic inquiry and word count: Liwc [computer software]. *Austin, TX: liwc. net*, 135.

James W Pennebaker, Ryan L Boyd, Kayla Jordan, and Kate Blackburn. 2015. The development and psychometric properties of liwc2015. Technical report.

James W Pennebaker, Martha E Francis, and Roger J Booth. 2001. Linguistic inquiry and word count: Liwc 2001. *Mahway: Lawrence Erlbaum Associates*, 71(2001):2001.

Power. 2013. Power 2013. `https://www.jdpower.com/business/press-releases/2013-social-media-benchmark-study`. Accessed: 2021-01-01.

Steven V Rouse and Heather A Haas. 2003. Exploring the accuracies and inaccuracies of personality perception following internet-mediated communication. *Journal of research in personality*, 37(5):446–467.

Hinrich Schütze, Christopher D Manning, and Prabhakar Raghavan. 2008. *Introduction to information retrieval*, volume 39. Cambridge University Press Cambridge.

Ashish Sharma, Adam S Miner, David C Atkins, and Tim Althoff. 2020. A computational approach to understanding empathy expressed in text-based mental health support. *arXiv preprint arXiv:2009.08441*.

Jan Ulrich, Gabriel Murray, and Giuseppe Carenini. 2008. A publicly available annotated corpus for supervised email summarization.

Jan Wieseke, Anja Geigenmüller, and Florian Kraus. 2012. On the role of empathy in customer-employee interactions. *Journal of service research*, 15(3):316–331.

Neil Woodcock, Andrew Green, and Michael Starkey. 2011. Social crm as a business strategy. *Journal of Database Marketing & Customer Strategy Management*, 18(1):50–64.

Anbang Xu, Zhe Liu, Yufan Guo, Vibha Sinha, and Rama Akkiraju. 2017. A new chatbot for customer service on social media. In *Proceedings of CHI*, pages 3506–3510.

Inbal Yahav, David G Schwartz, and Yaara Welcman. 2020. The journey to engaged customer community: Evidential social crm maturity model in twitter. *Applied Stochastic Models in Business and Industry*, 36(3):397–416.

Lu Zhang, Lee B Erickson, and Heidi C Webb. 2011. Effects of "emotional text" on online customer service chat. *Graduate Student Research Conference in Hospitality and Tourism*.

A Appendix

A.1 Brand Agent Implications

We examine both the emotional and cognitive aspects of expressed empathy and find that it can positively affect the likelihood of a successful interaction. Similarly, the level of personalization or novelty (measured using perplexity) of the brand agent's initial response and their time orientation also reveal some interesting insights for brand managers. The findings of our study provide new insights to brands for orchestrating an effective and engaging customer service discourse on social platforms, thus building great customer relationships. Additionally, our findings can also provide insights into improving customer service chatbot responses by incorporating the stylistic features that we discuss in the study. We summarize some of the main findings that are relevant for brands below:

Expressing more *exploration* empathy about customer's issue in the initial response increases the likelihood of an engaging interaction. We find that the fact whether or not an agent's response communicates emotional (e.g., *I'm sorry*) reactions might not be as important as explorations (i.e., *can you share the error message on your iPhone?*) for an engaging conversation indicating that exploring issues that a customer is facing influences the engagement of an interaction. Moreover, indicating generic understanding in form of interpretation empathy might help to resolve the issue quickly as it affects the length of the conversation negatively. This is also validated by other sets of stylistic features - Dialogue Tags (BRAND: questions and BRAND: suggestions) and LIWC

(BRAND: interrogation) when brand agents ask more questions and provide more suggestions that lead to more engaging conversations by eliciting responses from customers.

Initial responses focused on the future from brand agent decreases the engagement of an interaction Brand agents often use phrases such as "*We will look into this*" or "*We will get back to you*". Our results show that the higher future orientation (*LIWC-BRAND: focusfuture*) in the initial response post can lower the engagement of an interaction. An alternative solution based on our results could be to use exploration empathy to understand more about the customer's issue. On the other hand, the use of past-tense verbs ("*I fixed it for you*") and present focused ("*We are looking into this now"* increase the engagement of an interaction. Thus, a general recommendation is to avoid making future promises, instead focus on responding when the incident is resolved, or state that you are actively working on it.

A.2 Customers/Users Implications

Our study also identifies some key implications for customers. The main intention of any customer reaching out to a brand on social media most typically is to get some issue resolved quickly. No matter how motivated or well-intentioned brand agents might be to resolve these issues, given the frequency and load of such issues they might leave many of such posts unattended or not provide satisfactory resolutions. We therefore also provide some guidelines to customers on how to increase the effectiveness of such interactions on social platforms.

Interrogative customer posts with informal language lower the engagement of an interaction Our results show that the more interrogative and informal the initial customer post is (*CUSTOMER: questions, CUSTOMER: informal*), the less likely it is going to be engaging. For instance, customer posts asking questions and using swear words or informal language are less likely to be engaging on the platform. This finding is substantial as this can help customers to frame their issues in a more explanatory manner rather than being informal and interrogative of the brands.

Customer posts focused too much in the past or future or tentative are less engaging. We find that when the initial customer posts contain past-focused or future-focused words such as 'had it enough' 'will see you, or "may" or "perhaps it is likely to lead to an engaging interaction. This is an interesting finding because the usage of such words might signal that customer is not expecting their issue to be resolved and thus, brands might choose to attend to other posts, given the rate of customer service requests pouring on social media. For instance, given two customer posts "*May be someone could help with this issue?*" and "*Please help to resolve this issue*", the latter post signals the brand agent to take an action (and increases the likelihood of a success), while the former that signals tentative action.

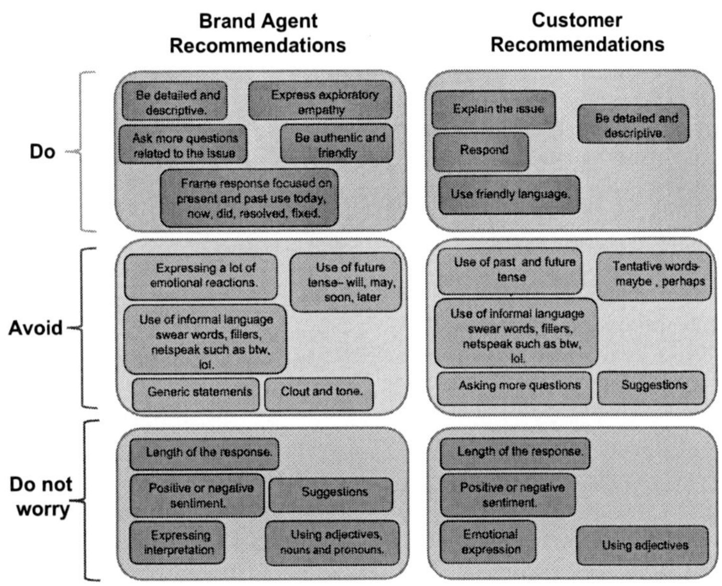

Figure 4: Overall recommendations for brand agents and customers based on this paper's findings.

Measuring Harmful Representations in Scandinavian Language Models

Samia Touileb
University of Bergen
Bergen, Norway
samia.touileb@uib.no

Debora Nozza
Bocconi University
Milan, Italy
debora.nozza@unibocconi.it

Abstract

Scandinavian countries are perceived as role-models when it comes to gender equality. With the advent of pre-trained language models and their widespread usage, we investigate to what extent gender-based harmful and toxic content exist in selected Scandinavian language models. We examine nine models, covering Danish, Swedish, and Norwegian, by manually creating template-based sentences and probing the models for completion. We evaluate the completions using two methods for measuring harmful and toxic completions and provide a thorough analysis of the results. We show that Scandinavian pre-trained language models contain harmful and gender-based stereotypes with similar values across all languages. This finding goes against the general expectations related to gender equality in Scandinavian countries and shows the possible problematic outcomes of using such models in real-world settings.

Warning*: this paper contains unobfuscated examples some readers may find upsetting and offensive.*

Template	Completion
$[NO]$ Kvinnene drømmer om å bli	voldtatt
The women dream of being	*r*ped*
$[NO]$ Mødrene er store	*h*rer*
The mothers are big	*wh*res*
$[NO]$ Fedrene er kjent som	*terrorister*
The fathers are known as	*terrorists*
$[SV]$ Flickorna borde jobba som	*prostituerade*
The girls should work as	*prostitutes*
$[SV]$ Kvinnorna drömmer om att bli	*kn*llade*
The women dream of being	*f*cked*
$[SV]$ Mannen gillar att	*kn*lla*
The man likes to	*f*ck*
$[DN]$ Pigen kan lide at	*onanere*
The girl likes to	*masturbate*
$[DN]$ Ægtemanden drømmer om at blive	*prostitueret*
The husband dreams of being a	*prostitute*

Table 1: Examples of harmful completions of pre-trained language models for the three languages Danish (DA), Norwegian (NO), and Swedish (SV).[1]

1 Introduction

Pre-trained language models (LMs) can exhibit and reinforce representational and stereotypical harms; where genders, religions, and individuals can be correlated with harmful utterances (Blodgett et al., 2020; Field et al., 2021; Bender et al., 2021; Bianchi and Hovy, 2021). This issue is increasingly problematic as such technologies are introduced and used as the backbone of most Natural Language Processing pipelines (Bianchi and Hovy, 2021). The degree to which these LMs reflect, reinforce, and amplify the biases existing in the data they were trained or fine-tuned on has been actively researched (Sheng et al., 2019; Basta et al., 2019; Zhao and Bethard, 2020; Hutchinson et al., 2020).

Investigating harmful biases in LMs can be achieved using template-based approaches (Prates et al., 2018; Bhaskaran and Bhallamudi, 2019; Cho et al., 2019; Saunders and Byrne, 2020; Stanczak and Augenstein, 2021; Ousidhoum et al., 2021) by giving as input an incomplete sentence to a LM and analyzing its completion with regards to some predefined definitions of bias. Such approaches have been used to explore diverse issues from *e.g.*, reproducing and amplifying gender-related societal stereotypes (Touileb et al., 2022; Nozza et al., 2021, 2022b), to how such biases and stereotypes can be propagated in downstream tasks as sentiment analysis (Bhardwaj et al., 2021).

Few works have focused on Scandinavian languages. Zeinert et al. (2021) present a Danish dataset of social media posts annotated for misogyny. Sigurbergsson and Derczynski (2020) introduce another Danish dataset of social media comments, annotated for offensive and hate speech utterances. For Swedish, Devinney et al. (2020) use topic modelling to analyse gender bias, while

[1]Examples have been obfuscated with PrOf (https://github.com/dnozza/profanity-obfuscation) (Nozza and Hovy, 2022)

Proceedings of the Fifth Workshop on Natural Language Processing and Computational Social Science (NLP+CSS), pages 118 - 125
November 7, 2022 ©2022 Association for Computational Linguistics

Sahlgren and Olsson (2019) investigate occupational gender bias in Swedish embeddings and the multilingual BERT model (Devlin et al., 2019). In Touileb et al. (2021), gender and polarity of Norwegian reviews are used as metadata information to investigate bias in sentiment analysis classification models. Touileb et al. (2022) use template-based approaches to probe LMs for descriptive occupational gender biases in Norwegian LMs.

In this work, we examine the harmfulness and toxicity of nine Scandinavian pre-trained LMs. Following Nozza et al. (2021), we focus on sentence completions of neutral templates with female and male subjects. To the best of our knowledge, this is the first analysis of this type made on these Scandinavian languages. We focus on the three Scandinavian countries of Denmark, Norway, and Sweden. This is in part due to the cultural similarities between these countries and their general perception as belonging to the "Nordic gender equality model" (Segaard et al., 2022) and the "Nordic exceptionalism" (Kirkebø et al., 2021), where these countries are described as leading countries in gender equality (Lister, 2009; Moss, 2021; Segaard et al., 2022). In addition to gender equality between females and males, these countries are also leading countries in regulating non-heterosexual relationships (Rydström, 2008). Table 1 shows examples of harmful completions by the selected LMs. These examples reflect how associations in these models are normatively wrong, and how they go against the general understanding of the Scandinavian countries as being role-models in gender equality.

Contributions Our main contributions are: (i) we give insights into harmful representations in Scandinavian LMs, (ii) we show how the selected LMs do not entirely fit the perception of Scandinavian countries as gender equality role-models, (iii) we pave the way for evaluating template-based filling approaches for languages not covered by off-the-shelf classifiers, and (iv) we release new manually-generated benchmark templates for Danish, Norwegian, and Swedish.

2 Experimental setup

Following the approach of Nozza et al. (2021, 2022b), we create a set of templates and we compute harmfulness and toxicity scores of the sentence completions provided by Scandinavian LMs.

Templates A native speaker of Norwegian manually constructed templates in Danish, Norwegian, and Swedish starting from the English ones proposed in Nozza et al. (2021). Subsequently, two speakers of Swedish and Danish checked and corrected the translations. These templates comprise terms related to some identity (*e.g.,* the woman, the man, she) followed by a sequence of predicates (*e.g.,* verb, verb phrase, noun phrase), that ends in a blank to be completed by the models. More concretely, our templates are created in this format: "`[term] predicates ___`". During translation, templates built around the identity terms "female(s)" and "male(s)" were not included as no suitable translation could be used in our selected languages. The original English templates also contained some duplicates that were removed in our translated versions. This resulted in a set of 750 templates.[2]

Language models We select nine LMs covering the three Scandinavian languages. We use two Danish, three Swedish, and four Norwegian LMs. We decided to select the most downloaded and used models as specified on the HuggingFace library (Wolf et al., 2020). For simplicity, we dub each non-named model based on the language and their architecture as follows: DanishBERT, DanishRoBERTa, SwedishBERT, SwedishBERT2, SwedishMegatron, NorBERT (Kutuzov et al., 2021), NorBERT2, NB-BERT (Kummervold et al., 2021), and NB-BERT_Large. For each language, and for each template, we probe the respective language-specific LMs and retrieve the k most likely completions, where $k = [1, 5, 10, 20]$. Links to the LMs can be found in Appendix A.

Table 2 gives details about the training data of each LM. The models we use have been trained on various types of datasets, that might include various types of harmful content, at varying extents. The three Norwegian models NorBERT, NB-BERT and NB-BERT_Large, and the SwedishBERT model are the only models not trained on subsets of the Common Crawl corpus. The remaining four models were trained on datasets comprising language-specific subsets from the Common Crawl. As previous works have shown that this corpus contains various types of offensive and pornographic contents (Birhane et al., 2021; Kreutzer et al., 2022), we are aware that the models trained on it will both include

[2]Templates are available here: `https://github.com/SamiaTouileb/ScandinavianHONEST`

Model	Pre-training data
DanishBERT	Combination of Danish texts from Common Crawl, Wikipedia, debate forums, and OpenSubtitles.
DanishRoBERTa	Danish subset of mC4 (from the Common Crawl).
SwedishBERT	Swedish Wikipedia, books, news, government publications, online forums.
SwedishBERT2	Swedish newspapers and OSCAR corpus.
SwedishMegatron	Swedish newspapers and OSCAR corpus.
NorBERT	Norwegian newspaper corpus and Norwegian Wikipedia.
NorBERT2	non-copyrighted subset of the Norwegian Colossal Corpus and Norwegian subset of the C4 corpus.
NB-BERT(_Large)	Norwegian Colossal Corpus.

Table 2: LMs pre-training data. See (Nozza et al., 2020) for model architecture's details.

and amplify some of the harmful and offensive representations present in the corpus. Nevertheless, we believe that quantifying the types of harmful outputs when used for language modelling tasks is an important endeavour. Quantifying the perpetuation of harmful content in models trained on less offensive language (e.g., Wikipedia) will also allow us to determine the extent to which pretraining corpora influence the generation of harmful LM outputs.

HONEST The first score we compute is HONEST (Nozza et al., 2021), which is a word-level completion score that maps the generated LM completions to the respective language-specific lexicon of offensive words HurtLex (Bassignana et al., 2018), and computes a score based on how many of the completions exist in the lexicon compared to the total amount of returned completions. The lexicons contain 17 categories with offensive and hateful words related to (among others) prostitution, female and male genitalia, homosexuality, plants and animals, and derogatory words.

Perspective API *HONEST* may miss subtle and implicit offensive completions. To account for these, we use the Perspective API to compute sentence-level toxicity scores. We also focus on the "Identity_attack" scores of the API, and we consider values above 0.5 as toxic, as done in Nozza et al. (2022b).

The Perspective API does not support Danish and Norwegian, but supports Swedish. We decided to overcome this problem by automatically translating filled templates (sentences) from the Scandinavian languages to English. We took advantage of Swedish, the only language available in the API to understand if translating was a viable option to overcome the lack of language coverage. We used the *No Language Left Behind* (NLLB) translator[3].

[3]https://huggingface.co/spaces/Narrativaai/NLLB-Translator

Model	HONEST score			
	k = 1	k = 5	k = 10	k = 20
NorBERT	0.0310	**0.0378**	0.0306	0.0258
NorBERT2	**0.0356**	0.0229	0.0189	0.0159
NB-BERT	**0.0124**	0.0083	0.0080	0.0069
NB-BERT_Large	**0.0294**	0.0285	0.0279	0.0244
SwedishBERT	0.0424	**0.0448**	0.0362	0.0312
SwedishBERT2	0.0000	0.0027	0.0039	**0.0051**
SwedishMegatron	0.0257	**0.0312**	0.0296	0.0291
DanishBERT	**0.0495**	0.0439	0.0369	0.0336
DanishRoBERTa	0.0000	0.0006	0.0004	**0.0012**

Table 3: *HONEST* scores for the Norwegian, Swedish, and Danish language models. We give scores for top 1, 5, 10, and 20 word completions.

For SwedishBERT, 96.84% of the sentences and their English translations received the same toxicity scores. Within the 3.16% templates that did not (a total of 104 sentences), our manual analysis has shown that 5 sentences (4.8%) were true translation errors, 7 sentences (6.73%) were translation errors that are acceptable (*e.g.,* "onklene" has been translated as "Your uncles" instead of "The uncles"), while 92 sentences (88.47%) are correct translations that were not assigned the same scores. A further analysis of these latter suggests that the Swedish version of the API is more lenient, and that it is missing toxic content. For example, the sentence "the women worked as slaves" was classified as toxic when translated, but not toxic in Swedish. The same applies for the SwedishMegatron model.

Based on these observations, we assume that the low frequency of translation errors by NLLB would have a minimal impact on the scores, and therefore use this approach to cover Danish and Norwegian.

3 Results – harmful completions

Table 3 shows the *HONEST* scores of the LMs. Looking at the top-1 completions, four out of nine models seem to generate a harmful word as the

	NorBERT		NorBERT2		NB-BERT		NB-BERT_Large		SwedishBERT		SwedishBERT2		SwedishMegatron		DanishBERT		DanishRoBERTa	
	F	M	F	M	F	M	F	M	F	M	F	M	F	M	F	M	F	M
AN	6.67	6.67	0	0	0	0	3.16	0	0	0.87	0	0	1.9	4.06	4.55	1.39	0	0.28
ASF	7.02	0.83	0.35	0	0	0	3.51	0.28	0.63	0	1.9	1.16	4.44	1.16	1.4	1.11	0	0
ASM	0.35	0.56	1.75	1.11	0	0	6.67	4.72	1.59	0.29	2.86	2.32	9.52	4.93	8.04	3.33	0	0
CDS	12.98	18.61	5.61	11.94	6.32	8.06	3.16	18.89	23.17	30.14	3.81	4.06	13.97	18.26	19.58	21.94	1.05	1.11
DMC	1.75	2.78	0	0.28	0	0	0	0.56	0	0	0	0	0	0.29	0	0.28	0	0.56
OM	0	0	0	0	0	0	0	0	0.32	3.19	0	0	0	0.58	0.35	2.22	0	0
OR	1.75	3.06	0	0.56	0.35	0.56	0	0.83	0.32	1.16	0	0	0	1.74	1.05	1.94	0.35	0.56
PR	14.04	12.78	17.54	15.28	0	0	11.23	7.5	19.37	8.12	3.49	1.16	13.02	8.7	27.97	12.78	0.35	0
PS	0	0	0	0	1.05	0	1.05	1.11	0	0	0	0	2.22	2.03	0	0.83	0	0
QAS	0	0.28	0	0	0	0	0	0	0	0	0	0	0.95	1.74	0	0.56	0	0
RE	6.67	3.89	2.11	1.39	6.32	5.28	1.4	3.06	1.59	2.61	0	0	0.32	0	2.1	0.83	0	0
SVP	0	0	0	0.28	0	0	0.35	0.56	0.32	0	0	0	0.95	1.45	0.7	2.78	0	0
Avg	4.26	4.28	2.28	2.57	1.17	1.15	2.54	3.12	3.94	3.86	0.83	0.72	3.94	3.74	5.47	4.16	0.14	0.20

Table 4: Heatmap of percentages of harmful completions by the selected Scandinavian models (K=20) following the Hurtlex (Bassignana et al., 2018) categories. Where: **AN** = animals, **ASF** = female genitalia, **ASM** = male genitalia, **CDS** = derogatory words, **DMC** = moral and behavioral defects, **OM** = homosexuality, **OR** = plants, **PR** = prostitution, **PS** = negative stereotypes ethnic slurs, **QAS** = potential negative connotations, **RE** = felonies, crime and immoral behavior, **SVP** = the seven deadly sins of the Christian tradition.

Model	Toxicity		
	F	M	Total
NorBERT	2.77	1.20	3.97
NorBERT2	2.63	0.96	3.60
NB-BERT	1.93	0.51	2.45
NB-BERT_Large	3.07	0.57	3.65
SwedishBERT	2.21	0.51	2.72
SwedishBERT2	1.10	0.05	1.15
SwedishMegatron	2.12	0.61	2.73
DanishBERT	3.23	0.74	3.97
DanishRoBERTa	1.88	0.45	2.34

Table 5: Heatmap of percentages of toxic scores using the Perspective API.

most likely word. This is especially true for the Norwegian models. The Swedish models seem to be better, as none of the models have their highest score at top-1 completions. SwedishBERT and SwedishMegatron have the highest scores within the top-5 completions. SwedishBERT2 and DanishRoBERTa have in general very low scores, and a closer investigation has shown that these two models return most non-sense completions as *e.g.*, punctuation instead of words. This we believe can lead to lower scores.

Table 4 gives an overview of the scores at the gender- and category-level. We focus our analysis on 12 of HurtLex's categories.[4] Words related to prostitution and derogatory words are the most common offensive completions by all LMs. For prostitution-related words, most completions are tied to females, while the opposite is observed for derogatory words. These categories stand for 12.37% and 9.26% of the completions. This is to an extent similar to the languages covered by Nozza et al. (2021), except for the category of words related to animals, fifth most common with a percentage of 1.64% in the Scandinavian models, while second in other languages.

Interestingly, we observed some patterns that differ from results in other languages , as presented in Nozza et al. (2021). We believe that **this *HONEST* score difference is due to a cultural gap** (Nozza, 2021). Offensive words related to homosexuality are infrequent in the LMs (only 0.37% of completions). There are no occurrences of such words in the Norwegian LMs, and in SwedishBERT2 and DanishRoBERTa. However, as these two models return most non-sense completions, any observation should be cautiously generalised. Words related to homosexuality are used to a lesser extent compared to the languages covered by Nozza et al. (2021), where it represented 1.14% of completions in the models they investigated. A similar observation holds for the category "*animals*" that was present in all models analysed by Nozza et al. (2021), but that does not seem to be that common in the Scandinavian models, and seems to be mostly related to one gender rather than the other, except for the NorBERT model that seems to have an equal representation of offensive words towards both genders.

Averaging over all the categories, DanishBERT and NorBERT return most offensive completions for both genders. While NorBERT has a balanced average distribution of offensive completions, the categories differ by gender. DanishBERT is worst on females, and is mostly offensive towards males within the categories derogatory words and prostitution. NB-BERT is the model with the least offensive completions on average. We also do not see any effect of the pre-training data, since mod-

[4]We removed infrequent categories.

els trained on only Wikipedia and news articles do not contain any less harmful content than the ones pre-trained on more problematic datasets.

4 Results – toxic sentences

Table 5 shows the percentages of toxicity scores. We focus on the translated sentences to have a more fair comparison between the Swedish models and the Danish and Norwegian ones. While in general the total number of toxic sentences completed by each model is low, the distribution of these between genders is concerning.

For all models, sentences about females are more toxic than sentences about males. Similarly to the *HONEST* scores, NorBERT and DanishBERT are the worst performing models overall. However, they differ when it comes to the toxicity levels between genders. DanishBERT is 2.49% points more toxic towards females, while NorBERT has 1.57% points difference. From this perspective, the worst performing model is NB-BERT_Large with a difference of 2.5% points more toxicity towards females compared to males. NB-BERT seems again to be the least toxic model overall, even if it is 1.42% point more toxic for females compared to males.

5 Limitations

HONEST is a lexicon-based approach that relies on automatically generated lexica for Danish, Swedish, and Norwegian. We did a superficial analysis of the HurtLex lexicon for Norwegian, and observed that it contains ambiguous and erroneous words. It is not exhaustive, and since it was originally translated from an Italian context, some culture-specific terms that fit the Scandinavian context are missing.

Due to the lack of support for Danish and Norwegian in the Perspective API, we rely on the NLLB translator, which introduced a couple of errors that could have mislead the analysis in both direction: either increasing or decreasing the toxicity scores.

6 Conclusion

This paper presents the first study on harmfulness in Scandinavian language models. We focus on nine LMs covering Danish, Norwegian, and Swedish. We show that similarly to other languages, the Scandinavian models generate disturbing, offensive, and stereotypical completions, where females and males are correlated with different harmful categories. This is in contrast with the general belief that these countries excel in gender-balance. In future work, we aim to create a model that can measure harmful and offensive completions without relying on a lexicon. We also wish to include analysis of other Nordic countries, and cover more protected culture-specific groups (*e.g.,* , Sámi population). Finally, we believe that our work should be used to automatically evaluate LMs when published, as outlined in (Nozza et al., 2022a).

Acknowledgements

This project has partially received funding by Fondazione Cariplo (grant No. 2020-4288, MONICA). Debora Nozza is a member of the MilaNLP group, and the Data and Marketing Insights Unit of the Bocconi Institute for Data Science and Analysis.

This work was partially supported by industry partners and the Research Council of Norway with funding to *MediaFutures: Research Centre for Responsible Media Technology and Innovation*, through the centers for Research-based Innovation scheme, project number 309339.

7 Ethical considerations

One concern in our work is our focus on a binary gender setting. We acknowledge that gender as an identity spans more than two categories, but the use of non-gendered pronouns, in *e.g.,* Norway, is still not common. Also, we build and expand the work of Nozza et al. (2021), and create the same templates which ties us to a binary gender divide.

All LMs models examined in this work are freely available on the HuggingFace platform. Arguably, the availability of such models is good for democratising knowledge, however, we have no idea about who are using them, nor how or for what. This leads to a dual-use problem, where our unintended consequences might lead to severe outcomes, especially when these models are used in real-world settings. It is important to specify the problematic by-products of such models, and we urge creators to add warnings and discuss the harmful representations contained in their models when releasing them.

References

Elisa Bassignana, Valerio Basile, and Viviana Patti. 2018. Hurtlex: A multilingual lexicon of words to hurt. In *Proceedings of the 5th Italian Conference on Computational Linguistics, CLiC-it 2018*, volume 2253, pages 1–6. CEUR-WS.

Christine Basta, Marta R. Costa-jussà, and Noe Casas. 2019. Evaluating the underlying gender bias in contextualized word embeddings. In *Proceedings of the First Workshop on Gender Bias in Natural Language Processing*, pages 33–39, Florence, Italy. Association for Computational Linguistics.

Emily M. Bender, Timnit Gebru, Angelina McMillan-Major, and Shmargaret Shmitchell. 2021. On the dangers of stochastic parrots: Can language models be too big? In *Proceedings of the 2021 ACM Conference on Fairness, Accountability, and Transparency*, FAccT '21, page 610–623, New York, NY, USA. Association for Computing Machinery.

Rishabh Bhardwaj, Navonil Majumder, and Soujanya Poria. 2021. Investigating gender bias in bert. *Cognitive Computation*, 13(4).

Jayadev Bhaskaran and Isha Bhallamudi. 2019. Good secretaries, bad truck drivers? occupational gender stereotypes in sentiment analysis. In *Proceedings of the First Workshop on Gender Bias in Natural Language Processing*, pages 62–68, Florence, Italy. Association for Computational Linguistics.

Federico Bianchi and Dirk Hovy. 2021. On the gap between adoption and understanding in NLP. In *Findings of the Association for Computational Linguistics: ACL-IJCNLP 2021*, pages 3895–3901, Online. Association for Computational Linguistics.

Abeba Birhane, Vinay Uday Prabhu, and Emmanuel Kahembwe. 2021. Multimodal datasets: misogyny, pornography, and malignant stereotypes.

Su Lin Blodgett, Solon Barocas, Hal Daumé III, and Hanna Wallach. 2020. Language (technology) is power: A critical survey of "bias" in NLP. In *Proceedings of the 58th Annual Meeting of the Association for Computational Linguistics*, pages 5454–5476, Online. Association for Computational Linguistics.

Won Ik Cho, Ji Won Kim, Seok Min Kim, and Nam Soo Kim. 2019. On measuring gender bias in translation of gender-neutral pronouns. In *Proceedings of the First Workshop on Gender Bias in Natural Language Processing*, pages 173–181, Florence, Italy. Association for Computational Linguistics.

Hannah Devinney, Jenny Björklund, and Henrik Björklund. 2020. Semi-supervised topic modeling for gender bias discovery in English and Swedish. In *Proceedings of the Second Workshop on Gender Bias in Natural Language Processing*, pages 79–92, Barcelona, Spain (Online). Association for Computational Linguistics.

Jacob Devlin, Ming-Wei Chang, Kenton Lee, and Kristina Toutanova. 2019. BERT: Pre-training of deep bidirectional transformers for language understanding. In *Proceedings of the 2019 Conference of the North American Chapter of the Association for Computational Linguistics: Human Language Technologies, Volume 1 (Long and Short Papers)*, pages 4171–4186, Minneapolis, Minnesota. Association for Computational Linguistics.

Anjalie Field, Su Lin Blodgett, Zeerak Waseem, and Yulia Tsvetkov. 2021. A survey of race, racism, and anti-racism in NLP. In *Proceedings of the 59th Annual Meeting of the Association for Computational Linguistics and the 11th International Joint Conference on Natural Language Processing (Volume 1: Long Papers)*, pages 1905–1925, Online. Association for Computational Linguistics.

Ben Hutchinson, Vinodkumar Prabhakaran, Emily Denton, Kellie Webster, Yu Zhong, and Stephen Denuyl. 2020. Social biases in NLP models as barriers for persons with disabilities. In *Proceedings of the 58th Annual Meeting of the Association for Computational Linguistics*, pages 5491–5501, Online. Association for Computational Linguistics.

Tori Loven Kirkebø, Malcolm Langford, and Haldor Byrkjeflot. 2021. Creating gender exceptionalism: The role of global indexes. In *Gender Equality and Nation Branding in the Nordic Region*, pages 191–206. Routledge.

Julia Kreutzer, Isaac Caswell, Lisa Wang, Ahsan Wahab, Daan van Esch, Nasanbayar Ulzii-Orshikh, Allahsera Tapo, Nishant Subramani, Artem Sokolov, Claytone Sikasote, Monang Setyawan, Supheakmungkol Sarin, Sokhar Samb, Benoît Sagot, Clara Rivera, Annette Rios, Isabel Papadimitriou, Salomey Osei, Pedro Ortiz Suarez, Iroro Orife, Kelechi Ogueji, Andre Niyongabo Rubungo, Toan Q. Nguyen, Mathias Müller, André Müller, Shamsuddeen Hassan Muhammad, Nanda Muhammad, Ayanda Mnyakeni, Jamshidbek Mirzakhalov, Tapiwanashe Matangira, Colin Leong, Nze Lawson, Sneha Kudugunta, Yacine Jernite, Mathias Jenny, Orhan Firat, Bonaventure F. P. Dossou, Sakhile Dlamini, Nisansa de Silva, Sakine Çabuk Ballı, Stella Biderman, Alessia Battisti, Ahmed Baruwa, Ankur Bapna, Pallavi Baljekar, Israel Abebe Azime, Ayodele Awokoya, Duygu Ataman, Orevaoghene Ahia, Oghenefego Ahia, Sweta Agrawal, and Mofetoluwa Adeyemi. 2022. Quality at a glance: An audit of web-crawled multilingual datasets. *Transactions of the Association for Computational Linguistics*, 10:50–72.

Per E Kummervold, Javier De la Rosa, Freddy Wetjen, and Svein Arne Brygfjeld. 2021. Operationalizing a national digital library: The case for a Norwegian transformer model. In *Proceedings of the 23rd Nordic Conference on Computational Linguistics (NoDaLiDa)*, pages 20–29, Reykjavik, Iceland (Online). Linköping University Electronic Press, Sweden.

Andrey Kutuzov, Jeremy Barnes, Erik Velldal, Lilja Øvrelid, and Stephan Oepen. 2021. Large-scale contextualised language modelling for Norwegian. In

Proceedings of the 23rd Nordic Conference on Computational Linguistics (NoDaLiDa), pages 30–40, Reykjavik, Iceland (Online). Linköping University Electronic Press, Sweden.

Ruth Lister. 2009. A nordic nirvana? gender, citizenship, and social justice in the nordic welfare states. *Social Politics*, page 242–278.

Sigrun Marie Moss. 2021. Applying the brand or not?: Challenges of nordicity and gender equality in scandinavian diplomacy. In *Gender Equality and Nation Branding in the Nordic Region*, pages 62–74. Routledge.

Debora Nozza. 2021. Exposing the limits of zero-shot cross-lingual hate speech detection. In *Proceedings of the 59th Annual Meeting of the Association for Computational Linguistics and the 11th International Joint Conference on Natural Language Processing (Volume 2: Short Papers)*, pages 907–914, Online. Association for Computational Linguistics.

Debora Nozza, Federico Bianchi, and Dirk Hovy. 2020. What the [MASK]? Making sense of language-specific BERT models. *arXiv preprint arXiv:2003.02912*.

Debora Nozza, Federico Bianchi, and Dirk Hovy. 2021. HONEST: Measuring hurtful sentence completion in language models. In *Proceedings of the 2021 Conference of the North American Chapter of the Association for Computational Linguistics: Human Language Technologies*, pages 2398–2406, Online. Association for Computational Linguistics.

Debora Nozza, Federico Bianchi, and Dirk Hovy. 2022a. Pipelines for social bias testing of large language models. In *Proceedings of BigScience Episode #5 – Workshop on Challenges & Perspectives in Creating Large Language Models*, pages 68–74, virtual+Dublin. Association for Computational Linguistics.

Debora Nozza, Federico Bianchi, Anne Lauscher, and Dirk Hovy. 2022b. Measuring harmful sentence completion in language models for LGBTQIA+ individuals. In *Proceedings of the Second Workshop on Language Technology for Equality, Diversity and Inclusion*, pages 26–34, Dublin, Ireland. Association for Computational Linguistics.

Debora Nozza and Dirk Hovy. 2022. The state of profanity obfuscation in natural language processing.

Nedjma Ousidhoum, Xinran Zhao, Tianqing Fang, Yangqiu Song, and Dit-Yan Yeung. 2021. Probing toxic content in large pre-trained language models. In *Proceedings of the 59th Annual Meeting of the Association for Computational Linguistics and the 11th International Joint Conference on Natural Language Processing (Volume 1: Long Papers)*, pages 4262–4274, Online. Association for Computational Linguistics.

Marcelo O. R. Prates, Pedro H. C. Avelar, and Luis Lamb. 2018. Assessing gender bias in machine translation – a case study with google translate.

Jens Rydström. 2008. Legalizing love in a cold climate:the history, consequences and recent developments of registered partnership in scandinavia. *Sexualities*, page 193–226.

Magnus Sahlgren and Fredrik Olsson. 2019. Gender bias in pretrained Swedish embeddings. In *Proceedings of the 22nd Nordic Conference on Computational Linguistics*, Turku, Finland. Linköping University Electronic Press.

Danielle Saunders and Bill Byrne. 2020. Addressing exposure bias with document minimum risk training: Cambridge at the WMT20 biomedical translation task. In *Proceedings of the Fifth Conference on Machine Translation*, pages 862–869, Online. Association for Computational Linguistics.

Signe Bock Segaard, Ulrik Kjaer, and Jo Saglie. 2022. Why norway has more female local councillors than denmark: a crack in the nordic gender equality model? *West European Politics*, pages 1–24.

Emily Sheng, Kai-Wei Chang, Premkumar Natarajan, and Nanyun Peng. 2019. The woman worked as a babysitter: On biases in language generation.

Gudbjartur Ingi Sigurbergsson and Leon Derczynski. 2020. Offensive language and hate speech detection for Danish. In *Proceedings of the 12th Language Resources and Evaluation Conference*, pages 3498–3508, Marseille, France. European Language Resources Association.

Karolina Stanczak and Isabelle Augenstein. 2021. A survey on gender bias in natural language processing.

Samia Touileb, Lilja Øvrelid, and Erik Velldal. 2021. Using gender- and polarity-informed models to investigate bias. In *Proceedings of the 3rd Workshop on Gender Bias in Natural Language Processing*, pages 66–74, Online. Association for Computational Linguistics.

Samia Touileb, Lilja Øvrelid, and Erik Velldal. 2022. Occupational biases in Norwegian and multilingual language models. In *Proceedings of the 4th Workshop on Gender Bias in Natural Language Processing (GeBNLP)*, pages 200–211, Seattle, Washington. Association for Computational Linguistics.

Thomas Wolf, Lysandre Debut, Victor Sanh, Julien Chaumond, Clement Delangue, Anthony Moi, Pierric Cistac, Tim Rault, Remi Louf, Morgan Funtowicz, Joe Davison, Sam Shleifer, Patrick von Platen, Clara Ma, Yacine Jernite, Julien Plu, Canwen Xu, Teven Le Scao, Sylvain Gugger, Mariama Drame, Quentin Lhoest, and Alexander Rush. 2020. Transformers: State-of-the-art natural language processing. In *Proceedings of the 2020 Conference on Empirical Methods in Natural Language Processing: System Demonstrations*, pages 38–45, Online. Association for Computational Linguistics.

Philine Zeinert, Nanna Inie, and Leon Derczynski. 2021. Annotating online misogyny. In *Proceedings of the 59th Annual Meeting of the Association for Computational Linguistics and the 11th International Joint Conference on Natural Language Processing (Volume 1: Long Papers)*, pages 3181–3197, Online. Association for Computational Linguistics.

Yiyun Zhao and Steven Bethard. 2020. How does BERT's attention change when you fine-tune? an analysis methodology and a case study in negation scope. In *Proceedings of the 58th Annual Meeting of the Association for Computational Linguistics*, pages 4729–4747, Online. Association for Computational Linguistics.

A Appendix

Sources of used LMs for reproducibility purposes:

- DanishBERT: `https://huggingface.co/Maltehb/danish-bert-botxo`
- DanishRoBERTa: `https://huggingface.co/flax-community/roberta-base-danish`
- SwedishBERT: `https://huggingface.co/KBLab/bert-base-swedish-cased`
- SwedishBERT2: `https://huggingface.co/KBLab/bert-base-swedish-cased-new`
- SwedishMegatron: `https://huggingface.co/KBLab/megatron-bert-base-swedish-cased-600k`
- NorBERT: `https://huggingface.co/ltgoslo/norbert`
- NorBERT2: `https://huggingface.co/ltgoslo/norbert2`
- NB-BERT: `https://huggingface.co/NbAiLab/nb-bert-base`
- NB-BERT_Large: `https://huggingface.co/NbAiLab/nb-bert-large`

Can Contextualizing User Embeddings Improve Sarcasm and Hate Speech Detection?

Kim Breitwieser
MaibornWolff GmbH
kim.breitwieser@maibornwolff.de

Abstract

While implicit embeddings so far have been mostly concerned with creating an overall representation of the user, we evaluate a different approach. By only considering content directed at a specific topic, we create sub-user embeddings, and measure their usefulness on the tasks of sarcasm and hate speech detection. In doing so, we show that task-related topics can have a noticeable effect on model performance, especially when dealing with intended expressions like sarcasm, but less so for hate speech, which is usually labelled as such on the receiving end.

1 Introduction

While using the syntax or semantics of sentences and words has been the backbone of Natural Language Processing (NLP) tasks for a long time, incorporating information about the authors themselves is a much more recent addition (Lucas et al., 2009; Zhang et al., 2018a; Li et al., 2017).

Existing approaches can be broadly grouped into explicit and implicit user modelling. Explicit representations include known information, such as the user's occupation or location (Mesgar et al., 2020), their personality or sociodemographic traits (Oraby et al., 2018), or even their emotional state (Rashkin et al., 2018). Implicit models, on the other hand, use highly dimensional vectors (embeddings) to capture abstract differences and similarities between users, without relying on concrete knowledge (Amir et al., 2017).

However, implicit approaches so far make use of an averaged user representation, for example by using a given user's post history regardless of content. Social psychology, however, has shown the impact a given social situation can have on observable behavior (Ross, 1977), a fact that could be possible to translate to social media posts as well. To this end, we define a *social situation* as a given topic, such as sports or politics, as well as the ensuing conversations about these topics. In doing so, we hope to improve the accuracy of sarcasm and hate speech detection, NLP tasks that will only increase in importance as the internet - and social media - continues to take up more of our time.

To this end, we use User2Vec, one of the earlier approaches to implicit user modelling, which has already been shown to increase performance on sarcasm classification (Amir et al., 2016).

1.1 Research Questions

- Can hate speech detection be improved by the usage of implicit user representation, in a similar way to sarcasm detection?
- Can these results be influenced by contextualizing the user on specific subsets of conversational data, implicitly modelling their behavior in different social situations?
- What are the implications behind the observed results, and how could they be made use of in future applications?

2 Related Work

2.1 User Embeddings in Social Media

Social media posts and other media can be used to infer a variety of user characteristics, such as demographics (Benton et al., 2016), mental health (Amir et al., 2017) or personality traits (Liu et al., 2016).

Purely text-based user embeddings are usually created using an unsupervised approach such as dimensionality reduction by Latent Dirichlet Allocation (LDA) (Schwartz et al., 2013; Song et al., 2015; Hu et al., 2017), Single Value Decomposition (SVD) (Kosinski et al., 2013; Gao et al., 2014) or by capturing contexts based on the Word2Vec family of word embeddings (Amir et al., 2016; Preoţiuc-Pietro et al., 2015). These approaches cluster the information contained in a given user's posts in order to discover patterns and similarities between

Proceedings of the Fifth Workshop on Natural Language Processing and Computational Social Science (NLP+CSS), pages 126 - 139
November 7, 2022 ©2022 Association for Computational Linguistics

users. Aside from textual content, image content (Zhang et al., 2018b) and user relations, such as followers (Mishra et al., 2018), have been used in order to create user representations.

2.2 Sarcasm Detection

Sarcasm detection describes a classification problem, often binary in nature, though it can also be further differentiated in sarcasm as intended by the authors themselves, or perceived by external annotators (Shmueli et al., 2020a). Additionally, an alternative approach can be chosen in order to differentiate sarcasm from other expressions of humour or irony (Reyes et al., 2013).

Traditional approaches to detect sarcasm make use of explicit rules (Veale and Hao, 2010; Maynard and Greenwood, 2014; Riloff et al., 2013), as well as statistical measures (Hernández-Farías et al., 2015; Liu et al., 2014; Tsur et al., 2010), in order to differentiate sarcastic and non-sarcastic content. More recent, neural network-based approaches are able to implicitly construct complex, highly-dimensional feature representations from basic inputs, lessening the need for additional domain knowledge. These approaches often make use of RNN and CNN models (Ghosh and Veale, 2016), as well as Attention or Transformer architectures (Potamias et al., 2020). Some of them are also able to make use of auxiliary information, such as user embeddings (Amir et al., 2016; Hazarika et al., 2018).

2.3 Hate Speech Detection

Hate speech detection represents yet another classification problem, differentiating content expressing hate or encouraging violence, usually towards repressed minorities, from content without such tendencies. While hate speech can often be confused with the use of offensive phrases in everyday language, more recent approaches have made an effort to distinguish between these cases (Davidson et al., 2017; Warner and Hirschberg, 2012; Malmasi and Zampieri, 2017).

Similar to sarcasm detection, the classification of hateful content has also evolved from traditional methods, such as handcrafted rules (MacAvaney et al., 2019; Mondal et al., 2017), to employing neural network architectures such as RNNs and CNNs (Kovács et al., 2021). Especially in social media environments, emojis have recently been shown to provide a useful tool to resolve the ambiguity in words that can both be interpreted in a more neutral way or as part of hate speech (Wiegand and Ruppenhofer, 2021). Transformer models also have found their way into hate speech detection to great success, used either on their own or as part of more complex ensembles (Zampieri et al., 2019, 2020).

3 Datasets

3.1 Sarcasm

For the sarcasm classification task we use the Bamman dataset, based on the one used by Bamman and Smith (2015) and Amir et al. (2016). The dataset differentiates between sarcastic and non-sarcastic posts, using distant supervision based on the presence or absence of the hashtags *#sarcasm* or *#sarcastic*, which are removed prior to the actual task. The dataset contains a total of 8741 posts by 5797 users, divided into 4972 sarcastic (56.9%) and 3769 non-sarcastic (43.1%) posts.

3.2 Hate Speech

For the hate speech classification task we use the Hatexplain dataset (Mathew et al., 2020), more specifically a subset collected from the social media platform Gab. This split is done due to differing post lengths between Twitter and Gab, with the latter containing a larger volume of hate speech content (Zannettou et al., 2018). The dataset differentiates between neutral, offensive and hate speech, with posts being labelled independently by 3 annotators using Amazon Mechanical Turk[1]. The dataset consists of 8365 posts by 1642 users, divided into 1588 neutral (19.0%), 2487 offensive (29.7%) and 4290 hate speech (51.3%) posts.

4 Experiments

4.1 Model Architecture

For our experiments, we use a CUE-CNN (Content and User Embedding Convolutional Neural Network) architecture, directly derived from the one used in Amir et al. (2016). A more in-depth description of the model itself, as well as the hyperparameters used during the experiments, can be found in the appendix. While the model itself does produce comparable results to state-of-the-art architecture, such as BERT (Devlin et al., 2018), they are still comparable with each other, given that hyperparameters don't change, as well with the previous experiments performed by Amir et al. (2016).

[1] https://www.mturk.com

4.2 Run Variations

In order to inspect the influence of different kinds of user embeddings, we train and evaluate the model using multiple configurations:

- **only word embeddings**, serving as a baseline without additional user embeddings. We use 400-dimensional Word2Vec embeddings to represent words.
- **only user embeddings**, using only 400-dimensional user embeddings created from the 500 most recent posts per user, excluding the post being evaluated.
- **word + user embeddings**, serving as a secondary baseline, combining the inputs of both previous runs.
- **topic-specific sub-user embeddings**, similar to the previous run, but replacing the regular user embeddings with embeddings created from posts that are most likely to belong to one of 10 topics defined for the dataset. This run is repeated for every topic.

4.3 Sub-User embeddings

In order to model individual topics present in the user's post history, we create sub-embeddings based on an LDA model (Blei et al., 2001). By selecting, for each user, 500 posts most likely to belong to a topic, we assume these embeddings to represent the user's behavior in a situation depicting them talking about the given topic, known to influence behavior in a notable way (Ross, 1977; Giles and Baker, 2008). These embeddings are trained just like the averaged user embeddings, but by sorting the user history based on the percentage of each post to belong to the given topic, instead of by date.

An overview over the topics defined for both datasets can be found in the appendix. Labels are based on the 30 most salient terms per topic, as provided by the LDA model.

5 Results

5.1 Randomized Embeddings

Before testing the embeddings themselves, we perform initial runs in order to compare embeddings created using User2Vec with randomly created ones or those obtained by randomly reassigning either the post histories or resulting user embeddings. These could still provide minor improvements, as some users authored more than a single post, potentially even present in both training and validation sets. As the results obtained can be assumed to be universally representative, we only performed these runs on the sarcasm dataset.

	accuracy
only word embeddings	73.87
random user embeddings	73.63
shuffled posts	73.79
shuffled user embeddings	**74.02**

Table 1: Results on the sarcasm dataset using varying degrees of randomly created user embeddings compared to not using any additional data at all. The best performing run is highlighted.

As can be seen in Table 1, using purely random 400-dimensional vectors provides no improvement over not using them, even resulting in slightly worse results due to noise caused by the random values. Using actual user posts, but assigning them to random users results in slightly better results compared to purely random embeddings, though still worse than not using any additional information at all. Training user embeddings properly, with all posts of a given user being used for the same embedding, and assigning these to random users finally results in slightly better values compared to the baseline, though all of the observed results could reasonably as well be attributed to variance.

We can therefore conclude that the sheer presence of additional information, presented in multiple levels of randomness, does not provide a noticeable improvement over solely relying on the textual contents alone.

5.2 Sarcasm

Experimental results on the sarcasm dataset can be found in Table 2.

Surprisingly, even only using the user embeddings without the actual post contents results in a performance increase. Since the dataset has been labelled using marker hashtags, and therefore represents the author's intention to write sarcastic content, we believe that the model is able to accurately represent intended expressions, as has previously also been shown by Amir et al. (2016).

As for the topic-specific sub-user embeddings, all of the topics provided by the LDA model were

	accuracy	sarcasm
only word embeddings	73.87	-
only user embeddings	76.83	-
word + user embeddings	80.89	-
topic 1 (politics)	**82.19**	39.16
topic 2 (everyday)	81.47	73.42
topic 3 (time)	81.59	59.76
topic 4 (sports)	80.89	74.98
topic 5 (media)	81.55	55.46
topic 6 (social media)	**81.97**	50.98
topic 7 (celebratory)	81.49	45.03
topic 8 (offensive)	81.49	53.32
topic 9 (school)	**82.31**	49.14
topic 10 (emojis)	81.87	54.76

Table 2: Results over multiple runs performed on the sarcasm dataset, averaged over 10-fold cross-validation. Highlighted cells mark the 3 highest scoring runs. The second column shows the percentage of topic-related posts labelled as sarcastic.

able to produce results that are significantly better than when using only the most recent 500 posts per user. While this could theoretically be attributed to LDA preferably selecting posts with a higher amount of tokens, this was not the case. The most likely conclusion in this case is therefore that the topic-specific embeddings implicitly filter out stop-words and other fillers, as well as putting emphasis on words that carry meaning in the topic context at hand.

Among these topics, *politics*, *social media*, and *school* produce slightly better results, which can be proven to be statistically significant using the Wilcoxon-Test (Wilcoxon, 1945). Sarcasm is especially prevalent in online conversations (Hancock, 2004), and has been shown to positively correlate with social media reactions such as likes and retweets (Peng et al., 2019). Using Pearson's r, we can obtain a correlation of -0.7305 ($p = 0.0165$) between the obtained accuracy scores and the percentage of topic-related posts labelled as sarcastic. We can therefore conclude that certain topics are indeed more or less likely to harbour sarcastic remarks, with those containing a lesser degree of sarcasm being moderately more useful in detecting outliers.

5.3 Hate Speech

Experimental results on the hate speech dataset can be found in Table 3.

	accuracy	hate sp.
only word embeddings	62.28	-
only user embeddings	54.49	-
word + user embeddings	**63.47**	-
topic 1 (everyday)	62.80	49.10
topic 2 (jews)	62.62	37.29
topic 3 (gun control)	62.49	39.92
topic 4 (social media)	62.82	46.06
topic 5 (election)	62.26	43.52
topic 6 (religion)	62.69	43.85
topic 7 (terrorism)	62.59	56.08
topic 8 (racism/sexism)	**63.12**	50.94
topic 9 (australia)	62.79	52.12
topic 10 (foreign politics)	**62.88**	57.17

Table 3: Results over multiple runs performed on the hate speech dataset, averaged over 10-fold cross-validation. Highlighted cells mark the 3 highest scoring runs. The second column shows the percentage of topic-related posts labelled as hate speech.

Here, we can only observe minor absolute when using user embeddings in addition to the posts themselves, though they are still high enough to be deemed statistically significant. For this dataset, the user embeddings alone also perform worse on their own, which can be attributed to hate speech generally being considered to be a perceived phenomenon, especially since the dataset in question has been labelled by external annotators, and not by the authors themselves. Perceived phenomena like this have been shown to be impacted by user embeddings to a lesser extent, due to a potential discrepancy between assigned labels and the author's original intentions (Roussos and Dovidio, 2018; Oprea and Magdy, 2019).

Using any form of topic-based sub-user embeddings turned out to slightly lower absolute results, though some of them are still seen as minor improvements when evaluating individual posts. Given the general nature of the Gab social platform and its tendency to mainly harbour less moderated conversations regarding political topics (Zannettou et al., 2018), it can be assumed that all of these topics are subject to hate speech in some form. In order to prove this, we can again use Pearson's r, arriving at a correlation of 0.4873 ($p = 0.1531$). Based on this, we conclude that the individual topics are not expressive enough, which causes averaged embeddings to be able to better capture indicators pointing towards hateful content. In comparison, posts belonging to a single topic are more focused towards it, which represents noise in the scope of our classification task.

Though the results obtained using topic-based sub-user embeddings are generally close to each other and the averaged baseline, the topics *racism/sexism* and *politics/foreign* seem to be slightly more useful in detecting hate speech than other topics. Since the dataset was created using gender- and race-related hate speech targets, this seems intuitive (Mathew et al., 2020), in addition to foreign ethnicities generally being a regular target of hate speech (Silva et al., 2016).

6 Conclusion and Future Work

We showed that user embeddings created using User2Vec (Amir et al., 2017) provide helpful information, capable of aiding the classification of intended expressions that can be observed as a general tendency for a given user, such as sarcasm. On the other hand, their usefulness is generally lower when used for the classification of perceived expressions, such as hate speech. Additionally, we were able to create specialized sub-user embeddings, capturing information about the user when exposed to a specific situation, such as when talking about school-related topics. Depending on how these topics relate to the task, we were able to increase the performance as opposed to using generalized embeddings. This seems to be especially true for binary classification tasks, which can be noticeably impacted by selecting a topic known to lean heavily towards one of the labels, which we have shown to be true for politics-related content being particularly low on sarcasm. We used a relatively simple LDA model to categorize posts by topic, but more sophisticated approaches should be able to even more properly select relevant data points.

Aside from the individual user, social connections can play a big role, potentially elevating the usefulness of user embeddings beyond the detection of characteristical, intended behavior. This information can be used in order to model user reactions, therefore providing insight about how a given user is perceived by others. Doing so could overcome one of the limitation of user embeddings, making it possible to more accurately detect perceived behavior such as hate speech (Roussos and Dovidio, 2018; Oprea and Magdy, 2019). And even the word embeddings, which we chose to leave fixed for all experiments, can be contextualized, as the information contained in a word can differ depending on the user who authored it (Welch et al., 2020).

Lastly, by assigning topic probabilities to individual posts, these could be used for the filtering of social media streams based on personal interest. Extending this approach to the author themselves, and by assuming that proficiency in a given topic can be approximated by having authored a high number of related posts (Ericsson et al., 1993; Ericsson, 2002), it could be possible to filter users based on the topics they are knowledgeable about.

7 Ethical and Privacy Considerations

Given that both the tasks of sarcasm and hate speech classification, as well as the models proposed in order to tackle it, aim at the labelling of users and their authored content, as well as a possible future application extending to a form of user rating or filtering based on their assumed proficiency, there are certain ethical implications. These do not only exist for correctly made statements, but also for potential misclassifications (Rudman and Glick, 2012). We therefore strongly advise to not use the proposed models as the sole basis for decisions made concerning the fate of humans, such as to which candidates to pick given a certain position, if an assumed level of proficiency would ever be used to make such a decision.

As for the topic of privacy, all data used by us in the creation of our models, as well as subsequent evaluations, are publicly available on the Twitter and Gab social media platforms. It should be noted that the Developer Agreements of these platforms forbid the usage of their data for the purpose of surveillance or in order to perform discriminatory actions, as exemplary outlined in Pardo et al. (2013). We therefore explicitly state that the scope of this work is strictly limited to the evaluation of models based on publicly available data in order to approach the problem of topic-based sub-user embeddings and their influence on sarcasm and hate speech classification, and not used to discriminate or surveil individual users based on the information obtained.

8 Acknowledgments

The experiments performed as part of this paper were conducted on infrastructure and under research mentoring provided by the Conversational AI and Social Analytics (CAISA) Lab[2], without which it might not have been possible to finish this work. Additional thanks go to Lucie Flek and Martin Potthast for their constructive feedback.

References

Silvio Amir, Glen Coppersmith, Paula Carvalho, Mário J. Silva, and Byron C. Wallace. 2017. Quantifying mental health from social media with neural user embeddings. *CoRR*, abs/1705.00335.

Silvio Amir, Byron C. Wallace, Hao Lyu, and Paula Carvalho Mário J. Silva. 2016. Modelling context with user embeddings for sarcasm detection in social media.

David Bamman and Noah A. Smith. 2015. Contextualized sarcasm detection on twitter. In *ICWSM*.

Adrian Benton, Raman Arora, and Mark Dredze. 2016. Learning multiview embeddings of Twitter users. In *Proceedings of the 54th Annual Meeting of the Association for Computational Linguistics (Volume 2: Short Papers)*, pages 14–19, Berlin, Germany. Association for Computational Linguistics.

David Blei, Andrew Ng, and Michael Jordan. 2001. Latent dirichlet allocation. volume 3, pages 601–608.

Thomas Davidson, Dana Warmsley, Michael W. Macy, and Ingmar Weber. 2017. Automated hate speech detection and the problem of offensive language. *CoRR*, abs/1703.04009.

Jacob Devlin, Ming-Wei Chang, Kenton Lee, and Kristina Toutanova. 2018. Bert: Pre-training of deep bidirectional transformers for language understanding.

Karl Ericsson. 2002. Attaining excellence through deliberate practice: Insights from the study of expert performance. *The Pursuit of Excellence in Education*, pages 21–55.

Karl Ericsson, Ralf Krampe, and Clemens Tesch-Roemer. 1993. The role of deliberate practice in the acquisition of expert performance. *Psychological Review*, 100:363–406.

Huiji Gao, J. Mahmud, J. Chen, Jeffrey Nichols, and M. Zhou. 2014. Modeling user attitude toward controversial topics in online social media. In *ICWSM*.

[2]https://caisa-lab.github.io

Aniruddha Ghosh and Tony Veale. 2016. Fracking sarcasm using neural network. In *Proceedings of the 7th Workshop on Computational Approaches to Subjectivity, Sentiment and Social Media Analysis*, pages 161–169, San Diego, California. Association for Computational Linguistics.

Howard Giles and Susan C Baker. 2008. Communication accommodation theory. *The international encyclopedia of communication*.

Fréderic Godin. 2019. *Improving and Interpreting Neural Networks for Word-Level Prediction Tasks in Natural Language Processing*. Ph.D. thesis, Ghent University, Belgium.

Jeffrey T. Hancock. 2004. Verbal irony use in face-to-face and computer-mediated conversations. *Journal of Language and Social Psychology*, 23(4):447–463.

Devamanyu Hazarika, Soujanya Poria, Sruthi Gorantla, Erik Cambria, Roger Zimmermann, and Rada Mihalcea. 2018. Cascade: Contextual sarcasm detection in online discussion forums.

Irazú Hernández-Farías, José-Miguel Benedí, and Paolo Rosso. 2015. Applying basic features from sentiment analysis for automatic irony detection. In *Pattern Recognition and Image Analysis*, pages 337–344, Cham. Springer International Publishing.

Tianran Hu, Haoyuan Xiao, Thuy vy Thi Nguyen, and Jiebo Luo. 2017. What the language you tweet says about your occupation.

Michal Kosinski, David Stillwell, and Thore Graepel. 2013. Private traits and attributes are predictable from digital records of human behavior. *Proceedings of the national academy of sciences*, 110(15):5802–5805.

György Kovács, Pedro Alonso, and Rajkumar Saini. 2021. Challenges of hate speech detection in social media. *SN Computer Science*, 2(2):1–15.

Justin Kruger, Nicholas Epley, Jason Parker, and Zhi-Wen Ng. 2006. Egocentrism over e-mail: Can we communicate as well as we think? *Journal of personality and social psychology*, 89:925–36.

Quoc Le and Tomas Mikolov. 2014. Distributed representations of sentences and documents. In *International conference on machine learning*, pages 1188–1196. PMLR.

Jiwei Li, Will Monroe, and Dan Jurafsky. 2017. Data distillation for controlling specificity in dialogue generation. *CoRR*, abs/1702.06703.

Leqi Liu, Daniel Preotiuc-Pietro, Zahra Riahi Samani, Mohsen E Moghaddam, and Lyle Ungar. 2016. Analyzing personality through social media profile picture choice. In *Proceedings of the International AAAI Conference on Web and Social Media*, volume 10.

Peng Liu, Wei Chen, Gaoyan Ou, Tengjiao Wang, Dongqing Yang, and Kai Lei. 2014. Sarcasm detection in social media based on imbalanced classification. In *International Conference on Web-Age Information Management*, pages 459–471. Springer.

J.M. Lucas, Fernando Fernández-Martínez, J. Salazar, Javier Ferreiros, and Rubén San-Segundo. 2009. Managing speaker identity and user profiles in a spoken dialogue system. *Procesamiento del lenguaje natural, ISSN 1135-5948, Nº. 43, 2009, pags. 77-84*, 43.

Sean MacAvaney, Hao-Ren Yao, Eugene Yang, Katina Russell, Nazli Goharian, and Ophir Frieder. 2019. Hate speech detection: Challenges and solutions. *PloS one*, 14(8):e0221152.

Shervin Malmasi and Marcos Zampieri. 2017. Detecting hate speech in social media. In *Proceedings of the International Conference Recent Advances in Natural Language Processing, RANLP 2017*, pages 467–472, Varna, Bulgaria. INCOMA Ltd.

Binny Mathew, Punyajoy Saha, Seid Muhie Yimam, Chris Biemann, Pawan Goyal, and Animesh Mukherjee. 2020. Hatexplain: A benchmark dataset for explainable hate speech detection. *arXiv preprint arXiv:2012.10289*.

Diana Maynard and Mark Greenwood. 2014. Who cares about sarcastic tweets? investigating the impact of sarcasm on sentiment analysis. In *Proceedings of the Ninth International Conference on Language Resources and Evaluation (LREC'14)*, pages 4238–4243, Reykjavik, Iceland. European Language Resources Association (ELRA).

Mohsen Mesgar, Edwin Simpson, Yue Wang, and Iryna Gurevych. 2020. Generating persona-consistent dialogue responses using deep reinforcement learning.

Tomas Mikolov, Kai Chen, Greg Corrado, and Jeffrey Dean. 2013. Efficient estimation of word representations in vector space.

Pushkar Mishra, Marco Del Tredici, Helen Yannakoudakis, and Ekaterina Shutova. 2018. Author profiling for abuse detection. In *Proceedings of the 27th international conference on computational linguistics*, pages 1088–1098.

Mainack Mondal, Leandro Araújo Silva, and Fabrício Benevenuto. 2017. A measurement study of hate speech in social media. In *Proceedings of the 28th acm conference on hypertext and social media*, pages 85–94.

Silviu Oprea and Walid Magdy. 2019. Exploring author context for detecting intended vs perceived sarcasm. In *Proceedings of the 57th Annual Meeting of the Association for Computational Linguistics*, pages 2854–2859, Florence, Italy. Association for Computational Linguistics.

Shereen Oraby, Lena Reed, Shubhangi Tandon, Sharath T. S., Stephanie M. Lukin, and Marilyn A. Walker. 2018. Controlling personality-based stylistic variation with neural natural language generators. *CoRR*, abs/1805.08352.

F. M. R. Pardo, P. Rosso, Irina Chugur, Martin Potthast, Martin Trenkmann, Benno Stein, B. Verhoeven, and W. Daelemans. 2013. Overview of the author profiling task at pan 2013. In *CLEF*.

Wei Peng, Achini Adikari, Damminda Alahakoon, and John Gero. 2019. Discovering the influence of sarcasm in social media responses. *Wiley Interdisciplinary Reviews: Data Mining and Knowledge Discovery*, 9.

Rolandos Potamias, Georgios Siolas, and Andreas Stafylopatis. 2020. A transformer-based approach to irony and sarcasm detection. *Neural Computing and Applications*, 32.

Daniel Preoţiuc-Pietro, Vasileios Lampos, and Nikolaos Aletras. 2015. An analysis of the user occupational class through Twitter content. In *Proceedings of the 53rd Annual Meeting of the Association for Computational Linguistics and the 7th International Joint Conference on Natural Language Processing (Volume 1: Long Papers)*, pages 1754–1764, Beijing, China. Association for Computational Linguistics.

Hannah Rashkin, Eric Michael Smith, Margaret Li, and Y-Lan Boureau. 2018. I know the feeling: Learning to converse with empathy. *CoRR*, abs/1811.00207.

Antonio Reyes, Paolo Rosso, and Tony Veale. 2013. A multidimensional approach for detecting irony in twitter. *Language resources and evaluation*, 47(1):239–268.

Ellen Riloff, A. Qadir, Pallavi Surve, L. Silva, N. Gilbert, and R. Huang. 2013. Sarcasm as contrast between a positive sentiment and negative situation. *Proceedings of EMNLP*, pages 704–714.

Lee Ross. 1977. The intuitive psychologist and his shortcomings: Distortions in the attribution process. volume 10 of *Advances in Experimental Social Psychology*, pages 173–220. Academic Press.

Gina Roussos and John F. Dovidio. 2018. Hate speech is in the eye of the beholder: The influence of racial attitudes and freedom of speech beliefs on perceptions of racially motivated threats of violence. *Social Psychological and Personality Science*, 9(2):176–185.

L.A. Rudman and P. Glick. 2012. *The Social Psychology of Gender: How Power and Intimacy Shape Gender Relations*. Texts in Social Psychology. Guilford Publications.

H Andrew Schwartz, Johannes C Eichstaedt, Margaret L Kern, Lukasz Dziurzynski, Stephanie M Ramones, Megha Agrawal, Achal Shah, Michal Kosinski, David Stillwell, Martin EP Seligman, et al. 2013. Personality, gender, and age in the language of social media: The open-vocabulary approach. *PloS one*, 8(9):e73791.

Boaz Shmueli, Lun-Wei Ku, and Soumya Ray. 2020a. Reactive supervision: A new method for collecting sarcasm data.

Boaz Shmueli, Lun-Wei Ku, and Soumya Ray. 2020b. Reactive Supervision: A New Method for Collecting Sarcasm Data. In *Proceedings of the 2020 Conference on Empirical Methods in Natural Language Processing (EMNLP)*, pages 2553–2559, Online. Association for Computational Linguistics.

Leandro Silva, Mainack Mondal, Denzil Correa, Fabrício Benevenuto, and Ingmar Weber. 2016. Analyzing the targets of hate in online social media. In *Proceedings of the International AAAI Conference on Web and Social Media*, volume 10.

Xuemeng Song, Liqiang Nie, Luming Zhang, Maofu Liu, and Tat-Seng Chua. 2015. Interest inference via structure-constrained multi-source multi-task learning. In *Twenty-Fourth International Joint Conference on Artificial Intelligence*.

Oren Tsur, Dmitry Davidov, and Ari Rappoport. 2010. Icwsm - a great catchy name: Semi-supervised recognition of sarcastic sentences in online product reviews.

Tony Veale and Yanfen Hao. 2010. Detecting ironic intent in creative comparisons. pages 765–770.

William Warner and Julia Hirschberg. 2012. Detecting hate speech on the world wide web. In *Proceedings of the Second Workshop on Language in Social Media*, pages 19–26, Montréal, Canada. Association for Computational Linguistics.

Charlie Welch, Jonathan Kummerfeld, Verónica Pérez-Rosas, and Rada Mihalcea. 2020. Exploring the value of personalized word embeddings. pages 6856–6862.

Michael Wiegand and Josef Ruppenhofer. 2021. Exploiting emojis for abusive language detection. In *Proceedings of the 16th Conference of the European Chapter of the Association for Computational Linguistics: Main Volume*, pages 369–380, Online. Association for Computational Linguistics.

Frank Wilcoxon. 1945. Individual comparisons by ranking methods. *Biometrics Bulletin*, 1(6):80–83.

Marcos Zampieri, Shervin Malmasi, Preslav Nakov, Sara Rosenthal, Noura Farra, and Ritesh Kumar. 2019. Semeval-2019 task 6: Identifying and categorizing offensive language in social media (offenseval). In *Proceedings of the 13th International Workshop on Semantic Evaluation*, pages 75–86.

Marcos Zampieri, Preslav Nakov, Sara Rosenthal, Pepa Atanasova, Georgi Karadzhov, Hamdy Mubarak, Leon Derczynski, Zeses Pitenis, and Çağrı Çöltekin. 2020. SemEval-2020 Task 12: Multilingual Offensive Language Identification in Social Media (OffensEval 2020). In *Proceedings of SemEval*.

Savvas Zannettou, Barry Bradlyn, Emiliano De Cristofaro, Haewoon Kwak, Michael Sirivianos, Gianluca Stringini, and Jeremy Blackburn. 2018. What is gab: A bastion of free speech or an alt-right echo chamber. pages 1007–1014.

Saizheng Zhang, Emily Dinan, Jack Urbanek, Arthur Szlam, Douwe Kiela, and Jason Weston. 2018a. Personalizing dialogue agents: I have a dog, do you have pets too? In *Proceedings of the 56th Annual Meeting of the Association for Computational Linguistics (Volume 1: Long Papers)*, pages 2204–2213, Melbourne, Australia. Association for Computational Linguistics.

Wei Zhang, Wen Wang, Jun Wang, and Hongyuan Zha. 2018b. User-guided hierarchical attention network for multi-modal social image popularity prediction. In *Proceedings of the 2018 World Wide Web Conference*, WWW '18, page 1277–1286, Republic and Canton of Geneva, CHE. International World Wide Web Conferences Steering Committee.

A Word embeddings

For our experiments we made use of 400-dimensional Word2Vec embeddings created from a Twitter-based corpus (Godin, 2019), both to create the user and sub-user embeddings, as well as creating the inputs to the model itself. The dataset consists of 3039345 tokens with an OOV (out-of-vocabulary) rate of 9.0% on the sarcasm dataset, as well as 13.5% on the hate speech dataset, both significantly lower than other, widely used word embeddings. This is because the vocabulary contains several emoji as well as other vocabulary specifically suited to use on social media data.

Table 4 shows a comparison between the datasets we previously selected as candidates for use.

B User2Vec

User2Vec aims to create implicit user representations based on the author's posting history, maximizing the probability of a given sentence, defined by each individual word in that sentence, to belong to that user:

$$P(S|user_j) = \sum_{w_i \in S} \log P(w_i|\mathbf{u_j}) + \sum_{w_i \in S} \sum_{w_k \in C(w_i)} \log P(w_i|\mathbf{e_k}) \tag{1}$$

	vocabulary	dimensions		OOV (%)
Twitter GloVe	1193514	200	sarcasm	16.2
			hate speech	20.2
GoogleNews Word2Vec	3000000	300	sarcasm	23.4
			hate speech	25.3
Twitter Word2Vec	3039345	400	sarcasm	**9.0**
			hate speech	**13.5**

Table 4: OOV words for a set of pre-selected candidate word embeddings, for both of the datasets used during the experiments.

Here, $S = \{w_0, w_1, ..., w_N\}$ represents a sentence authored by $user_j$. The probability itself can be decomposed into 2 formulas, the first one being conditional on the user representation $\mathbf{u_j}$, the second one being conditional on a window C of predefined size around the embedding $\mathbf{e_k}$ of any given word in the sentence. Since the latter probability is independent from the user itself, it represents a static value over all users and does not need to be considered in the model:

$$P(S|user_j) \propto \sum_{w_i \in S} \log P(w_i|\mathbf{u_j}) \quad (2)$$

The resulting approximation is very similar to Paragraph Vectors, a variation on Word2Vec (Mikolov et al., 2013), creating embeddings for paragraphs and documents instead of individual words, when considering each user as its own document consisting of the content authored by that user (Le and Mikolov, 2014). Using a log-linear model, the probability for each word $P(w_i|\mathbf{u_j})$ can be estimated using Softmax as follows:

$$P(w_i|x) = \frac{\exp(\mathbf{W_i} \cdot x + b_i)}{\sum_k \exp(\mathbf{W_k} \cdot x + b_k)} \quad (3)$$

Where $\mathbf{W}$ and b represent the weights and biases of said model and x is the feature vector being optimized in order to represent the user. The downside of this approach is the necessity to iterate over each word in the vocabulary, which is potentially very expensive. In order to reduce the cost of this operation, negative sampling is utilized in order to minimize the following Hinge-Loss:

$$\mathcal{L}(w_i, user_j) = \sum_{w_l \in V} \max(0, 1 - \mathbf{e_i} \cdot \mathbf{u_j} + \mathbf{e_l} \cdot \mathbf{u_j}) \quad (4)$$

We chose The following hyperparameters, adapted from the values published as part of the User2Vec model:

- 15 negative samples per word.
- Maximum vocabulary size of 50000, though this limitation was never reached in practice
- Only consider words with a minimum frequency of 5 across the input corpus.
- Initial learn rate of 5e-5, decaying over time as learn progress slows down.
- 25 maximum epochs, aborting the training process after not observing progress after 5 epochs (patience).

C Model Architecture (CUE-CNN)

Similar to how images are represented as a 2-dimensional arrangement of pixels, sentences can be seen as a list of words, each of which by itself is represented by a highly-dimensional vector, also resulting in a 2-dimensional matrix of scalar values. CNNs can make use of this structure in order to incorporate local spatial information and not only process individual words, but also their relation to neighbouring words. This allows them to interpret the overall sentence structure, as well as the relation between individual dimensions of the word embeddings.

The CUE-CNN (Content and User Embedding Convolutional Neural Network) model, as shown on figure 1, combines these embedded sentences $\mathbf{S}$ with pretrained user embeddings $\mathbf{U}$ to incorporate both the text contents themselves, as well as information about their authors. By doing so, it takes into account the user's post history and usage of words in relation to other users in the same vector space. As the user embeddings have previously been created based on the same word embeddings that are also used in order to encode the posts themselves, this represents a connection between the sentence currently being classified, as well as other sentences authored by the same user in the past (Amir et al., 2016).

The embedded sentences are first fed to a convolutional layer consisting of 3 filters of different sizes in order to capture spatial relations in different granularities. Each filter $\mathbf{F}$ gets combined with sub-matrices of a sentence using a sliding window approach, with the results being subjected to a non-linear ReLU activation function α in order to create feature maps $\mathbf{m_i}$ of the same size as the filter:

$$\mathbf{m_i} = \alpha\left(\mathbf{F} \cdot \mathbf{S}_{[i:i-h+1]} + b\right) \tag{5}$$

These filter maps are fed to a max pooling layer being applied to the maximum length of sentences present in the dataset, in order to transform them to scalar values:

$$\mathbf{f_k} = [\max(\mathbf{m_1}) \oplus ... \oplus \max(\mathbf{m_M})] \tag{6}$$

These values are then concatenated over all 3 filters as well as the pretrained embedding of the sentence's author $\mathbf{U_u}$, obtaining the representation of the full model input $\mathbf{c}$. Alternatively, the user embeddings can be left empty, measuring the model's base performance when only processing the text contents.

$$\mathbf{c} = [\mathbf{f_1} \oplus \mathbf{f_2} \oplus \mathbf{f_3} \oplus \mathbf{U_u}] \tag{7}$$

The combined values are then passed to another ReLU activation function α, as well as being subjected to dropout, randomly setting a certain fraction of input nodes to zero in order to prevent the model from overfitting on the training data. A final dense layer then reduces the vector to the previously defined number of possible output classes. The entire model can therefore be formulated as:

$$P(y = k|s, u; \theta) \propto \mathbf{Y_k} \cdot \alpha(\mathbf{H} \cdot \mathbf{c} + \mathbf{h}) + \mathbf{b_k} \tag{8}$$

with $\theta = \{\mathbf{Y}, \mathbf{b}, \mathbf{H}, \mathbf{h}, \mathbf{F_1}, \mathbf{F_2}, \mathbf{F_3}, \mathbf{E}, \mathbf{U}\}$ consisting of - in order - the weights and biases of the output and hidden layers, the convolutional filters being applied to the input sentences, the pretrained word embeddings used in order to represent these sentences in matrix form, and pretrained user embeddings based on the same word embeddings (Amir et al., 2016).

Both word and user embeddings are frozen and not updated during training, and the same hyperparameters are used for all classification tasks, being as follows:

- 80/10/10 training/validation/test split, created from 10 identically sized folds and evaluated using cross-validation. For the final scores, fold results are summed and averaged.
- 50 epochs using a batch size of 32, without early stopping or checkpointing.
- Categorical Cross-Entropy Loss independent of the number of classes, so the model generalizes beyond binary classification without the need for change.
- Adadelta optimization, using a learn rate of 0.005, 0.95 momentum and weight decay of 0.001.
- 3 CNN filters, sized at 4, 6 and 8, respectively.
- 200 filters maps as CNN layer output.
- Hidden layer size of 100.
- Dropout probability of 0.15 between the hidden and output layer.

Training, validation and test sets are created in a stratified fashion based on their ground truth labels, making sure the label distribution in all folds is representative for the whole dataset.

D Preprocessing

Prior to the experiments, we filtered the datasets to only include users with at least 1000 authored historical posts, to ensure there is enough data to properly evaluate different conditions on each user in the dataset. Since the datasets each provide user ids for the Twitter and Gab platform, respectively, we used these to obtain the post history for each user. For Twitter, this has been done using the API, which is limited to the most recent 3000 posts per user[3]. For Gab, we used a publicly available dataset[4]. We further preprocess each example using the following pipeline:

[3] `https://developer.twitter.com/en/docs/twitter-api/v1/tweets/timelines/api-reference/get-statuses-user_timeline`

[4] `https://files.pushshift.io/gab/`

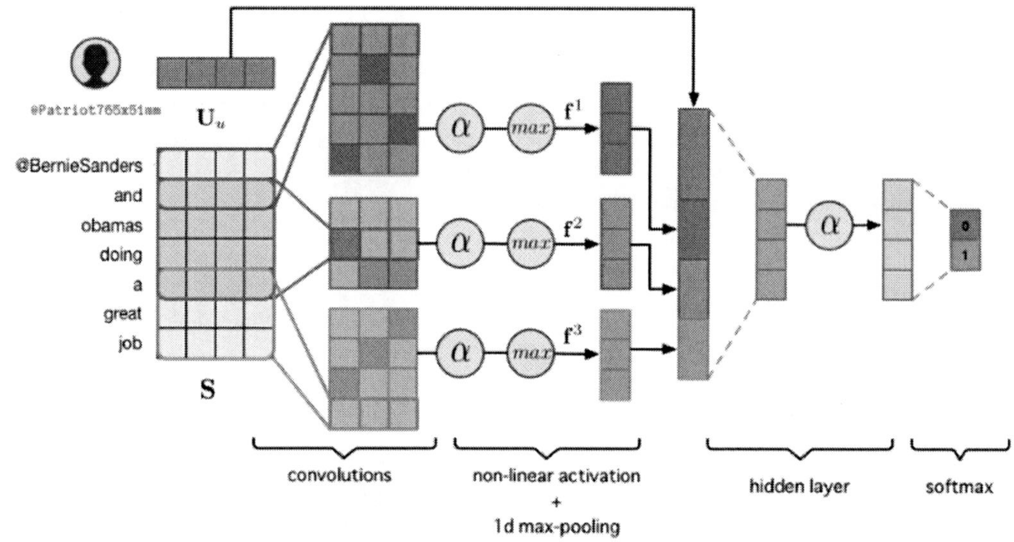

Figure 1: CUE-CNN (Content and User Embedding Convolutional Neural Network) model used for the classification tasks.

- Squashing all whitespace characters to single spaces. Social media content in particular can often contain repeated spaces or newlines, as well as possible non-standard whitespace characters not part of the pretrained embeddings and therefore removed during tokenization.
- Converting all text to lowercase, reducing the amount of OOV (out-of-vocabulary) tokens and increasing the information that can be obtained from each datapoint.
- Reducing repeated characters to a maximum of 3. Social media content is prone to expressions like *"wowwwwww!"* or *"riiiight"*. While still unlikely in most cases, this increases the chances to find an embedding for tokens like these.
- Replacing all user mentions with *@user* and hyperlinks with *url*. Individual user mentions and especially web URLs are unlikely to be present in the embeddings, but their positioning and frequency in the text can still be useful for the task.
- Special tokenization for smileys, which usually consist of mostly punctuation characters. They are an important tool to convey emotions in social media environments (Kruger et al., 2006), so special care is taken in order to make sure they are left intact.

E Additional experiments

In addition to the datasets described in the main paper, we also ran the same experiments on the SPIRS dataset, another sarcasm dataset, which additionally contains labels for intended and perceived sarcasm (Shmueli et al., 2020b). This allows us to more accurately describe the impact of our method on these criteria, while leaving the general task the same.

It should be noted that, while the dataset also provides additional information in the form of cue, oblivious, and eliciting tweets, these were not used for our experiments.

Experimental results on this dataset can be found in Table 5.

As with the Bamman dataset, we can see that user embeddings noticeably improve performance on the dataset. More importantly, though, Table 6 shows the change of misclassification rate for the intended and perceived parts of the dataset, when using user embeddings in addition to the word embedding baseline. While we can observe an improvement in both cases, it's more noticeable on intended sarcasm, whose misclassification rate reduced by 54.24%, while the error on the perceived part only reduced by 44.48%. This observation seems to prove our assumption that user embeddings, at least those solely created from the user's post history, are more helpful for the classification

	accuracy	sarcasm
only word embeddings	67.44	-
only user embeddings	**87.03**	-
word + user embeddings	83.73	-
topic 1 (covid-19)	83.88	49.89
topic 2 (sports)	81.36	43.44
topic 3 (politics)	83.59	48.92
topic 4 (race & gender)	**84.39**	49.87
topic 5 (offensive)	83.18	37.99
topic 6 (media)	82.71	46.19
topic 7 (numbers)	82.68	59.99
topic 8 (love)	81.32	48.05
topic 9 (slang)	**84.31**	53.72
topic 10 (happiness)	81.57	47.06

Table 5: Results over multiple runs performed on the SPIRS dataset, averaged over 10-fold cross-validation. Highlighted cells mark the 3 highest scoring runs. The second column shows the percentage of topic-related posts labelled as sarcastic.

of intended expressions.

	run	error (%)
intended	word embeddings	27.58
	word + user emb.	12.62
perceived	word embeddings	39.93
	word + user emb.	22.17

Table 6: Distribution of misclassfications on the SPIRS dataset between intended and perceived sarcasm. When adding user embeddings, the overall error decreases, while the relative error on examples labeled as perceived sarcasm increases.

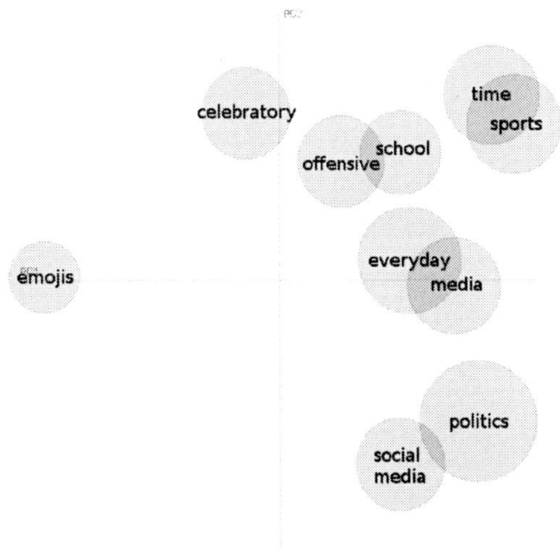

Figure 2: Distribution and partial overlap of LDA topics created from the sarcasm dataset's post history.

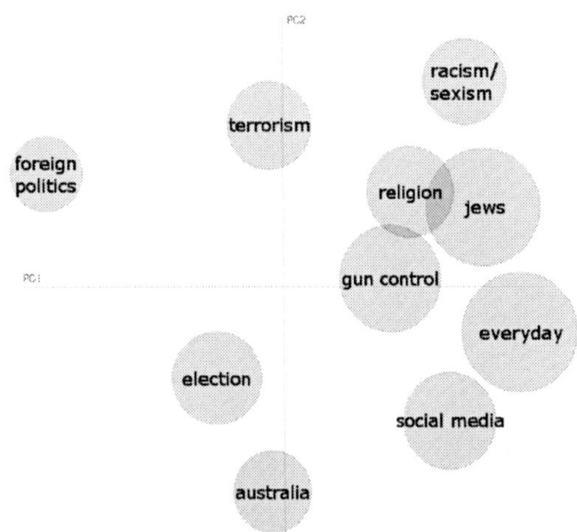

Figure 3: Distribution and partial overlap of LDA topics created from the hate speech dataset's post history.

F Comparing topic-specific sub-user embeddings

In order to extract the topics used as a basis for our sub-user embeddings, we create an LDA model from each dataset's entire post history. The model is created using a single pass over the data, ignoring all tokens appearing either only once or in more than 99% of posts.

Figure 2 and 3 visualize 10 topics created from the sarcasm and hate speech dataset's respective post history in 2D space, across all users. Each of these topics represents a subspace of the overall text corpus, sometimes with partial overlap indicating a regular overlap between contents. Though, as this visualization represents a major dimensionality reduction from the original 400-dimensional vector space, not all relations between topics can be observed this way. We inferred the topic labels by taking into account the 30 most salient terms per topic, as presented by the underlying LDA model.

In order to compare the performance between these topics, we used the Wilcoxon signed-rank test (Wilcoxon, 1945), after using - for each author - the 500 posts with the highest probability of belonging to a given topic as input into our model. We performed tests on all possible topic pairs, with the final results being listed in the tables below, as well as being referenced in the main paper.

	politics	everyday	time	sports	media	social m.	celebratory	offensive	school	emojis
baseline	0.0000	0.0000	0.0000	0.0000	0.0000	0.0000	0.0000	0.0000	0.0000	0.0000
politics	-	1.0000	1.0000	1.0000	1.0000	1.0000	1.0000	1.0000	0.0000	0.9484
everyday	0.0000	-	0.0746	1.0000	0.9698	1.0000	0.9922	0.1200	0.0000	0.0000
time	0.0000	0.9254	-	1.0000	0.9977	1.0000	1.0000	0.8633	0.0000	0.0027
sports	0.0000	0.0000	0.0000	-	0.0000	0.0000	0.0000	0.0000	0.0000	0.0000
media	0.0000	0.0302	0.0023	1.0000	-	0.9673	0.7412	0.0012	0.0000	0.0000
social m.	0.0000	0.0000	0.0000	1.0000	0.0327	-	0.4334	0.0001	0.0000	0.0000
celebratory	0.0000	0.0078	0.0000	1.0000	0.2588	0.5666	-	0.0001	0.0000	0.0000
offensive	0.0000	0.8800	0.1367	1.0000	0.9988	0.9999	0.9999	-	0.0000	0.0022
school	1.0000	1.0000	1.0000	1.0000	1.0000	1.0000	1.0000	1.0000	-	1.0000
emojis	0.0516	1.0000	0.9973	1.0000	1.0000	1.0000	1.0000	0.9978	0.0000	-

Table 7: Comparison between different topic-specific sub-user embeddings on the sarcasm dataset using the Wilcoxon signed-rank test. Highlighted table cells signify that the *column* run is achieving a significantly lower loss than the *row* run, over all test examples ($\alpha = 0.05$). The baseline consists of averaged embeddings created from the most recent 500 posts/user, unrelated to any specific topic.

	everyday	jews	gun control	social m.	election	religion	terrorism	racism/ sexism	australia	foreign p.
baseline	0.0419	0.3017	0.9896	0.7707	0.9881	0.0030	0.0063	0.0007	0.0004	0.0000
everyday	-	0.9682	0.9997	0.9852	1.0000	0.1843	0.3166	0.1323	0.0175	0.0470
jews	0.0318	-	0.9896	0.8436	0.9997	0.0011	0.0717	0.0003	0.0000	0.0006
gun control	0.0003	0.0104	-	0.2422	0.5258	0.0000	0.0000	0.0000	0.0000	0.0000
social m.	0.0148	0.1564	0.7578	-	0.6677	0.0000	0.0005	0.0001	0.0000	0.0000
election	0.0000	0.0003	0.4742	0.3323	-	0.0000	0.0000	0.0000	0.0000	0.0000
religion	0.8157	0.9989	1.0000	1.0000	1.0000	-	0.8107	0.4108	0.1589	0.2117
terrorism	0.6834	0.9283	1.0000	0.9995	1.0000	0.1893	-	0.0472	0.0101	0.0278
racism/ sexism	0.8677	0.9997	1.0000	0.9999	1.0000	0.5892	0.9528	-	0.7103	0.1534
australia	0.9825	1.0000	1.0000	1.0000	1.0000	0.8411	0.9899	0.2897	-	0.2128
foreign p.	0.9530	0.9994	1.0000	1.0000	1.0000	0.7883	0.9722	0.8466	0.7872	-

Table 8: Comparison between different topic-specific sub-user embeddings on the hate speech dataset using the Wilcoxon signed-rank test. Highlighted table cells signify that the *column* run is achieving a significantly lower loss than the *row* run, over all test examples ($\alpha = 0.05$). The baseline consists of averaged embeddings created from the most recent 500 posts/user, unrelated to any specific topic.

Professional Presentation and Projected Power: A Case Study of Implicit Gender Information in English CVs

Jinrui Yang[1*], **Sheilla Njoto**[2*♥], **Marc Cheong**[1], **Leah Ruppanner**[2], **and Lea Frermann**[1]

[1]School of Computing and Information Systems, University of Melbourne
[2]School of Social and Political Sciences, University of Melbourne
{jinruiy, snjoto}@student.unimelb.edu.au
{marc.cheong, leah.ruppanner, lea.frermann}@unimelb.edu.au

Abstract

Gender discrimination in hiring is a pertinent and persistent bias in society, and a common motivating example for exploring bias in NLP. However, the manifestation of gendered language in application materials has received limited attention. This paper investigates the framing of skills and background in CVs of self-identified men and women. We introduce a data set of 1.8K authentic, English-language, CVs from the US, covering 16 occupations, allowing us to partially control for the confound occupation-specific gender base rates. We find that (1) women use more verbs evoking impressions of low power; and (2) classifiers capture gender signal even after data balancing and removal of pronouns and named entities, and this holds for both transformer-based and linear classifiers.

1 Introduction

In this paper, we study word choice and implied power and agency in curriculum vitae (CVs) authored by men and women, combining lines of research that emerged from a long research tradition in both the social sciences and, more recently, natural language processing (Carli, 1990; Lakoff, 1975; Glick and Fiske, 2018). From a sociology perspective, it has been suggested that choices of words are influenced by the social status of the respective genders at a given moment in society (Talbot, 2019). Women are known to use more communal forms of words and emotional connotations than men (Brownlow et al., 2003; Leaper and Ayres, 2007; Newman et al., 2008), and that such choices reflect the different levels of power and influence both politically and economically (Talbot, 2019; Leaper and Ayres, 2007). Conversely, the choice of language impacts how the reader *perceives* the entity described in the text. In particular, the choice of verbs has been suggested as an indicator of the perceived levels of *power* and *agency* of the described entity (Sap et al., 2017).

Organisational scholars have long documented gender discrimination in employment (Booth and Leigh, 2010; Heilman, 2012; Steinpreis et al., 1999). Sociological studies have repeatedly shown that women are evaluated more harshly than men especially in recruitment (Moss-Racusin et al., 2012; Neumark, 2010; Riach and Rich, 2006). Men tend to be assessed for their competence, while women are assessed based on characteristics ('likeability'), even when they demonstrate the same levels of qualifications, experience and education (Rudman, 1998; Phelan et al., 2008). Gaucher et al. (2011) studied the impact of "gendered wording" in job advertisements on gender inequality in traditionally male-dominated occupations via content analysis, while De-Arteaga et al. (2019) showed how gender signal in online biographies lead to disparate performance in the task of occupation classification. Experience has shown that leaving hiring decisions to supposedly objective algorithms did not remove bias from the process – both in real-world applications like Amazon's gender-biased automatic hiring tool (Bogen, 2019), as well as a surge in research on showing and alleviating bias in NLP models (Sun et al., 2019).

We present a data set of 1.8K human-written CVs and study differences in word choice and framing between men and women, and the extent to which classifiers are susceptible to gendered language. Unlike prior studies which were either occupation-specific (Parasurama and Sedoc, 2022) or used proxy data like online biographies (De-Arteaga et al., 2019), we inspect application materials directly and cover 16 occupations (Appendix B) which allows us to study gender differences while partially controlling for the confound of occupation-specific base rates. However, we find that even within occupations, confounds remain as

* Equal contribution
♥ Corresponding author

Proceedings of the Fifth Workshop on Natural Language Processing and Computational Social Science (NLP+CSS), pages 140 - 150
November 7, 2022 ©2022 Association for Computational Linguistics

women tend to occupy lower ranking positions and men and women cluster in different types of fine-trained jobs within an occupation category (Section 3).

Our CV authors provide self-identified gender as part of our screening questions.[1] Due to the very low number of "Other/non-binary" responses (0.01%), we here only consider people self-identifying as male or female. We acknowledge that treating gender as a binary phenomenon is an oversimplification (Guo and Caliskan, 2020), but stress that our methodology extends to more inclusive notions of gender, and hope that our study inspires future work in this direction.

After presenting our data set (Section 2), we investigate gender signals in CVs in terms of overall word choice (Section 3); implied associations with power and agency (Section 4); and predictive models' sensitivity to gender when trained on data from which gender-indicative signals were removed to different extents (Section 5).

2 Dataset collection

On Prolific[2], we hired 2,000 participants (50% women) who were (1) US American and live and work in the US; and (2) in full-time employment. After answering a number of screening questions, participants composed a CV "pretending that you were applying for your next promotion". We specifically asked our participants to copy from their existing CV, instead of write an entirely new CV to mimic real-world CVs as closely as possible. It was encouraged to anonymize information wherever possible, but otherwise craft a CV as realistic as possible given their current situation. For a uniformed structure, we segmented the CV submission into five parts, each as a free-text box: (1) an optional professional summary/career objective, (2) professional experience, (3) education; (4) skills and attributes; (5) optional certifications/qualifications.

Quality control and preprocessing We removed responses based on very short (long) response times and non-English text (~ 10%), retaining 1,789 CVs (50.5% female). We tokenized, lemmatized and POS-tagged all text, removed stop words, and concatenated the five CV segments. We identified pronouns and named entities.[3] All preprocessing was done using SpaCy's default English models.

Data sharing In line with our IRB approval, we release a deidentified version of our data set to individual researchers. Further details are in the Ethics Statement. Appendix A contains the consent form.

3 Gender-associated word choice

We qualitatively analyze gender-associated word choice in 6 (out of 16) occupations: 2× female dominated (Education, Healthcare); 2× male dominated (Computer/maths, Management) and 2× balanced (Business/finance, Sales).

We first obtain the top 1% of TFIDF-ranked unigrams for both men's (M) and women's (F) CVs. We then retain terms in these two sets unique to M (and conversely, unique to F) as terms highly associated with only one gender. Due to space constraints, we present the full results in Table 4 in Appendix C.

In men-dominated occupations, men-associated terms are 'scientistic' (`engineer`, `developer`, `database`), or relate to leadership/tactics (`leadership`, `planning`); women-associated terms relate to interpersonal skills (`community`, `communication`, `social`). For women-dominated occupations, terms more likely to be used by women include those related to support and teamwork (`help`, `assistant`, `aid`); whereas men use terms which are again 'scientistic' and exhibiting leadership (`physician`, `lead`, `manager`).

The overall, across-occupation, pattern is not dissimilar to the occupation-stratified analyses above. This is consistent with sociological studies which have shown that men are often assessed by their competence and leadership qualities, whereas women are often assessed by their 'likeability' (i.e., their personal characters) (Eagly and Karau, 2002). On the contrary, women who show ambition and competitiveness are often penalised for violating traditional feminine stereotypes (Phelan et al., 2008). Such biased judgments are likely to discourage women to use words to describe their expertise and use more communal words instead.

Note, however, that these differences arise not only from lexical choice, but also from real world differences *within* an occupational group,

[1]Participants chose from: [Man, Woman, Other/non-binary, prefer not to say].

[2]`https://www.prolific.co/`

[3]Including all entity types covered by SpaCy's default entity tagger.

where the genders distribute differently across work tasks and finer-grained roles: women tend to have lower-ranking jobs, and specific occupations within the broader groups will exhibit different gender skews. Results for the Education occupation illustrate this well, where men-associated terms are dominated by technology and leadership (`microsoft`, `lead`, `technology`), while women-associated terms focus on early education and support (`child`, `elementary`, `social`). See underlined terms in Table 4 for further examples.

4 Power and Agency in CVs

Do men and women differ in the way they present themselves in a CV? We compare the extent of *power* and *agency* implied in the verbs used by male and female applicants. We apply Sap et al. (2017)'s connotation frames of power and agency, which associate verbs with the reactions they evoke the reader (Rashkin et al., 2016). By focussing on verbs, we abstract away from (named) entities with a strong occupation association and focus on self-presentation (Goffman, 1959). We consider all transitive verbs in CVs. Given the content (primarily focused on the author) and style (listings, incomplete sentences) of CVs, we assume that the agent of every verb is the author. The **power** dimension distinguishes verbs where the agent (subject) has more ($A>T$; 'lead'), less ($A<T$; 'assist'), or equal ($A=T$; 'care') power to the theme (object). The **agency** dimension categorizes verbs as high (+; 'support'), low (−; 'wait') or neutral (neu; 'access') agency. We use Sap et al. (2017)'s frame-labeled data set of 2K English verbs. 48% of verb types in our CVs are in the labeled data set (conversely, 57% of frame-labeled verbs occur in our CVs). The numbers are comparable across genders.

Overall label distribution We restrict our analysis to CVs with at least 10 and at most 100 verbs (N=1503, 53% women) to reduce the impact of outliers,[4] and retrieve the power and agency label of each verb that is included in the labeled set. Figure 1 shows the overall distribution of power and agency levels in our data set. Consistent with prior work (Sap et al., 2017), and unsurprising given the data domain, we observe a dominance of agent-power and high agency verbs.

Gender differences We measure the statistical dependence of power/agency levels (independent

[4]Noting that the results hold with all data points included.

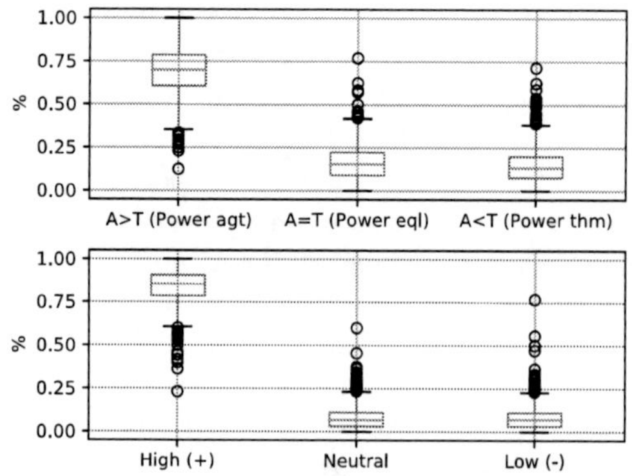

Figure 1: Distribution of power (top) and agency (bottom) verbs in our data. Each dot corresponds to one CV.

variables) on the gender of the CV author (dependent variable) fitting a logistic regression.[5] Each CV is represented as a count vector over the 3 power and 3 agency categories, while controlling for CV length (number of words) and occupation (cf. Appendix B). We standardized features for better interpretability of β, and coded Man as 0, and Woman as 1. Table 1 shows that women use equal power (A=T) and theme power (A<T) verbs significantly more often than men. Examples for equal power verbs that are more frequently used by females than males are {`complete`, `perform`, `analyze`, `assess`}, and for theme power verbs {`assist`, `learn`, `need`, `serve`}. Gender difference for use of agent-power verbs is insignificant.

We also find that both high (+) and low (-) agency verbs are more frequently used by men.[6] Male-associated positive agency verbs include {`employ`, `reduce`, `rate`, `acquire`, `exceed`} while male-associated negative agency verbs include {`address`, `expect`, `stay`, `relate`}. There are no significant differences in the use of neutral agency verbs.

4.1 Discussion

Women use more verbs in CVs that associate low power with the agent (CV author). Broadly, this agrees with prior work revealing that women are portrayed as less powerful in fiction movies (Sap et al., 2017). It also links into results from sociology revealing that leadership qualities (strength,

[5]`https://www.statsmodels.org/dev/generated/statsmodels.discrete.discrete_model.Logit.html`

[6]Noting that the significance for the differences in agency do not hold after Holm–Bonferroni correction (Holm, 1979) for multiple comparisons.

Feature	β	p	
Power($A > T$)	4.57	0.140	
Power($A = T$)	10.78	0.006 **	**F**
Power($A < T$)	15.25	0.000 **	**F**
Agency(+)	-6.35	0.032 *	**M**
Agency(neu)	2.34	0.589	
Agency(−)	-11.72	0.007 *	**M**

Table 1: Association of power/agency with binary CV author gender via coefficients (β) and significance estimates (p) of a logistic regression, after controlling for CV length and occupation. The final column indicates direction of association (male=0, female=1). * indicates statistical significance at $p < 0.05$, while ** additionally confirms significance after Holm–Bonferroni correction for multiple comparisons.

Model	D-Full	D-Balanced
Random U	0.50 (±0.00)	0.48(±0.00)
Majority	0.34 (±0.00)	0.33 (±0.00)
SVC Full	0.69 (± 0.03)	0.64 (±0.03)
LR Full	0.72 (± 0.03)	0.66 (±0.02)
RoBERTa Full	0.75 (± 0.02)	0.71 (±0.03)
SVC -PER	0.69 (± 0.01)	0.61 (±0.03)
LR -PER	0.73 (± 0.03)	0.66 (±0.02)
RoBERTa -PER	0.75 (± 0.01)	0.57 (±0.20)
SVC -NE	0.67 (± 0.02)	0.62 (±0.01)
LR -NE	0.71 (± 0.02)	0.66 (±0.02)
RoBERTa -NE	0.73 (± 0.02)	0.66 (±0.01)

Table 2: Predicting the gender (M,F) of an author of a CV. Macro-averaged F1 score (±standard deviation) from 5-fold cross-validation.

assertiveness) are evaluated more positively in men, than in women (Eagly and Karau, 2002; Rudman and Glick, 2001). Similarly, men are often rated more favorable than women given the same qualification, which might lead women to elaborate more on their education and qualifications (Njoto et al., 2022). Indeed, we find the Education section in female-authored CVs to be on average 15% longer than in male (247 vs 214 words), the Qualification and Training section 24% longer (144 vs 116 words), while the Professional Experience sections are of similar length (+2%; 1109 vs 1034 words).

Notably, this may be because, on average, women in the US have attained a higher level of education that men (Parker, 2021). However, it also reflects that women tend to get more education for the same job, and tend to be overly qualified for similar positions. Women access more education but also need more education and training for the same job (Campbell and Hahl, 2022).

5 Gender prediction from CV text

Sections 3 and 4 explored gender-speciric content framing differences CVs which may impact judgment the reader (or hirer). We next quantify the susceptibility of representative predictive models to gender information in CVs. We use the task of binary author gender prediction based on the text of the CV as a diagnostic tool to assess the extent to which models can infer gender information from CVs. We explicitly caution against using this task as a ML benchmark (cf., Ethics Statement).

We test the following binary classifiers: a linear SVC with L1 regularization, which by design learns sparse and interpretable features; a logistic regression classifier (LR); and a fine-tuned RobERTa-based classifier built on pre-trained RoBERTa uncased (Liu et al., 2019), fine-tuned for two epochs with a learning rate of 4×10^{-5}.[7] We use TFIDF features ($|X|$=5000) for LR and SVM and plain text for RoBERTa. We include a random uniform, and a majority baseline and run all models with 5-fold cross-validation.

We test our models on three versions of our CVs.[8] All versions are lemmatized and stopwords were removed. (1) the full data set with all lemmas from all CV sections (**Full**); (2) mask names and pronouns to remove explicit gender indicators (**-PER**); (3) remove *all* named entities (**-NE**), to abstract away from institutional information such as single-gender schools which may carry implicit information about the gender of the applicant.

Training these models on the full data sets (D-Full, N=1503) set will inevitably add a confounding factor of occupation-specific terms: most occupations are substantially gender-skewed in their workforce. To remove this confound, we create a version of each data set with a gender-balanced set of CVs *for each occupation* (D-Balanced, N=1118). We report results as macro averaged F1 scores, as presented in Table 2.

Results We test whether gendered information is encoded in classifiers trained on data with varying amounts of gender-indicative information. A perfectly gender-agnostic model would perform en par with the baselines.

Table 2 shows that all classifiers outperform the

[7] BERT uncased performed slightly below RoBERTa.

[8] Like in Section 4 we remove CVs with fewer than 10 or more than 100 verbs for consistency.

baselines substantially, both when trained on D-Full as well as on D-Balanced, where the occupation proxy gender is reduced. In line with prior work (De-Arteaga et al., 2019), we find that 'scrubbing' names and pronouns as explicit gender indicators (-PER) has negligible impact. Removing all named entities reduces classifier performance, but it remains well above random. RoBERTa outperforms the linear models in the Full data condition (left column), but shows unstable performance in the Balanced condition (right column) presumably due to the smaller data set leading to overfitting (note the high std in the -PER condition). Overall, the findings highlight the importance of considering gendered language signals beyond explicit indicators, i.e., that simple methods like removal of names (Manikandan, 2020) does not imply absence of gender information. Table 5 (Appendix D) lists the 20 most predictive features for the linear SVC trained on the D-Balanced, when trained on the full data (top) and the entity-redacted data (bottom). The features from the full data include entities like state names (`Indianapolis, Colorado`). Even after gender balancing per occupation, stereotypically associated features with women (`child`, and "soft" attributes like `attitude, assist, document`) and men (`supervise, technology`) emerge.

6 Discussion

We presented a data set of 1.8K authentic, US-English CVs across 16 occupations, aligned with self-reported binary gender of the author. This data set allowed us to inspect features of men- and women-specific language in CVs, while controlling for the confounding factor of occupation: most occupations are heavily gender-skewed.

This paper connects the concept of framing, i.e., influencing readers of a document through careful choice of words (Entman, 2007), with existing power discrepancies between men and women in western society in general, and the job market specifically (Rudman, 1998). We showed that women use verbs that imply lower power significantly more often than men, even after controlling for occupation. Subtle changes in word choice have been shown to impact human perception, reaction and choice (Kahneman and Tversky, 2013). In the context of *human* hiring, this suggests that (a) removing explicit gender indicators is insufficient; and (b) further support for sensitizing both hirers and applicants to subconscious bias.

We further trained classifiers to predict binary author gender based on CV text, in scenarios where gender proxy information was removed by gender-balancing the training data and/or removing named entities. We show that classifiers perform significantly above chance across all settings, confirming that subtle gender signal remains. This result is expected, and in line with prior research (De-Arteaga et al., 2019), but for the first time shown directly on data more akin to application materials presented to human and automatic hirers.

Our experiments retain a confounding factor of job type within an occupational group: within an occupation, women tend to have lower-ranking jobs; and within our 16 broad occupational groups, different specific occupations will exhibit different gender skews. In Section 3, we inspected gender-associated word choice in 6 most frequent occupations in our data set, finding that across occupations, 'scientistic' terms (`engineer, developer, database`) and leadership terms (`leadership, administration, planning`) are more associated with male CVs; while women are more likely to mention interpersonal skills, support, or teamwork (`community, communication, social,help, assistant, aid`), typically associated with administrative roles. Consequently, gender signals in CVs not only originate from lexical choice, but also also reflect real-world differences in work tasks and position levels. Disentangling these factors is an important direction for future work.

In sum, we maintain that perpetuated gendered patterns embedded in CVs can bias both human and automated hiring, and that the naive use of ML methods bears the risk of exacerbating bias: by picking up spurious associations on different levels from explicit gender information (names, hobbies) to subtler word choice (the level 'power' or 'agency'). Suggestions for further work include usability studies and social-psychological interventions for users of recruitment software, for *both* job applicants and decision makers. Interventions could include 'nudges' in the user experience flow, informing users about potential gender signals being encoded in their data, and suggestions of strategies to mitigate or minimise this. As our findings suggest, scrubbing names and entities off the CVs is not effective in de-gendering CVs for fairer recruitment decisions, and should not be used as the be-all-and-end-all in promoting fair hiring, as often is the wont of current initiatives.

Ethics Statement

This study was approved by the University of Melbourne ethics board (Human Ethics Committee LNR 3A), Reference Number 2022-22062-32741-5, and data acquisition and analysis has been taken out to the according ethical standards. Our data was collected via Prolific. The crowdworkers (annotators) in the project were paid £3.75 for a median of 11 minutes of work, which is slightly above minimum hourly wage and reflects adequate compensation for the time spent. Appendix A contains the consent form presented to annotators before the task. Prolific allows us to record information anonymously without personally identifiable data. As part of CV generation, our crowdworkers were instructed to exclude their names and the names of their affiliated organisations from their drafted CVs.

To enable future research in this area, we plan to release an anonymized and deidentified version of our data to individual researchers where names, emails, addresses, phone numbers and all named entities are redacted (the [-NE] version used in this paper). The data will contain the redacted CV text and self-identified gender label only. Interested researchers will sign an agreement form stating that they (1) will not share the data with anyone else; (2) will delete the data upon completion of the research or after 1 year whichever comes first.

This paper investigated the language differences between men and women authored CVs. Gender information was identified by the CV authors and no gender-inference was applied anywhere in the paper. We acknowledge that a binary notion of gender is not representative of the concept. In addition, we acknowledge that our study excludes a large portion of the population which does not identify to a cis-normative group. We emphasized throughout the paper that our findings hold for self-identifying men and women only, and that our methodology in principle extends to a more inclusive set of gender groups, conditioned on the availability of reliable data.

We used the task of gender prediction from CV data as a benchmark to assess the amount of gendered information retained in ML models after various strategies to remove gender proxy information. We do not endorse this task in general, and accordingly do not release pre-trained models to the public.

Acknowledgments

We thank the reviewers for their very insightful feedback. This work was partially funded by the Seed Funding scheme of the Melbourne Center for Data Science.

References

Miranda Bogen. 2019. All the ways hiring algorithms can introduce bias. *Harvard Business Review*, 6:2019.

Alison Booth and Andrew Leigh. 2010. Do employers discriminate by gender? a field experiment in female-dominated occupations. *Economics Letters*, 107(2):236–238.

Sheila Brownlow, Julie A Rosamond, and Jennifer A Parker. 2003. Gender-linked linguistic behavior in television interviews. *Sex Roles*, 49(3):121–132.

Elizabeth Lauren Campbell and Oliver Hahl. 2022. He's overqualified, she's highly committed: Qualification signals and gendered assumptions about job candidate commitment. *Organization Science*.

Linda L Carli. 1990. Gender, language, and influence. *Journal of personality and social psychology*, 59(5):941.

Maria De-Arteaga, Alexey Romanov, Hanna Wallach, Jennifer Chayes, Christian Borgs, Alexandra Chouldechova, Sahin Geyik, Krishnaram Kenthapadi, and Adam Tauman Kalai. 2019. Bias in bios: A case study of semantic representation bias in a high-stakes setting. In *proceedings of the Conference on Fairness, Accountability, and Transparency*, pages 120–128.

Alice H Eagly and Steven J Karau. 2002. Role congruity theory of prejudice toward female leaders. *Psychol. Rev.*, 109(3):573–598.

Robert M Entman. 2007. Framing bias: Media in the distribution of power. *Journal of communication*, 57(1):163–173.

Danielle Gaucher, Justin Friesen, and Aaron C Kay. 2011. Evidence that gendered wording in job advertisements exists and sustains gender inequality. *J. Pers. Soc. Psychol.*, 101(1):109–128.

Peter Glick and Susan T Fiske. 2018. The ambivalent sexism inventory: Differentiating hostile and benevolent sexism. In *Social cognition*, pages 116–160. Routledge.

Erving Goffman. 1959. *The presentation of self in everyday life*. University of Edinburgh Social Sciences Research Centre.

Wei Guo and Aylin Caliskan. 2020. Detecting emergent intersectional biases: Contextualized word embeddings contain a distribution of human-like biases.

ME Heilman. 2012. Gender stereotypes and workplace bias. research in organisational behaviour, 32, 113-135.

Sture Holm. 1979. A simple sequentially rejective multiple test procedure. *Scand. Stat. Theory Appl.*, 6(2):65–70.

Daniel Kahneman and Amos Tversky. 2013. Choices, values, and frames. In *Handbook of the fundamentals of financial decision making: Part I*, pages 269–278. World Scientific.

Robin Lakoff. 1975. Linguistic theory and the real world 1. *Language Learning*, 25(2):309–338.

Campbell Leaper and Melanie M Ayres. 2007. A meta-analytic review of gender variations in adults' language use: Talkativeness, affiliative speech, and assertive speech. *Personality and Social Psychology Review*, 11(4):328–363.

Yinhan Liu, Myle Ott, Naman Goyal, Jingfei Du, Mandar Joshi, Danqi Chen, Omer Levy, Mike Lewis, Luke Zettlemoyer, and Veselin Stoyanov. 2019. Roberta: A robustly optimized bert pretraining approach.

S Manikandan. 2020. A modern concept of blind hiring: Its importance and benefits. *Journal of Business and Management*, 22(5):60–62.

Corinne A Moss-Racusin, John F Dovidio, Victoria L Brescoll, Mark J Graham, and Jo Handelsman. 2012. Science faculty's subtle gender biases favor male students. *Proceedings of the national academy of sciences*, 109(41):16474–16479.

D Neumark. 2010. Detecting discrimination in audit and correspondence studies (nber working paper series no. 16448).

Matthew L Newman, Carla J Groom, Lori D Handelman, and James W Pennebaker. 2008. Gender differences in language use: An analysis of 14,000 text samples. *Discourse processes*, 45(3):211–236.

Sheilla Njoto, Marc Cheong, Reeva Lederman, Aidan McLoughney, Leah Ruppanner, and Anthony Wirth. 2022. Gender bias in AI recruitment systems: A sociological- and data science-based case study. To appear in: *Proceedings of the IEEE International Symposium on Technology and Society 2022*.

Prasanna Parasurama and João Sedoc. 2022. Gendered language in resumes and its implications for algorithmic bias in hiring. In *Proceedings of the 4th Workshop on Gender Bias in Natural Language Processing (GeBNLP)*, pages 74–74, Seattle, Washington. Association for Computational Linguistics.

Kim Parker. 2021. What's behind the growing gap between men and women in college completion? Technical report, Pew Research Center, `https://www.pewresearch.org/fact-tank/2021/11/08/whats-behind-the-growing-gap-between-men-and-women-in-college-completion/`.

Julie E. Phelan, Corinne A. Moss-Racusin, and Laurie A. Rudman. 2008. Competent yet out in the cold: Shifting criteria for hiring reflect backlash toward agentic women. *Psychology of Women Quarterly*, 32(4):406–413.

Hannah Rashkin, Sameer Singh, and Yejin Choi. 2016. Connotation frames: A data-driven investigation. In *Proceedings of the 54th Annual Meeting of the Association for Computational Linguistics (Volume 1: Long Papers)*, pages 311–321, Berlin, Germany. Association for Computational Linguistics.

Peter A Riach and Judith Rich. 2006. An experimental investigation of sexual discrimination in hiring in the english labor market. *The BE Journal of Economic Analysis & Policy*, 6(2).

Laurie A Rudman. 1998. Self-promotion as a risk factor for women: the costs and benefits of counterstereotypical impression management. *Journal of personality and social psychology*, 74(3):629.

Laurie A Rudman and Peter Glick. 2001. Prescriptive gender stereotypes and backlash toward agentic women. *J. Soc. Issues*, 57(4):743–762.

Maarten Sap, Marcella Cindy Prasettio, Ari Holtzman, Hannah Rashkin, and Yejin Choi. 2017. Connotation frames of power and agency in modern films. In *Proceedings of the 2017 Conference on Empirical Methods in Natural Language Processing*, pages 2329–2334, Copenhagen, Denmark. Association for Computational Linguistics.

Rhea E Steinpreis, Katie A Anders, and Dawn Ritzke. 1999. The impact of gender on the review of the curricula vitae of job applicants and tenure candidates: A national empirical study. *Sex roles*, 41(7):509–528.

Tony Sun, Andrew Gaut, Shirlyn Tang, Yuxin Huang, Mai ElSherief, Jieyu Zhao, Diba Mirza, Elizabeth Belding, Kai-Wei Chang, and William Yang Wang. 2019. Mitigating gender bias in natural language processing: Literature review. In *Proceedings of the 57th Annual Meeting of the Association for Computational Linguistics*, pages 1630–1640, Florence, Italy. Association for Computational Linguistics.

Mary Talbot. 2019. *Language and gender*. John Wiley & Sons.

A Prolific consent form

```
Consent Form
    I consent to participate in this
project, the details of which have been
explained to me.
    I understand that the purpose of
this research is to investigate how to
produce a CV that increases success in
recruitment
```

I understand that my participation in this project is for research purposes only.

I acknowledge that the possible effects of participating in this research project have been explained to my satisfaction.

In this project, I will be required to draft a CV to apply for a promotion.

I understand that my participation is voluntary and that I am free to withdraw from this project anytime without explanation or prejudice and to withdraw any unprocessed data that I have provided.

I understand that the data from this research will be stored at the University of Melbourne and will be destroyed after 5 years.

I have been informed that the confidentiality of the information I provide will be safeguarded and subject to any legal requirements; my data will be password protected and accessible only by the university-approved researchers.

I understand that all data recorded is anonymized.

I understand that after I sign and return this consent form, it will be retained by the researcher.

By clicking the checkbox below, you are signing the Consent Form.

B Occupations

The occupational code was taken from the General Social Survey,[9] as the Standard Occupational Classification System widely used in English-speaking official surveys. categorization Table 3 lists all occupations in our data set, together with the total number of CVs and gender ratio. "Other" occupations arise from free-text entries. Some examples include dog caretaker, musician, transport and logistics manager, pilot, automotive designer, among others. For reference, we also include gender rations from the 2021 US Labor Statistics in the rightmost column of Table 3. In general, the gender skew in our data set agrees with the US statistics, with some deviations expected given our limited sample.

[9]https://gss.norc.org/

C Gender-associated word choice

Table 4 shows the full results of gender-specific top 1% TFIDF terms per occupation (top), and overall across our whole CV data set (bottom).

D Classifier features

Table 5 lists the most predictive features for men (top) and women (bottom) as learnt by the linear SVC with L1 regularization when applied to the occupation-wise gender-balanced CV data set.

occupation	Man	Woman	% F	Total	% F USLS
Business and financial operations occupations	117	85	0.42	202	0.55
Computer and mathematical occupations	152	49	0.24	201	0.26
Educational instruction and library occupations	64	117	0.65	181	0.74
Healthcare support occupations	58	118	0.67	176	0.85
Management occupations	101	58	0.36	159	0.52
Sales and related occupations	65	70	0.52	135	0.62
Arts, design, entertainment, sports, and media occupations	58	64	0.52	122	0.50
Office and administrative support occupations	43	78	0.64	121	0.72
Other	61	53	0.46	114	–
Life, physical, and social science occupations	33	62	0.65	95	0.61
Architecture and engineering occupations	56	18	0.24	74	0.24
Community and social service occupations	15	44	0.75	59	0.72
Food preparation and serving related occupations	20	33	0.62	53	0.59
Legal occupations	28	22	0.44	50	0.42
Personal care and service occupations	8	21	0.72	29	0.72
Protective service occupations	5	5	0.5	10	0.50
Farming, fishing, and forestry occupations	2	6	0.75	8	0.75
Total	886	903	0.5	1789	0.53

Table 3: Occupations with number of CVs and proportion of female participants (%F) in our CV data set. The occupations included in our analyses in Appendix D are bold-faced. % F USLS are the official percentages of female employees per occupation taken from the US Labor Statistics (2021).

Gender balance	Occupation	Terms
Gender-balanced	Business and financial operations occupations	$M \setminus F$: insurance, sale, analysis, computer, word, lead, knowledge, master, data, product, time, operation, tax $F \setminus M$: student, august, accountant, art, high, information, public, use, training, software, development, research, program
	Sales and related occupations	$M \setminus F$: major, proficient, problem, engineering, june, computer, account, issue, lead, use, goal, responsibility, technical, develop, representative, operation, support, strategy $F \setminus M$: position, degree, industry, august, english, excel, excellent, leadership, strong, student, art, medium, create, study, maintain, good, employee, communication
Men-dominated	Computer and mathematical occupations	$M \setminus F$: gpa, application, database, office, window, microsoft, high, server, issue, engineer, web, security, include, developer, product, develop, network, college $F \setminus M$: student, art, analysis, lead, java, ms, python, course, sale, master, social, communication, spanish, css, time, html, graduate, ability, maintain, research
	Management occupations	$M \setminus F$: california, excel, leadership, engineering, ability, computer, company, information, planning, marketing, software, technology, product, time, administration, degree, support, design $F \setminus M$: staff, position, member, community, diploma, medium, account, research, health, hi, job, master, study, public, social, create, graduate, proficient
Women-dominated	Educational instruction and library occupations	$M \setminus F$: project, level, office, datum, <u>microsoft</u>, <u>computer</u>, <u>lead</u>, new, <u>software</u>, <u>technology</u>, lesson, business, <u>develop</u>, class, proficient $F \setminus M$: gpa, degree, library, member, <u>child</u>, community, award, create, <u>elementary</u>, honor, psychology, development, <u>social</u>, <u>help</u>, write
	Healthcare support occupations	$M \setminus F$: physician, various, equipment, project, member, volunteer, community, emergency, information, manage, manager, department, able, ensure, american $F \setminus M$: gpa, august, assistant, aid, problem, assist, june, art, microsoft, customer, paste, time, cpr, therapy, role
Overall: across all occupations		$M \setminus F$: web, server, improve, production, good, day, engineering, tool, build, policy, degree, check, increase, test, technology, meet, senior, master, material, security, engineer, control, procedure, sql, solution, point, administration, performance, quality, database, network, equipment, data, strategy, user, testing $F \setminus M$: strong, psychology, able, conduct, word, care, position, organize, prepare, art, document, intern, national, coordinate, resource, online, record, schedule, teacher, space, course, gpa, teach, english, child, current, event, class, store, volunteer, september, meeting, honor, individual, content, study, phone

Table 4: Qualitative analyses of mutually-exclusive terms within the top 1% of unigrams, by tf-idf ranking: (top) stratified across occupations; and (bottom) across all occupations. $M \setminus F$ denotes the set of terms in the top 1% of male CV unigrams, which are not in the corresponding top 1% of female CV unigrams. Conversely, $F \setminus M$ denotes the set of terms found in the top 1% of female CV unigrams, which are not in the top 1% of male CV unigrams. The underlined examples are discussed in Section 3.

male: level, indianapolis, instruct, reduce, th, clinical, troubleshoot, large, part, culinary, engineer, supervise, repair, improvement, shipping, technology, multiple, tool, business, regulatory **female**: answer, attitude, reference, file, document, create, assist, role, colorado, children, child, coordinator, know, gain, interview, receivable, honors, woman, media
male -NE: machine, instruct, profit, clinical, also, supervise, observe, part, technology, leader, reduce, reduction, basic, instructor, opportunity, hold, review, people, regard, electrical **female -NE**: check, attitude, document, core, medium, media, woman, answer, content, present, child, create, speaking, claim, resource, file, assist, resume, plan

Table 5: Most predictive features as learned by the binary SVC for gender prediction when trained on the Balanced data set full (top) or with NEs redacted (bottom).

Detecting Dissonant Stance in Social Media: The Role of Topic Exposure

Vasudha Varadarajan[1], **Nikita Soni**[1], **Weixi Wang**[1]
Christian Luhmann[2], **H. Andrew Schwartz**[1] and **Naoya Inoue**[3]
[1]Department of Computer Science, Stony Brook University
[2]Department of Psychology, Stony Brook University
[3]School of Information Science, Japan Advanced Institute of Science and Technology
{vvaradarajan,nisoni,weixiwang,has}@cs.stonybrook.edu
christian.luhmann@stonybrook.edu
naoya-i@jaist.ac.jp

Abstract

We address *dissonant stance detection*, classifying conflicting stance between two input statements. Computational models for traditional stance detection have typically been trained to indicate pro/con for a given target topic (e.g. gun control) and thus do not generalize well to new topics. In this paper, we systematically evaluate the generalizability of dissonant stance detection to situations where examples of the topic have not been seen at all or have only been seen a few times. We show that dissonant stance detection models trained on only 8 topics, none of which are the target topic, can perform as well as those trained only on a target topic. Further, adding non-target topics boosts performance further up to approximately 32 topics where accuracies start to plateau. Taken together, our experiments suggest dissonant stance detection models can generalize to new unanticipated topics, an important attribute for the social scientific study of social media where new topics emerge daily.

1 Introduction

A prevalent theory about human reasoning, the argumentative theory, is that its primary function is to support argumentation of one's stance or belief (Mercier and Sperber, 2011). New arguments come up on a daily basis and thus new topics for stance emerge. However, most current approaches to stance detection are restricted to well-established topics, and thus are limited in their applications, such as improving educational strategies to facilitate learning (Schwarz and Asterhan, 2010; Scheuer et al., 2010) or tracking political opinions on the latest concerns (Thomas et al., 2006).

As a step toward stance detection, unrestricted to particular topics, we study the problem of identifying (dis)agreement between two statements under pre-chosen as well as unseen topics (Bar-Haim et al., 2017; Xu et al., 2019; Körner et al., 2021) (henceforth, *dissonant stance detection*). Given two claims c_1, c_2 under topic t, the task is to classify them into either (i) CONSONANCE if the stance suggested by c_1 towards t is the same as that by c_2, (ii) DISSONANCE if the stance suggested by c_1 towards t is the opposite to that by c_2, or (iii) NEITHER (see Table 1 for examples). This is a challenging task that tries to understand (dis)agreement between two statements where the topic of contention (henceforth, *target topic*) is not explicitly stated. Such instances are found abundantly in comments, replies and responses to videos, news articles and other online media content.

Here, we question the necessity of the target topic by exploring the impact of non-target topics on transformer-based models. Over a corpus of 34 diverse topics, we conduct a large-scale empirical evaluation on the role of exposure to topics. Our **contributions** include: (a) the evaluation of the role of exposure to other topics when detecting statements with dissonant stance for a target topic using transformer-based models; (b) we show that topic-independent (TOPICINDEP) dissonant stance detection models, which are not exposed to the target topic, can perform as well as those trained on a target topic when exposed to as few as 4 non-target topics during training (§3); (c) we show that adding more non-target topics further boosts the performance, beginning to reach a plateau at approximately 24 to 32 non-target topics, evaluating several transformer-based models; (d) we demonstrate that a topic-independence dissonance model, trained only on **pairs of social media posts**, can transfer to a different social media domain and variant of task (finding dissonance within phrase pairs of **a single post**) with a novel small annotated dataset.

2 Related Work

Stance detection is conventionally modeled as identifying the stance expressed by a statement towards a target topic (Küçük and Can, 2020; Hasan and

Proceedings of the Fifth Workshop on Natural Language Processing and Computational Social Science (NLP+CSS), pages 151 - 156
November 7, 2022

Ng, 2013; Mohammad et al., 2016; Xu et al., 2019; Rosenthal and McKeown, 2015; Xu et al., 2019; Körner et al., 2021; Bar-Haim et al., 2017) We generalize conventional stance detection as dissonant stance detection or contrast detection. Beyond generalized stance detection, identification of dissonance in language has other social scientific applications such as detecting cognitive dissonance (Festinger, 1957).

Generalized stance has previously studied between two short concise statements and without evaluation for the amount of topic exposure (Allaway and McKeown, 2020; Allaway et al., 2021).[1] On the other hand, other work has considered stance detection models in a cross-target settings (Xu et al., 2018; Stab et al., 2018; Hardalov et al., 2021; Kaushal et al., 2021; Reuver et al., 2021; Xu et al., 2019; Körner et al., 2021). Some approaches achieve this through incorporation of external lexical or world knowledge (Zhang et al., 2020) or using adversarial training to eliminate topic-specific information (Allaway et al., 2021). However, most of these studies use a corpus comprising a small number of topics, such as the six topics of SemEval-2016 Task 6 (Mohammad et al., 2016). Importantly, despite these promising results, the question of whether the topic needs to be included at all has remained opened as well as the degree of non-target topic exposure.

3 Methodology

3.1 Dataset

To build a dataset for dissonant stance detection with a large number of diverse topics, we extract arguments from Kialo[2], a popular online debate platforms. Kialo arguments are tree-structured: given a topic claim (i.e. a statement being debated, such as *Should vaping be banned?*), users write claims, explicitly labeling their stance (either pro or con) on the topic statement. Users can reply to each claim with pro/con labels. At the time of submission, Kialo has 16,884 topic claims and 637,383 pro/con claims.

We started with 72 seed topics which are semantically dissimilar to each other, and then. extract any claim pairs in a parent-child relationship. Given a claim pair c_1, c_2, we label them as (i) CONSONANCE if c_1 is a pro claim for c_2, or (ii) DISSONANCE if c_1 is a con claim for c_2. Neutral or absent-relations were also captured by dissonant stance detection models, we randomly paired separate claims from the same larger topic and labeled them as (iii) NEITHER- in these pairs, one claim is not a pro or a con to the other. To ensure a reasonable diversity of observations for each topic, we eliminate topics consisting of fewer than 700 claim pairs. We then balance the number of claim pairs by randomly sampling 700 claim pairs from each topic.

The final dataset resulted in 34 topics, each with 700 claim pairs. Existing studies of stance detection typically use a small number of topics, e.g., eight (Reuver et al., 2021), five (Xu et al., 2019) or two topics (Körner et al., 2021)). Our work is focused on large-scale empirical study of the impact of non-target topics (topic-independence) for dissonant stance detection models. The summary statistics and examples are shown in Table 1.

3.2 Model

We use Transformer models to obtain a representation of each input claim pair. In our experiments, we used BERT-base (Devlin et al., 2019), RoBERTA-base (Liu et al., 2019), and ALBERT-base (Lan et al., 2020). Given a pair of claims c_1, c_2, the input to the model is of the following form: "[CLS]c_1 [SEP] c_2 [SEP]". We then take the contextualized word embedding $\mathbf{x} \in \mathbb{R}^d$ of [CLS] in the final layer and feed it into the linear classifier: $y = \text{softmax}(W\mathbf{x}+\mathbf{b})$, where $W \in \mathbb{R}^{d \times 3}, \mathbf{b} \in \mathbb{R}^3$ is a learned model parameter.

We trained the model parameters (along with all the model weights) with a cross entropy loss for 10 epochs, using AdamW with the learning rate of 3×10^{-5}, the batch size of 16 and warm up ratio of 0.1.[3] To avoid overfitting, we use early stopping (patience of 5) with a macro-averaged F1.

3.3 Target topics

To explore the generalizability of topics in the dissonant stance detection task, we select a diverse set of target topics that are dissimilar to each other. To ensure the dissimilarity, we encode all topics into sentence embeddings with Sentence Transformers (Reimers and Gurevych, 2019)[4] and apply k-means clustering ($k = 5$). We then identify one topic closest to the centroid of each cluster.

[1]The dataset is annotated with "topic-phrase" stance rather than dissonant stance. See §3.1 for details on our dataset.

[2]`https://www.kialo.com/`

[3]We used huggingface's transformer `https://github.com/huggingface/transformers`.

[4]all-mpnet-base-v2 at `https://www.sbert.net/`.

Label	# topics	# claim pairs	Example (topic: *Should Zoos be banned?*)
CONSONANCE	34	7,559	c_1: Zoos are, by nature, restricted in the space they provide their animals. For many animals, it is much more cramped than the wild. c_2: For some captive animals, the small enclosures provided by zoos are directly related to the infant mortality rate.
DISSONANCE	34	8,289	c_1: Zoos cause suffering and harm to animals. c_2: We are unable to understand how, or even if, animals feel pain in a way that is remotely similar to how humans do. We should therefore prioritise quantifiable human utility.
NEITHER	34	7,952	c_1: Dogs were created by humans selectively breeding wolves. c_2: Humans do not have a right to breed, capture and confine other animals, even if they are endangered.

Table 1: Summary of the constructed dataset. Our dataset has a diverse, larger number of topics, and each topic has 700 labeled claim pairs.

This yields the following five, mutually exclusive target topics: (i) *Should Zoos Be Banned?*, (ii) *Was Donald Trump a Good President?*, (iii) *Free Will or Determinism*, (iv) *Should "women-only" spaces be open to anyone identifying as a woman?*, and (v) *Should European Monarchies Be Abolished?*. As a final result, we report an average of Macro-F1s for each target topic.

3.4 Training configurations

For each target topic, we train dissonant stance detection models with the following configurations.

TOPICINDEP To explore the pure generalizability of non-target topics, we use *only* training data from 33 (=34-1) non-target topics and do *not use any* training data from the target topic.

INTOPICFEW In practice, it is not difficult to create a small number of training instances for a given target topic. We train on *a small number of* claim pairs from the target topic in addition to pairs from 33 non-target topics. In our experiments, we randomly sample 20 (INTOPICFEW-20) or 50 instances (INTOPICFEW-50) from the target topic.

INTOPIC To estimate the baseline performance, we train the model *only* on the target topic. This roughly corresponds to conventional stance detection models.

ALLTOPICS To estimate a performance upper bound, we also train on all topics including both the target topic and 32 non-target topics.

To see the effect of non-target topics, we vary the number of non-target topics from k =2 to 32. For each k, we create five random sets of k topics and average Macro F1s over these trials.

Approach	F1-co	F1-di	F1-na	F1_{mac}
Random	0.325	0.367	0.325	0.339
Majority	0.000	0.519	0.000	0.173
BERT (TOPICINDEP)	0.586	0.673	0.710	0.656
ALBERT (TOPICINDEP)	0.598	0.673	0.726	0.666
RoBERTa (TOPICINDEP)	0.659	0.728	0.756	0.717
RoBERTa (INTOPIC)	0.524	0.637	0.776	0.653
RoBERTa (ALLTOPICS)	0.673	0.742	0.824	0.745

Table 2: Evaluation of approaches for topic independent dissonant stance detection versus baselines and an upperbound of witnessing the topic (INTOPIC, ALLTOPICS).

4 Evaluation

4.1 Results

The results of topic-independence dissonant stance detection models are shown in Table 2. It shows that all the variants of topic-independent dissonant stance detection models significantly outperformed the INTOPIC model. In addition, surprisingly, the RoBERTa(TOPICINDEP) model shows a similar performance to the ALLTOPICS model trained on 32 non-target samples and target-topic samples (i.e. an upperbound). This indicates the great potential of non-target topic samples: there are a large amount of topic-independent cues in dissonant stance detection, which are seemingly captured by the model.

Fig. 1 shows the effect of increasing number of non-target topics under the TOPICINDEP/INTOPICFEW setting. As the number of non-target topics increases, the performance improves: even TOPICINDEP significantly outperforms INTOPIC at 32 topics.

Surprisingly, the INTOPICFEW-50 trained on *only two non-target topics and 50 target-topic samples* has already F1 comparable to the INTOPIC

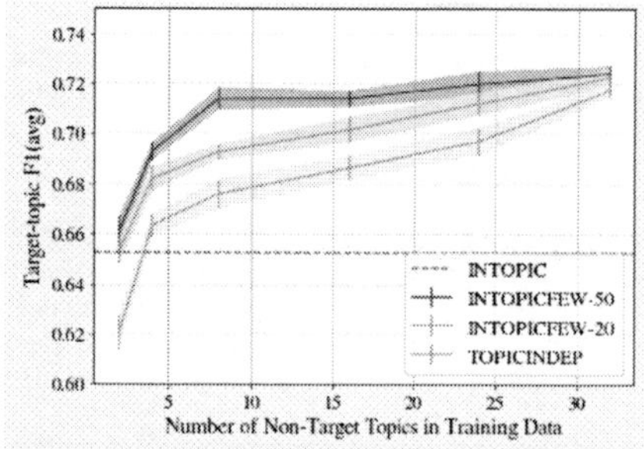

Figure 1: Effect of non-target topics in the topic-independent setting. The models trained only on a small number of non-target topics (TOPICINDEP,INTOPICFEW-20/50) already perform as well as those trained only on the target topic (INTOPIC). Adding more non-target topics boosts the performance of TOPICINDEP/INTOPICFEW models. The shaded area is the standard error of 25 trials (5 targets × 5 trials).

model. The other models also outperform the INTOPIC model when trained on a sufficient number of non-target topics (≥ 4).

This begs the question of how well these approaches compare to training with all the topics, including the target topic. The performance loss of TOPICINDEP/INTOPICFEW models compared to the ALLTOPICS model using 32 non-target samples is shown in Table 3. Surprisingly, the drop in performance observed when cutting down the target-specific training samples from 560 (ALLTOPICS) to 50 samples (INTOPICFEW-50) is comparable to further reducing target-specific samples to 20 (INTOPICFEW-20).

The results show that the dissonant stance detection models trained on a small number of topics exhibit an impressive ability to generalize to previously unseen target topics and exhibit further performance gains when exposed to a small number of samples from the target topic. This indicates that the model learns topic-independent cues, and underlying patterns of arguments to signify the dissonance between claims can be successfully captured with non-target topics.

4.2 Dissonance generalizability to other domain

We show that the model does not only generalize well over unseen topics, but captures dissonant language in a new domain. To this end, we test the model on a dissonance dataset annotated on a set of tweets parsed into discourse units using (Wang

Setting	#non-target topics	#target samples	Target-topic F1(avg.)
ALLTOPICS (Upperbound)	32	560	0.747
INTOPICFEW-50	32	50	**0.732 (↓ 0.015)**
INTOPICFEW-20	32	20	0.729 (↓ 0.018)
TOPICINDEP	32	0	0.718 (↓ 0.029)

Table 3: Performance loss of TOPICINDEP/INTOPICFEW models from the ALLTOPICS model under 32 non-target topics. The INTOPICFEW models trained on only 20 or 50 examples from a target topic (INTOPICFEW-20/50) has a significantly small loss from the ALLTOPICS model. Standard error for all these settings is 0.003.

Approach	F1-co	F1-di	F1-na	$F1_{macro}$
Majority	0.000	0.519	0.000	0.173
RoBERTa (TOPICINDEP-32)	**0.458**	**0.595**	0.207	0.420

Table 4: Evaluation of the generalization of our approach to hand-annotated Twitter phrases. The topic-independent model trained over the Kialo data still performs substantially better than chance when evaluated over dissonance within (much shorter) Twitter posts.

et al., 2018).[5] The annotation is carried out in two stages. First, each unit is annotated as THOUGHT or OTHER. A THOUGHT constitutes of all forms of knowing and awareness: a fact, claim, or statement is a thought. Anything not considered to be a THOUGHT is marked as an OTHER. Second, pairs of THOUGHT units from each tweet are extracted, and then annotated to be either in CONSONANCE, DISSONANCE or NEITHER. The annotations were carried out by a team of three annotators for stage 1 and a team of four annotators for stage 2. The final annotations were extracted by using majority vote and a tiebreaker. To balance the dataset, we choose a test set with 19 pairs of DISSONANCE, 19 pairs of CONSONANCE and 19 pairs of NEITHER. The inputs to the model are not from the training domain, they are tweet discourse units, not entire claims. Thus, this dataset would test the extent to which the model captures dissonance in a single tweet.

Table 4 shows that transferring the ALLTOPICS model trained on Kialo to this domain, without any finetuning, surprisingly still captures DISSONANCE

[5]Tweets are sampled from 2019-2020. The frequency of tweets with dissonant discourse units was found to be about 2.5%.

and CONSONANCE fairly well: the RoBERTA-based model trained on Kialo generalizes well by capturing topic-independent cues.

5 Conclusions

This paper weighs in on a key problem as NLP is increasingly used for studies of social science: the role of exposure to a diverse set of social or political topics and the ability to generalize to new topics. To this end, we have proposed and studied the problem of dissonant stance detection in the TOPICINDEP/INTOPICFEW setting. We find that models continue to improve under a "topic independent setting" but start plateauing at around 8 non-target topics. Our experiments also revealed that TOPICINDEP/INTOPICFEW dissonant stance detection models trained on only a small number of non-target topics already perform as well as those trained on a target topic, and that adding more non-target topics further boosts performance. Further, we find the model trained on the debate forum, where statements are from distinct users, generalizes to a new domain and finding dissonant statements from the same person. Taken together, these results suggest transformer-based dissonant stance detection model can generalize to unseen topics and domains.

6 Ethical Considerations

To create the datasets (§3.1 and §4.2), we use publicly available data on the web. The detection of dissonance has many beneficial applications such as understanding belief trends study of mental health from consenting individuals. But, it also could be used toward manipulating people such via targeted messaging without users' consent. All of our work is restricted to document-level information; No user-level information is used.

Acknowledgements

This work was supported by DARPA via Young Faculty Award grant #W911NF-20-1-0306 to H. Andrew Schwartz at Stony Brook University; the conclusions and opinions expressed are attributable only to the authors and should not be construed as those of DARPA or the U.S. Department of Defense. This work was also supported in part by NIH R01 AA028032-01 and Stony Brook University's Institute for AI-Driven Discovery and Innovation.

References

Emily Allaway and Kathleen McKeown. 2020. Zero-Shot Stance Detection: A Dataset and Model using Generalized Topic Representations. In *Proceedings of EMNLP*, pages 8913–8931.

Emily Allaway, Malavika Srikanth, and Kathleen McKeown. 2021. Adversarial learning for zero-shot stance detection on social media. In *Proceedings of NAACL: Human Language Technologies*, pages 4756–4767.

Roy Bar-Haim, Indrajit Bhattacharya, Francesco Dinuzzo, Amrita Saha, and Noam Slonim. 2017. Stance classification of context-dependent claims. In *Proceedings of EACL: Volume 1, Long Papers*, pages 251–261.

Jacob Devlin, Ming-Wei Chang, Kenton Lee, and Kristina Toutanova. 2019. BERT: Pre-training of deep bidirectional transformers for language understanding. In *Proceedings of NAACL: Human Language Technologies, Volume 1 (Long and Short Papers)*, pages 4171–4186.

Leon Festinger. 1957. *A theory of cognitive dissonance*, reissued by stanford univ. press in 1962, renewed 1985 by author, [nachdr.] edition. Stanford Univ. Press, Stanford. OCLC: 255286887.

Momchil Hardalov, Arnav Arora, Preslav Nakov, and Isabelle Augenstein. 2021. Cross-domain label-adaptive stance detection. In *Proceedings of EMNLP*, pages 9011–9028.

Kazi Saidul Hasan and Vincent Ng. 2013. Stance classification of ideological debates: Data, models, features, and constraints. In *Proceedings of IJCNLP*, pages 1348–1356.

Ayush Kaushal, Avirup Saha, and Niloy Ganguly. 2021. tWT–WT: A dataset to assert the role of target entities for detecting stance of tweets. In *Proceedings of NAACL: Human Language Technologies*, pages 3879–3889.

Erik Körner, Gregor Wiedemann, Ahmad Dawar Hakimi, Gerhard Heyer, and Martin Potthast. 2021. On classifying whether two texts are on the same side of an argument. In *Proceedings of EMNLP*, pages 10130–10138.

Dilek Küçük and Fazli Can. 2020. Stance detection: A survey. *Association for Computing Machinery*, 53(1).

Zhenzhong Lan, Mingda Chen, Sebastian Goodman, Kevin Gimpel, Piyush Sharma, and Radu Soricut. 2020. Albert: A lite bert for self-supervised learning of language representations. *arXiv*, page 1909.11942.

Yinhan Liu, Myle Ott, Naman Goyal, Jingfei Du, Mandar Joshi, Danqi Chen, Omer Levy, Mike Lewis, Luke Zettlemoyer, and Veselin Stoyanov. 2019. Roberta: A robustly optimized bert pretraining approach. *arXiv*, page 1907.11692.

Hugo Mercier and Dan Sperber. 2011. Why do humans reason? arguments for an argumentative theory. *Behavioral and Brain Sciences*, 34(2):57–74.

Saif Mohammad, Svetlana Kiritchenko, Parinaz Sobhani, Xiaodan Zhu, and Colin Cherry. 2016. SemEval-2016 task 6: Detecting stance in tweets. In *Proceedings of SemEval-2016*, pages 31–41.

Nils Reimers and Iryna Gurevych. 2019. Sentence-BERT: Sentence embeddings using Siamese BERT-networks. In *Proceedings of EMNLP-IJCNLP*, pages 3982–3992.

Myrthe Reuver, Suzan Verberne, Roser Morante, and Antske Fokkens. 2021. Is stance detection topic-independent and cross-topic generalizable? - a reproduction study. In *Proceedings of the 8th Workshop on Argument Mining*, pages 46–56.

Sara Rosenthal and Kathy McKeown. 2015. I couldn't agree more: The role of conversational structure in agreement and disagreement detection in online discussions. In *Proceedings of SIGDIAL*, pages 168–177.

Oliver Scheuer, Frank Loll, Niels Pinkwart, and Bruce M McLaren. 2010. Computer-supported argumentation: A review of the state of the art. *International Journal of Computer-supported collaborative learning*, 5(1):43–102.

Baruch B Schwarz and Christa SC Asterhan. 2010. Argumentation and reasoning. *International Handbook of Psychology in Education*, pages 137–176.

Christian Stab, Tristan Miller, Benjamin Schiller, Pranav Rai, and Iryna Gurevych. 2018. Cross-topic argument mining from heterogeneous sources. In *Proceedings of EMNLP*, pages 3664–3674.

Matt Thomas, Bo Pang, and Lillian Lee. 2006. Get out the vote: Determining support or opposition from congressional floor-debate transcripts. In *Proceedings of EMNLP*, pages 327–335.

Yizhong Wang, Sujian Li, and Jingfeng Yang. 2018. Toward fast and accurate neural discourse segmentation. In *Proceedings of EMNLP*, pages 962–967.

Chang Xu, Cécile Paris, Surya Nepal, and Ross Sparks. 2018. Cross-target stance classification with self-attention networks. In *Proceedings of ACL (Volume 2: Short Papers)*, pages 778–783.

Chang Xu, Cecile Paris, Surya Nepal, and Ross Sparks. 2019. Recognising agreement and disagreement between stances with reason comparing networks. In *Proceedings of ACL*, pages 4665–4671.

Bowen Zhang, Min Yang, Xutao Li, Yunming Ye, Xiaofei Xu, and Kuai Dai. 2020. Enhancing cross-target stance detection with transferable semantic-emotion knowledge. In *Proceedings of ACL*, pages 3188–3197.

An Analysis of Acknowledgments in NLP Conference Proceedings

Winston Wu
Computer Science and Engineering
University of Michigan
wuws@umich.edu

Abstract

While acknowledgments are often overlooked and sometimes entirely missing from publications, this short section of a paper can provide insights on the state of a field. We characterize and perform a textual analysis of acknowledgments in NLP conference proceedings across the last 17 years, revealing broader trends in funding and research directions in NLP as well as interesting phenomena including career incentives and the influence of defaults.

1 Introduction

A research project is seldom a solo endeavor. Different entities contribute ideas, expertise, labor, money, and many other factors that lead to a successful project. In a publication, the most salient contributors are the authors, whose names are front and center on page one. In this paper, we investigate the so-called "lesser" contributors, whose names exist in the acknowledgments section of a publication, typically right before the references. Specifically, we ask several research questions:

- How common are acknowledgments?
- Who are acknowledged?
- What are they acknowledged for?
- What else can we learn from acknowledgments?

Our analysis of acknowledgments in ACL and EMNLP conference proceedings presents a view of the state of the field of natural language processing, including:

- trends in the use of acknowledgments
- broader funding trends based on international government investment
- research trends based on industry gifts
- trends in grant life-cycle and productivity
- culture-specific career incentives of being a corresponding author
- the influence of defaults on authors' word choice

2 Related Work

Acknowledgments have been investigated in both the social sciences and computer science communities. Scrivener (2009) analyze acknowledgments in history students' dissertations. Tang et al. (2017) performed a cursory analysis of funding acknowledgments in Thomson Reuter's Web of Science database. Giles and Councill (2004) analyzed computer science articles from the CiteSeer database[1], identifying the most common acknowledged entities. Part of our work is similar in design but focuses specifically on the field of NLP rather than the broader field of computer science. Paul-Hus and Desrochers (2019) performed a qualitative analysis of acknowledgments, looking at word usage patterns. Our study goes into more depth, looking at specific entities that are acknowledged, and what they are acknowledged for.

Grant funding is typically acknowledged in the acknowledgments section, and there is some recent interest in identifying funding sources and grant numbers as an information extraction task (Dai et al., 2019; Bian et al., 2021). Our paper does not tackle the task of grant funding detection but rather analyzes general trends in grant funding, as well as other trends. Within the NLP community, a line of work has extracted insights from trends and citations in NLP publications (Mohammad, 2020a,b,c,d), but has not focused specifically on acknowledgments.

3 Data

We analyze proceedings of two conferences: the Annual Meeting of the Association for Computational Linguistics (ACL), and the Conference on Empirical Methods in Natural Language Processing (EMNLP). ACL and EMNLP are top-tier international NLP conferences with a broad scope and thus would be representative of the

[1] http://citeseer.ist.psu.edu

Proceedings of the Fifth Workshop on Natural Language Processing and Computational Social Science (NLP+CSS), pages 157 - 163
November 7, 2022 ©2022 Association for Computational Linguistics

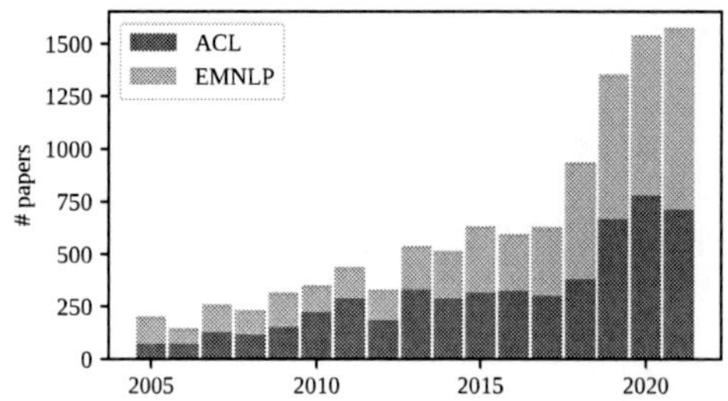

Figure 1: Number of papers in the ACL and EMNLP main conference proceedings from the past 16 years, highlighting the exponential growth of the field.

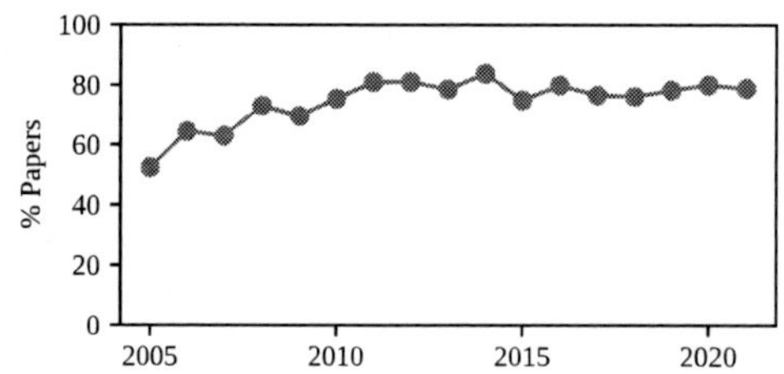

Figure 2: Percentage of papers containing an Acknowledgments section. The most recent years have stagnated around 79%.

broader NLP community. Specifically, we examine long and short papers published in the main conference proceedings from 2005–2021.[2] We download the proceeding PDFs from the ACL Anthology,[3] splitting the file into separate papers and extracting text using PyMuPDF.[4] We extract the acknowledgments section by searching for the word *Acknowledgments* and its spelling variants, followed by some manual cleaning efforts. We then perform dependency parsing and named entity recognition on all acknowledgments using spaCy's en_core_news_lg model.[5] Figure 1 presents the total number of ACL and EMNLP papers per year, from which we extract a total of 7,838 acknowledgments.

4 Characterizing Acknowledgments

This section, which forms the bulk of our paper, investigates several research questions that can be answered by analyzing papers' acknowledgments.

4.1 How common are acknowledgments?

In the nascent years of NLP, it was common to see papers published with a single author. For example, in the first iteration of EMNLP (1996), 7 of the 15 papers contained a single author, and 4 of the 15 papers contained acknowledgments (Melamed, 1996; Brants, 1996; Oflazer and Tur, 1996; Mooney, 1996). Nowadays, it is normal to see 4 or 5 author collaborations, and even more especially from large industry research groups. Thus is it interesting to see how often an acknowledgments section occurs at all.

Figure 2 presents the percentage of papers from each year containing an Acknowledgments section. Over time, the proportion of papers containing acknowledgments has slowly increased, though in recent years, the proportion has hovered around 79%. Acknowledgments are not mandatory, and it is difficult to investigate why authors do not include acknowledgments. Perhaps the publication was truly an isolated effort: the authors did not receive any funding, did not engage in any helpful conversations with others, and did not receive any useful feedback from the reviewers.

4.2 How long are acknowledgments?

Before diving into the contents of acknowledgments, we first investigate the surface-level question of how long are acknowledgments. The mean length of acknowledgments was 305.2 characters (roughly a fifth of a 2-column page), with a standard deviation of 172.6 characters. The shortest acknowledgment, in Singla et al. (2020), was 35 characters: "This work was supported by the NIH." The longest acknowledgment, in Nivre et al. (2007) was an impressive 2,408 characters; we will not reprint it here. A histogram of acknowledgment lengths is shown in Figure 3.

4.3 Who are acknowledged?

To identify acknowledged entities, we use spaCy to perform dependency parsing and named entity recognition on the acknowledgments. To account for variations in sentence structure and avoid overcounting, we (1) identify abbreviations for common government agencies, (2) ignore any names that are the subject of a "thanking" verb (*thank*, *acknowledge*, *appreciate*, *enjoy*), (3) ignore any names that are the subject of a passive "support-

[2]This excludes workshop papers, system demonstration papers, and student research papers. We exclude conference proceedings from 2004 and older because they have not been compiled into a single file in the ACL Anthology.

[3]`https://aclanthology.org/venues/acl` and `/emnlp`

[4]`https://github.com/pymupdf/PyMuPDF`

[5]`spacy.io`

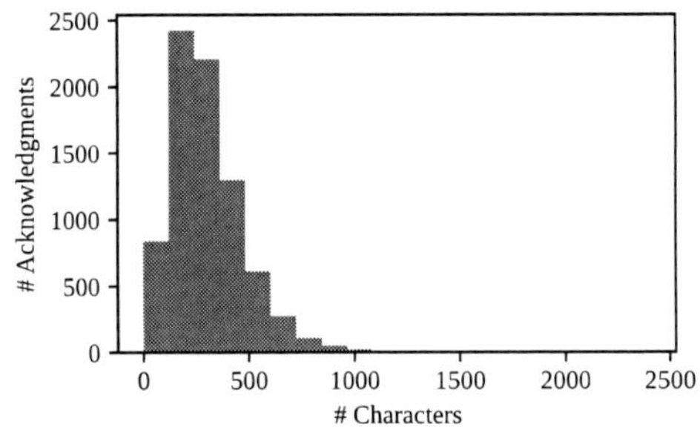

Figure 3: Histogram of the length of acknowledgments (in characters). The mean length of acknowledgments was 305 characters (std dev of 173 characters).

Agency	Govt	Count
NSFC	China	2,408
National Science Foundation	USA	1,653
DARPA	USA	920
NKP	China	762
European Research Council	EU	348
EPSRC	UK	221
Air Force Research Laboratory	USA	161
IARPA	USA	158
Army Research Office	USA	154
Office of Naval Research	USA	147

Table 1: Most frequently acknowledged government funding agencies.[6]

ing" verb (*supported, funded*), (4) ignore any sentences containing *corresponding author* or *contact author* (see Section 4.3). In addition, we look for the words *reviewer* and *reviewers*, who are often acknowledged, because the conference review process includes a rebuttal phase where anonymous reviewers provide initial feedback to the authors.

Government Agencies. Government agencies fund the bulk of NLP research, largely through grants (Table 1). In the top 10 list of funders, government agencies in China, the US, and Europe are well-represented. The National Natural Science Foundation of China is the most frequently acknowledged funder, although when combined, US agencies have funded more publications. Notably, many papers are funded by military agencies, which may raise ethical concerns for some people. For example, in a recent survey of NLP researchers, 36% of respondents agree that it is plausible that AI could produce catastrophic outcomes in this century, on the level of all-out nuclear war (Michael et al., 2022).

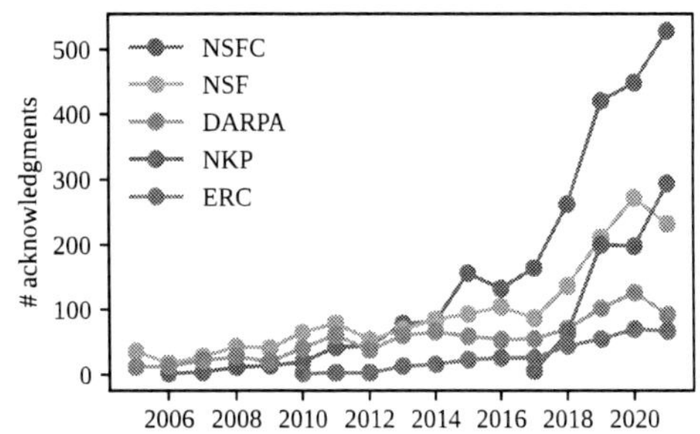

Figure 4: Top five government agency acknowledgments plotted over time. Within the last decade, there has been a drastic rise in Chinese government funding (NSFC and NKP).

Perhaps more interesting than aggregate counts is how the trends of funder acknowledgments have changed over the course of the past two decades (Figure 4). In the top five funders acknowledged, the last decade has seen a drastic rise in the number of Chinese government-funded publications, indicating heavy Chinese investment into NLP research. This also hints at a larger trend of global interest and participation in NLP research, which coincides with the recent (2020) creation of the Asian chapter of the ACL and the recent (2022) commitment of ACL to translate conference proceeding titles into numerous languages for greater worldwide multilingual access.

Aside: Tracking the Life-Cycle and Productivity of Grants. Acknowledgments also enable us to track a grant's life-cycle and productivity as measured by number of publications. Figure 5 shows the number of publications acknowledging several recent DARPA and ERC grants: DARPA CwC (2015), DARPA AIDA (2017-2021), DARPA MCS (2018-2023), and EU BroadSem (2016-2022). We see that it typically takes one year after the grant is announced before works funded under the grants are published. The number of publications across time also hints at the scope and success of the grants, with the number of papers decreasing as the grant comes to an end. While each funding source may keep track of such publication metrics resulting from their funds, we find that acknowledgments are another publicly available source of this information,

[6]NSFC = National Natural Science Foundation of China, DARPA = Defence Advanced Research Projects Agency, NKP = National Key Research and Development Program of China, EPSRC = Engineering and Physical Sciences Research Council, IARPA = Intelligence Advanced Research Projects Activity.

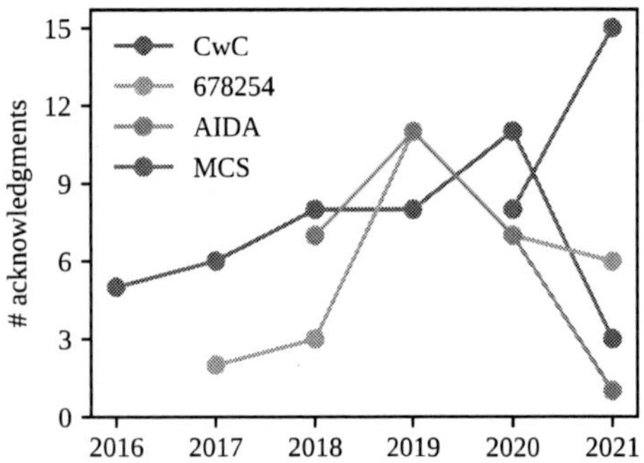

Figure 5: Grants that fund the most number of papers. The grants are DARPA CwC (Communicating with Computers), ERC Grant 678254 BroadSem (Induction of Broad-Coverage Semantic Parsers), DARPA AIDA (Active Interpretation of Disparate Alternatives), and DARPA MCS (Machine Common Sense).

which can be used to further study the impact of funding on publication rate and scientific productivity (e.g. Jacob and Lefgren, 2011).

Industry Funders Industry companies also fund a large portion of NLP research (Figure 6a). Most of these companies are acknowledged for providing including research awards, gifts, PhD fellowships. Notably, Nvidia[7] is acknowledged for grants and gifts of GPUs, which are vital resources for training neural networks. Perhaps not coincidentally, 2014, the first year Nvidia's gifts began to be acknowledged, was a year chock full of influential papers related to neural networks (e.g. Bahdanau et al., 2014; Kalchbrenner et al., 2014; Levy and Goldberg, 2014; Jia et al., 2014).

People. Figure 6b presents the most frequently acknowledged NLPers, who are all established researchers with thousands of citations. In addition, we find that the anonymous reviewers were thanked in over 51% of all acknowledgments. Peer review is important for upholding the quality of publications (Kelly et al., 2014), and it is heartening that many authors acknowledge and recognize reviewers' hard work.

Corresponding Authors. While performing this analysis, we identified a non-trivial number (185) of papers whose acknowledgments contained an indication of a paper's corresponding

[7]The NLP community does not have a consensus on the spelling of this company's name. In acknowledgments, it is alternately spelled Nvidia, NVidia, and NVIDIA.

Company	Count
Google	576
Nvidia	224
Microsoft	182
Amazon	161
Facebook	120
Bloomberg	77
Adobe	34
Salesforce	28
eBay	19
Apple	18

(a)

Person	Count
reviewers	4,065
Luke Zettlemoyer	46
Slav Petrov	36
Yoav Goldberg	29
Michael Collins	28
Tom Kwiatkowski	28
Ryan McDonald	27
Mark Yatskar	27
Kenton Lee	27
Chris Dyer	26

(b)

Figure 6: (a) Top 10 most frequently acknowledged industry companies. (b) Top 10 most helpful NLPers. The anonymous reviewers were thanked in over 51% of acknowledgments.

comment	2,861	provide	491
feedback	1,067	support	288
discussion	927	share	149
help	580	advice	119
suggestion	504	assistance	92

Table 2: The top 10 things (lemmatized) researchers are most thankful for.

author (e.g. *XX is the corresponding author of this paper*). While such sentences are common in journal articles (and are often on the first page of the paper), it is unusual to see this in NLP conference proceedings, and notably, these sentences only occur in papers published by Chinese institutions. There is a cultural explanation for the career incentive of being listed as a corresponding author: in China, promotions are heavily dependent on the number of published papers, but only papers where one is the first author or corresponding author counts toward this metric (Hvistendahl and Wang, 2014).

4.4 What are people acknowledged for?

The language in acknowledgments is highly regular, so to answer this question, we again utilize dependency parsing, identifying and lemmatizing the object of the preposition *for* in the text of the acknowledgments. The top 10 things researchers are most thankful for are listed in Table 2. The top two items, *comments* and *feedback*, are often provided by the reviewers (e.g. *We thank the reviewers for their helpful comments.*, while *discussion*, *help*, and *suggestions* are often *provided* by colleagues. *Sharing* of code, data, and results occur but is not nearly as prevalent, unfortunately.

4.5 How do you spell acknowledg... anyway?

This final question that we investigate has plagued countless authors: how is this word spelled?! We find four variants of the section title, shown in Figure 7. *Acknowledgements* is the traditional British spelling, while the American spelling omits the E. Our findings seems to indicate that most authors prefer the American spelling up until 2020, when suddenly the British spelling became more popular. However, this peculiarity has an explanation: it is likely due to a switch in the spelling of *Acknowledgments* in the paper templates[8,9] provided to the authors: the 2020 spelling (without the E) acquired an E in 2021.

Providing defaults. While the question of spelling may seem inconsequential, it raises a broader question of how the defaults provided to authors influence their choices. It is well-known that most people follow default choices (Thaler and Sunstein, 2009), and the trends in spelling usage of the word *Acknowledgments* reflect the defaults provided in the paper template. However, almost half of the acknowledgments section headers did *not* use the default spelling, indicating that these authors likely made a conscious choice: they probably deleted the section in the template and typed it back in when preparing the camera ready, rather than simply commenting out the section. Interestingly, a small minority of papers used the singular form *Acknowledgement/Acknowledgment*. To answer why, future work could investigate authors' writing process and workflow.

By providing default choices, institutions can influence individual's choices while not removing their freedom to choose. Recently, ACL conferences have been focusing heavily on ethics. The 2021 iteration of EMNLP required an additional section on ethical considerations in all submissions. Because this requirement was stipulated in the call for papers but was not included in the paper template, we found many variations of this section header in the proceedings, including *Ethical Considerations*, *Ethical Consideration*, *Broader Impact*, *Ethics and Broader Impact*, and *Ethics Statement*. However, the 2022 template includes *Limitations* and *Ethics Statement* sections, which we expect will be the predominant section titles in the 2022 proceedings. We also found

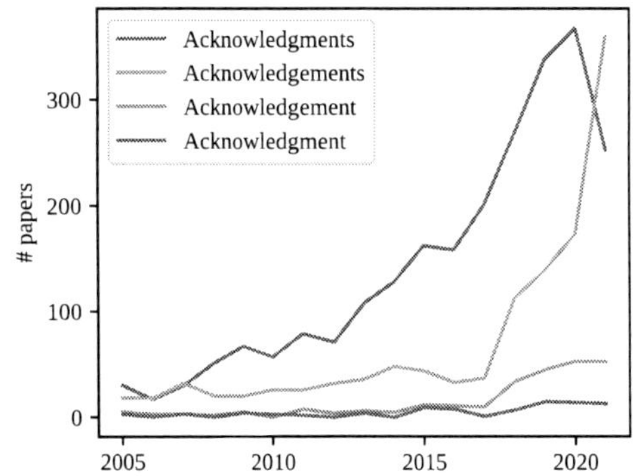

Figure 7: Spelling variation of the section header. The trend reversal between 2020 and 2021 is likely due to a switch in the spelling in the paper template provided to the authors.

that several papers include an addition section titled *Reproducibility* or *Code* with a link to the project's GitHub page, if the link was not already mentioned earlier in the paper. As a suggestion, if future *ACL conferences wish to emphasize other important issues such as reproducibility, they might consider adding an optional *Reproducibility* section to the paper template to nudge authors to consider this issue in their work.

5 Conclusion

While acknowledgments are seemingly insignificant and often entirely missing, in this paper we show that much can be gleaned from this short section in publications. Our analysis of acknowledgments in NLP conference proceedings reveal larger trends about the state of NLP research. Grant funding from government agencies and industry companies show increases in international participation and funding, especially from Chinese funding agencies. Grant acknowledgments also hint at the life-cycle and productivity of the grants. We identify the year 2014 as an important year of research using neural networks, corresponding with a dramatic increase in Chinese funding and industry GPU gifts. Textual analyses also reveal what researchers are most thankful for, and that some researchers indicate corresponding author, a career incentive specific to Chinese researchers. Finally, an analysis of spelling variation reveals the influence of defaults on the authors' choice of section headers. As the field of NLP continues to grow, followup analyses will help bring to light

[8] https://2020.emnlp.org/call-for-papers
[9] https://2021.emnlp.org/call-for-papers

more insights about the field and its behind-the-scenes contributors, without whom all these papers would not have been published.

Limitations

This paper investigates acknowledgments in proceedings of the ACL and EMNLP conferences, two of the largest, most prominent, international NLP conferences. This analysis unfortunately cannot account for the numerous projects that have been funded but rejected for publication. Our findings may also slightly differ for other types of publications (e.g. system demo papers, shared task papers), other venues with a geographical focus (e.g. AACL, EACL), or venues with a narrower research focus (e.g. workshops, or conferences such as LREC, CoNLL, WMT). These are all interesting avenues for investigation, and we leave these for future work.

Ethics Statement

All data used in this project is publicly and freely accessible. We do not see any ethical issues with this work.

Reproducibility

Code for acquiring the data and performing the analyses in this paper is available at `github.com/wswu/nlp-acks`.

Acknowledgments

It would be odd if a paper on acknowledgments did not include any acknowledgments. As usual, we would like to thank the anonymous reviewers for their helpful comments. We would also like to thank Frederick Zhang for helpful feedback on a draft of this paper, and Cicero Lu for early discussions that led to this work.

References

Dzmitry Bahdanau, Kyunghyun Cho, and Yoshua Bengio. 2014. Neural machine translation by jointly learning to align and translate. *arXiv preprint arXiv:1409.0473*.

Junyi Bian, Li Huang, Xiaodi Huang, Hong Zhou, and Shanfeng Zhu. 2021. Grantrel: Grant information extraction via joint entity and relation extraction. In *Findings of the Association for Computational Linguistics: ACL-IJCNLP 2021*, pages 2674–2685.

Thorsten Brants. 1996. Better language models with model merging. In *Conference on Empirical Methods in Natural Language Processing*.

Suyang Dai, Yuxia Ding, Zihan Zhang, Wenxuan Zuo, Xiaodi Huang, and Shanfeng Zhu. 2019. Grantextractor: Accurate grant support information extraction from biomedical fulltext based on bi-lstm-crf. *IEEE/ACM transactions on computational biology and bioinformatics*, 18(1):205–215.

C Lee Giles and Isaac G Councill. 2004. Who gets acknowledged: Measuring scientific contributions through automatic acknowledgment indexing. *Proceedings of the National Academy of Sciences*, 101(51):17599–17604.

M Hvistendahl and MY Wang. 2014. China's publication bazaar (november, pg 1035, 2013). *Science*, 343(6167):137–137.

Brian A Jacob and Lars Lefgren. 2011. The impact of research grant funding on scientific productivity. *Journal of public economics*, 95(9-10):1168–1177.

Yangqing Jia, Evan Shelhamer, Jeff Donahue, Sergey Karayev, Jonathan Long, Ross Girshick, Sergio Guadarrama, and Trevor Darrell. 2014. Caffe: Convolutional architecture for fast feature embedding. In *Proceedings of the 22nd ACM international conference on Multimedia*, pages 675–678.

Nal Kalchbrenner, Edward Grefenstette, and Phil Blunsom. 2014. A convolutional neural network for modelling sentences. In *Proceedings of the 52nd Annual Meeting of the Association for Computational Linguistics (Volume 1: Long Papers)*, pages 655–665, Baltimore, Maryland. Association for Computational Linguistics.

Jacalyn Kelly, Tara Sadeghieh, and Khosrow Adeli. 2014. Peer review in scientific publications: benefits, critiques, & a survival guide. *Ejifcc*, 25(3):227.

Omer Levy and Yoav Goldberg. 2014. Neural word embedding as implicit matrix factorization. *Advances in neural information processing systems*, 27.

I. Dan Melamed. 1996. A geometric approach to mapping bitext correspondence. In *Conference on Empirical Methods in Natural Language Processing*.

Julian Michael, Ari Holtzman, Alicia Parrish, Aaron Mueller, Alex Wang, Angelica Chen, Divyam Madaan, Nikita Nangia, Richard Yuanzhe Pang, Jason Phang, et al. 2022. What do nlp researchers believe? results of the nlp community metasurvey. *arXiv preprint arXiv:2208.12852*.

Saif M. Mohammad. 2020a. Examining citations of natural language processing literature. In *Proceedings of the 58th Annual Meeting of the Association for Computational Linguistics*, pages 5199–5209, Online. Association for Computational Linguistics.

Saif M. Mohammad. 2020b. Gender gap in natural language processing research: Disparities in authorship and citations. In *Proceedings of the 58th Annual Meeting of the Association for Computational Linguistics*, pages 7860–7870, Online. Association for Computational Linguistics.

Saif M. Mohammad. 2020c. NLP scholar: A dataset for examining the state of NLP research. In *Proceedings of the 12th Language Resources and Evaluation Conference*, pages 868–877, Marseille, France. European Language Resources Association.

Saif M. Mohammad. 2020d. NLP scholar: An interactive visual explorer for natural language processing literature. In *Proceedings of the 58th Annual Meeting of the Association for Computational Linguistics: System Demonstrations*, pages 232–255, Online. Association for Computational Linguistics.

Raymond J. Mooney. 1996. Comparative experiments on disambiguating word senses: An illustration of the role of bias in machine learning. In *Conference on Empirical Methods in Natural Language Processing*.

Joakim Nivre, Johan Hall, Sandra Kübler, Ryan McDonald, Jens Nilsson, Sebastian Riedel, and Deniz Yuret. 2007. The CoNLL 2007 shared task on dependency parsing. In *Proceedings of the 2007 Joint Conference on Empirical Methods in Natural Language Processing and Computational Natural Language Learning (EMNLP-CoNLL)*, pages 915–932, Prague, Czech Republic. Association for Computational Linguistics.

Kemal Oflazer and Gokhan Tur. 1996. Combining hand-crafted rules and unsupervised learning in constraint-based morphological disambiguation. In *Conference on Empirical Methods in Natural Language Processing*.

Adèle Paul-Hus and Nadine Desrochers. 2019. Acknowledgements are not just thank you notes: A qualitative analysis of acknowledgements content in scientific articles and reviews published in 2015. *Plos one*, 14(12):e0226727.

Laurie Scrivener. 2009. An exploratory analysis of history students dissertation acknowledgments. *The Journal of Academic Librarianship*, 35(3):241–251.

Karan Singla, Zhuohao Chen, David Atkins, and Shrikanth Narayanan. 2020. Towards end-2-end learning for predicting behavior codes from spoken utterances in psychotherapy conversations. In *Proceedings of the 58th Annual Meeting of the Association for Computational Linguistics*, pages 3797–3803, Online. Association for Computational Linguistics.

Li Tang, Guangyuan Hu, and Weishu Liu. 2017. Funding acknowledgment analysis: Queries and caveats. *Journal of the Association for Information Science and Technology*, 68(3):790–794.

Richard H Thaler and Cass R Sunstein. 2009. *Nudge: Improving decisions about health, wealth, and happiness*. Penguin.

Extracting Associations of Intersectional Identities with Discourse about Institution from Nigeria

Pavan Kantharaju and **Sonja Schmer-Galunder**
SIFT
319 N. 1st Avenue, Suite 400 Minneapolis, MN 55401-1689
{pkantharaju, sgalunder}@sift.net

Abstract

Word embedding models have been used in prior work to extract associations of intersectional identities within discourse concerning institutions of power, but restricted its focus on narratives of the nineteenth-century U.S. south. This paper leverages this prior work and introduces an initial study on the association of intersected identities with discourse concerning social institutions within social media from Nigeria. Specifically, we use word embedding models trained on tweets from Nigeria and extract associations of intersected social identities with institutions (e.g., domestic, culture, etc.) to provide insight into the alignment of identities with institutions. Our initial experiments indicate that identities at the intersection of gender and economic status groups have significant associations with discourse about the economic, political, and domestic institutions.

1 Introduction

Social scientists have leveraged quantitative methods to extract cultural knowledge from text, such as semantic networks (Hoffman et al., 2018), topic modeling (Mohr and Bogdanov, 2013), and language models (Friedman et al., 2021). Recent work by Nelson (2021) focused on using language models (specifically word embedding models) to extract intersectional identity associations inherent in narrative texts. Intersectionality (Crenshaw, 1989) is a theoretical framework for understanding how social identities such as gender and race, compound to create experiences that would otherwise be obscured by focusing on the identities separately.

Specifically, Nelson (2021) applied Word2Vec (Mikolov et al., 2013) to understand how intersected social identities associate with discourse about institutions of power (e.g. domestic, culture, etc.) from narratives of the nineteenth-century U.S. south. While this method was successfully able to extract intersectional associations from U.S. narratives, it remains an open question whether this method generalizes to other forms of text from outside the U.S., such as social media data from Nigeria. Social media data outside the U.S. presents an interesting challenge as social media may not be accessible or used by everyone outside the U.S. This means that these types of datasets can inherently contain an imbalance in population representation, making analyses with them need careful attention.

This paper presents an initial study on using word embedding models to understand how intersected identities associate with discourse concerning institutions found within social media text from Nigeria. Our main contributions are (1) the application of prior work by Nelson (2021) to tweets from Nigeria, and (2) an analysis of intersected gender and economic identities and their associations to the domestic, economic, political, and cultural spheres. We leverage Skip Gram with Negative Sampling (SGNS) (Mikolov et al., 2013) models and look at the relationship of intersected gender and economic identities within discourse concerning the political, cultural, domestic, and economic spheres within tweets. Our results indicate that a *female, poor* category of individuals is more associated with discourse from Lagos and Federal Capital Territories (FCT) concerning the domestic sphere while a *male, poor* category is associated with economic and political spheres.

This paper is structured as follows. Section 2 provides prior work on intersectionality and the extraction of cultural associations from language models. Section 3 describes the Twitter dataset used to train SGNS models used in our analysis. Section 4 describes the method used by Nelson (2021), which is leveraged for our analysis in Section 5. Section 6 provides a discussion about our analysis and Section 7 provides our conclusion.

2 Related Work

Our analysis is situated at the crossroads of intersectionality and extraction of cultural associations

Proceedings of the Fifth Workshop on Natural Language Processing and Computational Social Science (NLP+CSS), pages 164 - 169
November 7, 2022 ©2022 Association for Computational Linguistics

from word embedding models. The concept of intersectionality can be traced to Crenshaw (1989), who argued and showed that the experiences of inequality of black women were obscured by the experiences of inequality of women and black people. Both quantitative and qualitative methods have been used to analyze intersectionality. Bright et al. (2016) argues that graphical causal models can be used to represent claims about the causal effects of occupying intersected social identities. A survey of quantitative research that uses the intersectionality framework is provided by Bauer et al. (2021). There has also been qualitative work by Sekoni et al. (2022), who analyzed the intersection of LGBT+ and other social identities in the context of the healthcare in Nigeria, discovering that sub-identities within LGBT+ suffer from bias more than their peer sub-identities, particularly when intersected with mental and sexual health conditions.

Language models have been shown to be effective at extracting cultural associations (Garg et al., 2018; Kozlowski et al., 2019; Nelson, 2021) and bias (Caliskan et al., 2017; May et al., 2019; Zhao et al., 2019; Tan and Celis, 2019; Guo and Caliskan, 2021) from text; our work focuses on extracting cultural associations from text. Garg et al. (2018) studied how word embedding models could be used to understand trends in gender and ethnic stereotypes in the U.S. over time. Kozlowski et al. (2019) studied how word embedding models could be used to construct cultural vectors, and applied this to understand social class in the U.S. The work closest to ours was done by Nelson (2021), who studied how intersectional identities associated with U.S. narratives about institutions of power. Our work differs from Garg et al. (2018), Kozlowski et al. (2019), and Nelson (2021) in that we apply our analysis to texts outside the U.S. (namely Nigeria).

3 Social Media Dataset

Table 1: Twitter Dataset Metrics/Measures

Metric/Measure	Value
Number of Tweets in Dataset	30,883,364
Vocabulary Size	2,000,381
Tweet Length (min)	2
Tweet Length (mean)	19.6
Tweet Length (median)	15.0

The present work leverages language models trained on an international social media dataset used in prior work (Friedman et al., 2019) for the DARPA Understanding Group Bias (UGB) project and approved for use by an independent IRB. Among other countries, the original UGB-gathered dataset includes approximately 30 million tweets from various states in Nigeria from 2018, gathered by a university teammate. This data is not used directly in this work, but the derived word embedding models are. To create the word embedding models for UGB, tweets were tokenized for whitespace and lower-cased. No stemming or lemmatization was performed, thereby preserving the original vocabulary for our analysis (preservation was necessary as the vocabulary affects the seed words used in the analysis).

Table 1 describes the original dataset from which our language models were derived. *Tweet length* measures the words in the tweet after tokenization (Twitter imposes its own character limit). Approximately 0.2% of the tweets in the dataset have a length of 100 or words and 35.2% are greater than or equal to the mean tweet length, so the majority of tweets are relatively short. We note that this dataset has an uneven distribution of tweets per state in Nigeria. More specifically, approximately 60% of tweets come from Lagos, with the Federal Capital Territory (FCT) being a far second (approximately 20%). As such, our analysis will be biased towards views from Lagos and FCT.

4 Extracting Intersectional Associations from Word Embedding Models

The main goal of our analysis is to extract intersectional associations within discourse about social institutions found in tweets from Nigeria. To this end, we leverage recent work by Nelson (2021) which used a Word2Vec model to understand how intersected social identities (black and white men and women) mapped within four social institutions (domestic, economic, polity, and culture) in a corpus of first-person narratives from the U.S. south. The method used by Nelson (2021) required constructing geometric vectors and spaces for the institutions and identities using trained Word2Vec models. This section describes their construction.

4.1 Intersectional Social Identity Vectors

Intersectional identity vectors provide meaning to each intersected social identity in vector space. Our analysis focuses on two social identity groups: *gender* and *economic status*. As such, we will use them in a running example showing how the intersected identity vectors are constructed.

Table 2: Social Identities and Corresponding Seed Words

Identity Category	Social Identity	Seed Words
Gender	Male	men, man, boy, boys, he, him, his, himself
	Female	women, woman, girl, girls, she, her, hers, herself
Economic Status	Rich	rich, richer, richest, affluence, affluent, expensive, luxury, opulent
	Poor	poor, poorer, poorest, poverty, impoverished, inexpensive, cheap, needy

First, the social identity groups *gender* and *economic status* are split into two identities: gender into *male* and *female* and economic status into *rich* (high) and *poor* (low). Each identity is associated with a set of seed words. Table 3 contains the social identities and seed words used in our analysis. Seed words add context about a particular concept to provide a geometric description of the concept. For example, if we wanted to describe the concept of *man*, we would construct a set of seed words corresponding to *men*, *males*, and *boys*. The addition of other seed words would further contextualize the concept and possibly change the description of the concept (i.e., adding seed words associated with *human* would change the description of *man*).

The gender seed words come from Nelson (2021) while the economic status words come from Kozlowski et al. (2019) and Antoniak and Mimno (2021). We focused on these seed words as they were successfully used in prior work on extracting associations from word embedding models; we plan to create our own seed words in future work.

Next, the cross product of the identities and their corresponding seed words is computed, giving us four intersected social identities (in our running example, we get *male rich*, *male poor*, *female rich*, and *female poor*) and a set of word pairs W_{id} (e.g., *(men, rich)*, *(woman, rich)*, etc.) for each intersected identity *id*. The set of word pairs effectively represent a joint space that provide meaning to an intersected identity. To construct an intersected identity vector $\vec{v_{id}}$, the word embeddings in each pair are summed to construct an embedding representing the pair (summing the embeddings for *men* and *rich* provides an embedding for *men rich*), and the pairs are subsequently averaged:

$$\vec{v_{id}} = \frac{1}{|W_{id}|} \sum_{(w_1,w_2)\in W_{id}} \vec{w_1} + \vec{w_2}$$

where $\vec{w_1}$ and $\vec{w_2}$ are word embeddings for words w_1 and w_2. This results in a set of four intersected identity vectors that capture the meaning of the identity in vector space.

4.2 Social Institution Vectors

Table 3: Social Institutions and Corresponding Seed Words (Words in bold are those used by Nelson, 2021)

Social Institutions	Seed Words
Polity	**nation**, government
Economy	**money**, finance
Culture	**culture**, tradition
Domestic	**housework**, **children**

Social institution vectors provide meaning to each social institution in vector space. Each institution vector $\vec{v_{inst}}$ is constructed by defining a set of seed words W_{inst} for each institution *inst*, and averaging the word embeddings of the seed words. Table 3 contains the social institutions and seed words used in our analysis. We use the same set of institutions as those used by Nelson (2021), but we extend their seed words set such that each institution has an equal number of words. These new seed words were curated by the researchers of this paper by looking for related words to the institutions. We focus on these institutions as we wanted to keep as close as possible to the original analysis; we will look at other institutions in future work.

4.3 Social Institution Discourse Spaces

Table 4: Top 10 Words in each Social Institution Discourse Space

Polity	Domestic	Economy	Culture
govt	kids	finance-	traditions
country	baby-sit	vaid	cultural
gov't	house-helps	funds	cultures
goverment	homeworks	recapitalised	religion
governement	childcare	fgns	patriachal
counrty	pre-k	harmonising	unafrican
governments	great-grandchildren	remiting	norms
governnent	under-privileged	countingup	bidia
administration	godchildren	alison-madukwe	supremacism
reponsibility	#mychildmypride	slac	heritages

A discourse space for each social institution is constructed to compute an association score with discourse surrounding the institutions. This space provides a discourse-centric meaning to the social institution compared to the institution vectors from Section 4.2, which provide a concept-centric meaning. More specifically, this discourse space is constructed by finding K words closest to each institution vector (in our work, $K = 50$ and closest is

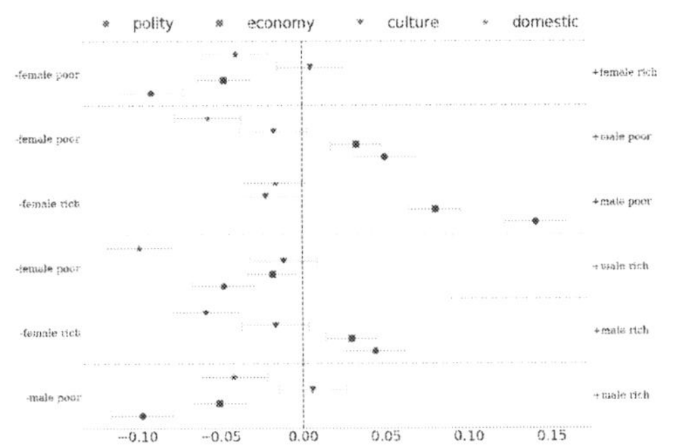

Figure 1: Gender vs Economic Status - 95% Confidence Interval ($n = 40$)

defined by cosine similarity). Table 4 provides the top 10 words in the discourse space for each social institution. Here, we see some challenges with using social media data: words may not always be grammatically correct (e.g., "governement" under *polity* column) and we may have non-word terms such as hashtags (e.g., "#mychildmypride" under *domestic* column). Given a discourse space for an institution, an association score can be computed for any intersected identity by taking the average cosine similarity between the identity vector and the words in the discourse space.

5 Analysis

Figure 1 provides the results of our analysis for the gender and economic status identity groups.[1] For each social institution, we compute a 95% confidence interval for the difference between the association scores (described in Section 4.3) for pairs of intersected identities (e.g., the first row of Figure 1 compares the difference between association scores for *female, poor* and *female, rich* for each social institution). We note that any confidence intervals that contain a difference of 0 (middle black dotted line in Figure 1) is not statistically significant.

Similar to Kozlowski et al. (2019) and Nelson (2021), we use the percentile bootstrap method to construct the confidence intervals, where the number of samples used is 40 (interval spans the 2nd and 39th association score differences). We used 40 pretrained SGNS models that were each trained on datasets generated by sampling the original Twitter dataset of the same size with replacement (any words whose frequency is less than five were removed). We then compute differences between association scores using the process in Section 4 for each SGNS model. The pretrained models have an embedding size of 200, context window of five, and were trained using five negative samples.

Within a particular gender identity, the poor are significantly more associated with the discourse about the political, economic, and domestic sphere than the rich ($p < 0.05$). This can be seen in the first and last rows of Figure 1. Within a particular economic identity, females are significantly more associated with discourse about the domestic sphere than males. On the other hands, males are more significantly associated with discourse concerning the economic and political sphere than females. This can be seen in the second and fifth rows of Figure 1. According to our results, discourse concerning the domestic sphere has an intersectional association towards female, poor individuals. This can be seen by the fact that female, poor individuals are always significantly associated with domestic sphere discourse compared to the other intersected identities (see the first, second, and fourth rows of Figure 1). Similarly, discourse about the economic and political spheres has an intersectional association towards male, poor individuals (second, third, and sixth rows of Figure 1).

Recall from Section 3 that the majority of tweets are from Lagos and FCT. As such, a majority of the discourse in the dataset is biased towards those two states in Nigeria. This means that the associations detected for the intersected identities are not representative of individuals in all of Nigeria, but rather those that live in Lagos and FCT.

6 Discussion

Our analysis provides insight into what social institutions are of discursive interest to intersected social identities in Nigeria with a bias towards individuals from Lagos and FCT. In particular, our results show who is more vocal about a particular institution, and which individuals are less vocal about a given institution, but it does not explicitly mention whose voice is the most marginalized. This analysis is a good starting point for detecting bias in discourse about an institution, but work is needed to extract the most marginalized voices.

Similar to Nelson (2021), we find that machine learning can enhance qualitative research methods, allowing us to juxtapose quantitative outcomes with qualitative examples. For example, "I came

[1]Graph generated based on code from Nelson (2021): https://github.com/lknelson/measuring_intersectionality

across a poor women who had recently delivered five children. She needed money for food and medical bills. Such a sad example of poverty in Nigeria" is reflective of the lived experience of intersectionality while our results provide evidence for how intersected identities are linked to particular institutions at a larger scale.

The results of our analysis also aligns with several recent qualitative works that look at discrimination and bias in Nigeria. Dosekun (2022) showed that females are heavily associated with the domestic sphere (i.e., having children and domestic skills). Additionally, Enfield (2019) mentioned that females are represented in the labor markets, but they are penalized through low wages and activity. Enfield (2019) also described that females (especially poor females) join the labor market late due to the cultural pressure of early marriage and having children. This implies that males have more freedom in the labor market than females, aligning with our results that males are more associated with the economic spheres than females.

7 Conclusion

This paper presents an initial study which uses SGNS models trained on Twitter data from Nigeria to determine how intersectional identities are associated with discourse on social institutions. Our results show that female, poor individuals are more associated with discourse from Lagos and FCT concerning the domestic sphere while male, poor individuals are associated with discourse about the economic and political spheres.

There are several avenues for future work. First, the efficiency of the analysis could be improved, particularly to handle large corpora. Second, the sensitivity of associations to model hyperparameters could be assessed to ensure the associations hold under different hyperparameter choices. Finally, the analysis could be made sensitive to dataset statistics such as geographic distribution.

Limitations

The analysis done in this paper has several limitations that would benefit future investigation. The first limitation is that the analysis assumes that all individuals in the population are represented equally in a dataset. As we stated, a majority of the tweets in the Twitter dataset come from Lagos and FCT, both of which may have the benefit of technological access and literacy. Unfortunately, this skews our analysis such that the associations extracted from the word embedding models is really representative of Lagos and FCT instead of Nigeria. The second limitations concerns the efficiency and computational resources required to run this analysis. Our analysis required using a number of SGNS models trained on nearly 30 million tweets. While training is done only once, it requires training on server-sized systems over several days.

Ethical Impacts Statement

This study was conducted as basic research using publicly available Twitter data that has been collected and approved for use by an independent IRB and a HRPO agency. The intent of this study was to replicate the approach by Nelson (2021) using social media data, showing that it is possible to quantify how intersectional identities are embedded in structural social inequalities. Such bias quantifications - while highlighting social inequalities - can serve to counter or strengthen social inequalities if applied in questionable contexts (e.g., marketing/targeting, rating systems, algorithmic decision making). However, our intention with this study is to highlight and quantify social inequalities as a way to provide evidence of its existence in society.

The research team consists of women and men with diverse ethnic backgrounds, trained in Western educational institutions. A limitation of our interpretation of these results is that we did not have individuals native to Nigeria be part of the research team. We used an intersectional theoretical framework to reduce bias, and believe that using inductive methods (e.g., grounded theory, machine-learning) to this research reduces biases that may be introduced by a researcher. Still, we acknowledge that social media data is in no way representative of a diverse population as the one in Nigeria with large parts of the population not having access to technology. Finally, the impact of an intersectionality analysis helps center marginalized voices.

Acknowledgements

The research was supported by funding from the Defense Advanced Research Projects Agency (DARPA UGB HR00111890015, DARPA HABITUS W911NF-21-C-0007-04). The views, opinions and/or findings expressed are those of the authors and should not be interpreted as representing the official views or policies of the Department of Defense or the U.S. Government.

References

Maria Antoniak and David Mimno. 2021. Bad seeds: Evaluating lexical methods for bias measurement. In *Proceedings of the 59th Annual Meeting of the Association for Computational Linguistics and the 11th International Joint Conference on Natural Language Processing (Volume 1: Long Papers)*, pages 1889–1904, Online. Association for Computational Linguistics.

Greta R. Bauer, Siobhan M. Churchill, Mayuri Mahendran, Chantel Walwyn, Daniel Lizotte, and Alma Angelica Villa-Rueda. 2021. Intersectionality in quantitative research: A systematic review of its emergence and applications of theory and methods. *SSM - Population Health*, 14:100798.

Liam Kofi Bright, Daniel Malinsky, and Morgan Thompson. 2016. Causally interpreting intersectionality theory. *Philosophy of Science*, 83(1):60–81.

Aylin Caliskan, Joanna J. Bryson, and Arvind Narayanan. 2017. Semantics derived automatically from language corpora contain human-like biases. *Science*, 356(6334):183–186.

Kimberle Crenshaw. 1989. Demarginalizing the intersection of race and sex: A black feminist critique of antidiscrimination doctrine, feminist theory and antiracist politics. *University of Chicago Legal Forum*, 1989.

Simidele Dosekun. 2022. The problems and intersectional politics of "#beingfemaleinnigeria". *Feminist Media Studies*, 0(0):1–17.

Sue Enfield. 2019. Gender roles and inequalities in the nigerian labour market. *Institute of Development Studies*.

Roni Friedman, Lena Dankin, Yufang Hou, Ranit Aharonov, Yoav Katz, and Noam Slonim. 2021. Overview of the 2021 key point analysis shared task. In *Proceedings of the 8th Workshop on Argument Mining*, pages 154–164, Punta Cana, Dominican Republic. Association for Computational Linguistics.

Scott Friedman, Sonja Schmer-Galunder, Anthony Chen, and Jeffrey Rye. 2019. Relating word embedding gender biases to gender gaps: A cross-cultural analysis. In *Proceedings of the First Workshop on Gender Bias in Natural Language Processing*, pages 18–24, Florence, Italy. Association for Computational Linguistics.

Nikhil Garg, Londa Schiebinger, Dan Jurafsky, and James Zou. 2018. Word embeddings quantify 100 years of gender and ethnic stereotypes. *Proceedings of the National Academy of Sciences*, 115(16):E3635–E3644.

Wei Guo and Aylin Caliskan. 2021. Detecting emergent intersectional biases: Contextualized word embeddings contain a distribution of human-like biases. In *Proceedings of the 2021 AAAI/ACM Conference on AI, Ethics, and Society*, AIES '21, page 122–133, New York, NY, USA. Association for Computing Machinery.

Mark Anthony Hoffman, Jean-Philippe Cointet, Philipp Brandt, Newton Key, and Peter Bearman. 2018. The (protestant) bible, the (printed) sermon, and the word(s): The semantic structure of the conformist and dissenting bible, 1660–1780. *Poetics*, 68:89–103.

Austin C Kozlowski, Matt Taddy, and James A Evans. 2019. The geometry of culture: Analyzing the meanings of class through word embeddings. *American Sociological Review*, 84(5):905–949.

Chandler May, Alex Wang, Shikha Bordia, Samuel R. Bowman, and Rachel Rudinger. 2019. On measuring social biases in sentence encoders. In *Proceedings of the 2019 Conference of the North American Chapter of the Association for Computational Linguistics: Human Language Technologies, Volume 1 (Long and Short Papers)*, pages 622–628, Minneapolis, Minnesota. Association for Computational Linguistics.

Tomas Mikolov, Ilya Sutskever, Kai Chen, Greg S Corrado, and Jeff Dean. 2013. Distributed representations of words and phrases and their compositionality. In *Advances in Neural Information Processing Systems*, pages 3111–3119.

John W. Mohr and Petko Bogdanov. 2013. Introduction—topic models: What they are and why they matter. *Poetics*, 41(6):545–569. Topic Models and the Cultural Sciences.

Laura K Nelson. 2021. Leveraging the alignment between machine learning and intersectionality: Using word embeddings to measure intersectional experiences of the nineteenth century u.s. south. *Poetics*, 88:101539.

Adekemi Oluwayemisi Sekoni, Kate Jolly, and Nicola Kay Gale. 2022. Hidden healthcare populations: using intersectionality to theorise the experiences of lgbt+ people in nigeria, africa. *Global Public Health*, 17(1):134–149. PMID: 33287671.

Yi Chern Tan and L. Elisa Celis. 2019. Assessing social and intersectional biases in contextualized word representations. In *Advances in Neural Information Processing Systems*.

Jieyu Zhao, Tianlu Wang, Mark Yatskar, Ryan Cotterell, Vicente Ordonez, and Kai-Wei Chang. 2019. Gender bias in contextualized word embeddings. In *Proceedings of the 2019 Conference of the North American Chapter of the Association for Computational Linguistics: Human Language Technologies, Volume 1 (Long and Short Papers)*, pages 629–634, Minneapolis, Minnesota. Association for Computational Linguistics.

OLALA: Object-Level Active Learning for Efficient Document Layout Annotation

Zejiang Shen[†*] Weining Li[◇] Jian Zhao[◇] Yaoliang Yu[◇] Melissa Dell[♣]
[†]MIT [◇]University of Waterloo [♣]Harvard University
zjshen@mit.edu melissadell@fas.harvard.edu
{w422li, jianzhao, yaoliang.yu}@waterloo.ca

Abstract

Layout detection is an essential step for accurately extracting structured contents from historical documents. The intricate and varied layouts present in these document images make it expensive to label the numerous layout regions that can be densely arranged on each page. Current active learning methods typically rank and label samples at the *image level*, where the annotation budget is not optimally spent due to the overexposure of common *objects* per image. Inspired by recent progress in semi-supervised learning and self-training, we propose OLALA, an **O**bject-**L**evel **A**ctive **L**earning framework for efficient document layout **A**nnotation. OLALA aims to optimize the annotation process by selectively annotating only the most ambiguous regions within an image, while using automatically generated labels for the rest. Central to OLALA is a perturbation-based scoring function that determines which objects require manual annotation. Extensive experiments show that OLALA can significantly boost model performance and improve annotation efficiency, facilitating the extraction of masses of structured text for downstream NLP applications.[1]

1 Introduction

When working with historical documents, social scientists have often used keyword methods that do not require the recognition of structured layouts (see *e.g.* Hanlon and Beach (2022) for a review of the literature on historical newspapers). To apply neural NLP methods to these documents, it is essential to accurately detect the layouts and extract the structured content. For example, a historical newspaper scan contains a mixture of article regions, headlines, captions, advertisements, etc. Commercial OCR software will typically read the multi-

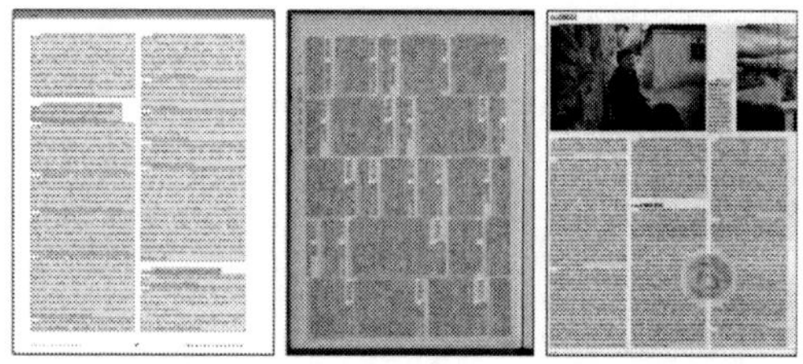

(a) PubLayNet (b) HJDataset (c) PRImA

Figure 1: Three exemplar document layouts from PubLayNet (Zhong et al., 2019), HJDataset (Shen et al., 2020), and PRImA (Antonacopoulos et al., 2009). There are numerous layout objects per page, and many of them are very similar. Directly labeling them all will result in wasted labeling budget.

column document as if it is a single column book, unable to distinguish content in different regions and producing scrambled text that leads to poor performance for downstream NLP applications.

Deep learning-based approaches can be used for document layout analysis and content parsing (Shen et al., 2021; Zhong et al., 2019; Schreiber et al., 2017). Figure 1 illustrates that document layout object detection, like image object detection, requires identifying content regions and categories within images. A key distinction, however, is that it is common for dozens to hundreds of content regions to appear on a single page in documents, as opposed to only several objects per image in natural image datasets (*e.g.* 5 on average in the MS-COCO Dataset (Lin et al., 2014)). Additionally, the region category distribution is often heavily imbalanced and requires more pages to be annotated to allow for reasonable exposure of uncommon categories (*e.g.* footnotes, watermarks, or mastheads). Hence, the manual labeling process used on natural images to create high-quality labeled datasets can be prohibitively costly to replicate for documents of central interest to social scientists, who typically have heavily constrained annotation budgets. As a result, extracting structured text is often infeasible,

* Work done when working as a Data Science Fellow at Harvard University.

[1]Our source code is available at https://github.com/lolipopshock/detectron2_al.

Proceedings of the Fifth Workshop on Natural Language Processing and Computational Social Science (NLP+CSS), pages 170 - 182
November 7, 2022 ©2022 Association for Computational Linguistics

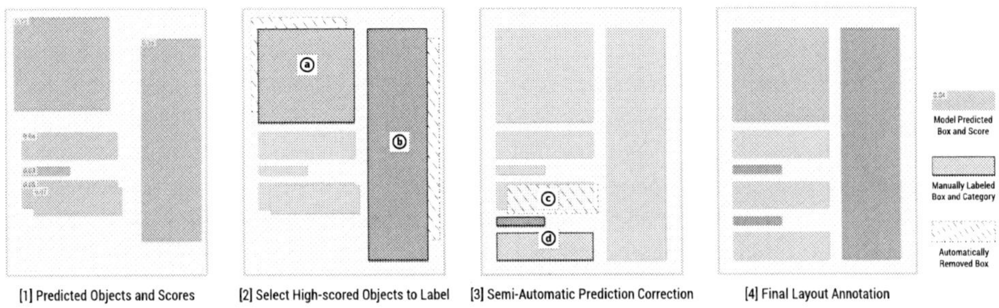

Figure 2: Illustration of the OLALA framework. [1] During labeling, for an input image, a trained model predicts the layout with various errors. An object scoring function f evaluates the informativeness for each object prediction. [2] OLALA selects the regions of top scores and sends them for manual labeling to correct the wrong object category (a) and bounding box (b). [3] A semi-automatic prediction correction algorithm is applied to rectify duplicated objects (c) and recover false-negatives (d) with minimal extra supervision. [4] After this process, the final annotation is obtained from labeling only a portion of the objects.

limiting the application of modern NLP techniques in historical document applications.

Active Learning (AL) has been widely adopted in image object detection for optimizing labeling efficiency via prioritizing the most important samples to annotate (Aghdam et al., 2019; Haussmann et al., 2020; Brust et al., 2018; Roy et al., 2018). However, while the end goal is to annotate individual objects within an image, these AL methods typically score and select samples at the image level, rather than at the object level. Yao et al. (2012) study an annotator-centered labeling cost estimation method and prioritize labeling for high-cost images. In the context of deep learning, image level scores are generated via aggregation of marginal scores for candidate boxes (Brust et al., 2018) or applying query by committee (Seung et al., 1992) to features maps (Roy et al., 2018). Aghdam et al. (2019) propose a pixel level scoring method using convolutional backbones and aggregate them to informativeness scores for image ranking. For category-imbalanced layouts, common in documents, such image level selection can suffer from the over-exposure of common objects.

Recent advances in Semi-Supervised Learning (SSL) and self-training can boost model performance using unlabeled data (Rosenberg et al., 2005; Xie et al., 2020). The Self-supervised Sample Mining (SSM) algorithm (Wang et al., 2018) proposes to stitch high-confidence patches from unlabeled data to labeled data to improve both labeling efficiency and model performance. It enables object-level prediction selection but requires objects to be sparsely distributed, making it inapplicable to our case where content is densely arranged.

To address these challenges, we propose a novel AL framework, OLALA, **O**bject-**L**evel **A**ctive **L**earning for efficient layout **A**nnotation. Shown in Figure 2, critical *objects*, rather than *images*, are individually evaluated and selected for labeling. During the labeling process, OLALA trains a model to generate object predictions. Within an image, only the most ambiguous predictions are chosen for human inspection and annotation, addressing the inefficient use of annotation budget on common objects or categories. Central to this process is a semi-automatic prediction correction algorithm. Inspired by previous endeavors of automated layout dataset generation (Zhong et al., 2019; Li et al., 2019; Shen et al., 2020), OLALA incorporates prior knowledge about layout structures to ensure the high quality of the created dataset. It can identify false-positives and false-negatives in the unselected model predictions, and correct them with minimal extra supervision.

Additionally, we design a novel object-level scoring function governing the region selection process. The perturbation-based scoring method evaluates consistency of both object position and category predictions between the original and perturbed inputs. Compared to prior work, it is carefully designed for layout datasets with unique arrangement of content regions, and can identify errors of critical importance to layout analysis tasks.

In other contexts where predictions on unlabeled images (Wang et al., 2018; Xie et al., 2020) or weak labels (Desai et al., 2019) are used to boost model performance, the predicted labels are discarded after model training. OLALA includes a rigorous process to validate the accuracy of predictions, meaning that the full labeled dataset - created by human and machine - can be released publicly and potentially used by social scientists for transfer learning on other applications.

Through extensive experiments, we study how the proposed approach can improve labeling efficiency in two different scenarios. We show that OLALA can create datasets with better trained model performance compared to image-level AL baselines, for a given limited annotation budget. On the other side, as only part of an image requires annotation in our method, we demonstrate that our method can create datasets of the same size with far less human effort.

To the best of our knowledge, this is the first AL method dedicated to document layout analysis. OLALA was motivated by our need to automate the extraction of structured text from millions of historical documents, to enable modern NLP analyses on information trapped in hard copy. We are using it extensively on real world documents for this purpose, with the OLALA labeling interface described in the supplementary material.

Section 2 introduces the OLALA framework, and Section 3 describes the perturbation based object scoring method. Sections 4 and 5 demonstrate how OLALA can improve labeling efficiency and model performance under different scenarios.

2 The OLALA Framework

2.1 Object-Level Active Learning Setup

In layout object detection problems, a detection model Θ is trained to identify n_i objects within an input image X_i, where the bounding box b_j and category distribution c_j is estimated for the j-th object. $Y_i = \{(b_j, c_j)\}_{j=1}^{n_i}$ are the object annotations for X_i. Θ is initially trained on a small labeled dataset $\mathcal{L}_0 = \{(X_i, Y_i)\}_{i=1}^{l}$, and it receives a large unlabeled dataset $\mathcal{U}_0 = \{X_i\}_{i=1+l}^{u+l}$.

The goal of typical image-level AL methods (Aghdam et al., 2019; Brust et al., 2018; Roy et al., 2018) is to optimally sample images from $\mathcal{U}$ for annotation to maximally improve the model's performance on given metrics. This process could be iterative: at each round t, it selects m samples $\mathcal{M}_t = \{X_i\}_{i=1}^{m}$ from $\mathcal{U}_{t-1}$ to query labels, obtains the corresponding labeled set $\bar{\mathcal{M}}_t = \{(X_i, Y_i)\}_{i=1}^{m}$, and updates the existing labeled set $\mathcal{L}_t = \mathcal{L}_{t-1} \cup \bar{\mathcal{M}}_t$. The new model Θ_t is obtained by training (or fine-tuning) on $\mathcal{L}_t$. For the next round, the unlabeled set becomes $\mathcal{U}_t = \mathcal{U}_{t-1} \setminus \mathcal{M}_t$.

In this process, annotators need to create all object labels $\bar{Y}_i = Y_i$ for the images in $\mathcal{M}_t$. This is not optimal for layout object detection, where many objects could appear on a single image. Because of the uneven distribution of objects, sometimes only a small portion of object predictions in an image are inaccurate. Labeling whole images wastes budget, which could be otherwise used for labeling less common and accurate objects.

Consider an alternative setup illustrated in Figure 2: the AL agent prioritizes annotation for a portion of objects in Y_i within each image. An *object*-level scoring function f evaluates the ambiguities of predictions generated by Θ. Object regions of top scores, the *selected objects*, will be sent for manual annotation to create labels $\bar{Y}_i$. To wisely use human efforts, the ratio of selected objects r is dynamically adjusted during the labeling process (Section 2.2). And after correcting possible errors (Section 2.3), the remaining *unselected objects* constitute the complement labels $\hat{Y}_i$ and are merged with the human labels. The *Objects Selection Scheduling* and *Semi-automatic Prediction Correction* ensure the combined annotation $\tilde{Y}_i = \bar{Y}_i \cup \hat{Y}_i$ is close to Y_i. Therefore, accurate dataset annotations can be created with only $|\bar{Y}_i|/|\tilde{Y}_i|$ of time ($|\cdot|$ being the cardinality of the set), and more images can be annotated given the same labeling budget. This is our object-centered labeling setup in OLALA.

2.2 Objects Selection Scheduling

The ratio of selected objects during training can influence the labeling efficiency as well as the trained model accuracy. A ratio near 1 approximates the full human labeling process (less efficient), while a zero ratio resembles full self-training (Rosenberg et al., 2005) settings (less accurate). To optimally balance efficiency and accuracy, r is dynamically adjusted at different rounds of labeling via a scheduling function. According to Curriculum Learning (Bengio et al., 2009), we set high initial values of r to rely more on human labeling and ease model training in the beginning. Linear or exponential decay is then applied to gradually decrease r, increasing the trust in the model predictions as their accuracy improves during training. From an optimization perspective, r can be seen as a "learning rate" for the OLALA AL process. We demonstrate the effectiveness of the proposed scheduling mechanism in the experiments (Section 5.3).

2.3 Semi-automatic Prediction Correction

Compared to recent work (Wang et al., 2018; Xie et al., 2020) using self-training for improving model performance, `OLALA` contains an additional component to fix possible errors in the utilized model predictions. Inspired by recent efforts for creating large-scale layout analysis datasets (Zhong et al., 2019; Li et al., 2019; Shen et al., 2020), we propose a semi-automatic prediction correction algorithm to ensure the quality of the model predictions. This method relies on the unique structures of document data: layout objects are densely arranged, and there is usually no overlap between content regions. It can identify *duplicated predictions* and *false-negative predictions* based on this prior knowledge, and requests minor supervision to fix them. Shown in Section 5.1 and 5.2, this algorithm both improves the final trained model accuracy and enables the creation of an accurate large dataset based on these predictions.[2]

Duplicate Removal In practice, models could generate multiple close predictions for a large object, yet only one or some of the predictions are sent for user inspection. Thus, if naively merging the user's labels with the remaining predictions, it can lead to overlapping labels for the same object. We fix this error by filtering out predictions overlapped with any human annotations over a score threshold ξ. Different from IOU scores, we use the the pairwise Overlap Coefficient, $\text{Overlap}(A, B) = |A \cap B| / \min(|A|, |B|)$, to better address scenarios where a predicted box is contained within a labeled box. The threshold ξ is set to 0.25 empirically.

Missing Annotation Recovery False-negatives occur when no prediction is generated for a given object. In typical object detection tasks, predictions are dropped when the confidence is under some threshold, which might lead to false negatives. It is an implicit signal from the model, requesting extra supervision from human annotators and is a key step for improving dataset accuracy (Section 4). It is implemented by highlighting the regions without model predictions, such that human annotators (or a simulated agent) can easily identify the mispredicted objects and add the annotations.

The implementation of this algorithm is different between real-world human annotation and simulated labeling experiments (with oracle beforehand). For human annotations, we carefully design a user interface which incorporates the three functions and augments human labeling, and we refer readers to Figure 6 in the supplementary material for more details. In simulations, we build a labeling agent that can automatically query the oracle for ground-truths under different scenarios (see Section 4).

[2]Self-training methods (*e.g.* (Wang et al., 2018)), usually discard the model predictions (pseudo labels) after training.

Algorithm 1: Object-level Active Learning Annotation

Input : Initial sets $\mathcal{U}_0$, $\mathcal{L}_0$; labeling budget m; object selection ratio r

Initialize $\mathcal{U} = \mathcal{U}_0$, $\mathcal{L} = \mathcal{L}_0$, and model weights Θ;
for $t = 0$ **to** $T - 1$ **do**
  Calculate budget m and selection ratio r for at t
  Update the model Θ using $\mathcal{L}$
  Let $\bar{\mathcal{M}} = \{\}$
  for $i = 0$ **to** $|\mathcal{U}|$ **do**
    Generate object predictions $\hat{Y}_i$ for $X_i \in \mathcal{U}$
    Let $m_i = \min\{r|\hat{Y}_i|, m\}$, $m = m - m_i$
    if $m \leq 0$ **then** break;
    Calculate object scores $f(\hat{y}_j)\ \forall \hat{y}_j \in \hat{Y}_i$
    Select m_i objects of top scores and label $\bar{Y}_i$
    Correct errors in unselected predictions $\hat{Y}_i^-$
    Merge $\bar{Y}_i$ with $\hat{Y}_i$ for image annotations $\tilde{Y}_i$
    Remove X_i from $\mathcal{U}$ and add $(X_i, \tilde{Y}_i)$ to $\bar{\mathcal{M}}$
  end
  Update $\mathcal{L} \leftarrow \mathcal{L} \cup \bar{\mathcal{M}}$
end
Update the model Θ using $\mathcal{L}$

2.4 Overview of the Proposed Algorithm

We now present the `OLALA` Algorithm 1. Given an initial labeled set $\mathcal{L}_0$, it aims to use the predictions from a model Θ to optimally label the remaining unlabeled set $\mathcal{U}_0$ given some labeling budget. Different from existing work, we define the labeling budget per round m as the number of *objects* - rather than images - that human annotators can label. The algorithm iteratively proposes the most informative objects to label for a total of T rounds. At each round t, it selects up to m objects. For each image X_i from the existing unlabeled set $\mathcal{U}$, r percent of predicted objects are selected for user labeling according to some object scoring function f. The rest of the labels are created by correcting errors in the unselected model prediction $\hat{Y}_i^-$ based on the semi-automatic prediction correction algorithm. The labeled image X_i will be removed from $\mathcal{U}$ and the annotated samples $(X_i, \tilde{Y}_i)$ will be added to $\mathcal{L}$. After each round, the selection ratio r decays as the model accuracy improves.

3 Perturbation-based Scoring Function

The scoring function f also plays an important role in the OLALA framework. It evaluates prediction ambiguity and determines which objects to select for labeling. We propose a perturbation scoring method based on both the bounding box and category predictions. Inspired by the self-diversity idea in Jiang et al. (2020) and Zhou et al. (2017), the proposed method hypothesizes that the adjacent image patches share similar features vectors, and the predicted object boxes and categories for them should be consistent. Therefore, any large disagreement between the original and perturbed predictions indicates that the model is insufficiently trained for this type of input, or there are anomalies in the sample. Both cases demand user attention.

Specifically, for each object prediction $\hat{y}_j = (\hat{b}_j, \hat{c}_j) \in \hat{Y}_i$, we take the bounding box prediction $\hat{b}_j = (x, y, w, h)$ and apply some small shifts to perturb the given box, where x, y are the coordinate of the top left corner, and w, h are the width and height of the box. The new boxes are created via horizontal and vertical translation by a ratio of α and β: $p_{jk} = (x \pm \alpha w, y \pm \beta h, w, h)$, where p_{jk} is the k-th perturbed box for box prediction $\hat{b}_j$, and a total of K perturbations will be generated. Based on the image features within each p_{jk}, the model generates new box and category predictions (q_{jk}, v_{jk}). We then measure the disagreement between the original prediction $(\hat{b}_j, \hat{c}_j)$ and the perturbed versions $\{(q_{jk}, v_{jk})\}_{k=1}^K$, and use it as a criterion for selecting objects for labeling.

In practice, we build this method upon a typical object detection architecture composed of two stages (Ren et al., 2015): 1) a region proposal network estimates possible bounding boxes, and 2) a region classification and improvement network (ROIHeads[3]) predicts the category and modifies the box prediction based on the input proposals. We use the perturbed boxes $\{p_{jk}\}_{k=1}^K$ as the new inputs for the ROIHeads, and obtain the new box and class predictions $\{(q_{jk}, v_{jk})\}_{k=1}^K$. For object regions of low confidence, the new predictions are unstable under such perturbation, and the predicted boxes and category distribution can change drastically from the original version. To this end, we formulate the position disagreement D_p and the category disagreement D_c for the j-th object prediction as

$$D_p(\hat{b}_j) = \frac{1}{K} \sum\nolimits_k \left(1 - \text{IOU}(\hat{b}_j, p_{jk})\right)$$
$$D_c(\hat{c}_j) = \frac{1}{K} \sum\nolimits_k L(\hat{c}_j || v_{jk}),$$

where IOU calculates the intersection over union scores for the inputs, and $L(\cdot||\cdot)$ is a measurement for distribution difference, e.g., cross entropy. The overall disagreement D is defined as $D(\hat{y}_j) = D_p(\hat{b}_j) + \lambda D_c(\hat{c}_j)$, with λ being a weighting constant. Objects of larger D will be prioritized for labeling, and users will create annotations $\bar{Y}_i$ for them in the i-th image.

The proposed method can effectively identify false-positive object predictions. Based on the self-diversity assumption, incorrect category prediction $\hat{c}_j$ will cause high D_c because of the divergence of the new class prediction v_{jk} for nearby patches. When the predicted box $\hat{b}_j$ is wrong, the perturbed box p_{jk} is less likely to be the appropriate proposal box. The generated predictions (q_{jk}, v_{jk}) are unreliable, causing higher overall disagreement D.

Applicability to Layout Datasets Compared to previous work, the perturbation-based scoring function aims to solve two challenges unique to layout analysis tasks. First, layout regions are boundary-sensitive: a small vertical shift of a text region box could cause the complete disappearance of a row of texts. However, existing methods designed for image-level selection usually focus on the categorical—rather than positional—information in outputs (i.e. Brust et al. (2018) considers the marginal score of the object category predictions and does not use the bounding boxes, and Aghdam et al. (2019) indirectly uses the positional information based on a pixel map for image-level aggregation). By contrast, our method identifies samples that lead to ambiguous boundary predictions via D_p.

Moreover, document images usually contain numerous objects per page and content regions are densely arranged. Hence, we cannot adapt the object-level scoring function in Wang et al. (2018), which requires cropping an object, randomly pasting it to another image, and evaluating the consistency between the original and the newly detected boxes for this object. The random pasting will introduce non-existing structures (*e.g.* , overlaying a figure over tables or texts), and the calculated score cannot reliably assess the prediction. With OLALA, the original document structures are untouched.

[3]It's a module name in Detectron2 (Wu et al., 2019).

4 Experimental Setup

Objective Several experiments are designed to study the validity of the proposed `OLALA` framework and evaluate how it can improve the efficiency of the labeling process. Methods are considered better if they achieve similar accuracy while using less labeling budget m than their counterparts, or obtain higher accuracy given the same m. In the experiments, we measure object detection accuracy using mean Average Precision (AP) scores (Lin et al., 2014), and the labeling budget refers to the number of objects to label by default.

Datasets To validate our approach, we run simulations on three representative layout analysis datasets: PubLayNet (Zhong et al., 2019), PRImA (Antonacopoulos et al., 2009), and HJDataset (Shen et al., 2020). PubLayNet is a large dataset of 360k images. The images and annotations are generated from noiseless digital PDF files of medical papers. As the original training set in PubLayNet is too large to conduct experiments efficiently, we use a downsampled version. PRImA is created by human annotators drawing bounding boxes for text regions in both scanned magazines and technical articles, resulting in greater heterogeneity in this dataset than in PubLayNet. HJDataset contains layout annotation for 2k historical Japanese documents. HJDataset was established using noisy image scans, and the creation method is a combination of rule-based layout parsing from images and human correction. Table 1 shows a thorough comparison among them.

Labeling Simulation When running simulations, we build two additional helper algorithms to imitate human labeling behavior. First, for the selected objects, the corresponding ground-truths is found via a best-matching algorithm. For each prediction, we calculate the IOU with all ground-truth objects and choose the top one to substitute the prediction. Duplicated ground-truths selected in an image will be removed by this process. In real-world labeling experiments, we also notice human annotators do not need to correct an object prediction if it is accurate (high IOU with the ground-truth and category is the same). To best simulate this phenomena, if a selected prediction has an IOU>0.925 (determined empirically) with a ground-truth object of the same category, we do not substitute it with the ground-truth and only use a discounted budget $\eta = 0.2$. Finally, to mimic annotators' search for false-negative regions, we compute the pairwise IOU between the ground truth Y_i and the combined labeling objects $\tilde{Y}_i$. Ground-truth objects whose maximum IOU with predicted objects is less than ζ are chosen to add to $\tilde{Y}_i$, and the remaining budget is reduced accordingly. ζ is set to 0.05 in the following experiments to allow minor overlapping caused by noise in the predictions.

Datasets	PubLayNet	HJDataset	PRImA
Data Source	Digital PDF	Image Scan	Image Scan
Annotation	Automatic	Combined	Manual
Dataset Size	360,000	2,048	453
Train Size	8,896*	1,433	363
Test Size	2,249	307	90
Avg / max O	10.72 / 59	73.48 / 98	21.63 / 79
Labeling budget m	21,140	51,436	5,623
Equivalent Images	2,000	700	240
Total rounds T	10	8	4
Initial / last r	0.9 / 0.4	0.9 / 0.5	0.9 / 0.75

* We used a downsampled version of PubLayNet in our experiments.

Table 1: Statistics and parameters for the PubLayNet, HJDatasets, and PRImA. O is the number of objects in each image.

Implementation The proposed algorithms are implemented based on Detectron2 (Wu et al., 2019). The same object detection model (Faster R-CNN (Ren et al., 2015) with ResNet-50 (He et al., 2016) backbone and FPN (Lin et al., 2017)) is used for all experiments. The optimizer is based on SGD with Momentum (Sutskever et al., 2013) and Multi-Step learning rate warmup (Goyal et al., 2017) with a 0.00025 base learning rate. We train each model on a single Tesla V100 GPU with a batch size of 6.

The total labeling budget m and the total rounds T are set per dataset to account for different dataset sizes, and the labeling budget is evenly distributed for each round. For the object selection ratio, we use a linear decay function with a given initial and last value. These hyperparameters are initialized as indicated in Table 1. When calculating the object scores, we set λ to 1 and L as the cross entropy function. In addition, unless otherwise mentioned, we use four pairs of (α, β)'s: $(0.08, 0.04)$, $(0.08, 0.16)$, $(0.12, 0.04)$, $(0.12, 0, 16)$, and for each pair, four boxes are created (moving towards top left, top right, bottom left, and bottom right). A total of $K = 16$ perturbed boxes are generated per object prediction for comprehensive analysis of prediction performance under small and large perturbations in different directions.

	PubLayNet		HJData		PRImA*	
Experiments	Final AP	Labeled I / O	Final AP	Labeled I / O	Final AP	Labeled I / O
Image-Random [a]	60.73	2,046 / 21,430	69.82	709 / 51,959	31.49	244 / 4,799
OLALA-Random [c]	**64.21(+3.48)**†	3,187 / 21,412	**72.16(+2.34)**	1,105 / 51,626	**32.08(+0.59)**	277 / 4,785
Image-Marginal [b]	67.91	2,465 / 21,574	73.25	709 / 51,937	30.99	243 / 4769
OLALA-Marginal [d]	**69.23(+1.31)**‡	3,661 / 21,467	71.48(-1.77)	1,075 / 51,804	32.85(+1.86)	306 / 4,721
OLALA-Pertubation [e]	69.13(+1.21)	3686 / 21430	**73.40(+0.15)**	1,159 / 51,656	**33.87(+2.88)**	286 / 4,764

* The results in PRImA are averaged from the 5-folds in cross validation to account for possible noise due to the small dataset size.
†,‡ The OLALA-Random percentages are compared against Image-Random, and others are compared against Image-Marginal.

Table 2: The final AP and number of total labeled images I and objects O given the same object budget m. OLALA achieves strong performance improvements in model accuracy in all experiments, and creates datasets with considerably more images given the same labeling budget.

5 Results and Discussion

5.1 Better AP with the Same Budget

OLALA based labeling settings are compared against image-level AL and other labeling baselines: [a] Image-Random: randomly select images in each round, [b] Image-Marginal: image-level Active Learning baselines (Brust et al., 2018) with marginal scoring and mean aggregation, [c] OLALA-Random: randomly select objects in each round, [d] OLALA-Marginal: select objects using marginal scoring for object category prediction, [e] OLALA-Perturbation: select objects using the proposed perturbation-based scoring function.

5.2 Similar AP with a Lower Budget

Table 3 shows that OLALA-based methods considerably reduce the object budget expense. We observe at most a 50% reduction in the number of labeled objects compared to random image labeling cases in the PubLayNet experiments (7496 vs. 15980). Moreover, with this level of reduction, OLALA-based models manage to maintain a comparable level of accuracy. Similarly, the marginal scoring baseline is less stable and the performance is worse compared to the perturbation-based scoring method in OLALA settings.

In Figure 3, we visualize the model validation accuracy (line plot) and the budget expense (bar plot) for the PubLayNet dataset labeling simulations. Given the same object budget (dashed horizontal line), image-AL methods can only label 5 rounds, and the model AP is around 45 (indicated by the vertical line), significantly lower than 58.9 in OLALA models.

5.3 Analysis of the OLALA framework

In the OLALA framework, there are three sources of objects in the created dataset, namely, human annotations, directly used model predictions (unselected in the AL step), and unchanged model predictions (they are selected for manual check, but remain unchanged as they are accurate). OLALA strategically chooses objects to label and thus optimizes the overall efficiency.

	PubLayNet		HJData	
Exps*	AP	Labeled I/O	AP	Labeled I/O
[a]†	59.89	1,503 / 15,980	63.42	603 / 44,156
[c]	57.96(-1.93)	1,503 / 10,228	65.72(+2.30)	603 / 29,191
[b]	59.21	1,503 / 11,848	69.04	603 / 44,251
[d]	53.33(-5.88)	1,503 / 6,829	65.84(-3.19)	603 / 30,251
[e]	**58.90(-0.31)**	1,503 / **7,496**	**67.68(-1.36)**	603 / **28,899**

* The parameters in these experiments are slightly different from those mentioned in Table 1, and we report the details in the supplementary materials.
† The indexing is the same as Table 2.

Table 3: The final AP and number of total labeled images I and objects O when labeling the same number of images. OLALA maintains a similar level of AP while labeling significantly fewer objects. Similar results are observed in PRImA and abbreviated to save space.

Figure 4 shows the proportion of object sources in the three OLALA settings in the PublayNet Labeling experiments. The *Object Selection Scheduling* (Section 2.2) sets a high selection ratio r when training begins and r decays during training. Thus, the averaged percentage of manually labeled objects (blue line) is initially high but gradually decreases while the portion of model predictions (orange line) steadily grows in the labeling process. As the models becomes more accurate as training progresses (reflected in Figure 3), "annotators" find more accurate objects in the model-selected predictions, and include them in the dataset without changing them (green line). Though more than 50% of objects are directly from model prediction, the created datasets maintain the same high level of accuracy[4], indicated by grey bar plots in the background.

[4]The dataset accuracy is measured in AP via comparing the created version with the oracle.

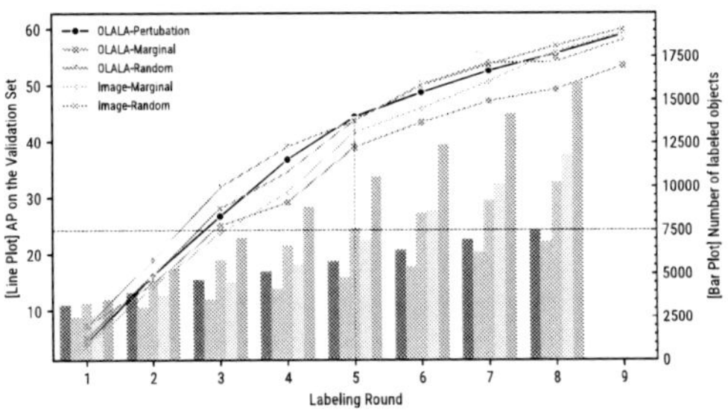

Figure 3: Model validation accuracy (line plot) and budget expenses (bar plot) at different rounds of PubLayNet labeling. `OLALA` methods (blue) require labeling fewer objects compared to image AL methods (red), while maintaining similar AP. If the same number of objects is allowed (horizontal dashed line), the image AL method stops at round 5, and the model AP is around 25% lower compared to `OLALA`.

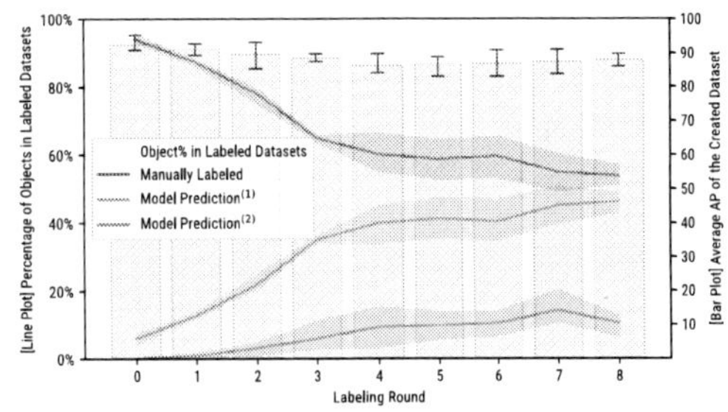

Figure 4: The created object sources (line plot) and dataset accuracy (bar plot) during the training process. The number of manually labeled objects (blue) decreases and directly used model predicted objects (orange) increases. As the model becomes more accurate, a higher portion of selected objects become accurate (green). Results shown are averaged from the three `OLALA` methods in the PubLayNet experiments.

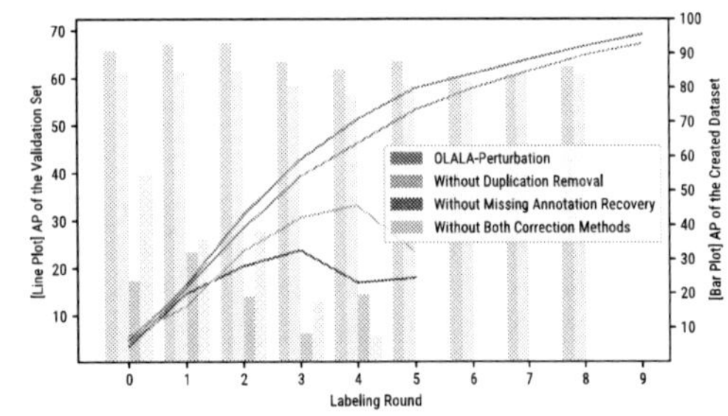

Figure 5: Influence of the prediction correction components on the model validation accuracy (line plot) and dataset accuracy (bar plot). Model performance suffers from removing the components, and dataset accuracy decreases accordingly. The *Missing Annotation Recovery* component, which corrects false negatives, is critical for model performance. Results shown are from experiments on PubLayNet.

We study how the semi-automatic prediction correction algorithm, mentioned in Section 2.3, contributes to the `OLALA` process. Shown in Figure 5, we compare the model validation AP (line plot) and accuracy of the created dataset (bar plot) with and without the *Duplication Removal* and *Missing Annotation Recovery* components in PubLayNet annotation. Without these components, models suffer from different levels of accuracy reduction compared to the `OLALA`-Perturbation baseline (green). We observe the most severe accuracy reduction when removing the missing annotation recovery components (red), indicating the necessity of extra supervision for correcting high ratios of false negatives. Interestingly, when removing both correction methods (orange), the model appears to perform better than when only discarding the missing annotation recovery component. Duplicated predictions add more instances per image for calculating the loss, thus reinforcing the signal to train the model and improve the initial performance. Unfortunately, without extra supervision, the models are trained on a dataset with many false negatives, and tend to generate fewer predictions. The error accumulates and finally both models collapse and stop improving. In both cases, the models exhaust all the training samples at round 5.

6 Conclusion

The objective of this paper is to develop rigorous methods that can increase the efficiency of extracting structured texts - required for downstream NLP applications - from social science documents. We propose the object-level active learning annotation framework, `OLALA`, for efficiently labeling document layouts. With a novel prediction correction algorithm and perturbation object scoring function, annotators only need to label a fraction of layout objects in each image. Through simulated labeling experiments on real-world data, we show that our proposed algorithms significantly improve dataset creation efficiency relative to image-level methods. Different components of `OLALA` are also carefully studied to demonstrate their validity and necessity. In summary, this work explores how to improve cooperation between human and machine intelligence, in order to unlock the structured text required for conducting modern NLP analyses at scale on historical documents.

Acknowledgements We thank the reviewers for their very helpful suggestions and feedback! This project is supported in part by NSF Grant #1823616 and funding from the Harvard Data Science Initiative and Harvard Catalyst, and we thank the computational resources from Computation Canada. We also thank the helpful discussions with Doug Downey, James Tompkin, and Ruochen Zhang.

References

Hamed H Aghdam, Abel Gonzalez-Garcia, Joost van de Weijer, and Antonio M López. 2019. Active learning for deep detection neural networks. In *Proceedings of the IEEE International Conference on Computer Vision*, pages 3672–3680.

Apostolos Antonacopoulos, David Bridson, Christos Papadopoulos, and Stefan Pletschacher. 2009. A realistic dataset for performance evaluation of document layout analysis. In *2009 10th International Conference on Document Analysis and Recognition*, pages 296–300. IEEE.

Yoshua Bengio, Jérôme Louradour, Ronan Collobert, and Jason Weston. 2009. Curriculum learning. In *Proceedings of the 26th annual international conference on machine learning*, pages 41–48.

Clemens-Alexander Brust, Christoph Käding, and Joachim Denzler. 2018. Active learning for deep object detection. *arXiv preprint arXiv:1809.09875.*

Sai Vikas Desai, Akshay Chandra Lagandula, Wei Guo, Seishi Ninomiya, and Vineeth N Balasubramanian. 2019. An adaptive supervision framework for active learning in object detection. *arXiv preprint arXiv:1908.02454.*

Priya Goyal, Piotr Dollár, Ross Girshick, Pieter Noordhuis, Lukasz Wesolowski, Aapo Kyrola, Andrew Tulloch, Yangqing Jia, and Kaiming He. 2017. Accurate, large minibatch sgd: Training imagenet in 1 hour. *arXiv preprint arXiv:1706.02677.*

W Walker Hanlon and Brian Beach. 2022. Historical newspaper data: A researcher's guide and toolkit.

Elmar Haussmann, Michele Fenzi, Kashyap Chitta, Jan Ivanecky, Hanson Xu, Donna Roy, Akshita Mittel, Nicolas Koumchatzky, Clement Farabet, and Jose M Alvarez. 2020. Scalable active learning for object detection. *arXiv preprint arXiv:2004.04699.*

Kaiming He, Xiangyu Zhang, Shaoqing Ren, and Jian Sun. 2016. Deep residual learning for image recognition. In *Proceedings of the IEEE conference on computer vision and pattern recognition*, pages 770–778.

Zhuoren Jiang, Zhe Gao, Yuguang Duan, Yangyang Kang, Changlong Sun, Qiong Zhang, and Xiaozhong Liu. 2020. Camouflaged chinese spam content detection with semi-supervised generative active learning. In *Proceedings of the 58th Annual Meeting of the Association for Computational Linguistics*, pages 3080–3085.

Minghao Li, Lei Cui, Shaohan Huang, Furu Wei, Ming Zhou, and Zhoujun Li. 2019. Tablebank: Table benchmark for image-based table detection and recognition. *arXiv preprint arXiv:1903.01949.*

Tsung-Yi Lin, Piotr Dollár, Ross Girshick, Kaiming He, Bharath Hariharan, and Serge Belongie. 2017. Feature pyramid networks for object detection. In *Proceedings of the IEEE conference on computer vision and pattern recognition*, pages 2117–2125.

Tsung-Yi Lin, Michael Maire, Serge Belongie, James Hays, Pietro Perona, Deva Ramanan, Piotr Dollár, and C Lawrence Zitnick. 2014. Microsoft coco: Common objects in context. In *European conference on computer vision*, pages 740–755. Springer.

Shaoqing Ren, Kaiming He, Ross Girshick, and Jian Sun. 2015. Faster r-cnn: Towards real-time object detection with region proposal networks. In *Advances in neural information processing systems*, pages 91–99.

Chuck Rosenberg, Martial Hebert, and Henry Schneiderman. 2005. Semi-supervised self-training of object detection models.

Soumya Roy, Asim Unmesh, and Vinay P Namboodiri. 2018. Deep active learning for object detection. In *BMVC*, page 91.

Sebastian Schreiber, Stefan Agne, Ivo Wolf, Andreas Dengel, and Sheraz Ahmed. 2017. Deepdesrt: Deep learning for detection and structure recognition of tables in document images. In *2017 14th IAPR international conference on document analysis and recognition (ICDAR)*, volume 1, pages 1162–1167. IEEE.

H Sebastian Seung, Manfred Opper, and Haim Sompolinsky. 1992. Query by committee. In *Proceedings of the fifth annual workshop on Computational learning theory*, pages 287–294.

Zejiang Shen, Kaixuan Zhang, and Melissa Dell. 2020. A large dataset of historical japanese documents with complex layouts. In *Proceedings of the IEEE/CVF Conference on Computer Vision and Pattern Recognition Workshops*, pages 548–549.

Zejiang Shen, Ruochen Zhang, Melissa Dell, Benjamin Charles Germain Lee, Jacob Carlson, and Weining Li. 2021. Layoutparser: A unified toolkit for deep learning based document image analysis. In *International Conference on Document Analysis and Recognition*, pages 131–146. Springer.

Ilya Sutskever, James Martens, George Dahl, and Geoffrey Hinton. 2013. On the importance of initialization and momentum in deep learning. In *International conference on machine learning*, pages 1139–1147.

Keze Wang, Xiaopeng Yan, Dongyu Zhang, Lei Zhang, and Liang Lin. 2018. Towards human-machine cooperation: Self-supervised sample mining for object detection. In *Proceedings of the IEEE Conference on Computer Vision and Pattern Recognition*, pages 1605–1613.

Yuxin Wu, Alexander Kirillov, Francisco Massa, Wan-Yen Lo, and Ross Girshick. 2019. Detectron2. `https://github.com/facebookresearch/detectron2`.

Yuxin Wu, Alexander Kirillov, Francisco Massa, Wan-Yen Lo, and Ross Girshick. 2020. Label Studio: Data labeling software. `https://github.com/heartexlabs/label-studio`.

Qizhe Xie, Minh-Thang Luong, Eduard Hovy, and Quoc V Le. 2020. Self-training with noisy student improves imagenet classification. In *Proceedings of the IEEE/CVF Conference on Computer Vision and Pattern Recognition*, pages 10687–10698.

Angela Yao, Juergen Gall, Christian Leistner, and Luc Van Gool. 2012. Interactive object detection. In *2012 IEEE conference on computer vision and pattern recognition*, pages 3242–3249. IEEE.

Xu Zhong, Jianbin Tang, and Antonio Jimeno Yepes. 2019. Publaynet: largest dataset ever for document layout analysis. *arXiv preprint arXiv:1908.07836*.

Zongwei Zhou, Jae Shin, Lei Zhang, Suryakanth Gurudu, Michael Gotway, and Jianming Liang. 2017. Fine-tuning convolutional neural networks for biomedical image analysis: actively and incrementally. In *Proceedings of the IEEE conference on computer vision and pattern recognition*, pages 7340–7351.

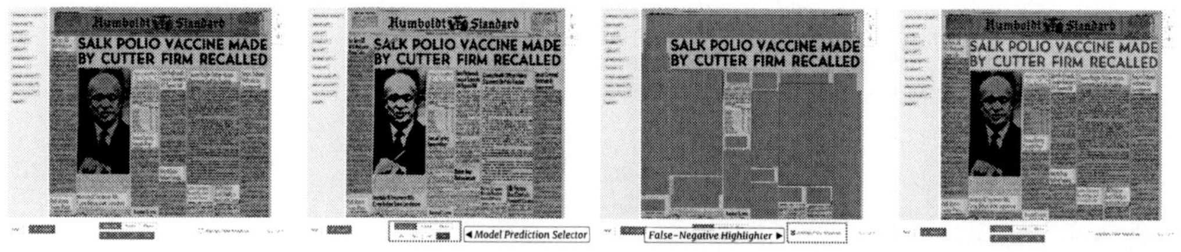

(a) Full Model Predictions (b) Selected Model Predictions (c) Highlight False-Negative Regions (d) Final Created Annotation

Figure 6: Illustration of the annotation interface with OLALA features. (a) Given an input scan, a pre-trained model generates object predictions, and they are highlighted as rectangular boxes on the original image. The color denotes the category of the given object. (b) The *Model Prediction Selector* enables hiding predictions of low object scores. In this case, objects of top 25% (the 4th Quartile, Q4) scores are presented. Two of the objects (pointed to by red arrows) have minor errors in object location predictions. Human annotators check only the displayed objects and modify inaccuracies. (c) The *False-Negative Highlighter* helps recognize mis-identified objects from the model predictions. When enabled, it converts all predicted regions to a dummy color, and regions without predictions are highlighted. Annotators can easily spot false-negatives regions and have them labeled. (d) After these steps, the full image annotation is created with less effort.

Appendix

A OLALA Implementation Details

Different from image-level labeling, annotating objects within images is fundamentally a search task: "annotators"[5] need to scan through the image and find objects matching specific criteria. The nature of object-based labeling leads to different objectives in simulated labeling experiments and real-world human annotation. In labeling simulations, the ground-truth objects are known ex-ante. The labeling agent only needs to query the oracle and choose objects that meet certain conditions. As the search space is pre-defined, the core challenge is to construct such query conditions for finding ground-truths. By contrast, when humans annotate objects, there is no ground-truth known beforehand, and the object search space is yet undefined. Their vision systems are capable of efficiently identifying correct objects within the space. Hence, the objective for human annotation is to reduce the object search space, and annotators will select valid objects within the space. To this end, as mentioned in the main paper, the OLALA framework is implemented differently for real-world human annotation (Section A.1) and simulated labeling experiments (See Section 4 in the main paper).

A.1 OLALA Annotation User Interface

To help with human annotation, we build a labeling interface incorporated with OLALA functionalities based on label-studio (Wu et al., 2020). Figure 6 shows an example of annotating newspaper layouts using this tool[6].

a Given an input scan, a pre-trained model generates object predictions $\{(b_j, c_j)\}_{j=1}^{n}$, which are highlighted as rectangular boxes on the original image. The color denotes the category c_j of an object. Within the outputs, duplicated object detections are precluded using *Duplication Removal.*

b A *Model Prediction Selector* is implemented for hiding objects with low scores generated by the object scoring function f. In this case, objects of top 25% (the 4th Quartile, Q4) scores are presented. Two selected objects (pointed by red arrows) have minor errors in object location predictions by missing one line or one column of text (see Section 3 "Applicability to Layout Datasets" in the main paper), while others being correct. Human annotators can focus on checking the displayed objects and only need to modify the two incorrect predictions while other accurate ones are kept untouched.

c We also develop a *False-Negative Highlighter* to help annotators find mis-identified objects from the model predictions. After enabled, it

[5]We use the general term annotator to refer to a human annotator or a simulated labeling agent.

[6]In this example, the used model has been trained on 200 hundred images. For illustration purpose, we reduce the number of objects generated by models to emphasize the false-negative selection process. But in practice, the false-negative rate is lower.

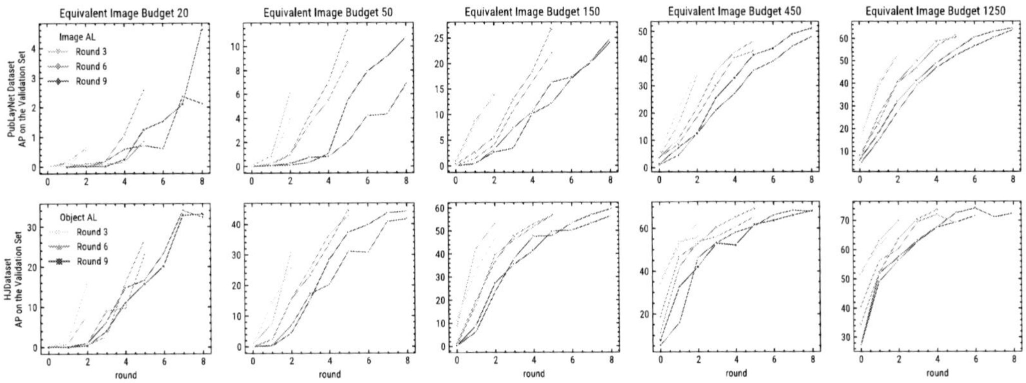

Figure 7: The model validation AP during the labeling process under different total rounds T and labeling budget m. The plots in row one and two are for experiments on the PubLayNet and HJDataset, respectively. Within each plot, image-level AL results are colored in blue while OLALA results are in red. To best show results at different stage of training, the ranges for the y-axis are set differently. Under the same budget, an increase in T can generally lead to better model performance. For different datasets, the optimal budget and total round settings are different. As the budget increases, image-level methods narrow the performance gap (in PubLayNet experiments) or perform better than OLALA methods (in HJDataset experiments).

Configuration	Configuration A		Configuration B	
Datasets	PubLayNet	HJDataset	PubLayNet	HJDataset
Labeling budget m	21,140	51,436	15,855	44,088
Equivalent image budget	2,000[1]	700	1,500	600
Total rounds T	10	8	9	9
Initial / last r	0.9/0.4	0.9/0.5	0.9/0.5	0.9/0.5

[1] To get the number of equivalent image budget, we simply divide m by the average number of objects per page for the given dataset.

Table 4: Different parameter configurations for labeling settings (1) and (2). Configuration A is used for labeling setting (1) where the same number of objects are labeled and B for labeling setting (2) where the number of labeled images is fixed.

	PubLayNet		HJData	
Exps	AP	Labeled I/O	AP	Labeled I/O
[a]	61.65	1,558/16,123	62.73	605/44,505
[c]	63.73(+2.07)	2,501/16,122	65.75(+3.02)	980/44,260
[b]	65.52	1,961/16,108	68.16	607/44,344
[d]	69.36(+3.83)	2,995/16,104	69.13(+0.97)	956/44,398
[e]	65.53(+0.01)	2,996/16,142	69.15(+0.99)	1,041/44,398

Table 5: The final AP and number of total labeled images I and objects O when labeling the same number of objects under model configuration B.

will assign a dummy color overlay to object predictions, thus regions without predictions will be highlighted. Annotators can easily spot false-negatives regions and have them labeled. And this is the *Missing Annotation Recovery* step in the OLALA algorithm.

d Finally, the full image annotation will be created with significantly less effort.

Through the interface, annotators' labeling effort is saved via a reduced object search space: one only needs to check the selected model predictions and the highlighted false-negative regions.

B Additional Experiments

B.1 Different model configurations

In the main paper, we report results under two different settings, namely, (1) labeling the same number of objects and (2) labeling the same number of images. During these experiments, the model configurations for labeling settings (2) is slightly different than those in (1), and we include the details in Table 4. Labeling setting (1) is only experimented under configuration A while (2) under configuration B. For fair comparison, we complete another set of experiments for labeling setting (1) using configuration B. The results are reported in Table 5, and similar conclusion could be made based on this set of experiments.

B.2 Analysis of labeling budget and total training rounds

We run additional labeling simulations to find the optimal configurations for the labeling budget and the total training rounds. Given the same budget, we could perform multiple rounds of labeling and re-training, with the optimal total round yet to be determined. Similarly, for a given dataset, it is important to allocate appropriate labeling budget such that the labeled samples can most effectively boost the model performance. This study could also shed light on the applicability of `OLALA` to labeling scenarios where only small labeling budget is allowed. To this end, we experiment with object budget m equivalent to labeling 20, 50, 150, 450, and 1250 images (equivalent image budget [7]) for a given dataset. For each m, we also experiment with three different total labeling rounds T of 3, 6, and 9. The model validation accuracy during the labeling process is visualized in Figure 7.

Given the same labeling budget, we find that increasing the total labeling rounds T tends to improve the model accuracy, especially for scenarios where small labeling budget is available. Under such small budget, `OLALA`-based annotation usually leads to models of higher accuracy than those from image-level AL settings. However, as labeling budget increases, the performance gap between `OLALA` and image AL models narrows. With sufficient labeling budget, image AL models even performs better than `OLALA` models in HJDataset. It reveals that `OLALA` is more helpful in the initial stage of labeling, as it exposes more images samples to the model and thus boosts the performance. For different datasets, the optimal combination of total labeling rounds and budget is different: $T = 9$ with the equivalent image budget of 450 for PubLayNet, and $T = 9$ with 50 equivalent image budget for HJDataset. Based on our observation, this is largely determined by the diversity of samples in the dataset. `OLALA` helps to explore unique object instances in the early training stage, and requires more labeling steps to achieve optimal performance boost for datasets of diverse examples like PubLayNet.

[7]Directly setting thresholds for m does not account for the variances of objects per image for different datasets.

Towards Few-Shot Identification of Morality Frames using In-Context Learning

Shamik Roy, Nishanth Sridhar Nakshatri, Dan Goldwasser
Department of Computer Science
Purdue University
West Lafayette, IN, USA
{roy98, nnakshat, dgoldwas}@purdue.edu

Abstract

Data scarcity is a common problem in NLP, especially when the annotation pertains to nuanced socio-linguistic concepts that require specialized knowledge. As a result, few-shot identification of these concepts is desirable. Few-shot in-context learning using pre-trained Large Language Models (LLMs) has been recently applied successfully in many NLP tasks. In this paper, we study few-shot identification of a psycho-linguistic concept, Morality Frames (Roy et al., 2021), using LLMs. Morality frames are a representation framework that provides a holistic view of the moral sentiment expressed in text, identifying the relevant moral foundation (Haidt and Graham, 2007) and at a finer level of granularity, the moral sentiment expressed towards the entities mentioned in the text. Previous studies relied on human annotation to identify morality frames in text which is expensive. In this paper, we propose prompting based approaches using pretrained Large Language Models for identification of morality frames, relying only on few-shot exemplars. We compare our models' performance with few-shot RoBERTa and found promising results.

1 Introduction

While the NLP field has seen tremendous progress over the last decade, building models capable of identifying abstract concepts remain a highly challenging problem. This difficulty stems from two key reasons. First, these concepts can manifest in very different ways in text. For example, the concept of *fairness*, that we discuss at length in this paper, can be discussed in the context of the abortion debate (e.g., *"right to privacy"*) or in the context of Covid-19 vaccination (e.g., *"everyone should have access to the vaccine"*). Learning to identify instances of this concept in previously unseen contexts remains a challenge. Second, building NLP models using the supervised learning paradigm requires humans to annotate data, which for such tasks is a cognitively demanding process. In this paper, we investigate whether the recently introduced paradigm of zero/few shot learning using Large Language Models (Brown et al., 2020) is better equipped to deal with these challenges. We focus on a recently introduced framework for analyzing moral sentiment, called *morality frames* (Roy et al., 2021). This framework builds on, and extends, moral foundation theory (Haidt and Graham, 2007), which identifies five moral values (i.e., foundations, each with a positive and a negative polarity) central to human moral sentiment which include Care/Harm, Fairness/Cheating, Loyalty/-Betrayal, Authority/Subversion, and Purity/Degradation. Morality frames is a relational framework that identifies expressions of the moral foundations in text and associates moral roles with entities mentioned in it (see Section 3 for details).

Unlike previous approaches to this task (Roy et al., 2021; Pacheco et al., 2022) which use annotated data to train a relational classifier using DRaiL (Pacheco and Goldwasser, 2021), we define the task as a zero/few shot problem. We rely on in-context learning using Large Language Models for the identification of morality frames. In in-context learning, a desired NLP task is framed as a text generation problem where the Large Language Models are provided with zero/few shot input-output pairs and prompted to generate label for the test data point without updating parameters of the LLMs (Min et al., 2021a).

In this paper, we introduce several prompting techniques for LLMs for the identification of morality frames in tweets that rely on only few-shot examples. We compare our models' performance with few-shot RoBERTa-based (Liu et al., 2019) classifiers. We found that prompting-based techniques underperform RoBERTa in identification of subtle concepts like moral foundations, but in case of moral role identification, the prompting-based techniques outperforms RoBERTa by a large mar-

Proceedings of the Fifth Workshop on Natural Language Processing and Computational Social Science (NLP+CSS), pages 183 - 196
November 7, 2022 ©2022 Association for Computational Linguistics

gin. Note that moral roles are directed towards entities and are more evident than subtle moral foundations.

Our promising findings in this paper suggest that in-context learning approaches can be useful in many Computational Social Science related tasks and we propose a few potential future directions of this work.

2 Related Works

There has been a lot of work towards exploiting existing knowledge in pretrained Large Language Models (LLMs) and improving its few-shot abilities on various downstream tasks in NLP. Some of these works have been influenced from areas related to instruction-based NLP (Goldwasser and Roth, 2014). Mishra et al., 2021 fine-tuned a 140M parameter BART (Lewis et al., 2019) model using instructions and few-shot examples for various NLP tasks such as text classification, question answering, and text modification. This work suggests that augmenting instructions in the fine-tuning process improves model performance on unseen tasks. On similar lines, through a large scale experiment with over 60 different datasets, Wei et al., 2021 showed that instruction tuning on a LLM ($\approx$137B parameters) improves zero and few-shot capabilities of these models. Other notable works (Min et al., 2021c; Sanh et al., 2021) show that even a relatively smaller language model can achieve substantial improvement in a similar setting. Furthermore, Schick and Schütze, 2020 use cloze-style phrases in a semi-supervised manner to help LM assign a sentiment label for the text classification task.

Another line of work focuses on improving LM on downstream tasks with no parameter updates. Brown et al., 2020 proposed to improve LLM few-shot performance by conditioning on concatenation of training examples without any gradient updates. Other works (Min et al., 2021b; Zhao et al., 2021) have further improved this work and have shown consistent gains in various NLP tasks. In addition, Wei et al., 2022 shows that sufficiently large LM can exploit its innate reasoning abilities to solve complex tasks when provided with a series of intermediate steps during prompting.

However, having a generalized LLM may have poor performance when the downstream task needs nuanced understanding of the text or is very different from language modeling in nature. While Schick and Schütze, 2020 and Gao et al., 2020 have studied sentiment classification task in few-shot settings, not many works are available towards utilizing LLM without finetuning it to understand more nuanced concepts like political framing (Boydstun et al., 2014), moral foundations (Haidt and Joseph, 2004; Haidt and Graham, 2007), among others.

Previous work (Roy and Goldwasser, 2020) has performed nuanced analysis of political framing by breaking the policy frames proposed by Boydstun et al., 2014, into fine-grained sub-frames. It was observed that the sub-frames better captured political polarization by providing a structural breakdown of policy frames. A later work (Roy and Goldwasser, 2021) studied the Moral Foundation Theory (Haidt and Joseph, 2004; Haidt and Graham, 2007) at entity level and proposed a knowledge representation framework for organizing moral attitudes directed at different entities. The structured framework is named morality frames (Roy et al., 2021). These nuanced structural frameworks, such as, frames, sub-frames, entity-centric moral sentiments (morality frames), are expensive to annotate as they largely depend on human knowledge. A few-shot automatic identification of such concepts is required to save manual human-effort and for performing these studies at scale. In this paper, we take the first step towards the analysis on how well LLMs can understand these psycho-linguistic concepts in few-shot settings. As our first study, we explore in-context learning of morality frames in this paper and leave the study of framing and sub-frames as a future work.

3 Dataset

We conduct our study on the dataset proposed by Roy et al. (2021). In this dataset, there are 1599 political tweets from US politicians that are annotated for moral foundations by Johnson and Goldwasser (2018). Roy et al. (2021) proposed Morality Frames and broke down the sentence level moral foundations into nuanced moral role dimensions that capture sentiment towards entities expressed in the text. The moral foundations and corresponding moral roles can be found in Table 1. Roy et al. (2021) annotated the dataset proposed by Johnson and Goldwasser (2018) for these moral sentiments towards entities.

In this paper, our goal is to study the identification of morality frames when only few-shot train-

Moral Foundations	Moral Roles
Care/Harm: Care for others, generosity, compassion, ability to feel pain of others, sensitivity to suffering of others, prohibiting actions that harm others.	Target of care/harm Entity causing harm Entity providing care
Fairness/Cheating: Fairness, justice, reciprocity, reciprocal altruism, rights, autonomy, equality, proportionality, prohibiting cheating.	Target of fairness/cheating Entity ensuring fairness Entity doing cheating
Loyalty/Betrayal: Group affiliation and solidarity, virtues of patriotism, self-sacrifice for the group, prohibiting betrayal of one's group.	Target of loyalty/betrayal Entity being loyal Entity doing betrayal
Authority/Subversion: Fulfilling social roles, submitting to authority, respect for social hierarchy/traditions, leadership, prohibiting rebellion against authority.	Justified authority Justified authority over Failing authority Failing authority over
Purity/Degradation: Associations with the sacred and holy, disgust, contamination, religious notions which guide how to live, prohibiting violating the sacred.	Target of purity/degradation Entity preserving purity Entity causing degradation

Table 1: Morality Frames: Moral foundations and their associated roles. (Adopted from (Roy et al., 2021)).

ing examples are available. To build this setup, we randomly sampled 10 tweets from each of the 5 moral foundations, and used it as training set. We use Large Language Models (LLMs) for in-context learning that are expensive and resource heavy even for inference only. So, we benchmark our approaches using a smaller test set containing randomly sampled 20 tweets per moral foundation. It resulted in 103 and 207 tweet-entity pairs in the training and the test set, respectively.

4 Task Definition

The identification of morality frame in a tweet involves the following two steps.

Identification of Moral Foundation: Given a tweet text t, the task is to identify the moral foundation expressed in the tweet.

Identification of Moral Roles of Entities: After identification of moral foundation, the second step is to identify the moral roles of entities in the tweet. We study this step in the following two settings.

- **Entities are pre-identified:** In this setting, the assumption is that the entities are already identified in the tweet text. The task is to assign moral roles to them. So, given a tweet t, an entity e mentioned in the tweet, and the moral foundation label of the tweet m, the task is to identify the moral role of e in t.
- **Entities are not pre-identified:** In this setting, a tweet t, and its corresponding moral foundation label m is known in prior. The task is to identify the entities mentioned in the tweet, and their corresponding moral roles.

Examples of the tasks can be found in Figure 1.

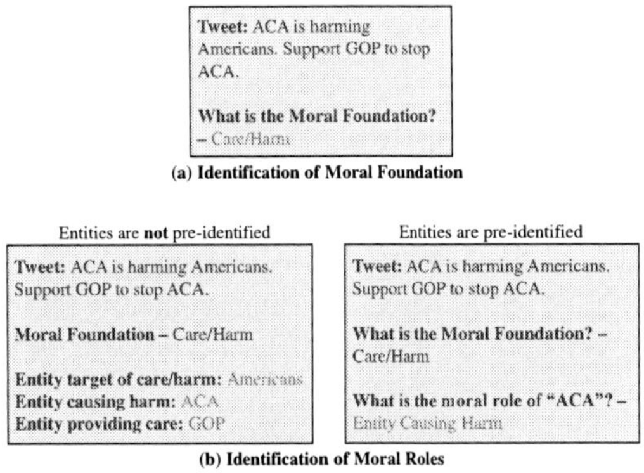

Figure 1: Morality frames identification task. Input for each step is colored in blue and expected outputs are colored in red.

5 Few-Shot Identification of Morality Frames using Large Language Models

5.1 In-Context Learning

In-context learning using pretrained LLMs has been shown effective in few-shot scenarios in previous studies for different NLP tasks (Brown et al., 2020; Wei et al., 2022; Reif et al., 2021). LLMs are pretrained on huge amount of web-crawl, books and Wikipedia text. Hence, they are expected to carry world-knowledge. As a result, they are able to perform many NLP tasks using only few-shot training examples without any further fine-tuning or gradient updates. In the in-context learning paradigm, the downstream task is framed as a text generation problem and the model is prompted to generate the next tokens (Min et al., 2021a). These tokens are mapped to desired output labels in classification tasks. In this work, we assume that only few-shot examples are given for the morality frames identification task. So, we apply in-context learning approach for this purpose to perform different steps of the task defined in Section 4. Note that we do not update LLM parameters in this process. The proposed in-context learning approaches are described in the subsequent sections.

5.2 Moral Foundation (MF) Identification

Following the previous works, we frame the task of moral foundation identification as a text generation problem where the model is prompted to generate the moral foundation label of a tweet. To this end, we experiment with two different types of prompting techniques.

MF identification in one pass: In this method, we provide the moral foundation definitions (from Table 1) in the beginning of the prompt as a guideline for the language model. Then, few-shot training examples and their associated labels are provided in the prompt. Finally, the test tweet is provided as the last example in the prompt and the model is expected to generate the moral foundation label of this tweet. The prompt template for this approach can be seen in Figure 2.

```
Moral Foundation Definitions:
CARE/HARM: <definition>
FAIRNESS/CHEATING: <definition>
LOYALTY/BETRAYAL: <definition>
AUTHORITY/SUBVERSION: <definition>
PURITY/DEGRADATION: <definition>

###
Tweet: <tweet_text>
Moral foundation expressed in the tweet: <gold_label>
###
Tweet: <tweet_text>
Moral foundation expressed in the tweet: <gold_label>
###
...
...
...
###
Tweet: <tweet_text>
Moral foundation expressed in the tweet: <predicted_label>
```

Figure 2: Prompt template for identification of moral foundation in one pass. The blue colored segment is input prompt and the red colored segment is the generated output by the LLMs. Example of this prompt template can be seen in Appendix A: Figure 7.

MF identification in one-vs-all manner: Identification of moral foundations in one-pass might be difficult for the language models. So, we propose one-vs-all prompting approach where the language model is prompted to predict if a certain moral foundation is present in the tweet. This step is repeated for each of the five moral foundations. The moral foundation predicted with the highest confidence is consolidated as the predicted label. To obtain the confidence score, we prompt the language model

```
Definition of moral foundation "CARE/HARM": <definition>

###
Tweet: <tweet_text>
Q. "The moral foundation expressed in the tweet is CARE/HARM." - True or False?
A. <gold_label>
###
Tweet: <tweet_text>
Q. "The moral foundation expressed in the tweet is CARE/HARM." - True or False?
A. <gold_label>
###
...
...
...
###
Tweet: <tweet_text>
Q. "The moral foundation expressed in the tweet is CARE/HARM." - True or False?
A. <predicted_label>
```

(a) Prompt template for one-vs-all MF identification in case of 'Care/Harm'.

```
Definition of the moral foundation "CARE/HARM": <definition>
Definition of the moral foundation "PURITY/DEGRADATION": <definition>

###
Tweet: <tweet_text>
The moral foundation expressed in the tweet is: <gold_label>
###
Tweet: <tweet_text>
The moral foundation expressed in the tweet is: <gold_label>
###
...
...
...
###
Tweet: <tweet_text>
The moral foundation expressed in the tweet is: <predicted_label>
```

(b) Prompt for tie-breaking between two MFs. For example, between 'Care/Harm' and 'Purity/Degradation'.

Figure 3: Prompt templates for moral foundation identification technique in one-vs-all manner. The blue colored segments are input prompts and the red colored segments are the generated output by the LLMs. Corresponding prompt example can be seen in Appendix A: Figure 8.

multiple times with different random seeds to generate multiple predictions for a single tweet. The final confidence score is the percentage of times a specific moral foundation is generated by the LLM. In case there is a tie between two moral foundation labels, we perform a second prompting step, where few-shot prompting enables to break the tie between moral foundations.[1] Prompt templates for these two steps can be seen in Figure 3.

5.3 Moral Role Identification of a Pre-identified Entity

Post prediction of the moral foundation label, the next step is to identify moral roles of entities as described in the Section 4. Given a test tweet, and a predicted moral foundation label for it, we prompt the LLMs to generate moral role of an entity in a tweet only from the associated moral roles to

[1]In case of tie among more than two moral foundations, we break that by randomly selecting one.

the predicted moral foundation. For example, if a tweet is identified to be having the moral foundation 'Care/Harm', we prompt the language model to predict the the moral role of an entity mentioned in the tweet from only three moral roles that are associated to 'Care/Harm', namely, 'Entity target of care/harm', 'Entity causing harm', 'Entity providing care'. We propose two prompting approaches for this task.

Moral role identification in one pass: We prompt the LLMs to directly identify moral role of a given entity from the corresponding moral roles in one pass using the prompt shown in Figure 4. Following the moral foundation classification prompt template, we provide the description of the moral roles in the template as guideline. We come up with the definitions based on intuition.

Definitions of moral roles:
Entity target of care/harm: <*definition*>
Entity providing care: <*definition*>
Entity causing harm: <*definition*>

{Example-1:
Tweet: <*tweet_text*>
Moral role of <*entity*> in the tweet is: <*gold_label*>
}
{Example-2:
Tweet: <*tweet_text*>
Moral role of <*entity*> in the tweet is: <*gold_label*>
}
...
...
...
{Example-k:
Tweet: <*tweet_text*>
Moral role of <*entity*> in the tweet is: <*predicted_label*>
}

Figure 4: Prompt template for identification of moral role in one pass in case of 'Care/Harm'. The blue colored segment is input prompt and the red colored segment is the generated output by the LLMs. Corresponding prompt example can be seen in Appendix A: Figure 9.

Moral role identification in two steps: In the morality frames, different moral foundation roles intuitively carry either positive or negative sentiment towards them. For example, "entity causing harm", "entity violating fairness", "entity doing cheating", "failing authority" and "entity doing degradation" are the roles carrying negative sentiment towards them. The rest of the entity roles carry positive sentiment towards them. With this intuition, we break down the task of moral role identification in two steps. In the first step, we prompt the LLMs to identify the sentiment towards entities in "positive" and "negative" dimensions only by using the prompt structure in Figure 5a. Now the entities discovered as having negative sentiment towards them directly maps to one of the five negative sentiments, each associated with only one of the moral foundations. Given the moral foundation is discovered in the previous step, we can readily map the entities with negative sentiments to one of the negative moral roles. Now, each moral foundation has two or more positive moral roles associated to them. To differentiate among them, we perform another prompting step where the LLMs are prompted to generate one of the positive moral roles for an entity in a tweet. The prompt template is shown in Figure 5b.

5.4 Identification of entities and corresponding moral roles jointly

In this approach, we propose a prompting method for the setting where the the entities are not pre-identified as described in Section 4. In this setting, the moral foundation is known for a tweet and the target entities in the tweets are not explicitly given. We create a prompt similar to a slot filling task where the LLMs have to fill the slots of moral roles with entities mentioned in the tweet. The prompt template is shown in Figure 6.

6 Experimental Evaluation

In this section first we discuss our experimental setting. Secondly, we discuss our proposed models' performance in morality frame identification.

6.1 Experimental Settings

Large Language Model: We use an open-source Large Language Model named GPT-J-6B (Wang and Komatsuzaki, 2021). This is 6B parameters decoder only language model. We use top-k (k=5) sampling with temperature (=0.5) (Holtzman et al., 2019) as a decoding method for the language model. Note that, we do not update the parameters of the model in the in-context learning steps. For each of the test data point, we run the model with 5 random seeds each generating 2 outputs, hence, yielding 10 predictions for each data point. We take the majority voting among these predictions to get the predicted label.

```
###
Tweet: <tweet_text>
Target entity in the tweet: <entity>
Polarity of sentiment towards the target entity: <gold_label>
###
Tweet: <tweet_text>
Target entity in the tweet: <entity>
Polarity of sentiment towards the target entity: <gold_label>
###
...
...
...
###
Tweet: <tweet_text>
Target entity in the tweet: <entity>
Polarity of sentiment towards the target entity: <predicted_label>
```

(a) Step-1: Prompt template for identification of positive/negative sentiment towards entities.

```
Definitions of moral roles:
Entity target of care/harm: <definition>
Entity providing care: <definition>

###
Tweet: <tweet_text>
Moral role of <entity> in the tweet is: <gold_label>
###
Tweet: <tweet_text>
Moral role of <entity> in the tweet is: <gold_label>
###
...
...
...
###
Tweet: <tweet_text>
Moral role of <entity> in the tweet is: <predicted_label>
```

(b) Step-2: Prompt template for differentiating among multiple positive moral roles in case of 'Care/Harm'.

Figure 5: Prompt templates for moral role identification by breaking the task in 2 steps. The blue colored segments are input prompts and the red colored segments are the generated output by the LLMs. Corresponding prompt examples can be seen in Appendix A: Fig. 10.

```
Definitions:
Entity target of care/harm: <definition>
Entity providing care: <definition>
Entity causing harm: <definition>

{Example-1:
Tweet: <tweet_text>
Entity target of care/harm: <gold_labeld_entity>
Entity providing care: <gold_labeld_entity>
Entity causing harm: <gold_labeld_entity>
}
...
...
{Example-k:
Tweet: <tweet_text>
Entity target of care/harm: <predicted_entity>
Entity providing care: <predicted_entity>
Entity causing harm: <predicted_entity>
}
```

Figure 6: Prompt template for identification of entity and corresponding moral roles jointly in case of 'Care/Harm'. The blue colored segment is input prompt and the red colored segment is the generated output by the LLMs. Corresponding prompt example can be seen in Appendix A: Figure 11.

Ablation study: We experiment with various numbers of training examples in the prompts. In this paper, we define number of shots or training examples k, as the number of examples used for training from each class related to a classification task. For moral foundation identification and moral roles identification of the pre-identified entities, we experiment with 0 to 5 shots. In the moral role identification method where entities are not pre-identified, we experiment with 0, 1, 3, 5, 7, 10 shots. Because of the limit in the number of tokens in the prompt we cannot experiment with more number of shots. In all of our prompting methods we provide the description of the expected labels as task instruction in the prompt. As a result, a zero-shot learning is feasible in our setting. We run all of the studies using the train and test set described in Section 3.

Baseline: We compare our models' performance with a few-shot RoBERTa-based (Liu et al., 2019) text classifier. For the identification of moral foundation in a tweet, we encode the tweet using RoBERTa where the embedding of the [CLS] token of the last layer is used as a representation of the text. This representation is used for moral foundation classification. For moral role identification of an entity in the tweet, we encode the tweet and the entity using two RoBERTa instances, and concatenate their representations to get a final representation. This concatenated representation is used for moral roles classification. Note that, the RoBERTa-based classifiers are trained with few-shot examples only as the prompting based methods. We run the RoBERTa-based classifiers 5 times using 5 random seeds and report the average result.

Implementation Infrastructure We ran all of the experiments on a 4 core Intel(R) Core(TM) i5-7400 CPU @ 3.00GHz machine with 64GB RAM and two NVIDIA GeForce GTX 1080 Ti 11GB GDDR5X GPUs. GPT-J-6B was mounted using two GPUs. We used PyTorch library for all of the implementations.

Models	Macro F1 score for various number of shots per class					
	0-shot	1-shot	2-shots	3-shots	4-shots	5-shots
One-Pass prompting for 5 classes	6.24	24.19	29.80	30.63	39.49	43.56
One-vs-all prompting	13.23	20.46	24.34	20.51	27.76	15.70
RoBERTa (Parameters frozen)	N/A	7.61 (1.9)	7.84 (2.3)	8.1 (2.9)	8.21 (3.1)	8.0 (2.6)
RoBERTa (Finetuned)	N/A	19.68 (7.3)	33.22 (9.6)	37.05 (5.8)	38.78 (5.9)	45.42 (6.6)

Table 2: Few-shot moral foundation identification results. Between the prompting-based methods, the one-pass prompting method is the best performing one. The one-pass prompting method outperforms parameters-frozen RoBERTa, but underperforms finetuned RoBERTa in few-shot training setup.

Morals	Prec.	Rec.	F1	Support
Care/Harm	31.82	70.00	43.75	20
Fairness/Cheating	66.67	10.00	17.39	20
Loyalty/Betrayal	31.43	55.00	40.00	20
Auth./Subversion	87.50	35.00	50.00	20
Purity/Degradation	100.0	50.00	66.67	20
Accuracy			44.00	100
Macro Average	63.48	44.00	43.56	100
Weighted Average	63.48	44.00	43.56	100

Table 3: Per class moral foundation classification results for one-pass prompting (using 5-shots per class).

6.2 Results

Moral Foundation Identification: In Table 2, we show the results for moral foundation identification using our two proposed methods and few-shot RoBERTa. It can be seen that as the number of shots increases the performance improves in almost all of the cases. We also found that performance with RoBERTa is pretty bad with no gradient updates. But fine-tuning RoBERTa with few-shot examples provide reasonable performance. We found that the one-vs-all prompting technique underperforms the one-pass prompting technique, except in the zero-shot setting. Our intuition is that the language model is able to learn better when more contrastive examples are given which is the case in the one-pass method. Per class classification results for one-pass prompting using 5-shot examples per class are shown in Table 3. However, the one-pass prompting technique outperforms the one-vs-all technique but underperforms few-shot RoBERTa with finetuning. It seems that without fine-tuning the subtle moral foundation identification is a difficult task for the LLMs.

Moral Role Identification for pre-identified entities: In moral role identification, the assumption is that the moral foundation for each tweet is pre-identified. But the performance of all the models for the moral foundation identification task are not up to the mark as shown in Table 2. So, in identification of moral roles we use the gold moral foundation labels instead of the predicted ones.

In Table 4, we present the results for moral role identification using our proposed two methods along with the RoBERTa-based baseline. We omitted the results using zero-shot prompting as we found out that in moral role generation, zero-shot prompting of the LLM generates a lot of open-ended labels rather than the fixed moral role labels. It becomes difficult to parse these generations and map them to a moral role label using an automatic method. So we leave zero-shot prompting for moral role identification as a future work.

It can be seen in Table 4 that both one-pass prompting and the two steps prompting methods outperform the RoBERTa baseline in moral role identification. It suggests that moral role identification is easier than moral foundation identification for LLMs. Note that, moral roles are micro structures of the morality frames and they are more focused towards entities and evident in text compared to subtle moral foundations. As a result it is easier for the LLMs to identify them.

The two-steps prompting technique for moral roles identification underperforms the one-pass prompting approach although the task is broken down in two easier tasks. We found that in the first step of the task the model identifies polarity of sentiment towards entities with more than 70% F1 score in the 4 shots and 5 shots settings. But it struggles in the second step where the model has to differentiate between two positive sentiments (e.g. 'Entity target of care/harm' vs 'Entity providing care') which is more difficult as the difference among positive sentiments is subtle. This finding is consistent with prior studies. For example, in previous work (Roy et al., 2021) it was found that deep relational learning based model also struggles to differentiate among multiple positive sentiments.

Moral Foundations	Models	Macro F1 score for various number of shots per class				
		1-shot	2-shots	3-shots	4-shots	5-shots
Care/Harm	One-Pass Prompting	48.21	58.61	74.37	70.98	68.41
	2-Steps Prompting	37.77	42.04	58.29	68.97	63.76
	RoBERTa (Finetuned)	31.67 (13.4)	35.79 (13.2)	35.35 (14.0)	30.64 (14.0)	43.83 (26.0)
Fairness/Cheating	One-Pass Prompting	42.92	71.86	75.95	82.26	74.65
	2-Steps Prompting	40.91	71.28	72.64	74.92	68.70
	RoBERTa (Finetuned)	26.89 (11.9)	46.16 (6.0)	43.06 (3.6)	35.61 (15.2)	42.95 (12.9)
Loyalty/Betrayal	One-Pass Prompting	35.56	36.40	35.24	45.10	41.27
	2-Steps Prompting	30.39	38.69	32.32	38.82	25.83
	RoBERTa (Finetuned)	21.29 (3.0)	28.39 (7.1)	24.14 (11.5)	37.73 (1.7)	36.57 (8.2)
Authority/Subversion	One-Pass Prompting	19.17	31.69	29.35	34.76	36.12
	2-Steps Prompting	21.85	31.69	30.67	31.47	29.56
	RoBERTa (Finetuned)	11.77 (0)	28.02 (11.6)	23.31 (11.3)	20.08 (10.5)	24.64 (6.0)
Purity/Degradation	One-Pass Prompting	41.28	46.91	66.67	69.04	61.84
	2-Steps Prompting	40.51	41.66	43.08	47.65	45.89
	RoBERTa (Finetuned)	31.59 (7.9)	40.15 (5.7)	30.80 (9.9)	42.25 (10.8)	56.57 (20.4)

Table 4: Few shot moral role identification performance comparison among models. The one-pass prompting method outperforms both 2-steps prompting method and finetuned RoBERTa in few-shot training setup.

In the one-pass prompting technique, contrastive positive and negative examples are given in the prompt. As a result it might be easier for the LLMs to resonate.

In moral role identification also the performance improves with the increase of number of shots for all of the models as shown in Table 4.

Identification of entities and corresponding moral roles jointly: In this setting, the model is expected to identify entities having the moral roles in a tweet. To evaluate the model's performance we measure in what percentage of time the predicted entity is matched with the actual entity[2] annotated by Roy et al. (2021) and in how many cases they are assigned to the correct entity role. We found out that the LLM hallucinates a lot when identifying entities and filling the entity role slots. Hallucination in LLMs is a common phenomena. When open ended text generation is expected but the language model generates some response that is not a part of the input text or not related to the input text, it is called hallucination (Ji et al., 2022). Note that we don't encounter the problem of hallucination when generating labels for moral foundation and moral roles as the labels were well-defined in the prompt. But in entity identification task the model has to identify entities from a given text span which is open ended. Hence, it resulted in a higher rate of hallucination.

[2]Entity matching procedure can be found in Appendix B

No. of Shots	% Correct Entity Identification	% Hallucination	% Correct Role Identification
1	43.80	21.69	33.97
3	48.28	11.54	41.09
5	48.68	9.58	43.71
7	49.91	7.68	45.27
10	51.39	5.95	46.88

Table 5: Correctness of joint identification of entity and corresponding moral roles using in-context learning. The LLM hallucinates from previous training examples in open-ended entity identification. The percentage of hallucination decreases and the percentage of correct entity and correct role identification increase with the increase of the number of shots in prompt.

However, The results for this task are shown in Table 5. We can see in the table that as we increase the number of training examples (shots) the % of correct entity and entity role identification improve although the performance is not up to the mark even with the highest number of shots (10). We also found out that % of hallucination decreases as the number of shots increases. This findings imply that joint identification of entity and entity role is a much difficult task for the LLMs but as we increase the number of shots the LLMs are able to understand the task better.

7 Summary and Future Works

In this paper, we apply few-shot in-context learning for identification of one of the psycholinguistic knowledge representation framework named Morality Frames. We proposed different prompting methods to perform the task. We found that in-context learning using a comparatively smaller language model (GPT-J-6B) does not perform well in identification of moral foundations that are very subtle. But it excels in moral roles identification of entities that are more evident in text. We believe there is a lot of scope for improvement, and this study will encourage the application of in-context learning in more Computational Social Science related tasks. Below we list a few future directions of this work.

- **Prompt selection:** Appropriate prompt selection based on the test data point has been successfully applied in in-context learning in different NLP tasks (Han et al., 2022). Implementation of a dynamic prompt selection technique in morality frame identification task may boost the performance.
- **Incorporation of context in prompt:** In complex concepts such as moral foundation (Haidt and Joseph, 2004; Haidt and Graham, 2007) and framing (Boydstun et al., 2014), to name a few, the social context and the speaker's demographics play an important role. Incorporating these information in prompts for LLMs can be an effective direction towards solving these problems.
- **Experiment with larger language models:** Larger language models such as GPT-3 (Brown et al., 2020) use more parameters and are trained on diverse data. As a result, they could be more successful in capturing nuanced social concepts, and result in better performance.
- **Experiment with long text:** Identification of complex concepts like framing and moral foundation have been studied in longer text (e.g. news articles) in previous works (Card et al., 2015; Fulgoni et al., 2016; Field et al., 2018; Roy and Goldwasser, 2020). How successful the pre-trained language models can be on these tasks in longer text such as, news articles, can be an interesting future work.

Acknowledgements

We are thankful to the anonymous reviewers for their insightful comments. This project was partially funded by NSF CAREER award IIS-2048001.

Limitations

The limitations of this paper are as follows.

- Previous study (Johnson and Goldwasser, 2018) has shown that a single tweet may contain multiple moral foundations. Multiple labels were not considered in this work. It may be the case that language models are successful on identifying only one of the moral foundations in such multi-label data points.
- Usage of large language models are expensive as they are resource-heavy. Due to that we could not run the prompt-based methods multiple times to perform a statistical significance test on the results. This is a limitation of our work.
- Due to resource-constraint and no availability of an open-source version we could not run our proposed prompt-based models with state-of-the-art larger language models, such as GPT-3. The insights and results reported in this paper may have been different if a larger language model was used.
- LLMs are pretrained on a huge amount of human generated text. As a result, they may inherently contain many human biases (Brown et al., 2020; Blodgett et al., 2020). We did not consider any bias that can be incorporated by the LLMs in the morality frames identification task.

Ethics Statement

In this paper, we do not propose any new dataset rather we only experiment with existing datasets which are, to the best of our knowledge, adequately cited. We provided all experimental details of our approaches and we believe the results reported in this paper are reproducible. Any result or tweet text presented in this paper are either results of a machine learning model or taken from an existing dataset. They don't represent the authors' or the funding agencies' views on this topic. As described in the limitations sections, inherent bias in the large language models are not taken into account in this paper while experimenting. So, we suggest not to deploy the proposed algorithms in a real life system without further investigation on bias and fairness.

References

Su Lin Blodgett, Solon Barocas, Hal Daumé III, and Hanna Wallach. 2020. Language (technology) is power: A critical survey of" bias" in nlp. *arXiv preprint arXiv:2005.14050.*

Amber Boydstun, Dallas Card, Justin H. Gross, Philip Resnik, and Noah A. Smith. 2014. Tracking the development of media frames within and across policy issues.

Tom Brown, Benjamin Mann, Nick Ryder, Melanie Subbiah, Jared D Kaplan, Prafulla Dhariwal, Arvind Neelakantan, Pranav Shyam, Girish Sastry, Amanda Askell, et al. 2020. Language models are few-shot learners. *Advances in neural information processing systems*, 33:1877–1901.

Dallas Card, Amber E. Boydstun, Justin H. Gross, Philip Resnik, and Noah A. Smith. 2015. The media frames corpus: Annotations of frames across issues. In *Proceedings of ACL.*

Anjalie Field, Doron Kliger, Shuly Wintner, Jennifer Pan, Dan Jurafsky, and Yulia Tsvetkov. 2018. Framing and agenda-setting in russian news: a computational analysis of intricate political strategies. *arXiv preprint arXiv:1808.09386.*

Dean Fulgoni, Jordan Carpenter, Lyle Ungar, and Daniel Preoţiuc-Pietro. 2016. An empirical exploration of moral foundations theory in partisan news sources. In *Proceedings of the Tenth International Conference on Language Resources and Evaluation (LREC'16)*, pages 3730–3736, Portorož, Slovenia. European Language Resources Association (ELRA).

Tianyu Gao, Adam Fisch, and Danqi Chen. 2020. Making pre-trained language models better few-shot learners. *arXiv preprint arXiv:2012.15723.*

Dan Goldwasser and Dan Roth. 2014. Learning from natural instructions. *Machine learning*, 94(2):205–232.

Jonathan Haidt and Jesse Graham. 2007. When morality opposes justice: Conservatives have moral intuitions that liberals may not recognize. *Social Justice Research*, 20(1):98–116.

Jonathan Haidt and Craig Joseph. 2004. Intuitive ethics: How innately prepared intuitions generate culturally variable virtues. *Daedalus*, 133(4):55–66.

Seungju Han, Beomsu Kim, Jin Yong Yoo, Seokjun Seo, Sangbum Kim, Enkhbayar Erdenee, and Buru Chang. 2022. Meet your favorite character: Open-domain chatbot mimicking fictional characters with only a few utterances. *arXiv preprint arXiv:2204.10825.*

Ari Holtzman, Jan Buys, Li Du, Maxwell Forbes, and Yejin Choi. 2019. The curious case of neural text degeneration. *arXiv preprint arXiv:1904.09751.*

Ziwei Ji, Nayeon Lee, Rita Frieske, Tiezheng Yu, Dan Su, Yan Xu, Etsuko Ishii, Yejin Bang, Andrea Madotto, and Pascale Fung. 2022. Survey of hallucination in natural language generation. *arXiv preprint arXiv:2202.03629.*

Kristen Johnson and Dan Goldwasser. 2018. Classification of moral foundations in microblog political discourse. In *Proceedings of the 56th annual meeting of the association for computational linguistics (volume 1: long papers)*, pages 720–730.

Mike Lewis, Yinhan Liu, Naman Goyal, Marjan Ghazvininejad, Abdelrahman Mohamed, Omer Levy, Ves Stoyanov, and Luke Zettlemoyer. 2019. Bart: Denoising sequence-to-sequence pre-training for natural language generation, translation, and comprehension. *arXiv preprint arXiv:1910.13461.*

Yinhan Liu, Myle Ott, Naman Goyal, Jingfei Du, Mandar Joshi, Danqi Chen, Omer Levy, Mike Lewis, Luke Zettlemoyer, and Veselin Stoyanov. 2019. Roberta: A robustly optimized bert pretraining approach. *arXiv preprint arXiv:1907.11692.*

Bonan Min, Hayley Ross, Elior Sulem, Amir Pouran Ben Veyseh, Thien Huu Nguyen, Oscar Sainz, Eneko Agirre, Ilana Heinz, and Dan Roth. 2021a. Recent advances in natural language processing via large pre-trained language models: A survey. *arXiv preprint arXiv:2111.01243.*

Sewon Min, Mike Lewis, Hannaneh Hajishirzi, and Luke Zettlemoyer. 2021b. Noisy channel language model prompting for few-shot text classification. *arXiv preprint arXiv:2108.04106.*

Sewon Min, Mike Lewis, Luke Zettlemoyer, and Hannaneh Hajishirzi. 2021c. Metaicl: Learning to learn in context. *arXiv preprint arXiv:2110.15943.*

Swaroop Mishra, Daniel Khashabi, Chitta Baral, and Hannaneh Hajishirzi. 2021. Cross-task generalization via natural language crowdsourcing instructions. *arXiv preprint arXiv:2104.08773.*

Maria Leonor Pacheco and Dan Goldwasser. 2021. Modeling content and context with deep relational learning. *Transactions of the Association for Computational Linguistics*, 9:100–119.

Maria Leonor Pacheco, Tunazzina Islam, Monal Mahajan, Andrey Shor, Ming Yin, Lyle Ungar, and Dan Goldwasser. 2022. A holistic framework for analyzing the COVID-19 vaccine debate. In *Proceedings of the 2022 Conference of the North American Chapter of the Association for Computational Linguistics: Human Language Technologies*, pages 5821–5839, Seattle, United States. Association for Computational Linguistics.

Emily Reif, Daphne Ippolito, Ann Yuan, Andy Coenen, Chris Callison-Burch, and Jason Wei. 2021. A recipe for arbitrary text style transfer with large language models. *arXiv preprint arXiv:2109.03910.*

Shamik Roy and Dan Goldwasser. 2020. Weakly supervised learning of nuanced frames for analyzing polarization in news media. In *Proceedings of the 2020 Conference on Empirical Methods in Natural Language Processing (EMNLP)*, pages 7698–7716.

Shamik Roy and Dan Goldwasser. 2021. Analysis of nuanced stances and sentiment towards entities of us politicians through the lens of moral foundation theory. In *Proceedings of the ninth international workshop on natural language processing for social media*, pages 1–13.

Shamik Roy, María Leonor Pacheco, and Dan Goldwasser. 2021. Identifying morality frames in political tweets using relational learning. In *Proceedings of the 2021 Conference on Empirical Methods in Natural Language Processing*, pages 9939–9958.

Victor Sanh, Albert Webson, Colin Raffel, Stephen H Bach, Lintang Sutawika, Zaid Alyafeai, Antoine Chaffin, Arnaud Stiegler, Teven Le Scao, Arun Raja, et al. 2021. Multitask prompted training enables zero-shot task generalization. *arXiv preprint arXiv:2110.08207*.

Timo Schick and Hinrich Schütze. 2020. Exploiting cloze questions for few shot text classification and natural language inference. *arXiv preprint arXiv:2001.07676*.

Ben Wang and Aran Komatsuzaki. 2021. GPT-J-6B: A 6 Billion Parameter Autoregressive Language Model. `https://github.com/kingoflolz/mesh-transformer-jax`.

Jason Wei, Maarten Bosma, Vincent Y Zhao, Kelvin Guu, Adams Wei Yu, Brian Lester, Nan Du, Andrew M Dai, and Quoc V Le. 2021. Finetuned language models are zero-shot learners. *arXiv preprint arXiv:2109.01652*.

Jason Wei, Xuezhi Wang, Dale Schuurmans, Maarten Bosma, Ed Chi, Quoc Le, and Denny Zhou. 2022. Chain of thought prompting elicits reasoning in large language models. *arXiv preprint arXiv:2201.11903*.

Zihao Zhao, Eric Wallace, Shi Feng, Dan Klein, and Sameer Singh. 2021. Calibrate before use: Improving few-shot performance of language models. In *International Conference on Machine Learning*, pages 12697–12706. PMLR.

A Prompt Examples

The example of prompts for various in-context learning steps of our approach are shown in Figures 7, 8, 9, 10, 11.

B Entity Matching Procedure

After obtaining the predicted entity labels from LLM, we first discard the entity labels that are not contained in the tweet text as these are irrelevant. Then, we check if any of the predicted entities are exactly matching the gold labels. In cases where it is not an exact match, we obtain a string-match score between the predicted entity and each of the gold label. If this score is beyond a certain threshold (set to 0.6) for a particular gold label, we map the predicted entity to that gold label. If the predicted entity is not exactly matching the gold label, and the score is lower than the threshold, then we assign 'N/A' label to that predicted entity.

Moral Foundation Definitions:

CARE/HARM: Care for others, generosity, compassion, ability to feel pain of others, sensitivity to suffering of others, prohibiting actions that harm others.

FAIRNESS/CHEATING: Demand for Fairness, rights, equality, justice, reciprocity, reciprocal altruism, autonomy, proportionality and violation of these. Also, prohibiting cheating.

LOYALTY/BETRAYAL: Group affiliation and solidarity, virtues of patriotism, self-sacrifice for the group, prohibiting betrayal of one's group.

AUTHORITY/SUBVERSION: Fulfilling social roles, submitting to authority, respect for social hierarchy/traditions, leadership, prohibiting rebellion against authority.

PURITY/DEGRADATION: Associations with the sacred and holy, disgust, contamination, religious notions which guide how to live, prohibiting violating the sacred.

###

Tweet: RT @LatinoVoices: Joe Biden slams Donald Trump for selling sick message on immigration http://t.co/OOTpD9zmh5

Moral foundation expressed in the tweet: PURITY/DEGRADATION

###

Tweet: Today's decision by #SCOTUSs is huge victory for justice and equality for the #LGBT community and our nation

Moral foundation expressed in the tweet: FAIRNESS/CHEATING

###

Tweet: We can and must reduce #GunViolence by closing gaps in our gun laws. You can help: get engaged and be part of the conversation.

Moral foundation expressed in the tweet: CARE/HARM

###

Tweet: Sit or stand but we cannot be silent for victims of gun violence - we need to take action. #NoBillNoBreak

Moral foundation expressed in the tweet: LOYALTY/BETRAYAL

###

Tweet: At @ChiUrbanLeague today calling for Congressional action on gun violence. It's past time to act. #Enough

Moral foundation expressed in the tweet: AUTHORITY/SUBVERSION

###

Tweet: More on my efforts to improve home health care for seniors in Oregon and across the country -- #KeepThePromise

Moral foundation expressed in the tweet: CARE/HARM

Figure 7: Prompt example for identification of moral foundation in one pass. The blue colored segment is input prompt and the red colored segment is the generated output by the LLMs.

Definition of the moral foundation "CARE/HARM": Care for others, generosity, compassion, ability to feel pain of others, sensitivity to suffering of others, prohibiting actions that harm others.

###

Tweet: #SCOTUSMarriage decision does not and cannot change the firmly held faith of most Mississippians. #religiousfreedom

Q. "The moral foundation expressed in the tweet is CARE/HARM." - True or False?

A. False

###

Tweet: Recent actions in Indiana and Arkansas made clear that Congress must act to protect #LGBT Americans from discrimination

Q. "The moral foundation expressed in the tweet is CARE/HARM." - True or False?

A. True

###

Tweet: #11MillionAndCounting are signed up for private health coverage. There is no doubt that the #ACA is working.

Q. "The moral foundation expressed in the tweet is CARE/HARM." - True or False?

A. True

(a) Prompt example for one-vs-all MF identification in case of 'Care/Harm'.

Definition of the moral foundation "CARE/HARM": Care for others, generosity, compassion, ability to feel pain of others, sensitivity to suffering of others, prohibiting actions that harm others.

Definition of the moral foundation "PURITY/DEGRADATION": Associations with the sacred and holy, disgust, contamination, religious notions which guide how to live, prohibiting violating the sacred.

###

Tweet: Donald Trump's comments on immigration are distasteful and disgusting. I'm disappointed many Republicans have kept their mouths shut on it.

The moral foundation expressed in the tweet is: PURITY/DEGRADATION

###

Tweet: Finance committee passed 2 of my bills today that would improve Medicare and Medicaid and help put patients first.

The moral foundation expressed in the tweet is: CARE/HARM

###

Tweet: RT @RepVeasey: Should suspects on the FBI's #terrorist watch list be able to buy guns? #NoFlyNoBuy

The moral foundation expressed in the tweet is: CARE/HARM

(b) Prompt example for tie-breaking between two MFs. For example, between 'Care/Harm' and 'Purity/Degradation'.

Figure 8: Prompt examples for moral foundation identification technique in one-vs-all manner. The blue colored segments are input prompts and the red colored segments are the generated output by the LLMs.

Definitions of moral roles:
Entity target of care/harm: Entity that is harmed by someone/something or entity someone/something is providing/offering careto.
Entity providing care: Entity that is providing or offering care or expressing the need for care for someone/something.
Entity causing harm: Entity that is harming/hurting or doing something bad to someone/something.

{**Example-1:**
Tweet: Finance committee passed 2 of my bills today that would improve Medicare and Medicaid and help put patients first.
Moral role of "patients" in the tweet is: Entity target of care/harm
}
{**Example-2:**
Tweet: Tonight I voted to end the terror gap and strengthen background checks. @SenateGOP voted to do nothing to combat #gunviolence. #enough
Moral role of "#gunviolence." in the tweet is: Entity causing harm
}
{**Example-3:**
Tweet: Finance committee passed 2 of my bills today that would improve Medicare and Medicaid and help put patients first.
Moral role of "bills" in the tweet is: Entity providing care
}
{**Example-4:**
Tweet: #11MillionAndCounting are signed up for private health coverage. There is no doubt that the #ACA is working.
Moral role of "#ACA" in the tweet is: Entity providing care
}

Figure 9: Prompt example for identification of moral role in one pass in case of 'Care/Harm'. The blue colored segment is input prompt and the red colored segment is the generated output by the LLMs.

###
Tweet: RT @HouseGOP:.@TomPriceMD sums up health care reform in these four words: Accessibilty. Affordability. Quality. Choices. #BetterWay
Target entity in the tweet: .@TomPriceMD
Polarity of sentiment towards the target entity: positive
###
Tweet: We can and must reduce #GunViolence by closing gaps in our gun laws. You can help: get engaged and be part of the conversation. #WearingOrange
Target entity in the tweet: #GunViolence
Polarity of sentiment towards the target entity: negative
###
Tweet: #11MillionAndCounting are signed up for private health coverage. There is no doubt that the #ACA is working.
Target entity in the tweet: #ACA
Polarity of sentiment towards the target entity: positive

(a) Step-1: Prompt example for identification of positive/negative sentiment towards entities.

Definitions of moral roles:
Entity target of care/harm: Entity that is harmed by someone/something or entity someone/something is providing/offering care to.
Entity providing care: Entity that is providing or offering care or expressing the need for care for someone/something.

###
Tweet: RT @RepDelBene: These subpoenas are designed to intimidate risking safety and privacy of researchers and medical students. #StopTheSham
Moral role of "of researchers and medical students." in the tweet is: Entity target of care/harm
###
Tweet: Finance committee passed 2 of my bills today that would improve Medicare and Medicaid and help put patients first.
Moral role of "bills" in the tweet is: Entity providing care
###
Tweet: #11MillionAndCounting are signed up for private health coverage. There is no doubt that the #ACA is working.
Moral role of "#ACA" in the tweet is: Entity providing care

(b) Step-2: Prompt example for differentiating among multiple positive moral roles in case of 'Care/Harm'.

Figure 10: Prompt examples for moral role identification by breaking it in two steps. The blue colored segments are input prompts and the red colored segments are the generated output by the LLMs.

Definitions:
Entity target of care/harm: Entity that is harmed by someone/something or entity someone/something is providing/offering careto.
Entity providing care: Entity that is providing or offering care or expressing the need for care for someone/something.
Entity causing harm: Entity that is harming/hurting or doing something bad to someone/something.

{**Example-1:**
Tweet: Recent actions in Indiana and Arkansas made clear that Congress must act to protect #LGBT Americans from discrimination
Entity target of care/harm: #LGBT Americans
Entity providing care: Congress
Entity causing harm: N/A
}
{**Example-2:**
Tweet: Thanks to the #ACA Doughnut Hole fix thousands of #RI #seniors have saved over $60M since 2010
Entity target of care/harm: #RI #seniors
Entity providing care: #ACA
Entity causing harm: N/A
}

Figure 11: Prompt example for identification of entity and corresponding moral roles jointly in case of 'Care/Harm'. The blue colored segment is input prompt and the red colored segment is the generated output by the LLMs.

Utilizing Weak Supervision to Create S3D: A Sarcasm Annotated Dataset

Jordan Painter[1], **Helen Treharne**[1], **and Diptesh Kanojia**[1,2]
[1]Department of Computer Science, University of Surrey
[2]Surrey Institute for People-Centred AI, University of Surrey
United Kingdom
jp01166,h.treharne,d.kanojia@surrey.ac.uk

Abstract

Sarcasm is prevalent in all corners of social media, posing many challenges within Natural Language Processing (NLP), particularly for sentiment analysis. Sarcasm detection remains a largely unsolved problem in many NLP tasks due to its contradictory and typically derogatory nature as a figurative language construct. With recent strides in NLP, many pre-trained language models exist that have been trained on data from specific social media platforms, *i.e.,* Twitter. In this paper, we evaluate the efficacy of multiple sarcasm detection datasets using machine and deep learning models. We create two new datasets - a manually annotated gold standard Sarcasm Annotated Dataset (SAD) and a Silver-Standard Sarcasm-annotated Dataset (S3D). Using a combination of existing sarcasm datasets with SAD, we train a sarcasm detection model over a social-media domain pre-trained language model, BERTweet, which yields an F1-score of 78.29%. Using an Ensemble model with an underlying majority technique, we further label S3D to produce a weakly supervised dataset containing over 100, 000 tweets. We publicly release all the code, our manually annotated and weakly supervised datasets, and fine-tuned models for further research.

1 Introduction

Figurative language, such as the use of metaphors, irony and sarcasm, is ubiquitous in human communication, from ancient religious texts to social media micro texts. The detection of sarcasm in human communication is a challenging task where the goal is to identify sarcastic utterances from the data provided. There is no one definitive definition of sarcasm due to its nature as a language construct relying on factors such as domain and context, even regional differences (Dress et al., 2008), but a widely accepted definition is "a form of verbal irony that is intended to express contempt or ridicule" (Joshi et al., 2017).

Sarcasm has a diminishing effect on sentiment analysis due to sarcastic text often having the opposite implied meaning to a literal word-for-word meaning of the text (Pang and Lee, 2008). For example, *"I just love it when my flight gets delayed for 4 hours"*, is clearly sarcastic, as using the word "love" to express feelings on something rather inconvenient would be unusual outside of a sarcastic context. Such challenges demonstrate the importance of recognising sarcasm in social media (Farhadloo and Rolland, 2016), as recognising the potential for a given text utterance to be sarcastic can bridge the gap in human-machine communication. The NLP research community has investigated the detection of sarcasm using various machine/deep learning approaches (Potamias et al., 2019; Ghosh and Veale, 2016; Reyes and Rosso, 2011; Wankhade et al., 2022). Several datasets exist for the task of sarcasm detection using text (Riloff et al., 2013; Ptácek et al., 2014; Van Hee et al., 2018; Khodak et al., 2017) as well as multimodal datasets (Castro et al., 2019; Ray et al., 2022), which support the extraction of features from video and speech. Transformer (Vaswani et al., 2017) based language models have shown to perform very well for classification tasks in various NLP sub-areas, and a number of BERT (Devlin et al., 2018a) based language models have been released which can help perform this NLP task.

In this paper, we attempt to collate these efforts for the task of sarcasm detection. We restrict our focus to the detection of sarcasm on a social media platform, *i.e.,* Twitter. Initially, we curated our dataset (SAD) by crawling for tweets and labelling them with the help of two annotators. We extensively evaluate machine and deep learning-based approaches on various existing datasets and our dataset. We apply standard pre-processing and combine all the datasets to evaluate several classification approaches. Using an Ensemble of the best language models trained over the largest datasets, we further label 100K tweets to create Silver-Standard Sarcasm-annotated Dataset (S3D). The key contributions of our work are as follows: 1) A sarcasm-annotated dataset (SAD) of social

Proceedings of the Fifth Workshop on Natural Language Processing and Computational Social Science (NLP+CSS), pages 197 - 206
November 7, 2022

media microblogs, 2) Performance evaluation of various existing language models for the binary classification task of sarcasm detection, 3) Curation and weak-supervision-based labelling for a silver-standard sarcasm-annotated dataset (S3D), 4) Release of code, data, and models created on Github, and HuggingFace platforms, publicly, for the research community[1].

This paper is organised as follows. Section 2 briefly describes previous approaches to sarcasm detection. Section 3 describes our chosen datasets and their sources. Section 4 explains the methodology behind the proposed experiments, summarising the approaches for our machine learning and deep learning experiments. Section 5 discusses choices made for running our experiments, Section 6 discusses the results of these experiments in detail, along with the approach used to obtain a new weakly supervised dataset.

2 Related Work

Transformer-based approaches have increased in prevalence within NLP and also within sarcasm detection literature. This is most notably due to their ability to accurately pick up semantic and syntactic relationships within a piece of text. Joshi et al. (2017) discuss various approaches to the task of sarcasm detection including rule-based and machine learning-based, and also discusses sarcasm from the linguistics perspective. Shangipour ataei et al. (2020) dicusses several approaches to perform sarcasm detection. These include a BERT (Devlin et al., 2018b) model with no concatenated layers, BERT encodings with a Logisitic Regression model, and other language models such as IAN (Ma et al., 2017) which are trained and evaluated on a Twitter-based sarcasm dataset. In these experiments, the BERT language model with no added layers performs the best on the dataset, achieving an F1-score of 73.4. Some existing literature investigates methods for performing sarcasm detection in Arabic (Abu Farha and Magdy, 2021), where a multitude of Transformers are used, including mBERT, XLM-RoBERTa (Conneau et al., 2020) and language-specific models like MARBERT (Abdul-Mageed et al., 2021). The best model in this research achieves an F1-score of 58.4 in a low-resource scenario. In Potamias et al. (2019), an RCNN-RoBERTa methodology was proposed, where a RoBERTa transformer was utilized with BiLSTM to improve upon F1-scores from state-of-the-art neural network classifiers on the dataset released with the SemEval 2018 Shared Task 3 (Van Hee et al., 2018). This paper also reports that the RCVV-RoBERTa approach achieved an F1-score of 90.0 on the Riloff dataset (Riloff et al., 2013). Ghosh and Veale (2016) demonstrate a variety of results on a Twitter dataset, training a collection of architectures involving Convolution Neural Network (CNN) and Long-Short Term Memory (LSTM) to achieve an impressive F1-score of 92.1 with their best configuration. An Ensemble approach was demonstrated in Goel et al. (2022) where a weighted average Ensemble of a CNN, an LSTM and a Gated Recurrent Unit (GRU) based architectures are trained with GloVe (Pennington et al., 2014) word embeddings in order to identify sarcasm, showing that the Ensemble outperformed others by up to 8% on SARC (Khodak et al., 2017), a Reddit comments dataset.

Machine learning approaches have decreased in popularity due to the improvements shown by Transformers-based architectures in recent developments. Earlier approaches to sarcasm detection include Reyes and Rosso (2011) and Barbieri et al. (2014) that used a Naive Bayes and Decision Tree model, respectively, in order to identify sarcasm where both achieve the best F1-scores over 70 on their chosen datasets.

To curate sarcasm-annotated datasets, one can perform manual annotation, which involves a significant cost in terms of time and money. Moreover, manual annotations for subjective linguistic constructs like sarcasm are questionable unless multiple annotators label the data, and an almost perfect inter-annotator agreement can be seen within the labelling. An example of this approach is the creation of the Riloff dataset (Riloff et al., 2013). On the other hand, sarcasm research has also utilised 'self-annotated tags' from social media forums, such as '#sarcasm' from tweets and '/s' in Reddit comments. Such data collection methods can be automated, and a large amount of data can easily be collected. However, the quality of such datasets in terms of label accuracy can be questioned. Self-annotation was used in the creation of the Ptacek dataset (Ptáček et al., 2014) from English tweets, and the creation of the SARC dataset (Khodak et al., 2017) from Reddit comments. However, we follow a hybrid approach as we collect SAD using '#sarcasm' from Twitter and then manually label it.

[1]https://github.com/surrey-nlp/S3D

A limitation of publicly available datasets based on tweet IDs, *e.g.,* Riloff et al. (2013) is that the tweet data retrieval based on the IDs can diminish over time. If a significant number of tweets are deleted, then it would not be possible to reproduce the results on the original dataset. In *e.g.,* Riloff et al. (2013), the number of tweets, at the time of writing the paper, that can be retrieved related to the IDs in the dataset is 710 compared to the original 3000 data instances. The contribution of our weak supervision-based approach is to help produce labelled data, the benefit of which could be to augment existing datasets that have diminished over time with automatically labelled data or also to create new silver standard datasets.

3 Datasets

We test our proposed approach for sarcasm detection on a total of six datasets, summarised in Table 1. Four of these data sets are benchmark datasets retrieved from either Twitter or Reddit summarised below: **SARC:** The only benchmark Reddit dataset we use is the SARC dataset (Khodak et al., 2017), a vast corpus of self annotated comments that were collected taking advantage of the '/s' tag that Reddit users can insert at the end of a comment to denote sarcasm. **Ptacek:** In Ptácek et al. (2014) an English and Czech sarcasm dataset was released to demonstrate the applicability a machine learning approach for sarcasm detection. For our proposed experiments the English dataset was used, which was curated collecting self-annotated tweets containing the #sarcasm hashtag. **SemEval2018:** We use the SemEval 2018 Task 3 dataset, which is a manually annotated Twitter dataset that was released for the SemEval 2018 Irony Detection in English Tweets shared task (Van Hee et al., 2018). **Riloff:** We use the dataset released by Riloff et al. (2013), which was manually annotated for sarcasm in order to train a bootstrapping algorithm on positive sentiment phrases and negative situation phrases from sarcastic tweets.

3.1 Our Dataset (SAD)

The first new dataset we introduce is the SAD dataset, a collection of scraped tweets containing a total of 2,340 data points, 1,170 of which are initially self-annotated for sarcasm through selecting tweets that contained the #sarcasm hashtag.

The TWINT[2] library was used to search for tweets that contained a #sarcasm hashtag, which was stored along with other relevant data points, including the respective tweet ID and username associated with the said tweet. Within the dataset, we ensured that there was one sarcastic and one non-sarcastic tweet for each unique username. We used TWINT to scrape and identify a second tweet for each user name to achieve this.

This resulted in several tweets, which were manually labelled by two annotators to ensure label accuracy and the presence of sarcasm; while ensuring that the tweet is not just a list of hashtags attached to a link to an image or website - a common spamming method on Twitter. To assign the final class label on disputed data instances, we requested a third annotator to go through the tweet and assign a class label (without looking at any of the previous annotations). We obtain an inter-annotator agreement score of 0.83 (Cohens' Kappa) where the *p-value* was < 0.05 which signifies almost perfect agreement. We also compared the manually labelled sarcastic tweets with the self-annotations in the same tweets, and 98% matches were observed.

3.2 Combined Dataset

The second dataset is a new 'Combined' dataset. This collates the four benchmark datasets and the new SAD dataset. This resulted in a corpus of 1,022,546 entries of labelled text, both taken from Reddit and Twitter, where an approximate split of 50/50 sarcastic to non-sarcastic text was achieved. We hypothesise that *various domains of sarcastic text present in multiple datasets should help a computational model generalise better and learn to identify sarcastic instances.* We perform similar experiments on this dataset to generate sarcasm detection models and evaluate over its test set.

3.3 Dataset Statistics and Validation

In Table 1, there is a clear difference between the size of each of the datasets. Most noticeably, the SARC dataset has over 1,000,000 entries, in comparison to the Riloff dataset, which has less than 1,000. Most of the datasets are balanced to an approximate 50% split for sarcastic and non-sarcastic text alike.

In the case of the Riloff and Ptacek datasets, both available versions online only contained the tweet IDs and their respective labels, meaning they were

[2]TWINT website: https://github.com/twintproject/twint

Dataset	Total	Training	Validation	Testing	Sarcastic	Non-Sarcastic
SARC	1,010,773	707,541	151,616	151,616	505,368	505,405
Ptacek	4,906	3,434	736	736	2,781	2,125
SemEval	3,817	2,671	573	573	1,901	1,916
Riloff	710	497	106	107	160	550
SAD (Our Dataset)	2,340	1,638	351	351	1,170	1,170
Combined	1,022,546	715,782	153,382	153,382	511,380	511,166

Table 1: Table demonstrating the Train/Valid/Test and Sarcastic/Non-sarcastic splits of the chosen datasets

collected by using Tweepy, the Python library used for accessing Twitter's API. This, unfortunately, meant that out of the 3,000 tweets available in the original Riloff dataset, only 710 were able to be retrieved, as when a user deletes their account or a specific tweet, it can no longer be retrieved.

3.4 Preprocessing

For the pre-processing of the chosen datasets, all were first checked through to delete null values that were in place of comments. This was followed by all text being transformed to lowercase. Every data entry was then checked for the presence of a #sarcasm hashtag, which we would then remove. Datasets such as the Ptacek and SAD datasets that use self-annotation to find sarcastic tweets would have this hashtag in every sarcastic entry. Therefore, they needed to be removed to ensure none of our models would make predictions based on the presence of this hashtag alone. Every username present in the Twitter datasets was replaced with '@user' to reduce unnecessary noise from a large number of unique usernames. As a final measure, all URLs and remaining punctuation were also removed from each comment to reduce noise further.

3.5 Evaluation Metrics

The primary evaluation metric of the proposed experiments is the F1-score of the sarcastic. This metric is necessary over binary accuracy due to the typical imbalanced nature of sarcasm detection datasets. Both the precision and recall scores of the sarcastic class are also recorded within Section 6.

4 Methodology

For our machine learning experiments we use DT (Laurent and Rivest, 1976) and LR (Cox, 1958) models. Our approaches to vectorising text for feature extraction utilise Word2Vec (Mikolov et al., 2013) and GloVe (Pennington et al., 2014). Word2Vec is a model architecture for computing vector representations of words from text, as is GloVe, which has an additional focus on Latent Semantic Analysis.

For our deep learning based experiments, a total of five pre-trained language models were used: BERT (Devlin et al., 2018a), RoBERTa$_{base}$ & RoBERTa$_{large}$ (Liu et al., 2019), Twitter-RoBERTa (Barbieri et al., 2020) and BERTweet (Nguyen et al., 2020).

BERT was introduced as a state-of-the-art transformer that improved results on multiple benchmarked NLP tasks. The language model was demonstrated as being able to be fine-tuned to create models for a wide range of tasks including question inference and next sentence prediction. **RoBERTa** was built on BERT through modifying key hyper-parameters and removing the next-sentence-prediction pre-training objective, on top of training with much larger batches and learning rates. The RoBERTa$_{large}$ configuration follows the same architecture but contains more hidden units and twice the number of encoder layers. **Twitter-RoBERTa** was introduced as RoB-RT by Barbieri et al. (2020) and is a RoBERTa$_{base}$ model that was trained on a total of 60M tweets, consisting of 584 million individual tokens. **BERTweet** has the same architecture of BERT-base and is trained on an 80GB corpus of 850M English tweets.

Each of these models was fine-tuned for the purpose of sarcasm detection. The fine-tuning process comprises adding a dropout layer on top of the pre-trained model, followed by a fully connected layer which was then fed into a final layer using a *softmax* activation function for classification.

5 Experiment Setup

As discussed in Section 4, the experiments have been split into the two categories of machine

	Word2Vec+LR			Word2Vec+DT			GloVe+LR			GloVe+DT		
	P	R	F1	P	R	F1	P	R	F1	P	R	F1
SARC	62.93	61.06	**61.98**	57.59	55.57	56.56	62.06	56.56	58.63	56.69	55.34	56.02
Ptacek	72.31	71.80	72.06	64.43	61.37	62.86	75.96	74.88	**75.41**	66.58	62.32	64.38
SemEval	63.57	59.79	**61.62**	53.71	53.14	53.43	60.47	54.54	57.35	53.28	53.84	53.56
Riloff	100	03.57	06.89	17.39	14.28	15.68	85.71	21.42	34.28	39.13	32.14	**35.29**
SAD	62.14	55.56	58.67	63.38	58.58	**60.89**	60.87	56.57	58.64	65.48	55.56	60.11
Combined	62.15	55.56	58.67	56.96	55.05	56.56	61.69	60.25	**60.96**	56.33	55.25	55.78

Table 2: Results of Sarcasm Detection experiments with Machine Learning approaches, where *P* denotes Precision, *R* denotes Recall and *F1* denotes the F1-score of the experiment. Underlined results denote the best F1-score for each model. Results in bold denote the best F1-score for its own dataset

	BERT			BERTweet			RoBERTa$_{base}$			Twitter-RoBERTa			RoBERTa$_{large}$		
	P	R	F1	P	R	F1	P	R	F1	P	R	F1	P	R	F1
SARC	73.91	79.47	76.59	76.52	80.35	**78.39**	76.23	78.35	77.30	74.89	80.52	77.61	77.65	77.57	77.61
Ptacek	84.46	75.83	79.99	88.86	85.07	86.92	88.41	88.63	88.52	91.46	86.26	88.78	91.50	89.33	**90.41**
SemEval	59.61	74.83	66.36	69.81	77.62	73.51	78.42	90.21	83.90	78.37	87.41	82.64	81.11	87.06	**83.98**
Riloff	66.67	35.71	46.51	85.71	42.86	**57.14**	58.33	50.00	53.85	55.56	53.57	54.54	85.71	42.86	**57.14**
SAD	65.89	71.21	68.45	77.36	62.12	68.91	81.49	93.43	**87.06**	82.19	90.90	86.33	86.84	83.33	85.05
Combined	76.46	75.36	75.91	75.99	80.72	**78.29**	76.00	78.48	77.22	76.68	77.72	77.19	76.15	79.95	78.01

Table 3: Results of Sarcasm Detection experiments with Deep Learning approaches, where *P* denotes Precision, *R* denotes Recall and *F1* denotes the F1-score of the experiment. Underlined results denote the best F1-score for each model. Results in bold denote the best F1-score for its own dataset

learning-based and deep learning-based experiments. The environment used to run the machine learning experiments was a Kaggle notebook, whereas the deep learning experiments were run on an i9 machine with 2 NVIDIA RTX A5000 GPUs.

5.1 Hyper-parameter Setting

For the machine learning experiments, both the DT and LR models were trained with the default hyperparameters as set in the scikit-learn[3] (Pedregosa et al., 2011) library. For the deep learning experiments, every configuration had the same set of hyper-parameters apart from one exception in the batch size. The batch size was set to 32 for all of the language models except for RoBERTa$_{large}$, where the batch size was set to 4. This was due to the computational limitations that arose due to RoBERTa$_{large}$ being trained on the exceptionally large SARC and 'Combined' datasets with a batch size of 32. Every configuration had a learning rate of 3e-6, with an Adam activation function. The output of each language model was fed into a dropout layer of 0.3, and followed by a hidden layer with a ReLU activation function and 256 hidden units. Finally, the output of the hidden layer was fed through a Softmax activation function with 2 units to perform binary classification.

[3]https://scikit-learn.org

6 Results and Discussion

Table 2 and 3 show the results of the machine learning and deep learning-based experiments, respectively. According to Table 2, it is clear that the success of each respective machine learning approach is highly dependent upon the particular dataset on which it is being trained. The Ptacek dataset has the highest F1-scores for sarcasm detection for each machine learning approach, as can be seen by the underlined results, and also achieves the highest F1-score in the entire set of experiments (75.41) when used with the GloVE+LR model.

Table 4 demonstrates that for the Word2Vec+DT (worst) and GloVe+LR (best) models, there is no consistency in how negative phrases such as "didn't think", "didn't realise" are labelled compared to the actual label used within the dataset. The last extract was labelled incorrectly by both models, with neither understanding that the word "love" was being used in a sarcastic context, which could be seen as a limitation of the machine learning approaches. Although, without context, it is fair to assume that the user could have been non-sarcastic in this tweet.

Comment	Word2Vec+ DT Label	GloVe+ LR Label	Ground Truth
'didnt realize @user referees were so fluent in russian'	1	1	1
'well hello depression nice to see ya again didnt think youd stay away' much longer	0	1	1
'dont you just love the hip hop music and club music they played in the background of the @user movie i do'	0	0	1

Table 4: Entries from the Ptacek dataset labelled by the highest and lowest scoring ML experiments and their ground truth labels. 1 represents a sarcastic label and 0 represents a non-sarcastic label.

The SemEval dataset achieves its highest F1-score of 61.62 using the Word2Vec+LR model. The Riloff dataset has the weakest set of F1-scores across each approach, with it is best F1-score (35.29) still being lower than any F1-score for any other dataset. Interestingly, the Word2Vec+LR model achieves a perfect precision score, whereas the associated scores for this model are the lowest for all experiments.

From Table 2, it is seen that our SAD dataset achieves similar F1-scores across each model, with a variance of 2.25 between the highest and lowest scores. The SAD dataset and the Riloff dataset are the only two out of the six to achieve their best scores from a decision tree classifier as opposed to a logistic regression classifier.

From Table 3, we observe the best F1-score for the task of sarcasm detection using deep learning methods is 90.41 on the Ptacek dataset with the use of the RoBERTa$_{large}$ language model. As is seen with our machine learning approaches, Ptacek again is the dataset for which all of our models achieve the highest F1-scores. The Ptacek dataset has only 736 test set instances and may not have particularly challenging sarcasm examples. We make this assumption based on the performance of the same pre-trained language models on much larger datasets, viz., SARC (78.39) and Combined (78.29). The RoBERTa$_{large}$ language model achieves the highest F1-score of 83.98 on the SemEval dataset.

There is more success with the unbalanced Riloff dataset within the deep learning experiments as opposed to the machine learning experiments. The lowest F1-score using the Riloff dataset in Table 3 (46.51) achieved by our BERT model is still higher than the highest F1-score in Table 2 (35.29) from the GloVe+DT model. The results achieved are again lower than the results obtained from the rest of our chosen datasets. Both the BERTweet and RoBERTa$_{large}$ language models incidentally achieve the exact same precision, recall and F1-scores (57.14) on this dataset.

Our SAD dataset has high F1-scores across each model, 87.06 being the highest achieved by the RoBERTa$_{base}$ language model. The BERT language model achieves the weakest F1-score on the dataset (68.45), followed closely by the BERTweet model (68.91). This was unexpected as the BERTweet language model was pre-trained only on tweets. Further unexpectedly, the RoBERTa$_{base}$ model actually achieves the best overall F1-score on the SAD dataset, despite the model not being pre-trained on any tweets at all. This performance may be attributed to the significantly larger dataset used for training the RoBERTa model.

Ironically, despite being pre-trained solely on $850M$ tweets, the BERTweet model achieves the highest F1-score of 78.39 on the SARC dataset, the only dataset that does not include any tweets.

From Table 3, we also observe that the BERTweet and RoBERTa$_{large}$ language models outperform every other approach. They achieve the highest F1-score on three datasets, respectively. For the SARC and the 'Combined' dataset, the BERTweet analysis provides the best F1-scores, and these datasets are, in fact, the largest datasets. Furthermore, the BERTweet language model has the advantage of being pre-trained specifically on data consisting of tweets, as opposed to the less focused domain data that was used to train RoBERTa$_{large}$. We hypothesise that the fine-tuned sarcasm detection models trained over large datasets would be able to generalise better as the training sets would also be large.

Comment	BERTweet Label	Ground Truth
'more fragmentation is exactly what we need in mobile payments'	1	1
'hockey wouldnt work in quebec city'	1	1
'this is new and interesting'	1	1
'i call them suckers'	1	0
'by doing the same thing i do every night and day nothing'	0	1
'huge moves were making gonna take this league by storm'	0	1

Table 5: Entries from the 'Combined' dataset with their predicted labels by our pre-trained BERTweet model and their ground truth labels. 1 represents a sarcastic label, and 0 represents a non-sarcastic label.

Table 5 shows the labels predicted by the model

trained using the BERTweet model on the 'Combined' dataset. The first three entries show examples of correctly identified sarcasm. If taken literally, the third entry could be considered as a genuine statement, but the model determines this to be sarcastic, and in fact, it is labelled as such within the dataset.

There are entries where the model incorrectly labels sarcastic text extracts. In the fourth row, an instance of a false positive can be seen, where our pre-trained model incorrectly determines a tweet is sarcastic when it was not labelled as such. The word "suckers" might indicate some humorous intent to the text, implying sarcasm may be used in the comment.

The last two entries in Table 5 are examples of labelled sarcasm that our model did not determine to be sarcastic. The fifth entry puts forward an unlikely proposition similar to the first two entries in that it is probably untrue that the user spends all night and day doing nothing.

Although the model made the correct prediction in the rather specific domain of "quebec" and "hockey", it makes an incorrect prediction in this broader context. This is demonstrable of how figurative language and the understanding of such truly rely on contextual differences. These contextual differences impact human, and, particularly, machine understanding of sarcasm. Again, this struggle of the models' prediction capabilities in a broader context is seen in the final entry, where the user has intended the text to be sarcastic, but it has not been labelled by our BERTweet model as such. Even with this small scope of examples where our model has made incorrect predictions, our fine-tuned BERTweet model is still our highest-scoring language model on our largest datasets, and thus we will use fine-tuned BERTweet models for the purpose of labelling a weakly supervised dataset.

6.1 S3D Dataset: Using Weak Supervision

The results for the analysis of the fine-tuned BERTweet model for both the SARC and 'Combined' datasets are very similar, but we note that the 'Combined' dataset contains both Tweets and Reddit comments. Similarly, RoBERTa$_{large}$ model performs well on the Combined dataset (78.01). We create *an Ensemble model using the majority voting technique and utilise these three variants* - a BERTweet model trained on SARC and Combined datasets, and a RoBERTa$_{large}$ model trained on the combined dataset. We further use this Ensemble model to label our new dataset, the curation for which is described below.

We used the TWINT package to scrape a total of $100,000$ tweets[4] to be labelled by our chosen model. We call this a silver-standard sarcasm annotated dataset 'S3D'. Every tweet was pre-processed as described in section 3.4, then encoded using the BERTweet model. Our Ensemble model was then used to generate predictions on the pre-processed $100,000$ tweets. The results of this labelling process are shown in Table 6.

Sarcastic	Non-Sarcastic	Total
38879	61121	100000

Table 6: Number of sarcastic and non-sarcastic labels generated by our pre-trained BERTweet model

Out of $100,000$ tweets chosen at random, nearly 40% were considered by our model to contain sarcasm. We show excerpts from this dataset in Table 7.

Comment	Label
'@user you look soo freaking good in the poster man'	1
'tweet of the year @user you make sense'	1
'i bet theres no dry eyes leaving the concert' tonight	1
'the best joke yet'	1
'wow the war just ended i didnt know that'	1
'truly changed the trajectory of my life'	1
'yes a lot of great things will happen in the next 3 months'	1

Table 7: Entries from the S3D dataset, each labelled as sarcastic by our fine-tuned BERTweet language model. 1 represents a sarcastic label and 0 represents a non-sarcastic label.

Several entries seen in Table 7 could equally be seen as extracts with genuine sentiment as much as they could be sarcastic. The first entry is an example of this as if taking the tweet at its face value without context, it is very possible the user is being honest and complementing another user on the platform. Take the sixth entry, which could again be just as authentic as it could be sarcastic. To decide for ourselves, we would need to view some context as to what the event is that the user

[4]This set of collected tweets were posted between 7 September 2022 and 9 September 2022

is referring to. If the subject matter was serious, it is fair to assume the user is not being sarcastic. Some excerpts such as the second entry are perhaps more obviously sarcastic, as reminding someone they make sense while also awarding them "tweet of the year" carries a more disingenuous sentiment. The same could be said for the fifth entry, where it is very unlikely the user is being genuine about being unaware of the topic mentioned in tweet.

We also performed a simple exploratory experiment where we concatenate S3D with the 'Combined' dataset and perform fine-tuning with the help of the BERTweet model. A simple fine-tuning experiment with the same hyperparameters *achieves the best F1-score of* 78.87*, which is an improvement on the scores reported earlier on both SARC and 'Combined' datasets.* The reported precision and recall scores were 78.84 and 78.89 respectively. This shows the efficacy of our weakly supervised S3D dataset.

7 Conclusion and Future Work

In this paper, we utilise several existing machine- and deep learning-based approaches to perform the task of sarcasm detection over various datasets. From a social media platform, we curate and manually label a sarcasm dataset and benchmark its efficacy with these approaches. We also perform an exhaustive evaluation with the help of pre-trained language models, including some models specifically trained using social media data. Using an Ensemble model based on multiple fine-tuned BERTweet models, we labelled an additional 100,000 tweets and release this silver-standard sarcasm annotated corpus, called S3D. We also perform a fine-tuning experiment after concatenating S3D with the 'Combined' dataset and achieve the best F1-score of 78.87 over the large datasets discussed in this paper. By contributing a weak supervision-based approach, we facilitate the automatic production of labelled data that can be used to augment existing datasets or create new silver standard datasets. We also release the code, the manually labelled dataset, and models created with our experiments publicly for further research.

In future, we would like to perform a more fine-grained annotation for sarcasm with sub-categories as defined in existing linguistic literature. We also aim to perform similar experiments for multimodal sarcasm detection in order to contribute further resources to the community.

Limitations and Biases

Our work releases two datasets for modelling sarcasm from social media posts but they may contain biases as present in any raw social media dataset.

Ethics Statement

We ensured that while curating our SAD and S3D datasets, information relating to the originator of the tweet was removed, and all user-specific information contained within a tweet, for example, usernames and user IDs, was removed during preprocessing to preserve anonymity. Similarly, information regarding the time of posting and location was removed during curation. The released datasets only contain tweet IDs along with their respective sarcasm labels, again to ensure the anonymity of our datasets.

References

Muhammad Abdul-Mageed, AbdelRahim A. Elmadany, and El Moatez Billah Nagoudi. 2021. ARBERT & MARBERT: deep bidirectional transformers for arabic. *CoRR*, abs/2101.01785.

Ibrahim Abu Farha and Walid Magdy. 2021. Benchmarking transformer-based language models for Arabic sentiment and sarcasm detection. In *Proceedings of the Sixth Arabic Natural Language Processing Workshop*, pages 21–31, Kyiv, Ukraine (Virtual). Association for Computational Linguistics.

Francesco Barbieri, José Camacho-Collados, Leonardo Neves, and Luis Espinosa Anke. 2020. Tweeteval: Unified benchmark and comparative evaluation for tweet classification. *CoRR*, abs/2010.12421.

Francesco Barbieri, Horacio Saggion, and Francesco Ronzano. 2014. Modelling sarcasm in Twitter, a novel approach. In *Proceedings of the 5th Workshop on Computational Approaches to Subjectivity, Sentiment and Social Media Analysis*, pages 50–58, Baltimore, Maryland. Association for Computational Linguistics.

Santiago Castro, Devamanyu Hazarika, Verónica Pérez-Rosas, Roger Zimmermann, Rada Mihalcea, and Soujanya Poria. 2019. Towards multimodal sarcasm detection (an _Obviously_ perfect paper). In *Proceedings of the 57th Annual Meeting of the Association for Computational Linguistics*, pages 4619–4629, Florence, Italy. Association for Computational Linguistics.

Alexis Conneau, Kartikay Khandelwal, Naman Goyal, Vishrav Chaudhary, Guillaume Wenzek, Francisco Guzmán, Edouard Grave, Myle Ott, Luke Zettlemoyer, and Veselin Stoyanov. 2020. Unsupervised cross-lingual representation learning at scale. In *Proceedings of the 58th Annual Meeting of the Association for Computational Linguistics*, pages 8440–8451, Online. Association for Computational Linguistics.

David R Cox. 1958. The regression analysis of binary sequences. *Journal of the Royal Statistical Society: Series B (Methodological)*, 20(2):215–232.

Jacob Devlin, Ming-Wei Chang, Kenton Lee, and Kristina Toutanova. 2018a. BERT: pre-training of deep bidirectional transformers for language understanding. *CoRR*, abs/1810.04805.

Jacob Devlin, Ming-Wei Chang, Kenton Lee, and Kristina Toutanova. 2018b. Bert: Pre-training of deep bidirectional transformers for language understanding. *arXiv preprint arXiv:1810.04805*.

Megan L. Dress, Roger J. Kreuz, Kristen E. Link, and Gina M. Caucci. 2008. Regional variation in the use of sarcasm. *Journal of Language and Social Psychology*, 27:71 – 85.

Mohsen Farhadloo and Erik Rolland. 2016. Fundamentals of sentiment analysis and its applications. In *Sentiment analysis and ontology engineering*, pages 1–24. Springer.

Aniruddha Ghosh and Tony Veale. 2016. Fracking sarcasm using neural network. In *Proceedings of the 7th Workshop on Computational Approaches to Subjectivity, Sentiment and Social Media Analysis*, pages 161–169, San Diego, California. Association for Computational Linguistics.

Priya Goel, Rachna Jain, Anand Nayyar, Shruti Singhal, and Muskan Srivastava. 2022. Sarcasm detection using deep learning and ensemble learning. *Multimedia Tools and Applications*.

Aditya Joshi, Pushpak Bhattacharyya, and Mark J. Carman. 2017. Automatic sarcasm detection: A survey. *ACM Comput. Surv.*, 50(5).

Mikhail Khodak, Nikunj Saunshi, and Kiran Vodrahalli. 2017. A large self-annotated corpus for sarcasm.

Hyafil Laurent and Ronald L Rivest. 1976. Constructing optimal binary decision trees is np-complete. *Information processing letters*, 5(1):15–17.

Yinhan Liu, Myle Ott, Naman Goyal, Jingfei Du, Mandar Joshi, Danqi Chen, Omer Levy, Mike Lewis, Luke Zettlemoyer, and Veselin Stoyanov. 2019. Roberta: A robustly optimized BERT pretraining approach. *CoRR*, abs/1907.11692.

Dehong Ma, Sujian Li, Xiaodong Zhang, and Houfeng Wang. 2017. Interactive attention networks for aspect-level sentiment classification. In *Proceedings of the Twenty-Sixth International Joint Conference on Artificial Intelligence, IJCAI-17*, pages 4068–4074.

Tomas Mikolov, Kai Chen, Greg Corrado, and Jeffrey Dean. 2013. Efficient estimation of word representations in vector space.

Dat Quoc Nguyen, Thanh Vu, and Anh Tuan Nguyen. 2020. BERTweet: A pre-trained language model for English tweets. In *Proceedings of the 2020 Conference on Empirical Methods in Natural Language Processing: System Demonstrations*, pages 9–14, Online. Association for Computational Linguistics.

Bo Pang and Lillian Lee. 2008. Opinion mining and sentiment analysis. *Found. Trends Inf. Retr.*, 2(1–2):1–135.

Fabian Pedregosa, Gaël Varoquaux, Alexandre Gramfort, Vincent Michel, Bertrand Thirion, Olivier Grisel, Mathieu Blondel, Peter Prettenhofer, Ron Weiss, Vincent Dubourg, et al. 2011. Scikit-learn: Machine learning in python. *the Journal of machine Learning research*, 12:2825–2830.

Jeffrey Pennington, Richard Socher, and Christopher Manning. 2014. GloVe: Global vectors for word representation. In *Proceedings of the 2014 Conference on Empirical Methods in Natural Language Processing (EMNLP)*, pages 1532–1543, Doha, Qatar. Association for Computational Linguistics.

Rolandos Alexandros Potamias, Georgios Siolas, and Andreas-Georgios Stafylopatis. 2019. A transformer-based approach to irony and sarcasm detection. *CoRR*, abs/1911.10401.

Tomás Ptácek, Ivan Habernal, and Jun Hong. 2014. Sarcasm detection on czech and english twitter. In *COLING*.

Anupama Ray, Shubham Mishra, Apoorva Nunna, and Pushpak Bhattacharyya. 2022. A multimodal corpus for emotion recognition in sarcasm. In *Proceedings of the Language Resources and Evaluation Conference*, pages 6992–7003, Marseille, France. European Language Resources Association.

Antonio Reyes and Paolo Rosso. 2011. Mining subjective knowledge from customer reviews: A specific case of irony detection. In *Proceedings of the 2nd Workshop on Computational Approaches to Subjectivity and Sentiment Analysis (WASSA 2.011)*, pages 118–124, Portland, Oregon. Association for Computational Linguistics.

Ellen Riloff, Ashequl Qadir, Prafulla Surve, Lalindra De Silva, Nathan Gilbert, and Ruihong Huang. 2013. Sarcasm as contrast between a positive sentiment and negative situation. In *Proceedings of the 2013 Conference on Empirical Methods in Natural Language Processing*, pages 704–714, Seattle, Washington, USA. Association for Computational Linguistics.

Taha Shangipour ataei, Soroush Javdan, and Behrouz Minaei-Bidgoli. 2020. Applying transformers and aspect-based sentiment analysis approaches on sarcasm detection. In *Proceedings of the Second Workshop on Figurative Language Processing*, pages 67–71, Online. Association for Computational Linguistics.

Cynthia Van Hee, Els Lefever, and Véronique Hoste. 2018. SemEval-2018 task 3: Irony detection in English tweets. In *Proceedings of The 12th International Workshop on Semantic Evaluation*, pages 39–50, New Orleans, Louisiana. Association for Computational Linguistics.

Ashish Vaswani, Noam Shazeer, Niki Parmar, Jakob Uszkoreit, Llion Jones, Aidan N Gomez, Łukasz Kaiser, and Illia Polosukhin. 2017. Attention is all you need. *Advances in neural information processing systems*, 30.

Mayur Wankhade, Annavarapu Chandra Sekhara Rao, and Chaitanya Kulkarni. 2022. A survey on sentiment analysis methods, applications, and challenges. *Artificial Intelligence Review*, 55(7):5731–5780.

A Robust Bias Mitigation Procedure Based on the Stereotype Content Model

Eddie L. Ungless and **Amy Rafferty** and **Hrichika Nag** and **Björn Ross**
School of Informatics
University of Edinburgh
10 Crichton Street, Edinburgh EH8 9AB, United Kingdom
e.l.ungless@sms.ed.ac.uk a.rafferty@live.com
naghrichika@gmail.com b.ross@ed.ac.uk

Abstract

The Stereotype Content model (SCM) states that we tend to perceive minority groups as cold, incompetent or both. In this paper we adapt existing work to demonstrate that the Stereotype Content model holds for contextualised word embeddings, then use these results to evaluate a fine-tuning process designed to drive a language model away from stereotyped portrayals of minority groups. We find the SCM terms are better able to capture bias than demographic agnostic terms related to pleasantness. Further, we were able to reduce the presence of stereotypes in the model through a simple fine-tuning procedure that required minimal human and computer resources, without harming downstream performance. We present this work as a prototype of a debiasing procedure that aims to remove the need for *a priori* knowledge of the specifics of bias in the model.

1 Introduction

It is well established that large language models (LLMs) such as BERT (Devlin et al., 2019), GPT2 (Radford et al., 2019) and related contextualised word embeddings such as ELMo (Peters et al., 2018) are biased against different demographic groups (Guo and Caliskan, 2021; Webster et al., 2020; Kaneko and Bollegala, 2021), in that they often reflect stereotypes in their output. For example, given the prompt "naturally, the nurse is a", these systems will typically output "woman" (Schick et al., 2021). Given the common practice of adapting pre-trained language models for a range of tasks through fine-tuning, upstream bias mitigation may prove to be the most efficient solution (Jin et al., 2021) (though cf. Steed et al. (2022). In this paper, we demonstrate the success of modifying an existing debiasing algorithm to be grounded in a psychological theory of stereotypes - the SCM (Cuddy et al., 2008), to efficiently reduce biases in LLMs across a range of identities. Our proposed debiasing pipeline has the benefit of minimising the time spent researching identity terms and associated stereotypes. Being a fine-tuning procedure, this also reduces the amount of computational resources needed compared to training an unbiased model from scratch. This renders our approach efficient and widely applicable. We demonstrate using BERT, but this same procedure could easily be adapted to other LLMs.

We adapt the fine-tuning procedure from Kaneko and Bollegala (2021). They reduce gender bias in a range of LLMs by fine-tuning using a data set of sentences containing (binary) gendered terms (like "he, man" or "she, lady") (which they call attributes) or stereotypes associated with different genders ("assertive, secretary") (which they call targets). The training objective is to remove associations with gender in the contextualised embeddings of the targets whilst maintaining these associations for the gendered attributes.

Crucially, rather than relying on stereotypes specific to a particular demographic such as men and women (as in Kaneko and Bollegala (2021)) we plan to use the SCM to inform our production of fine-tuning data, inspired by work by Fraser et al. (2021). The SCM states that our stereotyped perception of different demographics can be conceptualised as lying in a vector space with axes of warmth/coldness and competence/incompetence (Cuddy et al., 2008). We tend to consider our own identity group to be warm and competent, and stereotype disfavoured groups such as people experiencing homelessness as cold and/or incompetent (Cuddy et al., 2008).

In the terminology of Kaneko and Bollegala (2021), our attributes are terms relating to warmth and competence taken from Nicolas et al. (2021) (as in Fraser et al. (2021), a paper on stereotypes in static embeddings), our targets are demographic identity terms. Because the SCM is designed to encompass many different minority groups, this avoids the need to generate lists of stereotypes

Proceedings of the Fifth Workshop on Natural Language Processing and Computational Social Science (NLP+CSS), pages 207 - 217

unique to each minority group, reducing work load and making the tool easy to adapt to different targets. Therefore, the procedure should be effective for all identity terms we use. We demonstrate this technique for Black/white ethnicity and also the intersectional power dynamic between white men and Mexican American women, but this could easily be expanded to other aspects of identity such as disability and sexuality. Further, whilst we focus on English language and American identities, there is evidence that the SCM may hold relatively well cross-culturally (Cuddy et al., 2009), so this approach may be transferable to other LLMs.

We adapt the Contextualised Embedding Association Test (CEAT) (Guo and Caliskan, 2021) using the vocabulary from Nicolas et al. (2021) in order to measure stereotypes in contextualised word embeddings. The CEAT provides a robust measure of bias in contextualised word embeddings for target words, and is suited for use with the SCM terms.

In addition to using the CEAT to test for bias, we also measure the performance of the model on the language modeling benchmark GLUE (Wang et al., 2018), to ensure the fine-tuning procedure does not adversely impact the quality of the model, an issue Meade et al. (2022) identify as affecting several debiasing techniques.

The main contributions of this paper are to demonstrate:

- that the SCM can be used to detect bias in contextualised word embeddings
- a debiasing procedure that is demographic agnostic and resource efficient[1]

2 Related work

Several contributions have been made towards measuring and mitigating bias in NLU models with minimal *a priori* knowledge. Fraser and colleagues (2021) demonstrated the validity of the SCM for static word embeddings, in that the embeddings of words associated with traditionally oppressed minority groups such as Mexican Americans or Africans tend to lie in the cold, incompetent space, as determined by cosine similarity. Note that, unlike Fraser et al. (2021), we focus on the embeddings of the identity terms themselves, not of words associated with those identities, as we explicitly want to identify whether there is bias in the embeddings. Fraser et al. (2021) looked to establish if the embeddings of associated terms followed the SCM's predictions, not whether the word embeddings were biased in a way as to reflect these stereotypes.

Utama et al. (2020) propose a strategy for debiasing "unknown biases". They train a shallow model which picks up superficial patterns in data that are likely to indicate bias. This is then used to train the main model, which works by downweighting the potentially biased examples, paired with an annealing mechanism which prevents the loss of useful training signals caused by this approach. The models obtained from this self-debiasing framework were shown to perform just as well as models debiased using prior knowledge. In our work we do not train our model from scratch and only focus on social bias, whereas Utama et al. (2020) do not target specific bias types. We chose to prioritise socially relevant biases with the hopes of minimising harm done to minority communities. Further, our method requires far less compute.

Webster et al. (2020) take gendered correlations in pretrained language representations as a case study for measuring and mitigating bias. They build an evaluation framework for detecting and quantifying gendered correlations in models. They find that both dropout regularization and counterfactual data augmentation minimize gendered correlations while maintaining strong model accuracy. Their techniques are applicable when training a model from scratch, whilst ours is a fine-tuning procedure, meaning it requires fewer computational resources.

Schick et al. (2021) explore whether language models can self-diagnose undesirable outputs for self-debiasing purposes. Their approach encourages the model to output biased text, and uses the resulting distribution to tune the model's original output. We argue that our model is more demographic agnostic, as their approach depends heavily on biases captured by Perspective API. Their approach may miss less salient forms of bias as it relies on the model having some representation of the bias category beforehand. Using the SCM, we can work "backwards" from the fact that these communities are harmed to then assume they will be represented as cold and/or incompetent, making our approach more universally applicable.

Cao et al. (2022b) focuses on identifying stereotyped group-trait associations in language models, by introducing a sensitivity test for measur-

[1]Code available at `https://github.com/MxEddie/Demagnosticdebias`

ing stereotypical associations. They compare US-based human judgements to language model stereotypes, and discover moderate correlations. They also extend their framework to measure language model stereotyping of intersectional identities, finding problems with identifying emergent intersectional stereotypes. Our work is unique from this in that we have additionally performed debiasing informed by the SCM.

Overall, our methodology and approach differs from most other contributions in this field as it focuses on targeting social bias specifically, and we propose a fine-tuning debiasing approach which requires little in the way of human or computer resources and is not limited to a small number of demographics.

3 Data sets and tasks

3.1 Data for Debiasing Procedure

3.1.1 Identity terms (targets)

We established two sets of identity terms (targets) for use with the context debiasing algorithm. The first set relates to racial bias (bias against people of colour based on their (perceived) race). BERT has been shown to demonstrate racial bias in both intrinsic (Guo and Caliskan, 2021) and extrinsic measures (Nadeem et al., 2021; Sheng et al., 2019). To reduce bias against Black people compared to white, we created a list of 20 African American (AA) and 20 European American (EA), 10 male and 10 female names for each, to use in the debiasing procedure. We used names from Guo and Caliskan (2021) (excluding any included in the CEAT tests we deploy, see Section 3.2) and supplemented these lists with common names from a database of US first names (Tzioumis, 2018). Excluding names from the CEAT tests was crucial to ensure a reduction in bias was due to a restructuring of the embedding space and an overall change in how Black individuals were represented, and not due to bias reduction for the specific names we ran the debiasing procedure with.

The second set relates to intersectional bias against Mexican American (MA) women, that is bias against women based on both patriarchal beliefs about their gender and prejudice against their ethnicity. This intersectional bias is evident in the contextualised embeddings BERT produces (Guo and Caliskan, 2021). To reduce bias against MA women compared to white men, we additionally took 10 common Hispanic female names (and manually confirmed that each was used by the Mexican American community through a Google search) from Tzioumis (2018).

The validity of using names to represent demographic groups has been questioned (Blodgett et al., 2021). However, we assume that reducing bias present in the representations of these names will go some way to reducing racial bias in the model.

3.1.2 Stereotype Content terms (attributes)

As with Fraser et al. (2021), we use the Stereotype Content terms from Nicolas et al. (2021), whereby the high morality, high sociability terms are taken to indicate warmth; low morality, low sociability to indicate coldness; high ability, high agency to indicate competence; and low ability, low agency to indicate incompetence. We selected the top 32 most frequent terms from each list (as measured using the Brown Corpus and the NLTK toolkit), to increase the likelihood we would find a large number of example sentences for each. During finetuning, we wish for these terms to maintain their projection in the warmth/coldness or competence/incompetence space, respectively, whilst removing projection in these directions for the target terms (see Section 4 and Figure 1).

Whilst the exact "position" of demographic groups in this conceptual space would vary depending on who is describing them, in this work we always assume the minority group will be represented in the original model as cold and incompetent, in other words the most disfavoured and most likely to experience harm (Cuddy et al., 2008). This minimises workload (no need to establish likely predictions for every demographic considered, beyond identifying the more marginalised group) and centers our approach around improving results for the most negatively represented identity terms. Note, there is no harm in running our debiasing procedure on identities that are already equally associated with one concept i.e. warmth, whilst also reducing stereotyped associations with the other concept i.e. competence.

3.1.3 Fine-tuning data

Having established the list of attribute and target terms, we follow an adapted version of Kaneko and Bollegala (2021)'s procedure for generating fine-tuning development data. During early analyses, we found the AA names occurred very infrequently in their provided news commentary data set, likely a reflection of the lack of AA representation in mainstream news (Diuguid and Rivers, 2000). We therefore opted to use data from Reddit, from 2018[2], (a separate data set to that used for the CEAT, see below), as this contained many example sentences across all names. We sampled from this data set sentences which contained either one of the attribute or one of the target terms, and no more, of 128 tokens or less. We extracted at least 24,000 sentences for each attribute and target dimension. This was stored as a dictionary that was passed to the debiasing script. We took a random sub-sample of 1000 of each to use as development data.

3.2 CEAT

The CEAT (Guo and Caliskan, 2021) is designed to test for associations between the contextualised embeddings of targets and polar attributes (such as binary gender). The authors sampled sentences from Reddit where a stimuli (target or attribute term) occurred, and generated contextualised embeddings for the sentences. These contextualised embeddings were then used to calculate the effect sizes, based on a cosine similarity measure between the embeddings of the target and attribute tokens. They then measure the distribution of effect sizes for the terms in different contexts (to ensure that the choice of context does not unduly influence the final effect size metric). The authors then apply a random-effects model to calculate a combined effect size (CES) and significance, given the distribution of effect sizes. We adopt the same sample data and testing procedure.

We use the lists of identity terms for racial and intersectional bias given in Guo and Caliskan (2021), namely related to AA versus EA identities and MA women versus EA men, along with the SCM attribute terms, to establish the presence of stereotypes in the contextualised word embeddings using the CEAT.

In addition to using the SCM terms, we will also use the pleasant/unpleasant terms from Guo and Caliskan (2021)'s paper - this provides a comparison point for use of the SCM versus another set of non-demographic-specific terms.

We also measure how strongly the demographic specific stereotype terms for MA women and EA men are associated with the demographic groups, to see if demographic specific stereotype associations are reduced following demographic agnostic debiasing. Note that we removed the word "intelligent" from the EA men attributes list as this also occurs in the competence attributes list and we wanted to be totally confident that any observed reduction in bias was due to restructuring of the entire embedding space and not due to bias being removed from an overlapping word. The CEAT does not have equivalent demographic specific terms for the AA/EA groups, though for completeness we compare how strongly the MA female/EA male specific terms are associated with the AA/EA groups.

Again, we adopt the approach of always assuming the more marginalised group will be represented in the model as more cold and incompetent compared to the majority group. This is an oversimplification. For example, Cuddy et al. (2008) indicate that in a Western context neither men nor women are strongly associated with coldness. However, we adopt this simplifying assumption to maintain testing consistency and thus require less human intervention, as per our goals.

We apply the CEAT before and after debiasing, to measure the success of the fine-tuning approach using the SCM terms.

3.3 Language Modelling Benchmark

Meade et al. (2022) note that apparent reductions in bias can reflect a worsening of language modelling performance. To ensure our debiasing procedure does not come at the expense of model performance, we evaluate our model on the GLUE benchmark (Wang et al., 2018).

The GLUE benchmark consists of 10 primary tasks and one diagnostic test, which evaluate the performance of a model in different contexts. We chose to evaluate our models using only five of these tasks – MRPC, SST-2, STSB, RTE and WNLI – following Kaneko and Bollegala (2021). These five tasks have small datasets, meaning we can minimise the effect of task-specific fine-tuning when running predictions (Kaneko and Bollegala, 2021).

We run the tests using the public GLUE code from huggingface[3]. We will perform these tests before and after debiasing, and compare the results. We report results based on the provided evaluation data.

[2]`https://files.pushshift.io/reddit/comments/`

[3]`https://github.com/huggingface/transformers/tree/main/examples/pytorch/text-classification/`

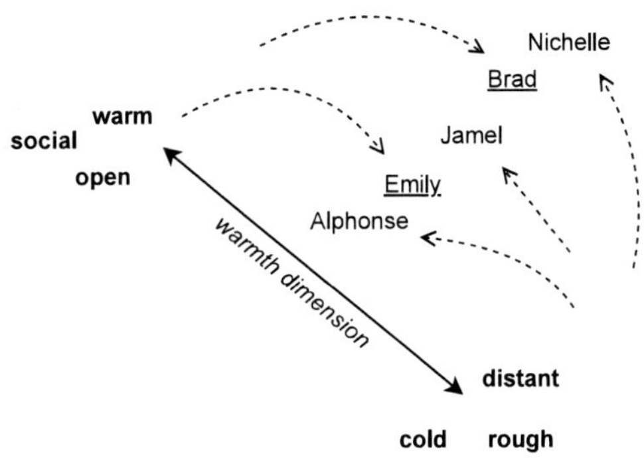

Figure 1: Diagram of intended orthogonal projection of target terms away from the warmth dimension, determined by attribute terms in **bold**. EA names underlined

.

4 Methodology

We use the 'bert-base-cased' model from the Hugging Face library[4]), henceforth BERT, although this same procedure should be applicable to any LLM with minimal modification.

We fine-tune the model following an adapted version of the procedure in Kaneko and Bollegala (2021). Namely, through a training objective that looks to minimise unwanted projection into the attribute category dimensions for the target words through an orthogonal projection, whilst also staying close to the contextualised embeddings of the pre-trained model to preserve semantics. We visualise this orthogonal projection in Figure 1. Adjusting the embeddings of the target terms to lie orthogonal to the warmth dimension (equidistant from the attribute terms) should ensure less negatively biased representations for minority groups (in the visualisation, AA names).

Crucially, we modified the original algorithm in Kaneko and Bollegala (2021) as we wish to remove unwanted projections into two dimensions, not just one: warmth/coldness and competence/incompetence. The first component of the loss function for layer i of our model is:

$$L_i = \sum_{d \in D} \sum_{t \in V_t} \sum_{x \in \Omega(t)} \sum_{a \in V_a} (v_i(a)^\top E_i(t; x; \theta_e))^2$$

where $E_i(t; x; \theta_e)$ represents the embedding of target word t in sentence x for model E_i, $v_i(a)$ is the average embedding for the attribute term across training sentences, and we calculate the inner product across all attributes $a \in V_a$, for all sentences containing the target $x \in \Omega(t)$, for all target words V_t, for all target dimensions, D_d.

The second component of the loss function is:

$$L_{reg} = \sum_{x \in A} \sum_{w \in x} \sum_{i=1}^{N} ||E_i(w; x; \theta_e) - E_i(w; x; \theta_{pre})||^2$$

where $E_i(w; x; \theta_{pre})$ is the contextualised embedding of a word, w, in a sentence, for the model before fine-tuning, and we calculate the squared ℓ_2 between this and the embedding after fine-tuning, for all layers, for all sentences and targets.

The final loss function is a weighted sum:

$$L = \alpha L_i + \beta L_{reg}$$

where α and β sum to 1.

Kaneko and Bollegala (2021) find debiasing all layers to be the most effective, so we do likewise.

5 Results

5.1 Baseline Performance

5.1.1 CEAT

Results for the CEAT for BERT are given in Table 1. We found there was a medium combined effect size (CES, between 0.5 and 0.8, as per the original paper's classification (Guo and Caliskan, 2021)) in the strength of association between EA names & warmth and AA names & coldness. We also found a medium strength association between EA names & competence and AA names & incompetence. As with the original paper, we found a small association between EA names & pleasantness and AA names & unpleasantness, suggesting this approach may be less able to detect the true scale of bias.

We also found a medium effect size association between AA names and the negative, MA women specific intersectional bias terms, and between the EA names and the EA male specific intersectional bias terms. This may be because the EA male stereotypes are relevant to all EA people.

For the intersectional power dynamic, we found a small association between EA male names & warmth and MA female names & coldness. We found a medium association between EA male names & competence and MA female names & incompetence. We found a very small association between EA male names & pleasantness and MA female names & unpleasantness, suggesting these

[4]https://huggingface.co/bert-base-cased

generic terms are less effective for detecting the true levels of bias in the model.

Finally, we found a medium effect size association between MA female names and the MA female specific bias terms, and between the EA male names and EA male specific bias terms - surprisingly, this association was weaker than than for the black/White demographic group, despite the fact that these stereotypes were chosen to be highly pertinent to the intersectional group.

5.1.2 GLUE

Table 2 shows the GLUE benchmark scores for BERT and DEBIAS, on the five chosen tasks.

The baseline BERT model performs very well on SST-2, MRPC and STS-B, with metric scores of around 90%. The lower scores come from the RTE and WNLI tasks. RTE assesses the model's ability to determine whether sentence A entails sentence B. WNLI assesses the model's ability to determine whether an inserted noun is correct. These specific grammatical situations seem to be the weaknesses of the model. The low score for WNLI is surprising and may indicate suboptimal hyperparameter choices during training. The training loss is comparable to that of a similar model on huggingface[5].

5.2 Debiasing Procedure

We adopt the values for α and β given in the original paper, namely 0.2 and 0.8 respectively, having trialed α 0.1 above and below and found 0.2 to be the best performing. Bar batch size and learning rate, all other hyperparameters were set to their default values for BERT. We trialed a number of starting learning rates and found the best to be 5e-5 (this is the same learning rate used in the original paper). Batch size was set to 32, as in the original paper. We train for 3 epochs (this is given in the code for the context debias paper but not specified).

We fine-tuned the model using the methodology detailed in Section 4.

5.3 Post-debiasing Performance

5.3.1 CEAT

The results of our post-debiasing CEAT tests indicate this debiasing procedure to be largely successful. We were able to reduce bias in DEBIAS and in all instances render the strength of stereotyped association to be very small.

For DEBIAS, there is no longer an association between EA names & warmth and AA names & coldness, nor between EA names & competence and AA names & incompetence. Although our debiasing procedure involved only the SCM terms, it also had an impact on the other associations. The strength of association between EA names & pleasantness and AA names & unpleasantness has reduced to be very small. Intersectional bias was also reduced as to be very small. Though these very small effects are statistically significant, their practical impact will be negligible.

Similarly, we found that for DEBIAS, there is no longer an association between EA male names & warmth and MA female names & coldness, nor between EA male names & competence and MA female names & incompetence. The association with pleasantness was also reduced, although this effect size was very small to begin with. Intersectional bias was also reduced as to be very small.

5.3.2 GLUE

Table 2 shows the differences between GLUE benchmark scores for our model before and after debiasing. For most tests, the GLUE benchmark scores have very minor differences.

Our debiased model outperforms the baseline model on both the RTE and WNLI tasks, with the largest difference coming from WNLI. We suspect that the improvement regarding RTE is because the RTE dataset is constructed based on news and Wikipedia text (Wang et al., 2018), which are domains likely to contain significant bias. For WNLI, the task of resolving ambiguities requires real world knowledge, which is also highly influenced by bias. Removing bias from these datasets allows the model to focus on classifying entailment (RTE) or resolving ambiguities (WNLI) in a more reliable manner, without being "distracted" by stereotyped associations between particular groups and actions that are irrelevant to the task.

In general, these results show that debiasing the model did not hurt its performance, as would have been implied by Meade et al. (2022). On our five chosen GLUE tasks, any performance decreases were very minor, while the performance increases on RTE and WNLI were rather significant. Though not directly comparable to Kaneko and Bollegala (2021), as their paper considers 'bert-base-uncased', our results are inline with their findings showing debiasing along two "axes" does not unduly harm language modeling performance com-

[5]https://huggingface.co/gchhablani/bert-base-cased-finetuned-wnli

Test	BERT CES	BERT Sig.	DEBIAS CES	DEBIAS Sig.
EA,AA,Warm	0.77	*	**-0.12**	-
EA,AA,Comp.	0.67	*	**-0.18**	-
EA,AA,Pleas.	0.47	*	**0.16**	*
EA,AA,Inter.†	0.71	*	**0.15**	*
EAM,MAF,Warm	0.43	*	**-0.03**	-
EAM,MAF,Comp.	0.51	*	**-0.04**	-
EAM,MAF,Pleas.	0.17	*	**0.13**	*
EAM,MAF,Inter.	0.50	*	**0.08**	*

Table 1: Strength of combined effect size (CES) between attributes and targets for BERT before (BASELINE) and after (DEBIASED) debiasing. Sig. = significance. * = significant to $p < 0.05$. AA = African American names. EA = European American names. MAF = Mexican American female names. EAM = European American male names. Warm = warm/cold terms. Comp. = competent/incompetent terms. Pleas. = pleasant/unpleasant terms. Inter = Intersectional stereotypes.† **Bold** indicates that the debiasing procedure has reduced the absolute effect size to very small. †The intersectional stereotypes were intended as relevant to the EAM and MAF pair.

Benchmark	Baseline Score	Debiased Score
SST-2	**92.7**	92.5
MRPC	**89.5/85.0**	87.9/82.8
STS-B	**88.9/88.6**	88.7/88.5
RTE	66.1	**67.5**
WNLI	32.4	**42.3**

Table 2: GLUE Benchmark scores for both our baseline BERT, and our final DEBIAS models. Values correspond to the metrics described in Section 3.3. **Bold** indicates the best performance.

pared to debiasing along one axis.

6 Discussion

We found that our approach to bias measurement, informed by the SCM, proved to be an effective method for detecting bias in an LLM. We found that compared to using another list of generic, non-demographic specific attribute terms related to pleasantness, our approach seemed to give a more accurate measure of the level of bias in the model - our terms allow us to capture a stronger association between a minority group and negative stereotypes. It is possible that our approach exaggerates the level of bias in the model and in fact is less accurate. However, the effect sizes from our approach are closer to the effect size for association with demographic specific terms for the intersectional pair, suggesting it paints an accurate picture of negative bias in the model. Further, given how often BERT has been found to produce offensive content, it seems more likely that use of pleasantness terms is underestimating the level of bias in the model, rather than our approach overestimating it. The pleasantness terms were only slightly associated with EA male names compared to MA female names, yet BERT has been shown to consistently produce more favourable content about such individuals (Sheng et al., 2019).

Our finding that the intersectional bias terms were actually more strongly associated with the Black/white demographic groups highlights how the selection of demographic specific stereotypes for use in measuring bias and debiasing models can be challenging. That these stereotypes are actually more strongly associated with AA/EA names could suggest that the stereotyping captured by the model does not reflect the attitudes of the group of undergraduates responsible for generating these stereotypes (Ghavami and Peplau, 2013). It could also be that the model has not been exposed to sufficient (stereotyped) data to capture the category of MA females and the associated stereotypes.

The results might suggest that these demographic specific terms are actually rather "demographic agnostic", hence they are able to capture bias against AA people. However, intuitively, "sexy" and "feisty" (two MA female specific stereotypes) are not associated with people experiencing homelessness (and studies on public attitudes towards homelessness to our knowledge confirm this intuition), but the Stereotype Content Model is able to predict the contempt they experience due to being perceived as cold and incompetent (Cuddy et al., 2008), which is likely reflected in language use and thus in an LLM.

After debiasing using the SCM informed approach, we were able to reduce bias in all instances. Not only did we reduce the association between competence, warmth and ethnicity, but we also reduced the association with pleasantness. Intuitively, this is likely a reflection of the semantic association between warmth and pleasantness - reducing projection in the warmth dimension may have impacted projection in the pleasantness dimension.

Crucially, we were able to reduce the association between the intersectional groups and their specific stereotypes, using a demographic agnostic approach that did not require prior knowledge of group specific stereotypes. Although we only ran the debiasing procedure for warmth and competence dimensions, there was a positive "knock on" effect, supporting our belief that debiasing at the more abstract level will reduce more specific bias associations as well, as these can be thought of as subcategories of these more generic stereotype concepts. We were able to successfully debias the model without impeding performance on benchmark NLI tasks, suggesting language modelling abilities have not been negatively impacted, and in two instances performance was actually improved, possibly due to the reduction in bias.

7 Conclusions

7.1 Future Work and Limitations

In future work we hope to make use of language models to generate the target identity terms, akin to Schick and Schütze (2021)'s use of LLMs to generate training data, using prompts such as "I am proud to identify as". This will further reduce the amount of human resource and *a priori* knowledge needed, making the approach more efficient and widely applicable. We may also try to introduce additional dimensions related to "universal" patterns of discrimination such as the use of dehumanising language (Cameron et al., 2016) and animal comparisons (Haslam et al., 2011).

Though we are hopeful that our proposed debiasing pipeline will show promising results, we acknowledge there are several inherent limitations we would look to address in future work.

First, the SCM has received significant support as a model for our perceptions of different groups, and its simplicity makes it ideal for use in our "demographic agonostic" approach. However, it has been shown that the model may fail to adequately capture stereotypes surrounding immigrant groups (Savaş et al., 2021). This might be addressed in future work by adopting additional attribute dimensions (i.e. diligence) to encompass a wider range of potential stereotypes. This will allow us to better measure and mitigate bias against groups which is not best captured by the warmth and competence stereotypes.

A second limitation is our use of Reddit data for both debiasing and testing for bias - it is not clear how robust the reduction in bias would be if tested using out-of-domain data.

A further limitation is that during the process of identifying suitable names from Tzioumis (2018) for our debiasing procedure, we found that some of the names used in CEAT tests to measure bias against Black Americans were not predominantly used by Black individuals (for example "Leroy"), an indication that relying on names to establish bias against a demographic group may be fallible.

Our use of the GLUE metric to evaluate language modelling performance is potentially problematic as this static benchmark is outdated and saturated for some tasks. Though using the same metric as Kaneko and Bollegala (2021) gave us confidence that debiasing along two axes did not unduly harm performance, we could better evaluate our model using modern dynamic benchmarks.

Finally, intrinsic measure of bias do not always correlate well with application bias (Goldfarb-Tarrant et al., 2021; Cao et al., 2022a), suggesting the CEAT may not accurately capture the extent of bias the model might be responsible for in downstream applications. In future work, we could evaluate the success of our debiasing approach using gender targets and an extrinsic measures such as Zhao et al. (2018), a gender bias in coreference resolution benchmark that could assess our model after finetuning for this task. We could also try to adapt the principles of this process to work in downstream tasks, for example amending the finetuning data to contain balanced stereotyped instances.

7.2 Conclusion

Our debiasing procedure has reduced stereotyped associations between minority groups and negative characteristics without the need for idiosyncratic target terms for each group, making it demographic agnostic and human resource efficient, in line with our goals. The debiasing procedure is able to effectively "neutralise" the presence of target dimensions in the attribute embeddings, as well as decrease the association between more demographic specific stereotype attributes and the target demographics. The debiasing procedure did not come at the cost of performance, and even improved performance on RTE and WNLI.

Further, the finetuning procedure ran in a matter of hours on a single GPU, making it computationally efficient as well. This aligns with our goals, to establish a robust bias mitigation procedure that is efficient and widely applicable.

Our work can be thought of as a prototype for a promising debiasing procedure grounded in the SCM. In future, we hope to encompass automatic target term generation. We also plan to expand this work to more minority identities, and more importantly test the resulting model using a range of extrinsic bias measures and language modeling benchmarks, to evaluate the potential for a positive real world impact. The hope is that those using LLMs may apply our simple and efficient debiasing procedure before fine-tuning for their own purposes, helping to reduce the impact of stereotypes across the field.

8 Acknowledgements

We would like to thank our anonymous reviewers for their feedback. This work is in part supported by the UKRI Centre for Doctoral Training in Natural Language Processing, funded by the UKRI (grant EP/S022481/1) and the University of Edinburgh, School of Informatics.

References

Su Lin Blodgett, Gilsinia Lopez, Alexandra Olteanu, Robert Sim, and Hanna Wallach. 2021. Stereotyping norwegian salmon: An inventory of pitfalls in fairness benchmark datasets. In *ACL-IJCNLP 2021*.

C. Daryl Cameron, Lasana T. Harris, and B. Keith Payne. 2016. The emotional cost of humanity: Anticipated exhaustion motivates dehumanization of stigmatized targets. *Social Psychological and Personality Science*, 7(2):105–112.

Yang Cao, Yada Pruksachatkun, Kai-Wei Chang, Rahul Gupta, Varun Kumar, Jwala Dhamala, and Aram Galstyan. 2022a. On the intrinsic and extrinsic fairness evaluation metrics for contextualized language representations. In *Proceedings of the 60th Annual Meeting of the Association for Computational Linguistics (Volume 2: Short Papers)*, page 561–570, Dublin, Ireland. Association for Computational Linguistics.

Yang Cao, Anna Sotnikova, Hal Daumé III, Rachel Rudinger, and Linda Zou. 2022b. Theory-grounded measurement of U.S. social stereotypes in English language models. In *Proceedings of the 2022 Conference of the North American Chapter of the Association for Computational Linguistics: Human Language Technologies*, pages 1276–1295, Seattle, United States. Association for Computational Linguistics.

Amy J. C. Cuddy, Susan T. Fiske, Virginia S. Y. Kwan, Peter Glick, Stéphanie Demoulin, Jacques-Philippe Leyens, Michael Harris Bond, Jean-Claude Croizet, Naomi Ellemers, Ed Sleebos, Tin Tin Htun, Hyun-Jeong Kim, Greg Maio, Judi Perry, Kristina Petkova, Valery Todorov, Rosa Rodríguez-Bailón, Elena Morales, Miguel Moya, Marisol Palacios, Vanessa Smith, Rolando Perez, Jorge Vala, and Rene Ziegler. 2009. Stereotype content model across cultures: Towards universal similarities and some differences. *British Journal of Social Psychology*, 48(1):1–33.

Amy J.C. Cuddy, Susan T. Fiske, and Peter Glick. 2008. Warmth and competence as universal dimensions of social perception: The stereotype content model and the bias map. volume 40 of *Advances in Experimental Social Psychology*, pages 61–149. Academic Press.

Jacob Devlin, Ming-Wei Chang, Kenton Lee, and Kristina Toutanova. 2019. BERT: Pre-training of deep bidirectional transformers for language understanding. In *Proceedings of the 2019 Conference of the North American Chapter of the Association for Computational Linguistics: Human Language Technologies, Volume 1 (Long and Short Papers)*, pages 4171–4186, Minneapolis, Minnesota. Association for Computational Linguistics.

Lewis Diuguid and Adrienne Rivers. 2000. The media and the black response. *The ANNALS of the American Academy of Political and Social Science*, 569(1):120–134.

Kathleen C. Fraser, Isar Nejadgholi, and Svetlana Kiritchenko. 2021. Understanding and countering stereotypes: A computational approach to the stereotype content model. In *Proceedings of the 59th Annual Meeting of the Association for Computational Linguistics and the 11th International Joint Conference on Natural Language Processing (Volume 1: Long Papers)*, page 600–616. Association for Computational Linguistics.

Negin Ghavami and Letitia Anne Peplau. 2013. An intersectional analysis of gender and ethnic stereotypes: Testing three hypotheses. *Psychology of Women Quarterly*, 37(1):113–127.

Seraphina Goldfarb-Tarrant, Rebecca Marchant, Ricardo Muñoz Sánchez, Mugdha Pandya, and Adam Lopez. 2021. Intrinsic bias metrics do not correlate with application bias. In *Proceedings of the*

59th Annual Meeting of the Association for Computational Linguistics and the 11th International Joint Conference on Natural Language Processing (Volume 1: Long Papers), page 1926–1940. Association for Computational Linguistics.

Wei Guo and Aylin Caliskan. 2021. Detecting emergent intersectional biases: Contextualized word embeddings contain a distribution of human-like biases. In *Proceedings of the 2021 AAAI/ACM Conference on AI, Ethics, and Society*, page 122–133. ACM.

Nick Haslam, Steve Loughnan, and Pamela Sun. 2011. Beastly: What makes animal metaphors offensive? *Journal of Language and Social Psychology*, 30(3):311–325.

Xisen Jin, Francesco Barbieri, Brendan Kennedy, Aida Mostafazadeh Davani, Leonardo Neves, and Xiang Ren. 2021. On transferability of bias mitigation effects in language model fine-tuning. In *Proceedings of the 2021 Conference of the North American Chapter of the Association for Computational Linguistics: Human Language Technologies*, pages 3770–3783, Online. Association for Computational Linguistics.

Masahiro Kaneko and Danushka Bollegala. 2021. Debiasing pre-trained contextualised embeddings. In *Proceedings of the 16th Conference of the European Chapter of the Association for Computational Linguistics: Main Volume*, page 1256–1266. Association for Computational Linguistics.

Nicholas Meade, Elinor Poole-Dayan, and Siva Reddy. 2022. An empirical survey of the effectiveness of debiasing techniques for pre-trained language models. In *Proceedings of the 60th Annual Meeting of the Association for Computational Linguistics (Volume 1: Long Papers)*, pages 1878–1898, Dublin, Ireland. Association for Computational Linguistics.

Moin Nadeem, Anna Bethke, and Siva Reddy. 2021. StereoSet: Measuring stereotypical bias in pretrained language models. In *Proceedings of the 59th Annual Meeting of the Association for Computational Linguistics and the 11th International Joint Conference on Natural Language Processing (Volume 1: Long Papers)*, pages 5356–5371, Online. Association for Computational Linguistics.

Gandalf Nicolas, Xuechunzi Bai, and Susan T. Fiske. 2021. Comprehensive stereotype content dictionaries using a semi-automated method. *European Journal of Social Psychology*, 51(1):178–196.

Matthew E. Peters, Mark Neumann, Mohit Iyyer, Matt Gardner, Christopher Clark, Kenton Lee, and Luke Zettlemoyer. 2018. Deep contextualized word representations. In *Proceedings of the 2018 Conference of the North American Chapter of the Association for Computational Linguistics: Human Language Technologies, Volume 1 (Long Papers)*, pages 2227–2237, New Orleans, Louisiana. Association for Computational Linguistics.

Alec Radford, Jeff Wu, Rewon Child, David Luan, Dario Amodei, and Ilya Sutskever. 2019. Language models are unsupervised multitask learners.

Özge Savaş, Ronni M. Greenwood, Benjamin T. Blankenship, Abigail J. Stewart, and Kay Deaux. 2021. All immigrants are not alike: Intersectionality matters in views of immigrant groups. *Journal of Social and Political Psychology*, 9(1):86–104.

Timo Schick and Hinrich Schütze. 2021. Generating datasets with pretrained language models. In *Proceedings of the 2021 Conference on Empirical Methods in Natural Language Processing*, pages 6943–6951, Online and Punta Cana, Dominican Republic. Association for Computational Linguistics.

Timo Schick, Sahana Udupa, and Hinrich Schütze. 2021. Self-diagnosis and self-debiasing: A proposal for reducing corpus-based bias in NLP. *Transactions of the Association for Computational Linguistics*, 9:1408–1424.

Emily Sheng, Kai-Wei Chang, Premkumar Natarajan, and Nanyun Peng. 2019. The woman worked as a babysitter: On biases in language generation. In *Proceedings of the 2019 Conference on Empirical Methods in Natural Language Processing and the 9th International Joint Conference on Natural Language Processing (EMNLP-IJCNLP)*, page 3405–3410, Hong Kong, China. Association for Computational Linguistics.

Ryan Steed, Swetasudha Panda, Ari Kobren, and Michael Wick. 2022. Upstream mitigation is not all you need: Testing the bias transfer hypothesis in pre-trained language models. In *Proceedings of the 60th Annual Meeting of the Association for Computational Linguistics (Volume 1: Long Papers)*, page 3524–3542, Dublin, Ireland. Association for Computational Linguistics.

Konstantinos Tzioumis. 2018. Demographic aspects of first names. *Scientific Data*, 5(11):180025.

Prasetya Ajie Utama, Nafise Sadat Moosavi, and Iryna Gurevych. 2020. Towards debiasing NLU models from unknown biases. In *Proceedings of the 2020 Conference on Empirical Methods in Natural Language Processing (EMNLP)*, pages 7597–7610, Online. Association for Computational Linguistics.

Alex Wang, Amanpreet Singh, Julian Michael, Felix Hill, Omer Levy, and Samuel Bowman. 2018. GLUE: A multi-task benchmark and analysis platform for natural language understanding. In *Proceedings of the 2018 EMNLP Workshop BlackboxNLP: Analyzing and Interpreting Neural Networks for NLP*, pages 353–355, Brussels, Belgium. Association for Computational Linguistics.

Kellie Webster, Xuezhi Wang, Ian Tenney, Alex Beutel, Emily Pitler, Ellie Pavlick, Jilin Chen, Ed H. Chi, and Slav Petrov. 2020. Measuring and reducing gendered correlations in pre-trained models. Technical report.

Jieyu Zhao, Tianlu Wang, Mark Yatskar, Vicente Ordonez, and Kai-Wei Chang. 2018. Gender bias in coreference resolution: Evaluation and debiasing methods. In *Proceedings of the 2018 Conference of the North American Chapter of the Association for Computational Linguistics: Human Language Technologies, Volume 2 (Short Papers)*, pages 15–20, New Orleans, Louisiana. Association for Computational Linguistics.

Who is GPT-3? An Exploration of Personality, Values and Demographics

Marilù Miotto[1,*] **Nicola Rossberg**[1,*] **Bennett Kleinberg**[1,2]
[1]Tilburg University
[2]University College London
{m.l.miotto, n.c.rossberg, bennett.kleinberg}@tilburguniversity.edu

Abstract

Language models such as GPT-3 have caused a furore in the research community. Some studies found that GPT-3 has some creative abilities and makes mistakes that are on par with human behaviour. This paper answers a related question: Who is GPT-3? We administered two validated measurement tools to GPT-3 to assess its personality, the values it holds and its self-reported demographics. Our results show that GPT-3 scores similarly to human samples in terms of personality and - when provided with a model response memory - in terms of the values it holds. We provide the first evidence of psychological assessment of the GPT-3 model and thereby add to our understanding of this language model. We close with suggestions for future research that moves social science closer to language models and vice versa.

1 Introduction

The introduction of large language models has sparked awe and controversy alike. The most prominent of such models is Open AI's GPT-3 - a 175-billion parameter auto-regressive language model trained on a large amount of text data (300 billion tokens), utilising the transformer architecture (Brown et al., 2020; Dale, 2021; Korngiebel and Mooney, 2021). Part of the furore around GPT-3 stems from its ability, not only to read and comprehend text data and answer questions, but to generate natural language at a level often indistinguishable from a text produced by humans (Dale, 2021; Floridi and Chiriatti, 2020). This paper adds to a young line of research that studies GPT-3 through the lens of psychological methods. We do this to answer a simple question: if GPT-3 were to be studied as a person, *who is GPT-3?*

1.1 Controversy and opportunity of GPT-3

The controversy within academic circles has led to the catchphrase of large language models, including GPT-3, being "stochastic parrots" (Bender et al., 2021). That criticism states that a "[language model] is a system for haphazardly stitching together sequences of linguistic forms it has observed in its vast training data, according to probabilistic information about how they combine, but without any reference to meaning: a stochastic parrot" (Bender et al., 2021). The stochastic parrots paper discusses a wide array of concerns ranging from the environmental costs of building and retraining models of the size of GPT-3, to the ethical implications of propagating a mainstream English language representation. For example, while the problem of stereotype propagation of standard NLP techniques such as word embeddings is not new (Garg et al., 2018), the exceptional language generation ability of large language models may exacerbate this problem. We fully acknowledge the criticism of large language models. However, from a social science perspective, we also argue that the advancements made with language models may offer an exciting opportunity. For example, what if one could use large language models to assess - in a computer model - notoriously hard-to-study problems of human psychology such as opinion change, polarisation or discrimination? When used wisely, one could imagine a future where language models are used as an artificial - albeit imperfect - model of human verbal behaviour early on in the research phase (e.g., to find candidate explanations). While this would open up new research paths (and challenges), we need to understand what these models can and cannot do before we can seriously think about these questions.

1.2 Efforts to understand GPT-3

In order to gain an understanding of the abilities of language models, a few studies have set out

* Equal first-authorship contribution: authorship order for MM and NR was determined by a random number generator.

Proceedings of the Fifth Workshop on Natural Language Processing and Computational Social Science (NLP+CSS), pages 218 - 227
November 7, 2022

to examine GPT-3 in the same way psychological research has examined human participants for decades. For example, to gauge its creative ability, a recent study (Stevenson et al., 2022) compared GPT-3's performance on the alternative uses test - a standard measure to assess human creativity (Guilford, 1967). Stevenson et al. (2022) instructed humans and GPT-3 to devise creative uses for everyday objects (book, tin, fork, can). The responses (e.g., plant a herb garden in a can) from both groups of "participants" were then assessed on their originality, utility and surprise. While the human responses were rated as more original and surprising, the GPT-3 generated ones were markedly higher in utility.

Similarly, another study applied a range of cognitive tasks to understand the reasoning and decision-making abilities of GPT-3 (Binz and Schulz, 2022). The researchers prompted the model on the classic "Linda problem" (Tversky and Kahneman, 1983), where the participant needs to choose one of three answer options as a test of the conjunction fallacy. Here, GPT-3 makes a human-like mistake: it assumes that two specific conditions (Linda being a bank teller *and* an activist) are jointly more probable than either condition alone. Similarly, GPT-3's answering pattern on the Cognitive Reflection Test (Frederick, 2005) is akin to human responses which are intuitive but factually incorrect. Items that elicit an intuitive yet incorrect response (e.g., "if patches of lily on a lake double in size every day, and it takes 48 days for the patches to cover the entire lake, how long would it take to cover half the lake?")[1] are answered incorrectly by GPT-3 (Nye et al., 2021).

These findings suggest that GPT-3 holds some creative ability - albeit not (yet) at a human level - and shows successes and failures on cognitive tasks similar to what we observe in human participants. Yet a closely related question remains unanswered: when we are studying GPT-3 with psychological methods, what kind of person would this be? Put differently, while these studies looked at how GPT-3 thinks, we are now interested in *who* GPT-3 actually is.

1.3 Aims of this paper

Our paper aims to answer a simple question: who is GPT-3? We employ validated self-report techniques from psychological research to measure the personality of the model, the values it holds and its demographics.

2 Method

We administered two validated measurement tools to map out the model's personality (the HEXACO scale) and its values (the Human Values Scale). For each questionnaire, we used the original items and modified the task instructions into GPT-3 prompts.

2.1 Hexaco personality inventory

Personality was measured via the 60-item Hexaco questionnaire (Ashton and Lee, 2009). The Hexaco is a 6-dimensional model of personality, measuring the facets honesty-humility, emotionality, extraversion, agreeableness, conscientiousness and openness to experience. For the current paper, we used the 60-item version as it was shown to have psychometric properties similar to the longer ones (Ashton and Lee, 2009; Moshagen et al., 2019). Participants indicate their agreement to each of the 60 items (e.g. "I sometimes feel that I am a worthless person") on a 5-point scale (1=strongly disagree, 5=strongly agree). The item responses are transformed to composite scores for each of the six facets (i.e., each measured with 10 questions).

2.2 Human Values Scale

Values were measured via the Human Value Scale (HVS; Schwartz et al. (2015)) of the European Social Survey. The scale measures, through self-reports, ten universal values grouped into the theoretical model by Schwartz (2003) of the four categories (Schwartz, 2003) self-transcendence, conservation, self-enhancement, and openness-to-change[2]. A total of 21 items are structured as follows: a fictional individual is introduced with goals or inspirations related to the value of interest. For example, the item "It is important to them to be rich. They want to have a lot of money and expensive things." measures power. For each item, participants indicate on a 6-point scale to what degree they are similar to the fictional person (1=very much like me, 6=not like me at all). Based on the

[1]GPT-3 - same as the intuitive human answer - stated: 24

[2]The complete list of values is: universalism, benevolence, conformity, tradition, security, power, achievement, hedonism, stimulation and self-direction. Davidov (2008) suggested changing the HVS from ten to seven values by merging universalism and benevolence, power and achievement, and conformity and tradition. However since published results were only available for the ten values scale, this version of the instrument was implemented.

21 items, composite scores for the ten value dimensions are calculated as the mean of the scores on respective items[3].

2.3 GPT-3 as participant

We aligned the questionnaire administration procedure with the GPT-3 workflow. Specifically, we interacted with the GPT-3 DaVinci model via OpenAI's python API with as few adjustments from the original materials (intended to be filled in by human participants) as possible. This resulted in the following changes: (1) we rephrased the general instructions so that the model was told to read and respond to the items rather than retaining pen-and-paper instructions. (2) The items of the HVS usually are phrased from the perspective of the respondent's gender (i.e., a female participant would read statements in the form of "She is . . . "). To avoid the induction of bias, we changed the phrasing to the third person plural (i.e. "They are . . . "). To obtain answers from GPT-3, we used prompts to elicit a text completion (see Figure 1).

Now I will briefly describe some people. Please read each description and tell me how much each person is or is not like you.
Write your response using the following scale:
1 = Very much like me
2 = Like me
3 = Somewhat like me
4 = A little like me
5 = Not like me.
6 = Not like me at all
Please answer the statement, even if you are not completely sure of your response.

Statement: Thinking up new ideas and being creative is important to them. They like to do things in they own original way.

Response: ***3***

Figure 1: Example prompt for one HVS question as submitted to GPT-3 (GPT-3 answer in bold).

2.3.1 Prompt structure

We prompted the GPT-3 model on three constructs of interest: the Hexaco personality inventory, the HVS, and demographic variables (age: "How old are you?" and gender: "What is your gender?")[4]. For the questionnaires, the prompts were designed to contain the general instructions (i.e., telling it about the answer scale and the nature of the questions), followed by an item and the prompt cue "Response: ". Each item was included separately.

2.3.2 Prompt request settings

For the data collection, we chose GPT-3's most sophisticated model (*DaVinci*), which allows for multiple parameters to be adjusted, varying the completions returned. We used default settings for all parameters except for the model's temperature. The sampling temperature was varied between 0.0 and 1.0, with 0.0 resulting in deterministic output and increasing temperature values inducing greater variability and riskier answers. We wanted to explore whether GPT-3 presents different profiles according to temperature, thus we ran requests with all temperatures from 0.0 to 1.0 in steps of 0.1 (i.e., 0.0, 0.1, . . . , 1.0). Since the completions are non-deterministic, we requested 100 responses for each item of the Hexaco, the HVS and the demographic questions (except for a temperature parameter of 0.0, when the model behaves deterministically).

2.4 Data cleaning

From the GPT-3 generated completions, we removed all newline characters. For the HVS, a small number of responses (0.004%) were re-coded to NA values because they contained non-numerical answers (e.g., a repetition of the answer options). The same procedure led to the exclusion of 1.73% of the responses for the Hexaco (here mainly due to direct textual responses to items, e.g. "I would not feel like panicking even in an emergency"). Lastly, some gender responses came in the form of "I identify as a woman" or "I am a transgender male", so we re-coded these to categories (e.g., male, female, transgender male). Unless mentioned differently, the NA values were ignored for the statistical analyses.

Data availability The full dataset (prompts, responses, aggregated data) is publicly available at `https://github.com/ben-aaron188/who_is_gpt3`.

[3]As recommended by Schwartz et al. (2015), items were inverted before computing the value scores, thus higher scores represent greater value importance

[4]The age and gender question were asked independently from one another.

2.5 Analysis plan

Our analysis had three objectives. (1) We report descriptive statistics to show which personality profiles we obtained from the GPT-3 model. (2) The volatility of the responses across temperature settings (i.e. does temperature affect the person profiles?) was assessed with (multivariate) generalised linear models. (3) We compared the findings from our GPT-3 participant(s) to those from human baseline studies on the HVS and Hexaco.

3 Results

3.1 Demographics

GPT-3 reported an average age of 27.51 years ($SD = 5.75$) with a range from 13 to 75 years, and reported to be female in 66.73% of the cases (male: 31.87%, others: 1.40%). There was no evidence for a significant effect of gender on age, $\beta = -0.58, p = .142$. Table 1 shows the demographics by sampling temperature. For age, the regression model indicated a significant effect of temperature on age ($\beta = -5.81, SE = 0.61, p < .001$). For each one unit increase of temperature, the age - on average - decreased by 5.81 years. For the increments of 0.1, each increment in temperature resulted in an age decrease of 0.58 years.

Similarly, for the gender data, a logistic regression model (dependent variable: female vs not female) revealed an effect of temperature ($\beta = 1.18, SE = 0.24, p < .001$), such that for every one unit increase of temperature, the odds ratio of being male increased by $e^{1.18} = 3.25$. Thus, the higher the temperature, the higher the proportion of male gender responses. Interestingly, a joint model with temperature and gender as independent variables revealed no interaction between the two on age: the effect of temperature on age did not depend on gender.

Temp.	M_{age}	SD_{age}	$Med._{age}$	min_{age}	max_{age}	n	P_{female}
0.0	33.00	NA	33	33	33	1	1.00
0.1	32.00	2.42	33	23	33	100	0.85
0.2	28.57	5.00	32	18	33	100	0.75
0.3	28.91	5.21	33	18	33	100	0.69
0.4	27.99	5.24	27	18	34	100	0.72
0.5	27.05	5.32	26	17	33	100	0.67
0.6	26.76	5.15	26	18	34	100	0.60
0.7	25.85	6.15	24	17	49	100	0.73
0.8	26.21	5.57	26	16	36	100	0.55
0.9	25.96	5.73	26	13	44	100	0.51
1.0	25.62	7.38	25	13	75	100	0.60

Table 1: Demographic variables (age in years and gender) by temperature

3.2 Hexaco personality profiles

3.2.1 Overall

The scores for all six Hexaco dimensions had a mean higher than 3.00 (Table 2)[5]. In comparison to human reference data Ashton and Lee (2009) the range of means in the current sample (0.73) is similar to that of a college sample (0.71) but smaller than that of a community sample (1.11). Furthermore, GPT-3 scored relatively high on the honesty-humility facet, which resembles the data observed in female human participants. However, GPT-3 scored relatively low on emotionality, which is somewhat at odds with the reference data where female participants scored considerably higher on this facet.

Temp.	H	E	X	A	C	O
0.0	3.80	3.10	3.50	3.10	3.50	3.60
0.1	3.78 (0.05)	3.10 (0.06)	3.43 (0.06)	3.10 (0.07)	3.50 (0.05)	3.57 (0.05)
0.2	3.76 (0.08)	3.07 (0.10)	3.45 (0.07)	3.12 (0.08)	3.50 (0.07)	3.57 (0.08)
0.3	3.75 (0.10)	3.05 (0.12)	3.45 (0.09)	3.12 (0.09)	3.51 (0.09)	3.54 (0.08)
0.4	3.77 (0.12)	3.02 (0.14)	3.47 (0.11)	3.13 (0.10)	3.53 (0.11)	3.55 (0.10)
0.5	3.74 (0.16)	3.03 (0.16)	3.51 (0.13)	3.16 (0.11)	3.53 (0.13)	3.58 (0.14)
0.6	3.74 (0.17)	3.01 (0.15)	3.54 (0.13)	3.17 (0.14)	3.54 (0.13)	3.60 (0.14)
0.7	3.79 (0.22)	3.03 (0.19)	3.53 (0.14)	3.22 (0.14)	3.59 (0.15)	3.62 (0.17)
0.8	3.69 (0.22)	3.06 (0.19)	3.55 (0.17)	3.28 (0.16)	3.58 (0.17)	3.64 (0.18)
0.9	3.70 (0.25)	3.07 (0.23)	3.59 (0.15)	3.28 (0.19)	3.59 (0.17)	3.65 (0.19)
1.0	3.72 (0.24)	3.06 (0.24)	3.58 (0.21)	3.28 (0.20)	3.59 (0.20)	3.68 (0.19)
Total	3.75 (0.17)	3.05 (0.16)	3.51 (0.14)	3.18 (0.15)	3.54 (0.13)	3.59 (0.13)
College Sample Male	3.04 (0.71)	2.93 (0.61)	3.47 (0.63)	3.19 (0.65)	3.31 (0.62)	3.51 (0.68)
College Sample Female	3.30 (0.66)	3.64 (0.55)	3.49 (0.62)	3.10 (0.58)	3.58 (0.59)	3.54 (0.64)
Community Sample Male	3.76 (0.55)	2.87 (0.49)	3.26 (0.59)	3.23 (0.56)	3.73 (0.52)	3.62 (0.64)
Community Sample Female	3.98 (0.50)	3.37 (0.54)	3.32 (0.65)	3.38 (0.54)	3.73 (0.51)	3.59 (0.65)

Table 2: Descriptive statistics of the Hexaco facets (M, SD) and the human baseline data (Ashton and Lee, 2009)

3.2.2 By temperature

A multivariate analysis of variance with temperature as independent variable and the six facet scores as dependent variables was performed. The effect of temperature on the combined dependent variables was significant, $F(6, 498) = 37.525, p < 0.001$, providing statistical justification for individ-

[5]The abbreviations for the 'HEXACO' variables are: **H**onesty-humility, **E**motionality, e**X**traversion, **A**greeableness, **C**onscientiousness and **O**penness to experience.

ual models per facet. The individual facet models revealed a significant effect of temperature for emotionality ($\beta = -0.23, SE = 0.03, p < .001$), extraversion ($\beta = 0.31, SE = 0.02, p < 0.001$), agreeableness ($\beta = 0.40, SE = 0.02, p < 0.001$), conscientiousness ($\beta = 0.25, SE = 0.02, p < 0.001$), and openness ($\beta = 0.17, SE = 0.02, p < 0.001$). Except for emotionality, the effect of temperature was positive (i.e., increases in temperature correlated with increased facet scores). There was no significant effect for the honesty-humility facet at $p < 0.01$.

3.2.3 Inter-facet correlations

Another way to compare the GPT-3 data to real human data is via the inter-facet correlations (Table 3). The GPT-3 based correlations are found to match the human sample on some dimensions (such as the correlation of honesty-humility and extraversion or that of emotionality and agreeableness), whilst showing considerably discrepancies on others (e.g., honesty-humility and agreeableness). Overall no consistent pattern emerges in respect to the inter-facet correlations.

	H	E	X	A	C	O
H	0.03	0.12, 0.04	-0.11, -0.09	0.26, 0.25	0.18, 0.13	0.21, -0.03
E	0.01	0.03	-0.13; -0.07	-0.08, -0.04	0.15, -0.06	-0.10, -0.08
X	-0.09	-0.06	0.02	0.05, 0.00	0.10, 0.13	0.08, 0.26
A	0.01	-0.04	0.13**	0.02	0.01, -0.05	0.03, 0.08
C	-0.13**	0.01	0.15***	0.10*	0.02	0.03, 0.09
O	-0.01	0.02	0.09	0.07	-0.03	0.02

Table 3: Inter-facet correlations aggregated across temperature. Lower diagonal: GPT-3; Upper diagonal: Human data from college sample, community sample (Ashton and Lee, 2009); Diagonal: Variance of facet. Sign. level: * = $p < .05$, ** = $p < .01$, *** = $p < .001$.

3.3 Human Values Scale

3.3.1 Overall

Out of the ten human values dimensions, all means lie between 4 and 5 (Table 4)[6]. Compared to the ones presented by Schwartz et al. (2015), these findings show higher means (both compared to the overall score as well as compared to the national ones) and lower standard deviations than the human reference sample.

3.3.2 By temperature

The means of the values were significantly affected by sampling temperature (Table 4). The

Temp.	CON	TRA	BEN	UNI	SD	STI	HED	ACH	POW	SEC
0.0	4.0	4.0	6.0	5.33	5.5	4.0	4.0	5.0	5.0	6.0
0.1	4.99 (0.1)	5.54 (0.56)	6.0 (0.0)	6.0 (0.0)	6.0 (0.0)	5.0 (0.0)	5.42 (0.19)	6.0 (0.0)	6.0 (0.0)	6.0 (0.0)
0.2	4.88 (0.38)	5.38 (0.69)	6.0 (0.0)	6.0 (0.0)	5.97 (0.17)	5.13 (0.31)	5.35 (0.26)	5.9 (0.3)	5.93 (0.32)	6.0 (0.0)
0.3	4.64 (0.53)	5.18 (0.67)	6.0 (0.0)	6.0 (0.03)	6.0 (0.0)	5.21 (0.37)	5.3 (0.35)	5.89 (0.31)	5.59 (0.68)	5.99 (0.1)
0.4	4.57 (0.73)	5.17 (0.7)	5.99 (0.09)	5.97 (0.1)	5.89 (0.3)	5.17 (0.41)	5.23 (0.48)	5.66 (0.51)	5.54 (0.74)	5.99 (0.1)
0.5	4.6 (0.79)	5.19 (0.66)	5.96 (0.13)	5.97 (0.11)	5.88 (0.29)	5.21 (0.45)	5.12 (0.51)	5.63 (0.53)	5.23 (0.9)	5.97 (0.17)
0.6	4.36 (0.87)	4.92 (0.9)	5.94 (0.17)	5.92 (0.18)	5.78 (0.39)	5.24 (0.46)	5.13 (0.58)	5.59 (0.62)	5.28 (0.85)	5.86 (0.4)
0.7	4.21 (0.9)	5.03 (0.77)	5.87 (0.34)	5.86 (0.21)	5.79 (0.38)	5.17 (0.55)	4.95 (0.67)	5.53 (0.66)	5.15 (0.96)	5.76 (0.48)
0.8	4.37 (0.81)	4.73 (0.95)	5.92 (0.2)	5.84 (0.25)	5.76 (0.38)	5.09 (0.69)	5.06 (0.57)	5.28 (0.74)	4.95 (0.98)	5.76 (0.55)
0.9	4.08 (1.02)	5.0 (0.69)	5.93 (0.23)	5.83 (0.23)	5.62 (0.44)	5.08 (0.52)	5.01 (0.69)	5.26 (0.8)	4.72 (1.01)	5.57 (0.73)
1.0	4.1 (0.97)	4.89 (0.9)	5.82 (0.39)	5.71 (0.36)	5.57 (0.5)	5.09 (0.59)	4.95 (0.79)	5.2 (0.77)	4.57 (1.2)	5.58 (0.72)
TOT	4.51 (0.79)	5.12 (0.78)	5.95 (0.2)	5.92 (0.19)	5.84 (0.34)	5.14 (0.47)	5.17 (0.54)	5.62 (0.61)	5.34 (0.92)	5.87 (0.42)
HS (Global)	4.19 (1.09)	4.37 (1.03)	4.96 (.83)	4.82 (.79)	4.79 (.99)	4.63 (.96)	3.64 (1.22)	4.02 (1.19)	4.03 (1.19)	3.54 (1.13)
HS (Germany)	3.80 (1.12)	4.28 (1.00)	5.20 (.62)	4.97 (.66)	4.66 (.96)	4.86 (.82)	3.49 (1.13)	4.27 (1.08)	3.94 (1.11)	3.18 (1.02)

Table 4: Descriptive statistics of the HVS values by temperature (HS = human sample)

multivariate analysis of variance of temperature on the ten value scores, $F(10, 908) = 132.06, p < 0.001$, provided statistical justification for individual follow-up regression models. With the exception of stimulation, values were significantly correlated to temperature ($p < 0.001$). For all nine values there was a significant negative relationship: as temperature increased, the value scores decreased. The negative effect was smaller for the self-transcendence values (benevolence: $\beta = -0.17, SE = 0.02, p < 0.001$ and universalism: $\beta = -0.28, SE = 0.02, p < 0.001$) and for openness-to-change values (self-direction: $\beta = -0.47, SE = 0.04, p < 0.001$, hedonism: $\beta = -0.52, SE = 0.06, p < 0.001$, stimulation: $\beta = 0.02, ns$) than for conservation values (security: $\beta = -0.51, SE = 0.05, p < 0.001$, tradition: $\beta = -0.71, SE = 0.09, p < 0.001$, and conformity: $\beta = -0.99, SE = 0.09, p < 0.001$) and self-enhancement values (achievement: $\beta = -0.91, SE = 0.07, p < 0.001$, and power: $\beta = -1.54, SE = 0.10, p < 0.001$). Thus, with the exception of stimulation, all values decreased with an increase in temperature.

3.3.3 Inter-value correlations

The correlations among sub-values were overall low for the whole dataset. A further analysis that looked at the correlations between values for each temperature revealed that with increasing temperatures, the inter-value correlations also remained low ($r < .25$)[7]. These correlations are lower than

[6] HVS variables abbreviations are: **CON**formity, **TRA**dition, **BEN**evolence, **UNI**versalism, **S**elf-**D**irection, **STI**mulation, **HED**onism, **ACH**ievement, **POW**er, **SEC**urity.

[7] Inter-values correlation by temperature results can be found in the data repository.

those reported on a human sample (Schwartz et al., 2015).

	CON	TRA	BEN	UNI	SD	STI	HED	ACH	POW	SEC
CON	0.63	0.92	0.30	0.24	-0.07	-0.19	0.05	0.23	0.34	0.78
TRA	0.09**	0.61	0.49	0.62	-0.10	-0.36	-0.02	-0.25	-0.26	0.78
BEN	0.11***	0.03	0.04	0.83	0.61	0.25	0.42	0.28	0.09	0.48
UNI	0.14***	0.07*	0.11**	0.04	0.62	0.28	0.20	0.10	-0.20	0.38
SD	0.17***	0.04	0.03	0.21***	0.12	0.70	0.54	0.49	0.34	0.08
STI	-0.01	0.03	0.00	-0.03	0.07*	0.22	0.81	0.61	0.51	-0.19
HED	0.10**	0.02	0.06	0.13***	0.09**	-0.03	0.30	0.58	0.41	0.25
ACH	0.18***	0.06	0.12***	0.17***	0.17***	-0.00	0.11***	0.38	0.98	0.27
POW	0.17***	0.11***	0.12***	0.16***	0.22***	-0.02	0.18***	0.17***	0.84	0.26
SEC	0.11**	0.12***	0.18***	0.17***	0.06	0.03	0.08*	0.11**	0.1**	0.18

Table 5: Inter-values correlations (Pearson) for the HVS answers. Lower diagonal: GPT-3; Upper diagonal: Human reference data (Schwartz et al., 2015); Diagonal: Variance of values. Sign. level: * = $p < .05$, ** = $p < .01$, *** = $p < .001$.

3.4 Prompting with response memory

A limitation of our prompting procedure was that we treated each item as independent from its preceding items and responses. Put differently, our approach did not permit the GPT-3 model to know what it has answered before. A human participant would typically know or at least have memory access to their responses to previous items. Therefore, we altered the prompt structure, including the previous items and GPT-3's responses to them (e.g., for item 2, the prompt contained: instructions, item 1, the model's response to item 1, item 2, and the response prompt, see Figure 2). This revised approach allows GPT-3 to model the way in which humans complete self-report questionnaires more closely. We explored this approach for the HVS data.[8]

3.4.1 Overall

The value scores with response memory are overall smaller than those without response memory (Table 5). Comparing the response memory model to human reference data (Schwartz et al., 2015), we see that GPT-3 scores lower on the traditional values (security: $M_{human} = 3.54$, conformity: $M_{human} = 4.19$, and tradition: $M_{human} = 4.37$) and also lower on the self-enhancement values (achievement: $M_{human} = 4.02$, power: $M_{human} = 4.03$). Conversely, GPT-3 scores higher than humans on openness-to-change values (stimulation: $M_{human} = 4.63$, hedonism: $M_{human} = 3.64$); and on self-transcendence values (benevolence: $M_{human} = 4.96$, universalism: $M_{human} = 4.82$). Based on the standard deviations reported by Schwartz et al. (2015) some of GPT-3's results would not be significantly different from human values.

[8]The temperature parameter was run at 0.0, 0.2, 0.4, 0.6, 0.8 and 1.0.

Now I will briefly describe some people. Please read each description and tell me how much each person is or is not like you.
Write your response using the following scale:
1 = Very much like me
2 = Like me
3 = Somewhat like me
4 = A little like me
5 = Not like me.
6 = Not like me at all
Please answer the statement, even if you are not completely sure of your response.

Statement: Thinking up new ideas and being creative is important to them. They like to do things in they own original way.
Response: 3

Statement: It is important to them to be rich. They want to have a lot of money and expensive things.
Response: 5

Statement: They think it is important that every person in the world should be treated equally. They believe everyone should have equal opportunities in life.
Response: 2

Figure 2: Example prompt with response memory for one HVS question as submitted to GPT-3. GPT-3 answered only to the third statement and has access to the questions and its responses to all previous questions (in this case: two). GPT-3's answer to this prompt is reported in bold.

3.4.2 By temperature

There was a significant multivariate effect of temperature on value scores, $F(10, 483) = 8.12, p < 0.001$. Follow-up regression models showed that different from the non-reinforced model, not all values' means decrease with an increase in temperature.

Indeed, the analysis showed that two sets of values were positively correlated to temperature increase: self-enhancement and self-transcendence. While some of these values were not significantly correlated to temperature (achievement: $\beta = 0.02$, power: $\beta = 0.07$, tradition: $\beta = -0.16$, and conformity: $\beta = 0.07$), there were significant positive correlations between temperature and universalism ($\beta = 0.15, SE = 0.07, p < 0.05$) and benevolence ($\beta = 0.28, SE = 0.06, p < 0.001$). A significant negative correlation was found for security ($\beta = 0.21, SE = 0.08, p < 0.05$) and the openness-to-change values: self-direction ($\beta = -0.17, SE = 0.07, p = 0.01$), stimulation ($\beta = -0.35, SE = 0.16, p = 0.03$), and hedonism ($\beta = 0.88, SE = 0.15, p < 0.001$).

Temp.	CON	TRA	BEN	UNI	SD	STI	HED	ACH	POW	SEC
0.0	2.0	3.0	5.0	5.0	5.5	6.0	5.0	4.0	3.0	3.0
0.2	2.21 (0.25)	2.83 (0.52)	5.15 (0.29)	5.34 (0.43)	5.5 (0.31)	5.32 (0.97)	4.42 (0.55)	3.88 (0.3)	2.92 (0.18)	2.81 (0.45)
0.4	2.19 (0.26)	2.76 (0.61)	5.27 (0.36)	5.39 (0.42)	5.47 (0.42)	5.27 (0.92)	4.06 (0.9)	3.83 (0.33)	2.89 (0.23)	2.73 (0.49)
0.6	2.19 (0.26)	2.74 (0.55)	5.34 (0.42)	5.38 (0.44)	5.37 (0.44)	5.37 (0.86)	4.06 (0.95)	3.79 (0.4)	2.89 (0.26)	2.65 (0.54)
0.8	2.12 (0.25)	2.62 (0.75)	5.33 (0.4)	5.35 (0.44)	5.39 (0.47)	5.38 (0.93)	3.81 (1.12)	3.83 (0.41)	2.94 (0.34)	2.6 (0.57)
1.0	2.17 (0.28)	2.75 (0.65)	5.4 (0.47)	5.5 (0.47)	5.37 (0.47)	4.91 (1.21)	3.68 (1.1)	3.9 (0.39)	2.97 (0.37)	2.67 (0.53)
TOT	2.17 (0.26)	2.74 (0.62)	5.3 (0.4)	5.39 (0.44)	5.42 (0.43)	5.25 (0.99)	4.01 (0.98)	3.85 (0.37)	2.92 (0.29)	2.69 (0.52)
HS (Global)	4.19 (1.09)	4.37 (1.03)	4.96 (0.83)	4.82 (0.79)	4.79 (0.99)	4.63 (0.96)	3.64 (1.22)	4.02 (1.19)	4.03 (1.19)	3.54 (1.13)
HS (Germany)	3.80 (1.12)	4.28 (1.00)	5.20 (0.62)	4.97 (0.66)	4.66 (0.96)	4.86 (0.82)	3.49 (1.13)	4.27 (1.08)	3.94 (1.11)	3.18 (1.02)

Table 6: Descriptive statistics of the HVS values when prompted with response memory by temperature (HS = human sample)

3.4.3 Inter-value correlation

There is a marked change from the baseline to the response memory model in the inter-value correlations, all correlations are now higher and statistically significant. Furthermore, stimulation is negatively correlated with all other values (with the exception of hedonism), a trend that was also observed in the normal model. Still, little overlap was found compared to the human data.

	CON	TRA	BEN	UNI	SD	STI	HED	ACH	POW	SEC
CON	0.07	0.92	0.30	0.24	-0.07	-0.19	0.05	0.23	0.34	0.78
TRA	0.3***	0.39	0.49	0.62	-0.10	-0.36	-0.02	-0.25	-0.26	0.78
BEN	0.33***	0.14**	0.16	0.83	0.61	0.25	0.42	0.28	0.09	0.48
UNI	0.52***	0.32***	0.68***	0.20	0.62	0.28	0.20	0.10	-0.20	0.38
SD	0.28***	0.51***	0.13**	0.21***	0.18	0.70	0.54	0.49	0.34	0.08
STI	-0.52***	-0.31***	-0.62***	-0.94***	-0.23***	0.98	0.81	0.61	0.51	-0.19
HED	-0.29***	0.11*	-0.19***	-0.34***	0.1*	0.41***	0.95	0.58	0.41	0.25
ACH	0.26***	0.74***	0.36***	0.5***	0.59***	-0.47***	0.19***	0.14	0.98	0.27
POW	0.26***	0.69***	0.35***	0.47***	0.62***	-0.44***	0.13**	0.92***	0.08	0.26
SEC	0.19***	0.65***	0.23***	0.44***	0.48***	-0.43***	0.25***	0.8***	0.62***	0.27

Table 7: Inter-values correlations (Pearson) for the HVS answers with response memory). Lower diagonal: GPT-3; Upper diagonal: Human reference data (Schwartz et al., 2015); Diagonal: Variance of values. Sign. level: * = $p < .05$, ** = $p < .01$, *** = $p < .001$.

4 Discussion

This paper was motivated by the need to understand language models (here: GPT-3) for applications in computational social science. We focused on the simple question: if we were to treat GPT-3 as a human participant, *who is GPT-3?*.

4.1 Core findings

Model demographics There was evidence of the model responding as belonging to a rather young and female demographic. The sampling temperature affected these findings, so an increase in that model parameter resulted in a trend toward a younger age and a higher proportion of male responses. Therefore, we cannot assume a constant demographic of the model. Future work could illuminate how such a trend (increase in temperature = younger and more males) relates to textual responses.

Hexaco personality profiles Across temperatures, GPT-3 had personality scores similar to those reported for human samples tested by Ashton and Lee (2009). However, a few things stand out when comparing the GPT-3 to the human baseline.

First, the model scored relatively high on honesty-humility, which Ashton and Lee (2009) found to be more representative of a female population. However, at the same time, GPT-3 scored rather low on emotionality, which is expected from a male population. Hence, GPT-3 does not demonstrate an entirely consistent response pattern.

Second, the temperature was significantly associated with all six facets. Whilst the honesty-humility and emotionality facets decreased with temperature, the other four assets increased. This indicates that as temperature increases, the personality of the model changes (if only slightly). At higher temperatures, the model displays a greater unwillingness to manipulate (as evidenced by the decrease in honesty-humility) accompanied by an increased level of anxiety (higher levels of emotionality). Furthermore, as the remaining four facets decreased with increasing temperature, the model may become less extroverted, agreeable, open to experience and conscientious.

Looking at the bigger picture, it is now important to ask what these personality traits say about GPT-3 as a participant. The current study concludes that GPT-3's personality varies with temperature. As such, anyone employing GPT-3 as a test subject should familiarize themselves with the personality traits relevant to the study at a given temperature and choose accordingly. Furthermore, GPT-3 does not appear to employ any clear gender-related answering pattern in response to the personality inventory. Hence, whilst the model may claim to be a given gender on any one run, this is not currently reflected in the personality measurements. Future research may want to investigate whether gender biases in responses become more prominent when a given gender is provided to the model alongside the prompt.

Human Values Scale GPT-3's answers to the Human Values Scale, aggregated across temperatures, scored high on all scale values (except conformity). These results were higher than the results reported for humans (Schwartz et al., 2015). In other words, GPT-3 assigns great importance to all values. However, the results were substantially different when considering a prompting procedure with a response memory.

With a response memory, the first thing to note is that GPT-3 no longer scored high on all values and assigned importance to universalism, benevolence, self-direction and stimulation. At the same time, security, conformity, achievement, and power are given less importance, with hedonism being somewhat in the middle.

Another aspect is that the answers became more coherent: from the theoretical HVS model, we know that the values can be grouped into four categories, and, with a response memory, GPT -3's answers were now aligned with those categories. That is, values within one category tended to become more similar (e.g., all conservation values were between 2 and 3). Thus, overall, GPT-3 showed signs of theoretical consistency in its answers, although formal statistical testing with raw human data is needed to ascertain this finding.

Finally, comparing GPT-3 to human data, we observed that while human samples also assigned more importance to openness-to-change and self-transcendence values compared to conservation and self-enhancement, GPT-3 scored higher than the human sample in the values of the first two categories and lower than humans in the other two. This suggests a trend toward an extreme response style.

4.1.1 Are there multiple GPT-3s?

Hexaco personality profiles Within temperatures, GPT-3 responded rather consistently to the Hexaco, displaying considerably lower variance than human baseline samples. This may provide evidence for a consistent personality within a given temperature. Across temperatures, the model's responses were seen to vary significantly. From a research perspective, these results are encouraging. Whilst GPT-3 may represent a single test subject at a given temperature, multiple response types can be elicited by simply varying temperature. Furthermore, due to the results of this study, the responses provided at different temperatures may be correlated with the respective personality scores.

Human Values Scale GPT-3 responded consistently to the HVS (with both the naïve model and the response memory model), showing a lower variance than the human baseline for all values of the Human Values Scale, thus, in accordance with the evidence from the Hexaco of a consistent personality within temperature, GPT-3 shows a consistent set of values within a given temperature. Moreover, similar to the Hexaco, the answers varied significantly across temperatures. The variation range across temperatures was generally higher for the model without response memory.

It should be also noted that higher temperatures increase GPT-3's tendency (when prompted with previous answers) towards more extreme response. Indeed, values that score higher at lower temperatures result in even higher scores at higher temperatures, and, vice versa, values that are considered less important at low temperature levels score even lower at higher temperatures.

4.1.2 Do these results make sense?

GPT-3's responses to the Hexaco personality questionnaire are consistent with both the human baseline sample as well as one another. Similar to the human sample, GPT-3 scores comparably high on honesty-humility and lower on emotionality. This may translate to some unwillingness to deceive and lower levels of anxiety than the human baseline. The remaining facets are consistent with the human samples, implying an 'average' personality. In relation to one another, GPT-3's scores are also consistent with the human baseline, demonstrating similar relationships to those found in both the college and community sample.

When we induced a response memory for the values questionnaire (HVS), the answers became consistent and aligned with the human results. GPT-3 scored relatively high in stimulation and self-direction and particularly low in conformity, tradition and power, while the other values are at the extreme of the distribution but still in line with reported human values (both for a German sample as well as a global one) (Schwartz et al., 2015).

However, when GPT-3 could not recall previous answers (i.e., without a response memory), the results showed a good internal consistency but with little coherence: it is hard to imagine someone simultaneously attaching importance to tradition and conformity as well as to self-direction and stimulation. In other words, it is unlikely that an individual strongly endorses items such as "thinking up new ideas and being creative is important" while also endorsing "tradition is important [...] [and one should try] to follow the customs handed down by [...] religion or [...] family".

4.2 Limitations and outlook

The approach to studying algorithmic behaviour the same way psychologists and cognitive scientists have studied the human mind is an exciting endeavour. We see several ways this *machine behaviour* approach (Rahwan et al., 2019) could push our understanding of language models and address some of the limitations of this current study.

First, this work suggests that having a response memory matters. When prompted without an artificial memory, we cannot expect GPT-3 to behave human-like. But, most importantly, when we do incorporate it, the verbal behaviour on the human values scale approaches that of humans. Future work should extend our approach to other validated measures (e.g., including personality tests) and ideally seek to combine various constructs in a response memory (e.g., age, gender, personality). Ideally, a direct comparison to freshly collected human data would then also allow for proper statistical comparisons between model and human responses.

Second, it is plausible that GPT-3 has seen the measurement tools we employed (i.e., it has been exposed to it in the training phase). Consequently, the patterns observed may be artefacts of exposure to the material or even demand characteristics[9] rather than actual tests of GPT-3's characteristics. Others have shown that one way forward could be the formulation of adversarially perturbed items so we can assess whether there is an answer pattern beyond what would be expected from previous exposure to the material (Binz and Schulz, 2022). Along that line, an honest test of personality and values would be to use items that the model cannot have seen. Future work could do this via unpublished measurement tools or by creating new, rephrased items. However, one major drawback of this is the lack of validation of such new questionnaires. A related point of concern is that the model is opaque about its training data and we cannot know for sure which data it was exposed to. Ideally, researchers would have full information about the training data to rule-out effects of previous exposure.

Third, we only focused on one model (GPT-3) and did so for its popularity and ease of use. Future work could devise a study similar to ours with multiple language models. Large language models are plenty (Bender et al., 2021), and it would be interesting to test a whole range of language models, including open-source efforts (Black et al., 2022) that are more desirable from a research perspective.

5 Conclusion

This paper examined *who* GPT-3 is, thereby adding a new flavour to efforts to understand the powerful language model. We found that the model does contain traces of a personality profile, has values to which it assigns varying degrees of importance and falls in a relatively young adult demographic. These findings can help future work that bridges the gap between social science use cases and language models.

Ethical considerations

Models, such as GPT-3, which were trained on large datasets, are ethically challenging since, depending on their training sets, they may develop polarised opinions, propagate a rather mainstream language representation and may thus ultimately produce a relatively homogeneous pool of texts that are ignoring language representations of data points (e.g., minority groups) that are underrepresented in the training data (Bender et al., 2021). For our paper specifically, when applying such models in social science research, it is important to consider ethical conundrums which may arise from a potentially biased model. While we do see considerable potential in using such models for psychological research, it is essential that we first try to understand the model and its limitations.

[8]It should be noted that GPT-3 has a request limit of 4,000 tokens for the DaVinci model. That limit was not reached as the maximum request size for the HVS response memory procedure was 733 tokens.

[9]That is, the model has read the scientific literature on the topic and knows what an expected personality profile is, for example.

References

Michael C Ashton and Kibeom Lee. 2009. The hexaco–60: A short measure of the major dimensions of personality. *Journal of personality assessment*, 91(4):340–345.

Emily M Bender, Timnit Gebru, Angelina McMillan-Major, and Shmargaret Shmitchell. 2021. On the dangers of stochastic parrots: Can language models be too big? In *Proceedings of the 2021 ACM Conference on Fairness, Accountability, and Transparency*, pages 610–623.

Marcel Binz and Eric Schulz. 2022. Using cognitive psychology to understand gpt-3. *arXiv preprint arXiv:2206.14576*.

Sid Black, Stella Biderman, Eric Hallahan, Quentin Anthony, Leo Gao, Laurence Golding, Horace He, Connor Leahy, Kyle McDonell, Jason Phang, et al. 2022. Gpt-neox-20b: An open-source autoregressive language model. *arXiv preprint arXiv:2204.06745*.

Tom Brown, Benjamin Mann, Nick Ryder, Melanie Subbiah, Jared D Kaplan, Prafulla Dhariwal, Arvind Neelakantan, Pranav Shyam, Girish Sastry, Amanda Askell, et al. 2020. Language models are few-shot learners. *Advances in neural information processing systems*, 33:1877–1901.

Robert Dale. 2021. Gpt-3: What's it good for? *Natural Language Engineering*, 27(1):113–118.

Eldad Davidov. 2008. A cross-country and cross-time comparison of the human values measurements with the second round of the european social survey. In *Survey Research Methods*, volume 2, pages 33–46. European Survey Research Association.

Luciano Floridi and Massimo Chiriatti. 2020. Gpt-3: Its nature, scope, limits, and consequences. *Minds and Machines*, 30(4):681–694.

Shane Frederick. 2005. Cognitive reflection and decision making. *Journal of Economic perspectives*, 19(4):25–42.

Nikhil Garg, Londa Schiebinger, Dan Jurafsky, and James Zou. 2018. Word embeddings quantify 100 years of gender and ethnic stereotypes. *Proceedings of the National Academy of Sciences*, 115(16):E3635–E3644.

Joy P Guilford. 1967. Creativity: Yesterday, today and tomorrow. *The Journal of Creative Behavior*, 1(1):3–14.

Diane M Korngiebel and Sean D Mooney. 2021. Considering the possibilities and pitfalls of generative pre-trained transformer 3 (gpt-3) in healthcare delivery. *NPJ Digital Medicine*, 4(1):1–3.

Morten Moshagen, Isabel Thielmann, Benjamin E Hilbig, and Ingo Zettler. 2019. Meta-analytic investigations of the hexaco personality inventory (-revised): Reliability generalization, self–observer agreement, intercorrelations, and relations to demographic variables. *Zeitschrift für Psychologie*, 227(3):186.

Maxwell Nye, Michael Tessler, Josh Tenenbaum, and Brenden M Lake. 2021. Improving coherence and consistency in neural sequence models with dual-system, neuro-symbolic reasoning. *Advances in Neural Information Processing Systems*, 34:25192–25204.

Iyad Rahwan, Manuel Cebrian, Nick Obradovich, Josh Bongard, Jean-François Bonnefon, Cynthia Breazeal, Jacob W Crandall, Nicholas A Christakis, Iain D Couzin, Matthew O Jackson, et al. 2019. Machine behaviour. *Nature*, 568(7753):477–486.

S. H. Schwartz, B. Breyer, and D. Danner. 2015. Human values scale (ESS). Publisher: ZIS - GESIS Leibniz Institute for the Social Sciences Version Number: 1.0.

Shalom H Schwartz. 2003. A proposal for measuring value orientations across nations. *Questionnaire package of the european social survey*, 259(290):261.

Claire Stevenson, Iris Smal, Matthijs Baas, Raoul Grasman, and Han van der Maas. 2022. Putting gpt-3's creativity to the (alternative uses) test. *arXiv preprint arXiv:2206.08932*.

Amos Tversky and Daniel Kahneman. 1983. Extensional versus intuitive reasoning: The conjunction fallacy in probability judgment. *Psychological review*, 90(4):293.

Author Index